345 3129

American drama : the bastard

In *American Drama: The Bastard Art*, Susan Harris Smith looks at the many often conflicting cultural and academic reasons for the neglect and dismissal of American drama as a legitimate literary form. Covering a wide range of topics – theatrical performance, the rise of nationalist feeling, the creation of academic disciplines, and the development of sociology – Smith's study is a contentious and revisionist historical inquiry into the troubled cultural and canonical status of American drama, both as a literary genre and as a mirror of American society.

American Drama

CAMBRIDGE STUDIES IN AMERICAN THEATRE AND DRAMA

General Editor
Don B. Wilmeth, *Brown University*

Advisory Board
C. W. E. Bigsby, *University of East Anglia*
Errol Hill, *Dartmouth College*
C. Lee Jenner, *independent critic and dramaturge, New York City*
Bruce A. McConachie, *College of William and Mary*
Brenda Murphy, *University of Connecticut*
Laurence Senelick, *Tufts University*

Long a field for isolated research, yet too frequently marginalized in the academy, the American theatre has always been a sensitive gauge of social pressures and public issues. The American theatre and its literature are now attracting crucial attention from historians, theoreticians, and critics of the arts. Investigations into its myriad shapes and manifestations are relevant to students of drama, theatre, literature, cultural experience, and political development.

The primary aim of this series is to provide a forum for important and original scholarship in and criticism of American theatre and drama in a cultural and social context. Inclusive by design, the series is intended to accommodate leading work in areas ranging from the study of drama as literature (but without losing sight of its theatrical context) to theatre histories, theoretical explorations, production histories, and readings of more popular or paratheatrical forms. The series welcomes work grounded in cultural studies and narratives with interdisciplinary reach, encompassing books and monographs aimed at a more strictly scholarly audience as well as titles that will also appeal to the general reader.

With a specific emphasis on theatre in the United States (though worthy studies in the whole of the Americas will be considered), *Cambridge Studies in American Theatre and Drama* provides a crossroads where historical, theoretical, literary, and biographical approaches meet and combine, promoting imaginative research in theatre and drama from a variety of new perspectives.

Books in the series include:

1. Samuel Hay, *African American Theatre: An Historical and Critical Analysis*
2. Marc Robinson, *The Other American Drama*
3. Amy Green, *The Revisionist Stage: American Directors Re-Invent the Classics*
4. Jared Brown, *The Theatre in America During the Revolution*
5. Susan Harris Smith, *American Drama: The Bastard Art*
6. Mark Fearnow, *The American Stage and the Great Depression*
7. Rosemarie K. Bank, *Theatre Culture in America, 1825–1860*

American Drama
The Bastard Art

SUSAN HARRIS SMITH

University of Pittsburgh

PUBLISHED BY THE PRESS SYNDICATE OF THE UNIVERSITY OF CAMBRIDGE
The Pitt Building, Trumpington Street, Cambridge CB2 1RP

CAMBRIDGE UNIVERSITY PRESS
The Edinburgh Building CB2 2RU, United Kingdom
40 West 20th Street, New York, NY 10011-4211, USA
10 Stamford Road, Oakleigh, Melbourne 3166, Australia

First published 1997

Printed in the United States of America

Typeset in Adobe Caslon

Library of Congress Cataloging-in-Publication Data
Smith, Susan Harris.
American drama : the bastard art / Susan Harris Smith.
p.   cm. – (Cambridge studies in American theatre and drama)
Includes bibliographical references.
ISBN 0-521-56384-4
1. American drama – History and criticism. I. Title. II. Series.
PS332.S64   1997
812.009 – dc20   96-14765
                                                                         CIP

A catalog record for this book is available from the British Library.

ISBN 0-521-56384-4 hardback

Contents

Acknowledgments	*page* vi
1	Introduction: The Problem of American Drama	1
2	Generic Hegemony: The Exclusion of American Drama	9
3	No Corner in Her Own House: What Is American About American Drama?	57
4	Did She Jump or Was She Pushed? American Drama in the University Curriculum	114
5	Caught in the Close Embrace: Sociology and Realism	159
6	Conclusion: Beyond Hegemony and Canonicity	197
	References	208
	Index	232

Acknowledgments

I am grateful to the University of Pittsburgh for a sabbatical leave in 1992–1993, when I did much of the research for this project. I would like to thank my colleagues Dana Polan for reading the manuscript in an early stage and Jean Ferguson Carr for introducing me to the Nietz Collection of old textbooks in the University of Pittsburgh's Hillman Library. I would also like to thank the many people at Cambridge University Press who saw this project through to completion: Sarah Stanton and Don Wilmeth for their initial interest and sustained commitment, the anonymous readers of a late draft for their helpful advice, and T. Susan Chang, Anne Sanow, Edith Feinstein, and Nancy Landau for their expertise. And above all, my abiding thanks to Phil for his thoughtful advice, patient professionalism, and loving support.

I

Introduction

The Problem of American Drama

AMERICAN DRAMA is, for me, the canary in the mine shaft of American literary and cultural studies. That it lies gasping for air is a sign that something is wrong with the entire critical and educational apparatus that promotes, sustains, and generates disciplinary enterprises. Therefore, my project is an inquiry into the cultural reception and position of American dramatic literature, which, in my view, is marked by the extensive degree to which it has been marginalized, excluded, or "disciplined" in the culture in general and the university in particular. Although the use of "disciplined" necessarily invokes the historian Michel Foucault and his analyses of institutions and their discourses and processes, this study is not theorized along strict Foucauldian lines. Certainly I am concerned with the creation of academic disciplines and the organization and management of fields of study; but I am interested as well in the "punishing" power of disciplinary fields, in particular in the ability to hierarchize, denigrate, and exclude American drama.

Four major concerns have prompted me: first, the generic hegemony, that is, the dominance of poetry and prose, which has always characterized canonized American literature and literary histories; second, the debatable essential "Americanness" of American drama and its objectives as perceived and codified by literary critics, anthologizers, and historians; third, the use to which drama was put in early American educational texts and the problematic location of American drama in the developing higher-education curriculum; and fourth, the cultural "place" of American drama as created in part by the emerging discipline of American sociology and in part by the fraught status of realistic dramaturgy. It is my contention that, to a significant degree, the contested and uncertain location of American drama is the consequence of the rise of disciplinary fields in English and American literary studies and has far less to do with the intrinsic merits or demerits of the genre than with the struggles for authority and legitimation of emerging professionalisms.

I initially became concerned over the lack of attention paid to American drama by American literary historians and critics at the Salzburg Seminar in 1985; there, Emory Elliott and Sacvan Bercovitch, the editors of two then-forthcoming histories of American literature, one from Columbia University Press, the other from Cambridge University Press, led seminars addressing issues pertaining to the reevaluation of American literature. Welcome and needed though this reconsideration was, it focused exclusively on poetry and prose. The absence of drama from consideration at the seminar and from more than a passing reference in the planned histories troubled me, and since that time I have been asking questions about what has proved to be a complex cultural phenomenon. A short version of my preliminary study, "Generic Hegemony: American Drama and the Canon," first presented at the Modern Language Association in 1987, was the focal article for a discussion with three other scholars (C. W. E. Bigsby, Joyce Flynn, Michael Cadden) about the problem in *American Quarterly* (March 1989). That article, in a much expanded version, forms the first chapter of this study.

Focusing largely but not exclusively on both the late nineteenth century and the twentieth century, I document and examine the history of the academic and critical bias against American drama in anthologies and literary histories, college texts and curricula, literary magazines, scholarly journals, and critical histories. This prejudiced high-cultural attitude, which ignores the American drama as if it were an unwanted bastard child, has prevailed for at least one hundred years because teachers, scholars, and critics have been either the willing producers or the unreflexive, unquestioning inheritors of a long-standing, ingrained disposition to dismiss drama as unworthy or not "literary." To my surprise, some readers of that article have assumed either that I, too, believe that American drama is not literature or that I believe American drama should be understood only as literature. Neither is the case. Quite to the contrary: I believe that American dramatic literature has as much claim to literary status as any other genre, but I believe, as well, that although a study of dramatic literature should place the text at the center, dramatic literature must be understood in its widest possible manifestations and contexts, from production of texts to reception of performances. To do an evaluation of the literary and aesthetic qualities of American drama would be to focus on particular works at the expense of larger issues; my project has been to look at the ways in which American drama has been devalued by others, not to vindicate its status as literature. Nor, despite what some mistakenly see as my "negative" focus, is my work in any way meant to discount or discredit those who have worked to keep American drama alive as a serious subject for scholarly and critical, literary and historical, investigation. Far from it; my work has been illuminated by the vigilant flame of earlier studies, most notably the historical work done by C. W. E. Bigsby, Travis Bogard, Ruby Cohn, Walter Meserve, and Brenda Murphy.

American drama has been written almost out of the American literary canon because of enduring hostile evaluations and proscriptions that themselves need to be reassessed. I argue that for several reasons American drama has been shelved out of sight: in part because of a culturally dominant puritan distaste for and suspicion of the theatre; in part because of a persistent, unwavering allegiance to European models, slavish Anglophilia, and a predilection for heightened language cemented by the New Critics; in part because of a fear of populist, leftist, and experimental art; in part because of a disdain of alternative, oppositional, and vulgar performances; in part because of narrow disciplinary divisions separating drama from theatre and performance; and in part because of the dominance of prose and poetry in the hierarchy of genres studied in university literature courses and reproduced in American criticism. As a consequence, American dramatic literature has no "place" in the culture either as a "highbrow" literary genre or, surprisingly, as a "lowbrow" popular form of entertainment. As a sociocultural product, "literature" is not born, it is made by institutional processes, by disciplinary fiat, and by critical assertion. In the production of an American national literature, American drama has been a casualty of the wars of legitimation fought in the academy and has been so diminished that not even the revisionists have taken up the cause. Ultimately, however, I am interested not as much in arguing for American drama as literature as I am in examining the phenomenon of exclusion and in studying the tactics, discourse practices, and maneuvers employed to deal with American drama by those who were busy dominating and defining culture and legitimating their claim.

In an introductory note to a special issue of *Resources for American Literary Study* (Spring 1990), the editors, Jackson R. Bryer and Carla Mulford, observe that "inquiry about American drama and theater is just coming into its own" (iii). This is supported by the existence of and the work being done in three new academic journals, *American Drama, The*

Journal of American Drama and Theatre, and *Studies in American Drama, 1945–Present* as well as the continued attention paid to American drama in journals with a broader focus, such as *Modern Drama*, *Theatre Journal*, and *Theatre Annual*. The notion that American drama and theatre are only now achieving independent stature is both unsettling and welcome news: Those in the fragile field of American drama have been aggrieved by the long-standing neglect but have had little chance outside the fortress walls to challenge or engage their colleagues in American literary and cultural studies. It is gratifying and exciting to be part of an intellectual movement now riding the cresting wave of amplified contextualization and new methodologies. Work on the issues is currently being done in histories of American literary and theatrical practice by scholars such as David Grimsted in *Melodrama Unveiled: American Theater & Culture, 1800–1850*, Lawrence W. Levine in *Highbrow/Lowbrow: The Emergence of Cultural Hierarchy in America*, and Loren Kruger in *The National Stage: Theater and Cultural Legitimation in England, France, and America*. In *American Drama, 1940–1960: A Critical History* (1994), Thomas Adler reads the central motifs of American drama through the lenses of "the sociopolitical currents" and "the sociocultural milieu" (5). Gary Richardson, emphasizing the critical marginality of his subject in *American Drama from the Colonial Period Through World War I: A Critical History* (1993), argues that "the stepchild of American literary culture" has been marked by a distrust of the historical, critical, and economic forces that shaped a canon rich in "formal diversity and cultural complexity" (ix–xi). I hope to add to the useful work being done by my colleagues by basing my avowedly polemical reconstructive consideration on movements in academic institutions and on impulses in literary criticism.

Obviously, concern about American dramatic literature is but a small part of larger, related concerns about the professionalization of literary study, of the creation of disciplines, of the debatable Americanness of American literature, and of canon formation, concerns that have become increasingly central to any evaluation of literature. Given the recent proliferation of studies on the history of the creation of academic disciplines and the struggles to legitimate those disciplines, this is an opportune, even necessary, moment to join in the discussion. Valuable considerations include such recent work as Gerald Graff's pioneering *Professing Literature*; Arthur N. Applebee's *Tradition and Reform in the Teaching of English: A History*; Gerald Graff and Michael Warner's documentary anthology, *The Origins of Literary Studies in America*; Bruce Robbins's *Secular Vocations: Intellectuals, Professionalism, Culture*; Peter Carafiol's *The American Ideal:*

Literary History as a Worldly Activity; essays by Michael Colacurcio and William Spengemann; Paul Lauter's *Canons and Contexts*; and David Shumway's *Creating American Civilization: A Genealogy of American Literature as an Academic Discipline*, all of which have informed my work.

Of necessity, much of this book is the documentation of literary and cultural history; the rest must be informed speculation. The documentation, I insist, is a necessary step in calling back yesterday and in recovering those voices, many now forgotten though their traces linger on, which spoke so stridently or urgently against or for the drama. The particulars of those arguments are revealed as much in the discourse as in the thematics, and, at times the cacophony is staggering. Although many wrote against the drama as literature, they were far from coherent or uniform in their charges; in fact, I contend that the very evident dissensus of opinion – the posturing fatuousness, obvious biases, and not so hidden agendas in many of the arguments against the drama – support my contention that dramatic literature itself was not so much the issue as were the contriving of necessary hierarchies, the forming of boundaries, and the excluding of a troublesome and slippery literary form that resisted entrapment in a narrow genre. In fact, the very elusiveness speaks to a fundamental flaw in the whole concept of disciplining drama. Therefore, rather than presuming to have written a history with a narrative cohesiveness, I think of this reconstructive effort as an idiosyncratic trip through a museum with stops at significant exhibits, an effort to eschew a totalizing or organic history for an introductory investigation of related problems prevailing in American drama's cultural location.

The other part of this exercise, my informed speculation, admittedly is only a tentative first step toward an understanding of an enormously complex issue, but it is the best contribution I can make at this juncture. Although, from my perspective, to argue *for* American dramatic literature seems like a radical stance, I am fully aware that I open myself to a plethora of critical charges: of being superficial in taking such an approach, of not dealing in sufficient depth with any one issue, and of accepting outworn paradigms, to say nothing of employing the narrow generic term itself. In defense of my approach, I would respond that to investigate how and where the boundaries were framed, I have stayed within the narrow parameters of the "field" as it historically has been constituted by those who profess literature. In trying to construct my own mapping of the marginalization of, and embarrassed confusion in, cultural discourse about American drama, I have read, quite deliberately, for the exclusions, for the limited inclusions, for the defensive maneuvers, and for the nervous apologies in previous histories. What I found were discourses of legitimation anxiously and hegemonically focused around concerns for nationalism, gender, and the construction of disciplines, all conservative enterprises that stripped American dramatic literature of its potential academic and actual rich cultural capital. In my survey of cultural history, I make no claim to an unbiased reading, exhaustive scholarship, or complete "coverage," all of which are impossible; but I have tried to analyze the standard texts and some peripheral ones to reposition American drama, to take it out of the wings and put it, if only briefly, into the spotlight. Like many narrative contrivances, this may open avenues for discussion. I urge readers to consider the matrix of cultural, ideological, and aesthetic criteria that have resulted in the neglect of American drama. If a debate ensues, then the question of opening the American literary canon to drama may emerge as a first, though not the final, step in rethinking American drama.

I do not think this is a minor or peripheral problem. Given that the canon of American literature is currently undergoing an overdue scrutiny and revision, this is also an opportune moment to draw attention to the problem because it has wide ramifications in culture studies. If American drama in general has been buried, so, too, in particular have been the voices of the experimentalists, marginalized minorities, and ethnic groups who have tried to speak through the drama. The recovery of "lost" plays has been well under way for several decades, but these plays must be studied in a wider context. To a great extent the burgeoning interest in culture critique, culture studies, performance studies, and multicultural and interdisciplinary studies could act as a corrective to the narrow and ill-conceived dismissal of American drama from consideration.

Because I primarily study the texts of dramatic literature rather than records of theatrical productions or performance histories, I turn to theatre histories only when they have some direct bearing on the matter. I recognize that this is a difficult point of separation, a play being as much a script for full realization in production as it is a literary text. I feel strongly, however, that one great attraction of a play's printed text is that it can serve two masters, the reader and the audience, and that the dissemination of a text through print and through critical reception is as vital to its survival as is a well-received production, especially when one of the vexed questions is the literary status of the genre. Also, much of the material I study, such as the creation of a literary discipline, is built on the presumption of printed texts. That this model must be enlarged is one of my final arguments.

I am fully aware that the formation of canons and disciplines is the result of a complex interaction of forces, for example, institutional and professional debates over curriculum, critical rhetoric, economic and political objectives, and a dominant, cultural insistence on rational order. A "complete" study of the cultural situation of American drama would have to account for the intersections of theatrical and textual production, convergences with the other arts, government funding and censorship, educational systems, copyright laws, the book publishing industry, and a host of related problems, full considerations of which are beyond the horizons of this book. As a consequence, I have not attempted a comprehensive chronological narrative but, instead, have constructed my investigation around four problems with a substantive location in higher education and connected sites: generic hegemony, "Americanness," the academic curriculum, and sociology.

I recognize that teachers, critics, and historians and their canons of national literature can become agents of legitimation, sites for fixing dominant ideologies, and purveyors of self-aggrandizing myths for established or dominant interests or classes. I also recognize that the very idea of an essential "American" literature is being strenuously questioned. Nonetheless, until very recently, critics, historians, and anthologizers took it for granted that they could define and point to the central texts of American literature. Their enshrined values are implicit in the texts they chose to canonize; the desired image of a progressive America rested firmly in a preoccupation with historical situations and with topical verisimilitude, with native characters and indigenous forms rather than cosmopolitan imports. The few who wrote in favor of American drama valued and valorized a democratic hegemony through what they understood as "civilizing" discourse and dramaturgical strategies of containment. In the chapter devoted to the problem of the Americanness of American drama and its cultural work, I argue that these perceptions were illusions rigorously imposed in defiance of what was really happening in American theatres and in American drama. As a consequence of American literary historians ignoring or dismissing American drama in general, in particular the pluralistic voices of resistance, the voices of women, African Americans, ethnic groups, leftists, and experimentalists, to an astonishing degree, also have often been left out of the history.

Annette Kolodny has written that the delegitimation crisis "asserts as its central critical category not commonality but *difference*" and has urged critics to focus on the forces of exclusion (293). In studying the cultural history of the disciplining of American drama, we need to understand how drama exists within American culture, to explore the many dimensions of the relations between society and drama. We need to accept drama as a literary genre but not solely as a literary genre; drama is a complicated genre that is socially created, distributed, experienced, and shared in a multiplicity of ways. Drama is what theatre does, but it is not the only thing that theatre does. We need to reencounter both the plays themselves and the responses to them, the circumstances of publication, performance, and reception, to recover the historical narratives. By so doing, I hope to make a modest contribution to "re-placing" American drama in its literary and cultural framework.

2

Generic Hegemony

The Exclusion of American Drama

"IN THE FOUR QUARTERS of the globe, who reads an American book? or goes to an American play?" queried Sydney Smith in *The Edinburgh Review* in 1820 (79). More to the point, who *reads* an American play? The evidence would suggest that few have or do. The question has to be, Why? Even though the American literary canon has been "busted," the firm pronouncement from the pen of Dion Boucicault in 1890 that "there is not, and there never has been, a literary institution, which could be called the American drama" would provoke very little argument from most American critics more than a hundred years later (641). In fact, the neglect of American drama is so pervasive that Ruby Cohn, in her history of twentieth-century drama for the *Columbia Literary History of the United States* (1988), begins with the observation: "Given the chokehold on drama of a misnamed *Broad*way, given the lure of Hollywood, and given the power of some small-minded reviewers in the daily press, it is a virtual miracle that American drama merits admission to a history of American *literature*" (1101).

Despite its segregation from the main corpus of American literature, American drama has never been written in a vacuum. It has mirrored peculiarly American social, political, and historical issues in traditional as well as challenging forms and experimental styles. It has been the forum for a plurality of American voices. A reflexive cultural barometer, American drama has always responded to national and regional problems, either in reifying prevailing sentiments or by challenging dominant ideologies. Like

This chapter is based on "Generic Hegemony: American Drama and the Canon," *American Quarterly* 41 (1989). Reprinted by permission of the Johns Hopkins University Press.

other forms of American literature, drama embodies the American struggle. Certainly, American literature itself was for years excluded from or relegated to a minor role in higher education; in 1936, Howard Mumford Jones referred to it as the "orphan child of the curriculum" (376). Even with the expansion of American literature in the higher-education curriculum after World War II, for too many critics and historians American drama is still American literature's unwanted bastard child, the offspring of the whore that is theatre. For decades scholars and critics of American literature, engaged in establishing an academic discipline with canonical hierarchies and feeling embattled in the face of longer-lived English literary studies, have practiced generic hegemony; as a consequence, American drama historically has been the most devalued and overlooked area in American literary studies.

It is also the most maligned, vilified, and unjustly neglected area. For instance, to begin near the middle of the twentieth century, George Beiswanger's assertion about the drama, in an article entitled "Theatre Today: Symptoms and Surmises" written in 1944, captures the bias against American drama that has prevailed in American literary studies. "It is a fact," he writes, "that the American imagination is not at home in the medium of the drama. . . . Serious drama, I surmise, is not an American art. It has never been. We have no tradition of playwriting on the deeper things of life" (26–27). In the same year, in an acid assessment of the theatre season for *The Kenyon Review*, he wrote that "it has always been unwise to expect much of theatre . . . its task is show business; its mind essentially (and wisely) illiterate; its instincts that of a jade" (318–319). John Gassner in "'There Is No American Drama' – A Premonition of Discontent" (1952), worried about the New Critics' hostility to the drama but conceded that "the literary element was never the strong point of American playwriting" (84). Eric Bentley, in a 1954 article "The Drama: An Extinct Species?," drew a similar conclusion, "'there is no American drama.' There is a lack not only of Shakespeares and O'Caseys but also of Dekkers and Joneses. In America playwriting is not yet a profession" (413).

In 1963, Richard Gilman was as harsh: "The drama has suffered more than the other arts from the disjuncture between thought and activity that is so characteristic of our cultural life. The American drama is itself almost mindless," because of "a refusal to believe that intellect has anything to do with theater" (157). He continued by arguing that unlike European drama, which has undergone a modernist transformation, American drama continues to be at fault for "its refusal to take thought, its clinging to passion when passion is mere noise" (169).

Some still might agree with these harsh assertions that most American drama is not "high" literature, but given that the canon of American literature now is opening up to embrace a wide variety of material, these elitist vilifications should seem distastefully antiquated. The institutionalizing of cultural memory has depended to a large extent on the academics and critics who have codified the canon of American literature, itself a wholly artificial construct. The academic hegemony of genres that has marginalized drama should be exposed as another fossil of an outdated professional humanist attempt to mystify the best that has been thought and said as a substitute, via secular high cultural texts, for religion – the program outlined in Matthew Arnold's "The Study of Poetry" – and followed in various ways by a tradition of pedagogy and criticism whose published results, in considering American literature, I will describe. The problem spans the centuries; a bias against drama and theatre that was firmly in place in the nineteenth century only hardened in the twentieth. Dramatic texts did not fit the midcentury canons of modernist complexity and ahistorical philosophical ethos preferred by the New Critics; likewise, both early and late in this century, American drama as social text did not fit into the canons of high culture, as taught either by old-fashioned humanists or by trend-setting acolytes of new theoretical methodologies.

All the evidence suggests that this clear academic and critical bias against American drama remains current. Poetry, fiction, and nonfictional prose continue to dominate the canon of American literature while American drama hovers on the periphery. The most generous possible interpretation is that no intentional bias or active discrimination exists, but, rather, that academics and critics are simply the unreflective, unquestioning inheritors of a long-standing ingrained disposition to dismiss or ignore American drama. There is also a less generous interpretation, namely, that American drama deliberately has been buried alive in the cover-up of what was perceived embarrassedly and fearfully as a vital manifestation of cultural provincialism, feminine emotion, and unstable radicalism. Rather than debase or discredit the dominant ideology's romantic insistence on "progressive" civilization, on a domesticated, appropriated, and integrated bourgeoisie, the critics approved and continue to uphold only those literary forms which were sanctioned by the propertied, patriarchal culture, a culture that necessarily had to value the containment and restraint of exuberance or subversiveness.

Though the neglect of American drama has been noticed frequently, there has never been a full accounting of the phenomenon. Now that the canon of American literature is being given long-needed scrutiny and revision, this is an opportune moment to draw attention to the problem. As hitherto "marginal" works – that is, works by women and African Americans, Native Americans, and other ethnic groups – are being incorporated into the canon of American literature, so, too, should drama, especially by these marginalized groups, be reexamined and included on a scale commensurate with its importance as both literature and cultural artifact. Given that the narrowest traditional conception of and justification for literary study as being devoted to linguistic and aesthetic issues has been challenged by cultural materialism, new historicism, feminism, and ethnic studies, American drama can be reexamined from new perspectives in a reconstructed discipline. American drama has been written almost out of the canon because of enduring evaluative proscriptions that themselves need to be reassessed. In part because of a culturally dominant puritan distaste for and suspicion of the theatre; in part because of a persistent, unwavering allegiance to European models, slavish Anglophilia, and a predilection for heightened language cemented by the New Critics; in part because of a suspicion of populist, leftist, ethnic, and experimental art; and in part because of the dominance of prose and poetry in the hierarchy of genres studied in university literature courses, American drama nearly has been shelved out of sight.

It is impossible to solve all the mysteries surrounding the discrimination against American drama, but I would like to open an inquiry into the problem by documenting the astonishing extent of extant generic hegemony, and by initiating a discussion of the diverse academic and cultural issues pertinent to the exclusion of America drama, some of which the following chapters explore in greater depth. First, I chronicle at length the cultural and academic bias against drama. Second, I consider the history of this bias as it arose from the intersection of several conditions including cultural Anglophilia and a predilection for heightened language as the touchstone for admission to the category of "literature," the consequence of which has been a patterned isolation of the drama from other genres. Third, I try to account for that isolation by reviewing American literary histories. Fourth, I consider the ways in which American critics have been disdainful of, have disregarded, or have discriminated against American drama. Fifth, I examine the current status of the drama in the light of a revitalized American canon. Finally, I conclude with generalizations about the relationship between the genre and national culture.

Cultural and Academic Bias

The simplest explanation for generic hegemony and the discrimination against drama is that in the culture at large and in higher education few

Americans read plays, let alone American plays. The roots of genuinely native American drama lie in an spontaneous, oral tradition – honky-tonk, vaudeville, burlesque, and minstrel shows. The nonliterary origins are further prejudicial to readers because these always have been considered to be vulgar, lower-class, and, more recently, sexist and racist entertainments. But even when imported drama and American imitations of European models finally triumphed over lingering puritan prohibitions and became an accepted part of the literary output, drama still remained in the cultural shadows. To a large degree the unique constraints on production of texts and a retrograde copyright system limited the availability of a wide variety of dramatic material. Recently, dissemination of dramatic literature has depended on prominent (and usually popular) theatrical production; a published play is a secondary phenomenon, an afterthought in an economically driven system. This commodification also represents a simple confusion of "texts" in which a production supersedes and displaces the script and privileges a director over the playwright. Admittedly, reading a play is more difficult than reading a poem or a novel; it must be staged in the "theatre of the mind." Theatre is a mass medium in which a director manages and mediates the work of seeing and understanding for a passive audience; it produces the imposition of an interpreted vision. Reading a play, on the other hand, is an egocentric, solitary activity that requires active engagement; the reader produces the vision. This kind of reading presupposes an educated or theatrically knowledgeable reader. Most Americans lack the kind of dramaturgical literacy that makes reading a play possible, let alone pleasurable.

If the American reader lacks the necessary dramaturgical literacy, it would not seem to matter, given that many critics have suggested there is no substance in American drama to produce either pleasure or insight. For the next few pages, I revisit and summarize some of the arguments against American drama's claims to literary status. Richard Gilman, harsh though he was about the intellectual substance of American drama, pointed to a pattern of faulty thinking about drama that has skewed its position. If American theatre lacks "little that is permanent, revelatory and beautiful," it "also suffers from a great reluctance to being *thought about*, except in the most sanctified and unoriginal ways" (157). Noting that drama criticism has lagged behind advances in drama, Gilman faulted the critics for being mired in "a fixed notion of drama as the enactment of passions," an approach that precludes an examination of the real work of (modern) drama: "self-mockery, wit, fantasy, aggression, and irony," all attributes that did not find favor within the conservative program of academe, which especially in the early decades of the century, turned away from transgressive modes in favor of the respectability of "high" culture. Such attitudes were more prevalent in the early decades of the century than today, but the effect of prejudice continues; one might even suggest that the traces were etched with the diamonds of displeasure and distaste.

Carving out a place for American drama as literature was impeded by academic resistance to the genre during the nineteenth and twentieth centuries as well as by the refusal to accept the equality of text and production. The consequences of the divisiveness between theatrical production and performance versus the study of dramatic literature have been more harmful to the literature than the practice, but both have suffered. Bernard Beckerman, in "The University Accepts the Theatre: 1800–1925," and James H. Butler, in "The University Theatre Begins to Come of Age: 1925–1969," document the history of the struggle for the legitimation of theatre study within academe. As Beckerman notes, "a semi-curricular authority was achieved [when] professors of elocution or rhetoric selected passages from Shakespeare and other classical authors for illustration" (346). The consolidation of the study of physical theatre, as opposed to dramatic literature, was complete when George Pierce Baker, on the eve of opening his new drama department at Yale, announced that his twenty-five-year plan insured that the main emphasis would be on "plays as something to be acted – something to be judged with accuracy only when seen" ("University" 100). Although Baker had nurtured a number of American playwrights in his pioneering course at Harvard, "English 47," which he began in 1906, his forceful insistence on the importance of performance paved the way for the sidelining of dramatic literature in general and American drama in particular that has come to characterize most English departments. The general acceptance of Eugene O'Neill as America's first legitimate playwright notwithstanding, the received, codified, and operative assumption underlying most English departments' curricula in this century is that there is no American dramatic literature worthy of more than a contemptuous nod.

If people read fewer plays than novels or poems, therefore, it may be, in part, because few university teachers include plays in their literature courses. A commonsense rejoinder to the evidence of a bias against American drama might be that a play is really a script to be realized on the stage in performance and, as such, should be taught in Theatre departments. If this proposition were entirely true, however, Shakespeare would not be a hardy and popular perennial in English departments. Nevertheless, drama in general, with the exception of classical Greek works and the plays of Shakespeare, fares badly as canonical literature in academic institutions.

First, it is understood erroneously to fall between two stools; while some argue that a play is a score to be performed, others contend that it is a self-sufficient literature to be read. It should not be a matter of either/or; a play is both, but it is foremost a literary text. Furthermore, the text is permanent; productions leave only traces in reviews and photographs. Of the oft-repeated idea that a play is not a play unless it is performed, Barrett H. Clark, one of the few early-twentieth-century champions of the drama, remarked that it was "fallacious," "pernicious," and "preposterous," observing that few plays ever get more than a few productions and that they only survive through print (*Modern* 12).

Such protestations notwithstanding, the academic division of the study of drama into Theatre and English departments and the ensuing turf battles have only reinforced this artificial separation, disallowed either discipline's absolute claim to the drama, and diluted the extent to which drama is taught in English departments. But the academic division of the subject does not account for the impoverished standing of American drama in particular. The two disciplinary approaches should be not mutually exclusive but, rather, mutually reinforcing, because drama combines language and action. There is a long-standing cultural as well as academic context for this dichotomy but it has played itself out differently in America than in Europe.

In "Drama as Literature and Performance," Jiri Veltrusky traces the separation of the academic study of dramatic literature in Europe from the history of theatre to Max Herrmann in 1914, and claims this radical move to mark the beginning of the modern theory of theatre and the emancipation of theatre arts from literary study. He also claims that drama was equally freed, freed to be considered as literature, as it was, decisively, by Max Dessoir in 1908 and more recently by Peter Szondi in 1959 when he defined drama as a definitive form of poetry for the stage (12–13). But the linguistic analyses of dialogue that sustained scholars from Hermann Wunderlich in 1894 to Jan Mukarovsky in 1940 and formed the basis for the separation of literature and theatre were not the operative principle in America, where the link with the theatre was the central feature that differentiated the drama from other forms of literature. Certainly one important historian of American drama believed this to be the case. In his contribution to the *Cambridge History of American Literature* (1921), Montrose J. Moses observed, "Our modern native drama did not grow out of literature, as it did in England and France; it grew out of the theatre" (CHAL 271).

Beginning in the nineteenth century, that interest in theatre, as opposed to the drama, was reflected in the editorial practices of an important cultural journal, *The Dial*. From 1880 to 1883, books by and about actors were reviewed; a review of twenty years of American literature in the journal published in 1900 excluded the drama, and through the early decades of the twentieth century, *The Dial* published reviews of productions and followed the community work of the Drama League. Writing in 1914, Clayton Hamilton, in trying to account for "What Is Wrong with the American Drama?," observed, "It must be frankly stated that the public of America . . . is not at all interested in the drama. It is enormously interested in the theatre; but that is another matter altogether" (315). At midcentury, Richard Cordell echoed this idea that the life of the theatre in America was markedly different from that of the drama. Introducing his anthology of American drama in 1947, he observed that although theatre had enjoyed "a vigorous existence for more than a century," the drama was one of "incredible triviality," and that although the theatre "flourished," the drama "languished" (v–vi).

This separation of page and stage, of dramatic literature and performance site, is both unfortunate and inexact because a production is, after all, no more than a director's enacted interpretive reading of the script and a designer's imaginative visualization of the setting. A theatre's "health" cannot be severed credibly from the work performed there. But the mistaken perception that such a separation enhances study produces a peculiarly American problem that is not duplicated in Europe. Native dramas are taught in literature departments in European universities, and outside the United States, American drama is studied and read as seriously and extensively as any other form of American literature. Furthermore, in Europe texts of plays often are offered for sale in the theatre lobbies; the relationship between the theatre and the drama is as reciprocal, mutual, and inseparable as the relationship between reader and text, audience and performance.

The availability of texts and the desirability of being a published playwright were an issue until just before the turn of the century. In *The Old Drama and the New* (1923), William Archer looked at the problem from the English perspective: "During the middle years of the nineteenth century, the habit of reading plays became entirely extinct . . . and the greater the value of a play the more chary was the author of letting it get into print, since he thereby sacrificed American stage right, and became, potentially at all events, the defenceless prey of piratical producers beyond the Atlantic. In 1891 a new copyright convention put an end to this deplorable state of things. . . . It was literally true that, for the fifty years between 1840 and 1890, England had possessed nothing that could reasonably be called a dramatic literature" (309). But if England recovered the habit of reading plays, why didn't America? One problem was the availability of plays in print.

One of Irish playwright Dion Boucicault's contributions to the American drama was his effort in getting the U.S. Copyright Law of 1856 passed in order to produce and profit from his own plays. The previous, ineffective Copyright Law of 1836 had done nothing to protect American playwrights from unauthorized publication or production. In fact, once playwrights had published their plays or had sold them to a producer, they lost ownership of them. As a consequence, because some early-nineteenth-century playwrights simply refused to publish their plays, many have been lost. The 1856 law, because it required the registration only of a title but not the text, still did not provide complete protection for texts. Such protection was finally guaranteed under the Copyright Law of 1891, which was passed mainly through the efforts of Bronson Howard (1842–1908), the first American to make a full and profitable career as a professional playwright. Despite the passage of this protective law in 1891, guidelines established by the Dramatists Guild at its inception in 1912, and the Minimum Basic Agreement of 1926, playwrights were and continue to be at the mercy of directors whose interpretive productions radically could alter a script beyond recognition. But this recent phenomenon, stimulated in part by German theatrical practices, pertains to much modern drama and does not account for the unique neglect of American drama.

Arthur Hobson Quinn, in the preface to *A History of the American Drama from the Beginning to the Civil War* (1923), begins with the observation that the "one notable omission" in American literary histories had been the drama primarily because of the rarity of printed plays: "many of the stage successes, both of the past and the present, have been kept from publication by the protective instinct of the producing manager, who feared for his property rights and to whom the literary reputation of the playwright was of secondary importance" (xi). Quinn was not overstating the case; for instance, George Woodbury in *America in Literature* (1903) could make the pronouncement that "epic and drama, the two greatest literary forms, have been absent from [American literature]" (228). Therefore, for those who believed that there was such a thing as American dramatic literature, the creation of a body of works to be named "American drama" was as much a reclamation effort as it was one of identifying and canonizing texts. In 1939 in "Rediscovering American Drama," Eugene Page points first to the unprotected status of the dramatist as a major factor in the absence of printed plays, and second to the collecting of plays by the Dunlap Society and the recent teaching of American drama in colleges as two crucial steps in the recovery process.

Even when copyrighted texts were becoming available early in the century, the idea prevailed that American drama was not really literature. This point of view was argued even by those advocating appreciation and publication, such as Montrose Moses, who in his study course for the Drama League (1916) opens with equivocations about American drama's literary status. Advertising his own forthcoming edition of American plays, Moses notes the near impossibility of obtaining complete texts, pointing out the widespread practice of both the distilling and the novelizing of plays. He also points out that monthly magazines like *Current Opinion* and *Hearst's Magazine* published synopses and chunks of dialogue rather than whole plays. Further, popular plays not otherwise available in print, such as *The Girl of the Golden West, Kindling, The Lion and the Mouse, The Money Makers, Maggie Pepper, Paid in Full, The Wolf,* and *The Easiest Way* had been novelized ("Study" 24–25). The egregious practice did not die out even after full texts became available; "reading versions" of plays, that is, plays reduced to narrative lines and excerpts of dialogue, were produced by Random House in the 1950s.

The way in which drama has been and is currently being taught may also offer an answer to the question of American drama's readership. Arthur N. Applebee, in *Tradition and Reform in the Teaching of English: A History* (1974), notes two distinct phases in the appropriation of drama as a mode of instruction: The first began just before World War I when the progressives stressed oral presentation, and the second emerged in the 1960s when the British model of instruction using creative dramatics was valued as a means of fostering students' personal development. Both posed problems for the study of drama as literature; the former because it focused on self-expression, and the latter because it did not require a cognitive response. Neither called for analysis or criticism of texts in any depth. In *Theories of the Theatre* (1984), Marvin Carlson notes that after 1970, theorists increasingly focused on the text not as a dramatic piece but as a theatrical one, a "playscript" (486). The new critical concern with the dynamics of performance, as it affected the process of interpretation, again focused the greater pedagogical interest onto performance rather than literary analysis.

Because the new pedagogical approach also opens the way to teaching the plays not as essentialized classics but as performances that carry the traces of their own historical and social moments, as playscripts that also extend, critique, or deconstruct a whole tradition of performance, it would seem that the drama would be particularly appropriate for new literary studies emphasizing cultural and critical approaches to texts. In fact, this reappropriation has happened in Shakespeare studies, which have been rejuvenated by a panoply of new approaches such as feminist, psychoanalytic, New Historicist, and Marxist. The new approach to studying drama shares much with an analogous generic discipline, Film Studies, which takes quite seriously as canonized texts the popular productions of Hollywood. In fact, Film Studies criticism often brings to bear upon its subjects the methods of criticism suitable to popular culture and mass entertainment that can also illuminate the study of American drama. But cultural studies has not become a home for dramatic literature and, it is an irony worth noting, nor has it for theatre. In "Geographies of Learning: Theatre Studies, Performance, and the 'Performative'" (1993), Jill Dolan, disturbed by the "midnight raiding of our metaphors" by other disciplines, observes that "in a recently published, lengthy volume on cultural studies, none of the forty articles included is about theatre, although many look at popular forms like music, detective fiction, porn magazines, book clubs, and dancing. These exclusions and absences indicate theatre is still marked by 'high' art, in an academic moment which, through cultural studies in particular, is privileging the 'low'" (422).

The minimal presence of American dramatic literature in academe reflects larger cultural issues, such as the preference for popular and profitable performance pieces over serious drama with a strong literary and textual basis. For some historians, such as Arthur Hobson Quinn, the promise of an American dramatic literature in the nineteenth century had been altered by war. In *Representative American Plays* (1923), Quinn points out that under the guidance of the elder Wallack and Laura Keene, the late 1850s movement to bring into the theatre "pieces of significant dramatic literature" like Julia Ward Howe's *Leonora or The World's Own* (1857) was arrested by the Civil War and further frustrated by the system of traveling companies such as those managed by Dion Boucicault (387). In his account of nineteenth-century drama, William Reardon blames the "less than felicitous nature of national topics as content for the drama, as exemplified by the Barbary Wars" for the dominance of sentiment and spectacle (173). Certainly American drama has been tarnished by a strong association with commercialism since its dominance by managers in the nineteenth century and by Broadway in the twentieth, a taint that has concerned both playwrights and critics. For instance, Howard Taubman in *The Making of American Theatre* (1965) summarily dismisses the "mounting trash" of "frantic commercialism" in theatre (368). Walter J. Meserve marked in Americans a strong predilection from the beginning to the present day for "entertainment" in American theatre, a predilection he accounts for and documents in *An Emerging Entertainment: The Drama of the American People to 1828* (1977).

Broadway successes may be prominent in the general consciousness, but they are a small sample of the large output of dramatic writing in America and should have less to do with the status of drama in academe than with the culture in general. However, because newspapers and popular magazines focus mostly on Broadway triumphs and because production precedes publication, much regional and experimental drama that does not receive Broadway production and the ensuing publicity and publication is often lost as literature. Furthermore, despite an apparent love of entertainment, there is, in the Western tradition, a pervasive and long-standing cultural and social antipathy toward the theatre and, as a consequence, toward the drama. Here, for example, are four American manifestations: First, in *What a Young Husband Ought to Know* (1897), one of the "Self and Sex" series, Sylvanus Stall, D.D., addressing a paramount concern of late-nineteenth-century men, the conservation of sperm, offers the following advice: "If you wish to attain your greatest usefulness in life, avoid the undue use of foods which are calculated to stimulate the reproductive nature. Use eggs and oysters, pepper and condiments with reasonable moderation. Do not stimulate impure thinking by theatre-going, the reading of salacious books, participation in the round dance" (98). Second, in *The Great War on White Slavery or Fighting for the Protection of Our Girls* (1911), the author, Clifford G. Roe, locates the heart of the trade in the theatre, illustrating his text with line drawings of panders tricking young women (see Figures 1 and 2). "This is the most usual scheme used by white slave traders," he writes. "They pose as theatrical managers and go even into the homes of their victims to try their voices, etc. They are smooth talkers and tell what a great future awaits her. She leaves home and in a few days finds herself a white slave" (112). Third, in an examination of the division between literature and the stage in *The Atlantic Monthly* (1912), O. W. Firkins, positioning the former as spiritual and demonizing the latter as gross, sets forth the analogy that literature is to theatre as Christianity was to paganism, that is, a conversionary and purifying force. Fourth, Henri Bonnet in "Dichotomy of Artistic Genres" claims that there are only two fundamental, "pure" artistic genres, fiction and poetry: "The theater is nothing but a mode of presentation of the fictional or poetical substance. This is true to such a degree that one can transpose novels for the stage" (5). Even these four examples suggest that the idea of the contaminating "impurity" of theatre was culturally pervasive. Jonas Barish has thoroughly surveyed the history of this problem in *The*

"THE THEATRICAL SCHEME."

This is the most usual scheme used by white slave traders. They pose as theatrical managers and go even into the homes of their victims to try their voices, etc. They are smooth talkers and tell what a great future awaits her. She leaves home and in a few days finds herself a white slave.—Chapter X.

Figure 1

THE LURE OF THE STAGE—ANSWERING A WANT AD
Disreputable Theatrical Agents sometimes act as white slave traders,
alluring positions on the stage being the net used to catch young girls.

Figure 2

Anti-theatrical Prejudice (1981), but he explicitly avoids hazarding an explanation beyond observing that the intense and durable hostility toward mimicry and exhibitionism may be a worldwide phenomenon. But while this also may help explain the antidramatic bias in literary studies in general, it does not account for the neglected position of American drama in particular.

Historically, American drama has always suffered from a bad reputation. One might argue that the tradition of skepticism about drama, dating back to colonial America, suggests that the well-documented Puritan distaste for theatre and drama continues to hold strong sway over the general populace as well as academic institutions. But because Puritan strictures applied to other literary forms as well, this explanation does not adequately explain the drama's predicament. One could also look to the biases of early American critics who were instrumental in laying down patterns of taste in prominent journals and papers. For instance, in his study of the relationship between politics and literature from 1837 to 1850, John Stafford demonstrates the equation of "literature" primarily with poetry, but also with fiction and the essay; drama simply is not a consideration. As for later critical biases, Jonas Barish cites the influential "critical myopia" of Yvor Winters's rationalist, "antimimetic bias" as a strong force in American criticism, but does not go so far as to hold one critic responsible for the marginalized state of American dramatic literature (420).

The reasons espoused for the drama's lowly status have been many and various, ranging from the star system and vice in the theatre balconies to generic and critical standards and the failure of American playwrights. An anonymous article, "Decline of the Modern Drama," in *New England Magazine* (1835) raised the issue of "the prevailing practice of writing for popular actors, or 'Stars'" (105). T. R. Sullivan had similar thoughts in 1895, claiming that though the old prejudice, based on moral concerns, against the theatre was dead, nonetheless the combination of a "vicious star system," an uncritical audience, and the businessman as producer resulted in an art form seriously behind music, painting, and sculpture. Despite concerted efforts to clean up the image of theatre as a site for dissolute behavior, the association with prostitution persisted until the end of the nineteenth century and, as Claudia Johnson has shown, for good reason: It was not until the 1880s that those sympathetic as well as those antagonistic to the stage agreed that the third tier, the prostitutes' gallery, finally was closed. Johnson argues that the "degree of public, especially clerical, condemnation against which the nineteenth-century theatre had to struggle is hard to overstate" ("Tier" 583). Of the "divorce" of literature and the stage,

Charles Warner, in 1889, pointed to the displacement of "real dramas" that could be "read with pleasure" by plays of exaggerated "characters," largely dramatizations of novels, in which "the text is nothing, the action everything" (285). Detailing the extent to which the American drama adapted the native novel, Paul Wilstach in "The American Library and the Drama" (1898) documented the phenomenon from its beginning with a production of *Rip Van Winkle* in 1822 through more than fifty plays. Wilstach observed that the life of the novel often was extended by the practice and that some novels such as *Pudd'nhead Wilson*, "on account of the prohibitive price put upon it as a book," were better known as plays (137). Charles Warner's complaint was echoed in a similar one brought by Henry Davies in 1903, that the dramatization of novels confused literary forms and usurped the drama's independent creation of literature. In fact, it is clear that for some, drama meant only the superficial action on the stage and not the words, either spoken or read; in "Photography in Fiction: 'Miss Jerry,' the First Picture Play" (1895), Alexander Black published in *Scribner's Magazine* an experimental novelette accompanied by columns of photographs, which he analogized to action in a play and which freed the writer from the necessity to describe appearance or action (see Figure 3).

In 1914, Clayton Hamilton, neither the first nor the last to attack the critics and reviewers, laid the blame on the "so-called 'dramatic critics'" most of whom, he noted, were reporters (318). James Metcalfe lamented the absence of "scholarly critics to help in establishing standards for our theatre" but expressed no surprise given that Americans "are not an artistic people" and that "the theatre is not an institution we turn to for its literature" ("Criticism" 499). George Jean Nathan accused American critics of being "plush-covered" provincials suffering from "commercial Puritanism" (141). Most historians faulted the writers, who in many assessments were portrayed, probably with some accuracy, as venal panderers to public taste or as helpless pawns to managers. In 1890, Alfred Hennequin blamed the playwrights who pandered to the public for "producing mongrel compositions based upon French originals" (709). In another condemnation of American playwrights, Sheldon Cheney cites three primary reasons why they have failed: first, like Augustus Thomas, they are recruited largely from the ranks of newspaper writers; second, if they are not newsmen, then they are, like David Belasco, too schooled in theatrics, by which Cheney means insincerity; third, they have succumbed to the commercial sirens of Broadway; and, fourth, pointing out that the playwright was so inconsequential that his name was often omitted from the program, Cheney bemoans the state of affairs in which the playwright is not an artist but a "tradesman"

PHOTOGRAPHY IN FICTION

When she has gone Hamilton regrets that he has not refused to let her go alone. From a window overlooking the street he sees a man at the corner. It is Ward, who met Jerry on her way to the office, and who, in view of the quarrel, prefers not to enter. Hamilton sees her join him and walk away. Then he sends a telegram to the proprietor of the paper, who is in Washington, accepting the London commission.

When Jerry meets Ward in the street below she tells him about the strange letter, and adds, "You can't go with me."

"What will you do if I simply do go?"

"But you mustn't. I've already refused an escort. Good-by!"

"Let me walk a little way with you," says Ward, "and I'll be very good and go just when you tell me."

When they have reached Cherry Street he turns to her. "This is a horrible place. Can't I wait at the door for you?"

"No, that would make me nervous."

Ward paces the block waiting for her to come out. The house that Jerry enters is dark. In a room on the third floor she discovers the writer of the letter, who after recovering from the surprise of finding that the writer of the article is a woman, tells her the sad story of a sad life; of an early marriage and separation under the influence of her young husband's father. The young husband has been permitted to think that she is dead. "And he has made a great name now," says the woman, showing Jerry a newspaper clipping, with the Ward interview

Figure 3. "Miss Jerry" story sequence

and in which the "star system" places the drama itself beneath the acting
and the setting ("Sincerity" 502–4). The charge against the journalist-
turned-playwright also surfaces in Arthur Hobson Quinn's history of
American drama, in which he connects the phenomenon to the "wave of
melodrama which dramatized current events" around 1910. "Naturally," he
explains, "it was from newspaper offices that playwrights were recruited,"
and this episode is best forgotten in the history of drama because these plays
do not advance the "art" (*Present* I 109–12). But if this movement has been
written out of literary histories, it could and should be recovered and
reexamined in cultural histories and certainly should be connected to the
muckraking movement, the rise of realism, and the interaction between
theatre and journalism.

What is clear is that there was no one site, no one cause, no one
institution insisting on generic hegemony. However, several of the suggested causes merit closer attention, and it will be useful to begin with
playwrights who are, for some analysts, the root cause of drama's failure to
be literature. Of the many articles that have surveyed the problem, Robert
Brustein's "Why American Plays Are Not Literature" (1959) is the most
comprehensive and provoking of the modern diagnoses. Brustein touches
on the tyranny of Broadway and the taint of commercialism but places most
of the blame on the playwrights themselves. The dominance of Broadway
is, of course, a significant factor that many critics and playwrights have
cited. For instance, Arthur Miller acidly has observed that the "American
theater is five blocks long, by about one and a half blocks wide" (90). Even
those who are optimistic about noncommercial theatre recognize the power
of Broadway. Richard Kostelanetz is one of many who have expressed
concern that "tripe" is "entrenched" on Broadway ("New" 85). The concentration of the country's theatrical power and economy in such a small site
naturally has created a strong incentive if not necessity for many playwrights to conform to its values rather than to write out of a literary or
dramatic tradition.

"One of the unique features of postwar American drama," Brustein
insists, "is its cheerful isolation from a central literary tradition." Arguing
that the American dramatist would be unlikely to call himself a "literary
man," Brustein draws a grim picture of the writer "far removed, if not
completely cut off, from the mainstream of intellectual and literary discourse." Brustein goes on to suggest that this willful insularity differs
radically from the European tradition. "Besides plays," he says, "all the great
European playwrights of the past hundred years wrote poetry, epics, novels,
short stories, essays, or criticism. . . . With the exceptions of Thornton

Wilder, Tennessee Williams . . . and Arthur Miller, few American playwrights have made more than token gestures in the direction of non-dramatic literatures, while even fewer are aware of what is being attempted or said there." Finally, he argues that the split cuts both ways: "American literary culture generally scorns the stage," and novelists and poets rarely turn to the dramatic form (245–46). Nor did the passage of time and the emergence of alternatives to Broadway mellow Brustein; ten years later in his introduction to *The Third Theatre*, he rails against a host of theatrical sins including "anti-intellectualism," "sensationalism," "sexual obsessiveness," and "massacre of language," and levels the charge against the oppositional theatre challenging Broadway and the mainstream that "it may now spell as great a danger to dramatic art as the old theatre: it already embodies similar defects" (xii–xiii).

Brustein is far from the only critic to have accused American dramatists of lacking the stature of European writers. In 1916, Clayton Hamilton remarked, "Our wise men do not write for the theatre; and our playwrights are not wise" ("Something" 166). Hamilton, evaluating the range of American plays, considered only a few to be artistic achievements – *The Great Divide* (1906) by William Vaughn Moody; *The New York Idea* (1906) by Langdon Mitchell; *The Witching Hour* (1907) by Augustus Thomas; *Kindling* (1911) by Charles Kenyon; *The Scarecrow* (1911) by Percy MacKaye; *Romance* (1913) by Edward Sheldon; *Why Marry?* (1917) by Jesse Lynch Williams; and *Beyond the Horizon* (1918) by Eugene O'Neill. Of the plays he reviewed between 1906 and 1920, only *Why Marry?* by Jesse Lynch Williams and *Beyond the Horizon* by Eugene O'Neill, he believed, could bear comparison to European plays, and of those, only O'Neill's was "a great play" (Hunter 291). In 1953, Joseph Wood Krutch, in "How Modern Is the Modern American Drama?," made much the same complaint: "We have no one who has assumed a stature comparable to that of Shaw or Ibsen no matter by what standards you measure it. Several are worthy of serious consideration; several may be as good as any playwright writing today in any language. But no American of any time has been a really major figure in either the intellectual or the literary world. Four or five Europeans of the late nineteenth and early twentieth century were both" (106). To be sure, Krutch shot his poisoned dart at American drama before the posthumous productions sparked a revival of interest in O'Neill, but nonetheless O'Neill's work had been much heralded when he was alive. And even the presence of O'Neill did not dispel the dominant strain of dismissiveness. More recently, Morris Freedman in *American Drama in Social Context* (1971) wrote off American drama as only a form of "public entertainment," offering as proof that "the *Ziegfeld Follies* were theatrical happenings virtually empty of literary content" (1). He continues with his assessment: "We have not had a serious American political drama comparable to the works of Bertolt Brecht, Albert Camus, or Ugo Betti, no sustained examination of the moral complications of power, or of that large spiraling landscape lying between the lowest and highest levels of society," nothing like "Shakespeare's history plays" (7).

Though from a stringently elitist, Eurocentric perspective there might be some shadow of truth to Brustein's, Krutch's and Freedman's charges, their exaggeration of the lack of breadth and depth demonstrated by a number of American writers needs to be qualified and placed in a historical context. Most modern American playwrights have written or do write in several genres and no modern playwright, American or otherwise, produces "Shakespearean" plays. Furthermore, that American playwrights write in other genres may be the rule rather than the exception: It is true for a significant number of twentieth-century American playwrights, for instance, Paul Green, Imamu Amiri Baraka, John Howard Lawson, Arthur Miller, William Saroyan, Irwin Shaw, Lillian Hellman, Tennessee Williams, Thornton Wilder, Michael McClure, Rochelle Owens, Jack Gelber, David Mamet, and Sam Shepard.

The writing of plays in America is not limited to those who are primarily playwrights. An impressive number of writers who are known principally as novelists have, with varying degrees of success, written plays: Booth Tarkington, Bret Harte, Hamlin Garland, Stephen Crane, Harold Frederic, Henry James, Mark Twain, Joyce Carol Oates, Kurt Vonnegut, Gore Vidal, Upton Sinclair, John Dos Passos, Joseph Heller, Edna Ferber, Bruce Jay Friedman, Djuna Barnes, John Hawkes, Ayn Rand, Thomas Wolfe, Saul Bellow, Ernest Hemingway, Mary Roberts Rinehart, Truman Capote, William Dean Howells, Jane Bowles, Washington Irving, Carson McCullers, Alfred Hayes, Gertrude Stein, J. P. Donleavy, Mark Harris, James Purdy, Norman Mailer, Ray Bradbury, Robert Penn Warren, Toni Morrison, Zora Neale Hurston, and Conrad Aiken.

The diverse number of American poets who have written plays includes T. S. Eliot, Edgar Allan Poe, Edna St. Vincent Millay, Charles Olson, Anne Sexton, Wallace Stevens, Delmore Schwartz, e. e. cummings, Robinson Jeffers, Richard Eberhart, William Carlos Williams, Sylvia Plath, Randall Jarrell, Lawrence Ferlinghetti, Kenneth Koch, Robert Lowell, Robert Frost, Archibald MacLeish, James Merrill, and Kenneth Rexroth.

American writers from a great range of other disciplines also have written plays: literary critics Mark Van Doren and Edmund Wilson; drama critics Eric Bentley and Stanley Kaufmann; cultural critic Lewis Mumford; academics William Alfred and James Scheville; anthropologist Robert Ardrey; historians Martin Duberman and William Shirer; cartoonist Jules Feiffer; satirists S. J. Perelman, Dorothy Parker, and Woody Allen; and any number of newspaper journalists, such as Howard Bronson. It is also worth noting that Washington Irving (as Jonathan Oldstyle), Edgar Allan Poe, and Walt Whitman all wrote drama criticism for newspapers. Finally, no one should need to be reminded that Henry James, William Dean Howells, and T. S. Eliot contributed to dramatic theory and criticism. One tactic to resist the dominant idea that American drama is not literature would be to invoke verse drama and appreciative studies of it, such as Denis Donoghue's *The Third Voice*, but to do so would be to capitulate to the narrow, elitist assumptions about what constitutes "literature" and to make an exception for verse drama. American drama, in whatever form, is literature to the same degree as any other genre, although its patterned isolation is unique.

Patterned Isolation

The isolation of American dramatic literature from American literature was one of Arthur Hobson Quinn's concerns in *A History of the American Drama from the Civil War to the Present Day* (1936), one of the earliest and most comprehensive surveys of the genre. "One of the common errors in the discussion of American drama," he wrote, "is to assume its divorce from the main current of our literature." He points out the involvement of Irving, Willis, Bird, Boker, Longfellow, and Mrs. Howe with the pre–Civil War rise of romantic drama that paralleled the rise of other forms of romantic literature, and addresses the attempts of Twain, Harte, and Howells to write plays as an index of their regard for and attachment to the drama. For instance, Howells published his short farces about domestic and social values in *Atlantic Monthly*, *Harper's Weekly*, and *Harper's Magazine* and wrote essays on the drama from his editorial position. As far as Quinn is concerned, Howells was unsurpassed in the writing of English language farces, but "the fact that the one-act plays of Howells were acted chiefly by amateurs has obscured their significance" (66–67).

Lists of writers who have written plays should not be necessary, yet most major histories of American literature and many anthologies suggest or imply that there is no such thing as American dramatic literature. In fact, the widespread discrimination against American dramatic literature is of long standing; it is the sour leitmotif in American publishing, academic or commercial, highbrow or low, where drama in general is slighted to a great

extent but American drama virtually is erased. Even a few random examples
show the extent to which American drama is ignored and the degree to
which this neglect actually is a recent phenomenon. Both popular and
intellectual magazines used to publish plays. *Plays in Periodicals*, which
indexes the four thousand plays that were in print in ninety-seven magazines between 1900 and 1968, demonstrates the wide range of locations for
dramatic texts including: *Esquire, Ladies' Home Journal, Harper's Bazaar* and
*Harper's Monthly Magazine, House and Garden, Life, New Republic, The New
Yorker, Saturday Evening Post,* and *Saturday Review of Literature*. Fiction
and poetry are still published in most of these but not plays, a change
explained, in part, by an increased interest in an increasingly respectable,
bourgeois, and commercial theatre. For instance, the short-lived *The Seven
Arts*, later absorbed into *The Dial*, demonstrated its commitment to drama
by regularly publishing short plays. True, many were written by the editor,
James Oppenheim, but Robert Frost's *A Way Out* appeared in the February
1917 issue. *The Dial's* "Theatre Chronicle," however, regularly featured
reviewers of productions, such as Gilbert Seldes, Edmund Wilson, Padraic
Colum, and e. e. cummings. The same was true of *The Partisan Review*,
which in 1936 began a "Theatre Chronicle" column for notable reviewers
including James Farrell, Mary McCarthy, and Eric Bentley.

Learned journals that claim to be comprehensive often overlook American drama. In *TriQuarterly* magazine's special issue, "Twenty Years of the
Best Contemporary Writing and Graphics" (Spring/Summer 1985), there is
no drama. *The New Criterion's* special issue, "The Arts in America, 1945–
1985" (Summer 1985), ignores the drama. *The New York Review of Books* has
no regular drama reviewers, rarely reviews published plays, and even then
only in the form of a general retrospective, such as Robert Mazzocco's "Sam
Shepard's Big Roundup." The segregation extends even to publishers' catalogues; for instance, the 1993 Harcourt Brace Jovanovich catalogue places
novels, short stories, poetry, belles lettres, and biography under "literature,"
but puts drama, film, journalism, and African-American and Women's
Studies under "humanities." A striking exception to this bleak situation is
The Kenyon Review, which in the last few years, despite a preponderance of
poetry and fiction, nonetheless has published almost one play per issue and
has devoted an entire issue (Spring 1993) to the theatre.

Scholarly journals, with the notable exception of *American Quarterly*, also
slight American drama. Furthermore, at best the coverage will be of a
substantially canonized figure. The last article on American drama to
appear in *PMLA* was "Notes on the Antecedents of *Anna Christie*" by
Claude R. Flory in 1971. Before that, *PMLA* published Doris Alexander's

"Psychological Fate in *Mourning Becomes Electra*" in 1953. At the rate of one every twenty years, *PMLA* is about due for another article on American drama, although it recently published a special topics issue on performance (May 1992), a subject that seems to be pushing drama as literature further out of the picture. In the last two decades, *Contemporary Literature*, despite a pronounced proclivity for Samuel Beckett and one article each on Pinter and Friel, has included nothing on American drama. Only two articles on this subject, one on O'Neill and one on Stein, have appeared in the last twenty years of *Twentieth Century Literature*. Until the mid-eighties, only two articles on American drama, one on O'Neill, the other on Miller, had been published in *American Literature*. Since then, *American Literature* has published two articles on O'Neill in 1987, presumably to get a jump on the centennial of O'Neill's birth, and one on Adrienne Kennedy in 1991. In the newer journals animated by wide theoretical concerns, the drama in general and American drama in particular generally are ignored. *New Literary History*, founded in 1969, published a performance issue in Spring 1971 and has published articles on Beckett and medieval and Renaissance drama, but otherwise it gives priority to prose and poetry. Since its inception in 1974, *Critical Inquiry*, despite an interest in film and detective fiction as well as poetry and prose, has never dealt with American drama. Despite the announced intention of guest editor Donald Pease to explore the new interventionist, revisionist, and counterhegemonic moves against the American canon in *boundary 2* (Spring 1990), the "concrete fantasy" of the field-imaginary remains undisturbed by the reality of American dramatic literature.

Finally, if Richard Ohmann is correct in his analysis of canon formation for fiction in the 1960s and 1970s in *Critical Inquiry* (1983), the *New York Times* was the most influential agent for creating, disseminating, and sustaining the values and beliefs of the educated, professional, professorial, and upwardly mobile book market and for fixing certain works in the culture as "literature." So where does this leave dramatic literature? Apparently, out of the professional-managerial classes' social and academic experiences. Because the *New York Times* reviews theatrical productions, the *New York Times Book Review* never reviews published plays. In other words, a production is taken as equivalent to the text and is not understood to be only an interpretation by a director. Once again, the theatrical enactment, a temporary manifestation, is privileged over the author's direct statement, the permanent record.

Charles A. Carpenter has summarized the problem from a bibliographer's perspective: "In the context of American literature, drama surely ranks last among the major forms. Its status as an academic discipline is roughly but graphically conveyed by the space it occupies in *American Literary Scholarship*. . . . The discussions of noteworthy scholarship and criticism on drama and theater fill only 4 percent of the total space. Studies of Melville alone require 4.5 percent" (3). The critical energy devoted to Melville has less to do with the volume of his work than with his valorized place in the canon; after all, Gertrude Stein wrote seventy-seven plays but book-length studies didn't materialize until the 1990s. The discrimination against American drama, however, is not manifested in scholarly journals devoted to drama and theatre; in *Modern Drama* and *Theatre Journal*, for instance, articles on American drama figure regularly and prominently.

The problem of the discrimination against American drama is not just confined to scholarship and literary journals. The standard college anthologies employed to teach American literature exclude the drama to an astonishing degree. Howard Mumford Jones and Ernest Leisy's *Major American Writers* (1935) is typical of early anthologies in that it has no drama. The only play in Jay Hubbell's *American Life in Literature* (1951), a collection of the works of forty-seven "important writers" who were "thinking about American problems," is O'Neill's *The Emperor Jones* (xiii). Most first volumes of more recent two-volume anthologies of American literature, although they include a wide variety of materials such as meditations, letters, humor, folklore, and songs, simply omit drama. For example, the first volume of *The Norton Anthology of American Literature* (1979) contains no plays. Neither does the first volume of Blair, Hornberger, Stewart, and Miller's *The Literature of the United States* (1966).

This pattern of exclusion reflects the critics' constant refrain that American drama before Eugene O'Neill was, in Howard Mumford Jones's term, "subliterary," or in Eric Bentley's words, "almost moronic" (Jones "Orphan" 158; Bentley "Chronicle" 416). Even the inclusion of O'Neill in the American canon as the foremost of American dramatists often comes with a caveat. Edmund Wilson, reviewing American literature in 1926, remarked, "as for the dramatists, there is still only O'Neill who . . . remains a typical naturalistic dramatist of something under the very first rank." Of the others writing during the preceding fifteen years, Wilson says that "they forget critical standards in their devotion to the great common cause – the cause of an American national literature in independence of English literature, and of the contemporary American mind as against the mind of the last generation" (158–59). Homer Woodbridge, who in 1938 included O'Neill in the canon with trepidation, warned that "this is not as high praise as it sounds; for drama has always been the weak spot in American literature.

Up to the Great War we produced almost no plays of more than immediate contemporary interest – almost none which had literary value or prospect of permanence" (307). This judgment, of course, leaves aside the contextual interest of other genres and begs the question of what is literature.

But the situation is not much better for the later decades, when American drama is generally conceded to have come into its own. Eugene O'Neill's *The Hairy Ape* is the only play included in Walter Blair's 1,300-page textbook *The Literature of the United States* (1949). In the 1956 and 1962 editions of Bradley, Beatty, and Long's *The American Tradition in Literature*, Eugene O'Neill's *The Hairy Ape* is also the only play and O'Neill the only playwright included in a collection of seventy-four authors. Archibald MacLeish, T. S. Eliot, e. e. cummings, Robert Lowell, and Robinson Jeffers, all playwrights, too, are represented only as poets. The 2,043-page second volume of *Anthology of American Literature: Realism to the Present* (1974), edited by George McMichael, is marginally more comprehensive than most college anthologies because it includes not only the ubiquitous *The Hairy Ape* but also *Zoo Story* and *Dutchman*. In the nearly two thousand pages of Bradley, Beatty, and Long's *The American Tradition in Literature*, volume II of the fourth edition (1974), there is no nineteenth-century drama and the entire twentieth century is represented by two plays, O'Neill's *The Hairy Ape* and Williams's *The Glass Menagerie*. Furthermore, no drama is discussed under likely thematic headings such as "Literary Expressions of Social Thought: The 1930's and 1940's." *American Literature Survey* (1975), a four-volume anthology covering the colonial period to the present and edited by Milton Stern and Seymour Gross, includes only one play, O'Neill's *The Hairy Ape*.

Things got worse in 1979. The new, renamed *The Norton Anthology of American Literature*, edited by Ronald Gottesman et al., supposedly brought up-to-date by a more inclusive editorial policy, and now uniform in design and title with the rest of the "Nortons," was divided into four sections. Under literature from 1865 to 1914, there was no drama. From 1914 to 1945, there was no drama. The last two sections, covering 1945 to the present, were devoted exclusively to poetry and prose. Thus, any student using the two volumes of the 1979 edition during the six years they were current could have assumed there was no such thing as American drama in the entire history of American literature. John Benedict, vice-president and editor at W. W. Norton, later explained that the teachers who were consulted when the anthology was being compiled were "not interested in drama," and that in hindsight he recognized that the exclusion of plays was "a mistake" (personal correspondence). The problem for American drama, therefore, became one simply of representation, not just of distinctions based on literary merit.

Accounting for Neglect: Literary History

Why should American drama have been and continue to be discriminated against and neglected? Historically, American drama has always suffered from a bad reputation. The tradition of suspicion about drama, dating back to colonial America, suggests that the well-documented Puritan distaste for theatre and drama holds strong sway over general as well as academic inclinations. The dismissive tone is set in the first history of American literature, Samuel L. Knapp's *Lectures on American Literature* (1829), which makes descriptive, nonjudgmental, and passing references to only three playwrights: Thomas Godfrey, the first American playwright to be professionally produced in America with *The Prince of Parthia*; political satirist Mercy Otis Warren; and poet-preacher John Blair Linn. Joseph Gostwick's *Hand-Book of American Literature* (1856), which begins its coverage in 1620 and includes backwoods writings as well as religious pamphlets, has nothing on drama. Thirty years later, Charles Richardson in *American Literature 1607–1885* dismissed native American drama, which "has never risen into the place of true literature," as not fit "for the library lamp" (17). Though Richardson suggested that one hundred years earlier the prospects for an American drama seemed good, he blames William Dunlap, John Howard Payne, and Charles Taylor for pretentiousness and sentimentalism. In fact, Richardson admitted only two plays, George H. Boker's *Francesca da Rimini* (1855) and Dwight's "grave poem of the epic class," *Conquest of Canaan*, into the sacred confines of literature. In 1901, Barrett Wendell argued that no American drama could "claim serious consideration," although he then proceeded to document the extensive popularity of theatre in America (517). His Anglophilia was much in evidence because he said that theatres in New England "were held in such abhorrence that even so lately as 1850 the Boston Museum, whose stock company at that time *admirably preserved the old traditions of the English stage* [my emphasis], advertised its auditorium as a lecture-room and its performances of standard comedies as lectures" (247). Even Montrose Moses's contribution to the *Cambridge History of American Literature* (1918) wrote off the drama as tainted by journalism in the 1880s and by melodrama in the 1900s, and as a consequence either academic and aloof or commercial and popular. Its greatest fault was that it had "no philosophical body of ideas" (294). Even American critics who devoted themselves to the drama tended to focus on foreign playwrights. Percy Boynton documented the gradual shift in 1931: "In 1905 Hunecker's *Iconoclasts* dealt with Norwegian, French, German, Russian, Italian, Belgian and English dramatists, and Hale's *Dramatists of To-day* was of the same complexion. But by 1910 the drift was suggested in Eaton's *At the New Theater and Others*, about half of which was devoted to American themes" ("American" 484–85).

Literary historians writing in the thirties, though still contemptuous of American drama, began to make an effort to document the causes for its second-rate status, a status most accepted without question. Charles Angoff, in his four-volume *A Literary History of the American People* (1931), points an accusatory finger at persistent Puritanism. He notes that Harvard, though it modeled itself after Cambridge and Oxford, did not follow their example in including playwriting in its curriculum. The moral issue was compounded by a political one: From 1774 to 1783, the theatre was under full control of the British military. The moral bias against theatre persisted up to the Civil War. In 1824, Yale's president declaimed that to indulge in playgoing meant "'nothing more or less than the loss of that most valuable treasure, the immortal soul'" (375). Angoff did not regret the slighting of drama: "All of the plays by native Americans before 1815 have only historic interest today. They were considerably inferior to the contemporary fiction or verse, bad as they were" (377). V. F. Calverton observed that, because of the dominance of the Episcopal church in the South (with the exception of North Carolina) in the eighteenth century, the aristocracy (as opposed to the bourgeoisie) allowed the theatre to flourish. The mood shifted as the economic power base went north with industry: "Although after 1814 there were scarcely any states of the Atlantic Seaboard which still forbade stage performances, as late as 1845, Phineas T. Barnum found it necessary to call his theatre in New York a 'Moral Lecture Room' as a subterfuge to ward off attack" (*Liberation* 118). In *An Hour of American Drama* (1930), Barrett Clark was very severe about the shortcomings of early American drama. Of Herne, Howard, and Fitch, he observed: "It is not the quaintness of the language and the labored style of these plays that has caused them to be forgotten, it is the fundamental fact that they are the products of superficial writers, of men who could say and believe that 'plays are not written but re-written'" (20).

Russell Blankenship, in *American Literature as an Expression of the National Mind* (1931), making a distinction between "dramatic worth" and "theatrical effectiveness," notes that "the dearth of masterpieces in American drama before O'Neill" is really no different from the situation in English drama between the passing of Goldsmith and Sheridan and the rise of Wilde (709; 702). As to the reasons for the paucity of "fine native plays," Blankenship cites the "vague impropriety" of the stage suspected by large numbers of Americans, the slavish devotion to Shakespeare, the dominance of rhetorical declamation associated with romantic tendencies, and the lack of financial rewards for playwrights until long after the Civil War. Percy Boynton, in *Literature and American Life* (1936), echoes the other critics of the thirties in tracing the bias against drama to several causes, including Puritan repression, the prohibitions of the Continental Congress War Measure act of 1774, which discouraged colonists from horse racing, cockfighting, and playgoing, and the commercial and superficial manager-dominated theatres of the nineteenth century. Howard Mumford Jones and Ernest Leisy did not include playwrights in *Major American Writers* (1935), but they did argue that the "humorless reasonableness" of "sociological" drama, that is, the serious "problem" play, written before 1910 was simply a weak echo of the magazines that were excoriating modern industrial society: "When the American stage was reborn after its long immersion in false and theatrical romanticism, it became too accusatory" (20).

Of course, English taste dictated American taste to a large degree. For example, James Nelson Barker's theatricalization of *Marmion; or, The Battle of Flodden Field* (1812) was initially presented as being English in order to avoid the neglect accorded to native works (Bordman 52). Not everyone embraced English drama unequivocally. In 1827, early on in the establishment of a dramatic canon, James Kirk Paulding, a reviewer for the *American Quarterly Review*, expected that he was surprising his readers with the information that there were sixty American dramas, some of them "not entirely unworthy of being read" and quite the equal of their London counterparts. Noting the prevailing "decline in dignity and usefulness" of the stage now "notorious" in England, Paulding feared it was almost "inevitable" that American drama, too much lacking in "wholesome, manly and vigorous taste," would also slide into decline (332). Paulding's worries notwithstanding, the English drama prevailed. According to another historian, "it was not until the late nineteenth century that prejudice against an American-made play subsided. In fact, American plays were sometimes put on anonymously with the intent that the audience should think them foreign contributions" (Mayorga 75). Though Harold J. Nichols credited the War of 1812 and the ensuing rise of nationalism with the beginning of a decline in prejudice against native works, a persistent Anglophilia marred the reception of American drama by both audiences and critics.

Literary histories written after the 1930s pose another problem. The strident, engaged voices of dramatists from the radical Left that were rumbling in the twenties and howling in the thirties gave rise to critical unease; to the conservatives, when drama became a weapon, it was understood to be the enemy, if not also the antithesis, of literature. Leftist theatre focused on social issues, played to the proletarian masses, and had a decidedly didactic goal. Plays, such as George O'Neil's indictment of the middle class, *American Dream* (1933); John Wexley's assault on the courts' unjust prosecution of minorities, *They Shall Not Die* (1934); the protest about the plight of farmers, *Triple-A Plowed Under* (1936) by Arthur Arent and the editorial staff of the Living Newspaper; and Marc Blitzstein's *The Cradle Will Rock* (1937), were firmly rooted in historical and political consciousness, more often challenging than reaffirming received American values, taking an adversarial and critical position toward dominant ideologies. This form of American drama went up against both existing proscriptions about the style and dominant beliefs regarding the function of literature. And the hostility toward pageant drama, a prevalent phenomenon, tarred the drama further with a populist brush. Furthermore, in the struggle to validate English philology and literary history in the face of resistance from classicists, both scholars and generalists valorized the inclusion of American literature in university curricula by holding it up to the Arnoldian model. As a consequence of the New Criticism in particular, "literature" was limited to the stylistically subtle, psychologically intricate, and epistemologically complex. The result was a white, phallocentric, crypto-Christian cultural conservatism that slammed shut the door on an enormous body of works integral to American cultural history. This narrowing of the definition of "literature" marks a turning point in the critical treatment of American drama.

Traditionally, American critics have been defensive chauvinists or nervous apologists for native drama. Edgar Allan Poe, in a defense of American drama in the *American Whig Review* in 1845, insisted that the American drama had "*not declined*" but offered weak proof in his long approval of Willis's *Tortesa, the Usurer* and longer criticism of Longfellow's "dramatic poem," *The Spanish Student*. Poe argued that drama depended on imitative "spirituality," should only advance in terms of "mechanisms," and should never be adulterated with other genres, such as poetry. Walt Whitman is more representative of the critics who cast a cold eye on American theatre when he wrote, "of what is called the drama, or dramatic presentation in the United States, I should say it deserves to be treated with the same gravity, and on a par with the questions of ornamental confectionery at public dinners, or the arrangement of curtains and hangings in a ball-room, – nor more, nor less" (511). Arts critic James Gibbons Huneker, whom historian Glenn

Hughes named "the most important influence on American dramatic criticism" and whose tastes were formed in Europe, echoed this dismissive attitude with his own evaluation that the American stage "is beneath critical contempt" (Hughes 408; Norton 322). That he went on to write drama criticism from 1890 to 1921 suggests something of the love–hate relationship many critics have had with American drama, a tension thoroughly documented in Alan Downer's *American Drama and Its Critics* (1965) and in Moses and Brown's *The American Theatre as Seen by Its Critics, 1752–1934* (1934).

At the turn of the century, Percy MacKaye, playwright Steele's ambitious and idealistic son, sought the creation of a "Drama of Democracy" that would be neither an imitation of what he called the "Segregated Drama" based on European ideals nor the vaudevillean alternative. The former, MacKaye dismissed as drama for a sophisticated few, the anemic, "corroding remains of an aristocratic system now mingled with *bourgeoisie*"; the latter as an amusement as "coherent as shoes and sealing-wax" fit only for "aborigines of Patagonia." The "Drama of Democracy," on the other hand, would, like the Greek drama which, according to MacKaye, "infused generations of shepherds, bankers, and street gamins with a judicious enthusiasm for the fine art of dramatic poetic," speak of a New World optimism and wholesomeness to a community tightly bound by "science and inter-communication" (100–117). Unfortunately, MacKaye's own efforts as a playwright were too forced; Montrose Moses, calling for a "regeneration" by way of an intellectual improvement in the theatre, noted that the dialogue clogged with sentiment and allusion produced by MacKaye was not the answer ("Regeneration" 587).

But as early as 1914, Sheldon Cheney, the first editor of *Theatre Arts Magazine*, the voice of the theatre arts movement, was expressing concern that the promise of the revolution had not been realized: "No American Shaw or Yeats has been born of the struggle against the established order" (untitled editorial, 1). Cheney sought salvation for American drama in a Maeterlinckean symbolist "aesthetic" and a Galsworthian "psychologic" realism presented in a "re-theatricalized" style (16). Like Cheney, his successor, Kenneth Macgowan, a seminal influence on O'Neill, advocated imitation of the European models in the early 1920s, urging the movement away from realism to presentational or expressionistic drama, arguments he made in *The Theatre of Tomorrow* (1921) and with Robert Edmond Jones in *Continental Stagecraft* (1922). Because Europe was still the evaluative touchstone it was inevitable that the new American art theatre would be tested by that measure and, given that much of it was necessarily derivative, equally as inevitable that it would be found wanting.

A span of five decades reveals the pervasive neglect of drama in several of the important classic literary histories. Stanley Williams's *American Literature* (1933), F. O. Matthiessen's *American Renaissance* (1941), Harry Hayden Clark's *Transitions in American Literary History* (1953), Robert Spiller's *The Oblique Light* (1968), and Marcus Cunliffe's *American Literature to 1900* (1973) are silent on the drama. Histories with a narrower focus are equally culpable. Fred Lewis Pattee's *The New American Literature, 1890–1930* (1930) covers biography and criticism for this period but does not even mention Eugene O'Neill, let alone any other playwright. Even when the canon begins to be challenged in 1937, in such articles as Bernard De Voto's "At the Cannon's Mouth," drama is not the issue. The hierarchy of established "great" novelists and poets is shuffled, but playwrights are not included; it is still only a matter of "who's on first," because the players never change. None of this should come as much of a surprise, of course, because the canonical texts and critical dispositions were laid down early. In an analysis of early historics of American literature published between 1882 and 1912, Nina Baym summarizes the conclusions the historians regularly pointed to: "a striking increase in the production of long and short fiction along with a decrease in poetry; the dominance of the school of realism in fiction. . . ; the development of a distinct type of humorous literature; and . . . New York City as the chief American literary center" (475–76).

In and after the middle of the century, when the expectation might be for an opening up of the canon to include what is known as "marginal" works, the drama is still neglected. James D. Hart's survey *The Popular Book: A History of America's Literary Taste* examines works up to 1949. It includes everything from Norman Vincent Peale's *A Guide to Confident Living*, Toynbee's *A Study of History*, and Van Wyck Brooks's *The Flowering of New England*, along with lots of fiction and poetry – but it mentions not a single play. John McCormick's *The Middle Distance: A Comparative History of American Imaginative Literature: 1919–1932* (1971) and Everett Carter's *The American Idea: The Literary Response to American Optimism* (1977), like so many thematic studies, draw only on novels and poetry. Warner Berthoff, who might have been expected to use American drama as part of his ammunition in his 1979 survey *Literature Without Qualities: American Writing Since 1945*, does not even consider the drama. Alfred Kazin's ceremonial concatenation of modern "greats" in *An American Procession* (1984), a work that claims to examine the major American writers from 1830 to 1930, what he calls the "crucial century," for all intents and purposes excludes playwrights. For instance, Gertrude Stein is considered only to the extent to which she was an influence on Hemingway, and John

Dos Passos is examined only as a novelist. Eugene O'Neill is not mentioned.

Those few literary histories that do include the drama radically limit coverage. Out of 764 pages in Russell Blankenship's *American Literature as an Expression of the National Mind* (1949), only fifteen concern drama. Marcus Cunliffe in *The Literature of the United States* (1954) devotes a seventeen-page chapter to white male playwrights, beginning with what he terms the "bastard art-form" of the nineteenth century, but half the chapter is devoted to O'Neill. In Leon Howard's *Literature and the American Tradition* (1960), which spans the years from 1608 to 1956 in three hundred pages, six pages in the epilogue are given to brief mention of seven white male playwrights writing in the twenties and thirties (Odets, O'Neill, Anderson, Lawson, Rice, Saroyan, and Wilder). O'Neill is characterized as an exciting voice of frustration, but for Howard the year 1939 marks the end of his interest in drama. In *American Writing in the Twentieth Century* (1960), Willard Thorp calls the burst of dramatic activity between 1915 and 1940 only an "interlude." After World War II, he writes, there are only three playwrights of distinction: Inge, Williams, and Miller. For Thorp, "literary distinction" has everything to do with "ideological content," by which he means "social and political philosophy," organic themes far preferable to the mere vitiating theatricality of the Gilded Age (63–68). Willis Wager's *American Literature: A World View* (1968) contains plot summaries of plays by prominent male playwrights but makes no attempt to analyze or contextualize American drama. A recent four-volume history, Goldman's *American Literature in Context* (1983), which in the preface promises a "comprehensive sequence of interpretations of major American texts – fiction and non-fiction, poetry and drama," includes only one chapter on drama and that one, of course, is on O'Neill. Such concentration on O'Neill, understandable given his productivity and experimental range, seriously imbalances the history. The heralding of O'Neill as the savior of American drama, which marks so many histories, reveals the deep-seated desire for the victory of classical, namely hegemonic, values over threateningly unfamiliar and lower-class voices. Percy Boynton's assessment in 1936 is characteristic of the early reception of O'Neill; Boynton praises O'Neill for continuing "to dream the Greek dream in modern terms" (828).

At this point, it might seem like ungrateful carping to complain about any literary history that actually does deign to notice the drama, but those that are to some degree responsible about including the drama narrowly segregate it from the rest of American literature. Robert Spiller's *The Cycle of American Literature* (1955), a consideration of major writers in their historical context, makes an attempt to explain the lack of experimentation and originality in drama before 1920 by citing the commercial emphasis of the theatre and the dominance of Broadway spectacles. Of the five pages (of 2,280) that he devotes to drama, three are given to plot summaries of O'Neill's plays, the other two to a list of white male playwrights prominent in the twenties and thirties, a period he characterizes as "naturalist-symbolist." He has nothing to say about the forties and fifties. Such radically limited considerations of the drama are manifest. The Spiller revised fourth edition of *Literary History of the United States* (1978) excludes consideration of the drama from many likely general chapters such as "The Literature of Ideas," "The Hope of Reform," and "Delineation of Life and Character." Of the eighty-six chapters, four concern drama and three focus exclusively on the dominant white male playwrights. The *Harvard Guide to Contemporary American Writing* (1979) follows the familiar format: One chapter of twelve examines the drama, no plays are considered in the "Women's Literature" chapter, and only James Baldwin's *Blues for Mister Charlie* gets a one-sentence acknowledgment in the chapter entitled "Black Literature." Such compartmentalizing disallows the thematic connections with other genres, closes avenues of comparison, and generally impoverishes the study of American literature and culture. As editor of the new *Cambridge History of American Literature*, Sacvan Bercovitch addresses the concerns facing the new historians: "One is the recognition that questions of race and gender are integral to formalist analysis" ("Ideology" 637). One can only hope that questions of genre, linked as they are to race and gender, also will be recognized and that drama finally will be given an equal place in American literary history.

But if American drama is too low for literary historians of high culture, it also seems to be too high for low culture; in Russel Nye's *New Directions in Popular Culture* (1972), a collection of essays on popular culture that includes studies on dime novels and Sunday school books, drama is not considered. The historically pervasive disregard for the drama is proven repeatedly in Jay Broadus Hubbell's *Who Are the Major American Writers? A Study of the Changing Literary Canon* (1972). The only playwright who appears in Hubbell's lists of the "best" is Eugene O'Neill, and even then only infrequently. Nor does American drama fall under the rubric of mass media or communication arts in books on those subjects which do consider American television, radio, and film. Even critics critical of the critics don't trouble themselves over the question of drama in or out of the canon. In a 1967 consideration of critics from Irving Babbitt to F. O. Matthiessen, *The Rediscovery of American Literature: Premises of Critical Taste, 1900–1940*,

Richard Ruland does not examine why the earlier critics did not examine drama.

C. W. E. Bigsby, the British historian of American drama, observes that "the serious academic study of American drama is a comparatively recent phenomenon and did not start on any scale until the 1950s." He points to the establishment of major journals during this period, such as *Educational Theatre Journal* (1949), *Tulane Drama Review* (1955), *Modern Drama* (1958), and *Theatre Survey* (1960), and goes on to lament "that the failure of the American theatre to rise to a level of sustained seriousness has been matched by a corresponding failure of criticism to identify the nature of that theatre's actual achievements." As a consequence, "drama is relatively ignored by the serious critic" ("Cultural" 331–332).

Four Charges Against American Drama

Part of the problem of the second-rate status of American drama stemmed from an anxious desire to compete with the European models, a concern that preoccupied all the early American writers. The conflict between the felt need for a native, democratic drama and the artificial anxiety created by competition with the European models forms the basis for most of the arguments over the failure of American drama to be "literature." But, like the blind men describing the elephant, the critics, groping to assess an enormous puzzle, have touched only on parts of the problem. Of the many charges laid against American drama, four sweeping generalizations recur most often: that American drama is emotional rather than intellectual, subliterary rather than literary, theatrical rather than dramatic, and derivative rather than indigenous.

The first problem was anticipated by Alexis de Tocqueville when he wrote, "In democracies, dramatic pieces are listened to, but not read. Most do not go there to seek the pleasures of the mind, but the keen emotions of the heart" (349). Henry James made a similar observation in 1875: "'American' theatre is Irish, French or English and the public doesn't care if the images are true or not. It has gone to look and listen, to laugh and cry – not to think" (23). Writing in 1918 for *The Drama*, Chester Calder, directing his attention to the ways in which the drama could be made to work for the unified democracy felt to be at issue in postwar America, asserted that drama's "primary appeal is to the emotion, and that dramatist who would succeed with the largest number of people should study the psychology of the crowd. Humanity in the mass demands simplicity of story and treatment" (53). More recently, Saul Bellow, himself a playwright,

echoed this observation with his statement stressing the primacy of the
emotional appeal of dramatic performance: "I am not a highbrow, though
I do not disclaim intelligence, and I do not go to the theater in quest of
ideas but to be diverted, delighted, awed, and in search of opportunities to
laugh and to cry" (312). For Clayton Hamilton, the American demand for
entertainment meant that playwrights were technically advanced but basically empty. After all, he waspishly noted, "a dramatist is a playwright with
something to say" (*Conversations* 182). For critics such as John Simon and
Robert Brustein, this absence of "idea" is the fundamental flaw of American
drama. The acerbic Simon blames the audience: "The American people in
general and Broadway theatre-goers in particular, do not want drama" (55).
Brustein, on the other hand, faults the playwrights: "American drama often
seems to be the most mindless form of legitimate culture since eighteenth-
century sentimental comedy, a form to which it bears more than a little
resemblance . . . most playwrights are devoted to dramatizing sensations
which grow more hysterical and rarefied with every passing year" ("Why"
252). Sharing this view, Walter P. Eaton had earlier argued that because
"the end of drama is the emotional excitation of an audience in a theatre,"
the nature of any drama does not warrant a purely literary analysis and that
American drama in particular ought to be studied from the historical and
sociological point of view ("American" 82). Philip Rahv links the "romances" before Henry James with the state of the drama: "The literature of
early America is a sacred rather than a profane literature. Immaculately
spiritual at the top and local and anecdotal at the bottom, it is essentially,
as the genteel historian Barrett Wendell accurately noted, a 'record of the
national inexperience' marked by 'instinctive disregard of actual fact.' For
this reason it largely left untouched the two chief experimental media – the
novel and the drama" (364).

   As a consequence of addressing itself to the heart rather than the head,
a charge many critics and playwrights would take exception to, American
drama has been vilified as being "subliterary." In his long career as a theatre
critic, John Gassner worried this problem like a sore tooth. Accusing
American drama of "a want of language" and "a low-grade sensibility," he
concluded, in "A Hundred Years of American Theatre" (1963), that America did not get a literary theatre: "The poetry in the American drama has
been *poesie de theatre* rather than strictly verbal poetry, which does not give
the plays themselves distinction as dramatic literature," and "the twentieth-
century American drama may come to be known as the greatest *subliterary*
drama in the history of the Western theatre" (247–49). In a later lecture,
"An Appraisal of the Contemporary American Stage" (1964), he com-

pounded this criticism with the complaint that American drama was also "subtragic," echoing the received notion of the supremacy of a classical-style tragedy in the dramatic hierarchy (354). Gassner is not alone in his view. Brustein also cites "an indifference to language" that makes American drama "rarely readable"; most playwrights, he continues, "are charter members of a cult of inarticulacy" ("Why" 250).

The problem is fraught with ironies. American drama before World War I was thought to be empty spectacle; the commercial nature of manager-dominated theatre disallowed serious drama. As a consequence, American drama was slow to catch up with what had been the province of the novel, what James Salem characterizes as the honest and complex confrontation of the social, moral, and sexual problems of American life (54). But when American playwrights embraced realism as the means by which to dramatize the issues pertinent to modern American life, the critics continued to howl; only the tune changed. At least three critics blame the dramatists' commitment to realism for a lack of heightened or "literary" language. American theatre failed to "deliver genius" for Clive Barnes because "the impulse, the actual need for theatrical realism, persisted too long" (xii-xiii). Vivian Mercier pronounces American drama to be "moribund" because the "force of Realism" renders it "mechanical" (375). Mary McCarthy, too, finds that the dramatists "pledged to verisimilitude" (26) strive against the constraints of realism and write pretentiously and hollowly; as a consequence, such writers are "cursed with inarticulateness" (30).

Whatever the merits of the charge that modern American drama lacks "literary" language, it is certainly true that much contemporary drama increasingly has moved away from a purely literary text and toward performance values. For most critics, this development has simply worsened a bad situation. Bonnie Marranca identifies this movement as "the single most important feature of contemporary theatre." Of the changes in the sixties and seventies, she observes that "value came increasingly to be placed on performance with the result that the new theatre never became a literary theatre, but one dominated by images – visual and aural" (77). But most critics contend that America has never had a literary theatre. Herbert Blau, for instance, argues that the "tactile experimentation of the sixties and seventies" simply compounded the existing "faintness of mind" and "verbal and intellectual deficiencies" that characterize American drama in general (520). Even Ruby Cohn, a critic who has made a study of American drama from the point of view of its distinctive dialogue, insists that "only four American playwrights [O'Neill, Miller, Williams, and Albee] have produced distinctive dialogue" and concludes that "the best modern American dramas fall short of the best European" (314). The recent development of what Richard Kostelanetz calls "the theatre of mixed means," a theatre that has revolted against "the predominance of the word," marks, for him, a connection with the American tradition of a nonliterary stage that precludes the kind of "theatre of literature" that thrives in Europe: "What theatrical genius we have had in America would seem to express itself primarily not in playwriting but performance . . . we should recognize once and for all that a European tradition of a theatre of literature . . . will not thrive . . . on these shores" (*Theatre* 26–28).

As for the charge that American drama has been only a weak reflection of European models, John Gassner, who is on the defensive as often as he is on the offensive, argues that while it is too soon (in 1952) to judge whether a "vital American drama could arise from the new critics' specifications," at least American drama has ceased to be "provincial." Begging the real issue, he calls for an indigenous drama that would reflect its "rough, bouncing and democratic context" ("Answer" 59–61). Robert Brustein, who also calls for a native drama with its own identity, is less sanguine about the possibility. Though he places his hopes in the "American literary men" such as Lowell, Roth, Malamud, and Koch, all of whom were writing plays in the mid-sixties, he bemoans the fact that American drama is "stagnating in its parasitical dependence on the style and substance of foreign works," a complaint that can be traced back to the earliest critics of American drama ("New" 124, 138).

Critical Disdain

Ultimately, much of the blame for disregarding American drama, however legitimate the charges against it may have been given the proscriptions of any particular period, must be placed on the literary and cultural critics. At present, American drama has been out of the literary-critical and theoretical arena for so long that it no longer even figures in a general literary critic's vocabulary or frame of reference. Reginald Gibbons's approach is typical. In an essay on the current state of academic criticism and contemporary literature, he uses such phrases as "when neither fiction writers nor poets" and "what a writer of fiction or poetry misses" (15). In ignoring the drama he joins the bulging ranks of American critics who have turned American drama into an invisible genre. If the critics don't see it, it ceases to exist.

The disdainful, elitist attitude toward American drama was solidified firmly by the critics who turned American drama into a nonliterary, hence "invisible," genre. Historically, the "schools" of Americanist criticism have ignored American drama. The "New York Intellectuals," such as Irving

Howe, Alfred Kazin, and Lionel Trilling, do not consider American drama. Nor do Leo Marx, R. W. B. Lewis, and Charles Sanford, the American "Myth-symbol Critics." The "New Critics" are another matter. René Wellek and Austin Warren do analyze drama in *Theory of Literature* (1949), but all their examples are drawn from classical and European literature. The same is true of Cleanth Brooks and Robert Heilman in *Understanding Drama* (1945). When Eric Bentley, in *The Playwright as Thinker* (1946), legitimized serious critical attention to modern Western drama, he did so at the expense of American drama. Focusing on the giants of European drama, Strindberg, Ibsen, Brecht, et al., Bentley put O'Neill, Odets, and Wilder on hold, as it were, because he found them to be merely "promising" (xvi). Though critical appreciation of the drama in general benefited from Bentley's study, American drama in particular stayed in the shadows of academe.

Certainly within the academic community, the dominance of New Criticism's formalist, aesthetic, intratextual analysis has been the most damaging force against the consideration of American drama as literature. John Gassner anticipated the potential damage to be done in "'There Is No American Drama' – A Premonition of Discontent" (1952), observing that though American drama had never been exempt from criticism, "it was badgered rather than written off" (24). Those educated during the years when New Criticism held sway are those who fixed the American canon, created the texts, and edited the journals that froze the prejudice against American drama. Emphasizing the self-sufficiency of a work of art, New Criticism, by definition, had to struggle against the drama, the least autonomous and most contextual of literary forms. It is hardly surprising that the "best" drama would be the most "poetic" drama, that is, the classical and European models, and that American drama, especially during the period when realism was dominant, would be considered second-rate if it was considered at all.

Of the effect of New Criticism, R. P. Blackmur wrote presciently in "The Lion and the Honeycomb" that because it dealt either "with the executive technique of poetry (and only with a part of that) or with the general verbal techniques of language," it was inappropriate for the literature of an "unstable society like ours," one characterized not by a shared culture but by multiplicity, extensive and unfamiliar forms. "Applied to the drama [New Criticism] is disfiguring" (206–7). Yvor Winters's assault on the drama is another case in point. In *The Function of Criticism* (1957), Winters went after what he claimed were the "flaws which may be unavoidable in the medium" (51). Using *Macbeth*, "the greatest play with which I am acquainted and a great work of literature," Winters offered the flaws in this play as proof that the whole genre was flawed (55). The drama has three major and insurmountable defects. First, because it is "an imitation of an imitation," it can only ever be a "rough approximation." Second, because language is mediated by character, it cannot be sustained at a constantly high level of intelligent or poetic discourse. Third, in performance, drama depends on actors, and, Winters tartly observes, "In general I think the world would be well enough off without actors . . . they cannot read poetry, for they try to make it appear to be something else . . . which they themselves can understand" (85). If Shakespeare could not pass through the eye of Winters's needle, what chance had an American dramatist?

In a series of heated exchanges in the early fifties, John Gassner became a qualified defender of American drama against the three drama critics, Eric Bentley, Eleanor Clark, and William Becker, whom he charged with using Europe as the measure of excellence by which to judge the drama and whom he perceived as being influenced by New Critical doctrine. Gassner defined their method in an odd mix of contemptuous dismissal and begrudging praise: "It is European *cum* Eliot-sponsored aristocratic traditionalism *cum* erstwhile aristocratic southern agrarianism transposed into the key of so-called New Criticism. It is intellectually more selective, and it is more wary of theatricality (and of social passion, too) than the European intelligentsia was in the 'twenties. It is certainly more refined. It is intellectually subtler, too" ("No American Drama" 25). Concerning the danger implicit in this approach, Gassner wrote of Becker's attacks on O'Neill, that "with O'Neill demolished the entire American drama falls to pieces" (ibid. 84).

Gassner was right to be worried. The strongest attacks on American drama were loosed during this formative period of American literary study. Theodore Hoffman's answer to Gassner is representative of the vehement denunciations that marked this era. He points out that *Uncle Tom's Cabin* should have been the beginning of "powerful realistic theatre" and "native colloquial comedy"; instead, "literature got Hawthorne, Emerson, Melville and Whitman out of that renaissance, and the theatre got *East Lynne*, *Under the Gaslight* and *Ten Nights in a Bar Room*" (72). He charges American dramatists with opening a Pandora's box of ills: melodramatic clichés, mongrel Freudianism, misunderstood Aeschylean and Strindbergian oppression, bookish ideas, diaphanous symbolism, artificial and inert language, Marxist clichés, liberal platitudes, corny overtures, dependence on conventions and surface profundities (72–73). In a similarly denunciatory manner, Rufus Hallette Gardner, in *The Splintered Stage: The Decline of the American Theatre* (1965), simplifies the accusation by blaming Marx for the miserable state of American drama from the depression to 1945, and Freud for everything written since 1945.

The formalist, aesthetic focus of much criticism has precluded a serious consideration of American drama's strengths. In his analysis of what he calls "the paradox of American Literature," Russell Reising surveys theories of American literature and observes that "while many of them attempt to define the 'radical' or 'oppositional' nature of American literature, . . . the theorists tend to separate literary significance and reflection from social and political significance. . . . By declaring literature autonomous they tend to deprive it of its capacity to reflect critically on issues of social and political significance" (39). Certainly much modern American drama is firmly rooted in historical and political problems, more often challenging than reaffirming received American values, taking an adversarial and critical position toward current ideologies. Despite the recovery of the political dimension of literature by recent critical movements, however, American drama is still in the shadowy margins of the canon. A few more recent examples of the continued neglect, overt discrimination, and compartmentalization even in the work of theoretically aware critics and literary historians will suffice. Sandra Gilbert and Susan Gubar's lengthy *The Norton Anthology of Literature by Women* (1985), according to the jacket blurb, purports to be a "comprehensive" work that "encompasses all genres" and includes "the full range of women's writings." It is ironic, given the focus of this discussion, that the one and only play they include, *Trifles*, is by an American, Susan Glaspell. The recent *Columbia Literary History of the United States* (1988), under the general editorship of Emory Elliott, a history that might have been a site for the repositioning and reconsideration of drama, perpetuates the pattern of neglectful compartmentalization. Of the 1,199 pages, 17 are given to a chapter on early drama and 24 to contemporary drama. Apart from a few scattered references to some ethnic groups, once again the literary historians relegate American drama to a shadowy corner and do not integrate it wholly into the general history. In the first volume of Sacvan Bercovitch's long-awaited *Cambridge History of American Literature* (1994), covering 1590–1820, Michael Gilmore gives but 18 pages of the 690 total for the drama. Gilmore points to the lack of a dramatist of "international stature," explaining that the "republican and propagandistic" nature of the drama was "slow to accommodate the individualism" that became synonymous with the romantic phase (573).

The Current Status

Given that the entire canon of American literature is undergoing scrutiny and is opening up to include all kinds of "marginal" works, is dramatic literature finally being recognized? Many of the old charges against American drama remain current. In a 1980 symposium on American playwrights, critics Gautam Dasgupta, Michael Early, and Bonnie Marranca conclude that "American drama is very non-literary," and suffers from a lack of ideas, moral basis, humanist tradition, or analytical thrust (44). It would appear that academics also still hold to this view.

Reconstructing American Literature: Courses, Syllabi, Issues, a collection of syllabi, edited by Paul Lauter in 1983, that reflects the new concern for restructuring American literature courses in terms of content and organization, offers a dismal picture for the status of drama. In commendably and zealously trying to overturn the overrepresentation of works by white males characteristic of traditional courses, the teachers who contributed to this collection included works by blacks, women, and Native Americans. Judging from the descriptions, however, it would seem that few of the newly incorporated writers or any other Americans wrote plays. Susan Glaspell and Mercy Otis Warren turn up in supplementary reading lists. Only one teacher even assigns a writing topic on drama, and that is on nineteenth-century melodrama in a course on the nineteenth century.

The restructured courses outlined fall into four categories: introductory courses, advanced period, genre, and thematic. The odds should favor drama's turning up prevalently in all categories, but once again it is slighted, and to an astonishing degree. In only one general introductory course is drama included, and ironically enough, given the broad sweep implicit in the project, the plays are by two white men, Arthur Miller (*The Crucible*) and David Rabe (*The Basic Training of Pavlo Hummel*). Drama fares only a little better in the modern period; one course includes Arthur Miller's *Death of a Salesman* and Carson McCullers's *Member of the Wedding*.

Lauter includes a proposal drafted by a group of participants at the Yale Institute (May 31–June 11, 1982). In the project entitled "Reconstructing American Literature," two weeks out of sixteen are suggested for the study of drama. The participants proposed the following six plays: Odets' *Waiting for Lefty*, Hellman's *The Little Foxes*, Williams's *A Streetcar Named Desire*, Albee's *Zoo Story*, Baraka's *Dutchman*, and Shange's *for colored girls . . .* ; Megan Terry is listed as a possible inclusion. In the same proposal, under genre courses, the most obvious place for consideration of drama, there are no plays at all, even though courses on autobiography and "story-chronicle" are included along with the predictable novel and poetry courses. In the theme courses, again an obvious place for drama, only three dramatic writers are included in a list that covers ten broad areas: immigrant experience, black and ethnic, social justice, the new woman, the land, regionalism, urban frontier, the city, southern literature, and the American dream. Ntozake Shange is designated a "third-world" writer and placed in immigrant experience, Williams's *A Streetcar Named Desire* is placed in southern literature, and, most oddly, Arthur Kopit's *Indians* is consigned to regionalism.

Though there have been improvements in the numbers of plays included, generic hegemony continues to skew the balance of texts in college anthologies. *The Norton Anthology of American Literature* has been revised several times since the dramaless 1979 version edited by Ronald Gottesman et al. In the second edition (1985) four plays by four white, "canonized" men were added: Eugene O'Neill's *Long Day's Journey Into Night*, Tennessee Williams's *A Streetcar Named Desire*, Arthur Miller's *Death of a Salesman*, and Clifford Odets' *Waiting for Lefty*. In the third edition (1989) the Odets was dropped and Royall Tyler's *The Contrast*, Adrienne Kennedy's *A Movie Star Has to Star in Black and White*, and Sam Shepard's *True West* were added. American prose and poetry since 1945 have their own editors in the fourth edition (1994); under prose are included the four plays and one screenplay, all by men, which serve to represent modern drama: O'Neill's *Long Day's Journey into Night*, Williams's *A Streetcar Named Desire*, Miller's *Death of a Salesman*, Wilson's *Fences*, and Mamet's *House of Games*. But Tyler's *The Contrast* is the only premodern play in the two-volume anthology, and it would appear that no American women ever wrote plays. By way of introduction to modern American drama, the editors assert that "drama in America was slow to develop as a self-conscious literary form. It was not until 1920 – the year of Eugene O'Neill's *Beyond the Horizon* – that America produced a playwright" (949). Furthermore, they conclude that because "many of the poets and fictionists of this century have written plays . . . such work indicates that drama has moved decisively into the American literary mainstream" (950). The outrageous conclusions to be drawn from these assertions are, first, that no playwright before O'Neill was conscious of his art or craft and, second, that American drama gains credibility and recognition only because writers of the authorized and canonized genres, that is, *real* writers, have written plays.

Other textbook anthologies have undergone radical revisions with an eye toward redressing ethnic and gender imbalances, but once again the upgrading has slighted the drama. The recently released two-volume edition of *The Harper American Literature*, edited by Donald McQuade et al., makes a bold claim on the jacket that is unsupported by the contents: "The entire range of tradition is here, refreshed by bold and practical innovation." This means the inclusion of Native American and women writers, of "marginal" generic forms, but as for the drama, only O'Neill's *Hughie* is included. *Anthology of American Literature* (1989), a two-volume text edited by George McMichael, contains only four plays by four white men: *The Contrast, The Hairy Ape, The Glass Menagerie,* and *Zoo Story. The Heath Anthology of American Literature,* edited by Paul Lauter (1990), also addressed to incorporating women and minorities, allows seven plays into the 5,514-page double volume, but five of these are only one-act plays: *The Contrast, Trifles, The Hairy Ape, Waiting for Lefty, Portrait of a Madonna, A Raisin in the Sun,* and *Zoo Story.*

As a recent corollary, some critics have modified their perspective on drama in general and American drama in particular. For example, in his encyclopedic *Theories of the Theatre* (1984), Marvin Carlson notes that "one of the most important directions that American theorists took after 1970 was toward a consideration of the theatre as a performed art, though without rejecting a critical interest in the written text (significantly, some began to speak of the text not as a play but a 'playscript')" (486). This new critical concern with the structure of drama, the dynamics of performance, and the process of interpretation has been paralleled by new approaches to teaching dramatic literature. A 1984 survey of twenty-seven universities by Mary Anderson, *Drama in the English Department,* reveals that the greatest emphasis is being placed on performance rather than on literary analysis or critical interpretation. But this is a recent pedagogical phenomenon that pertains to the study of *all* drama and does not explain or remedy the unique bias against American drama.

Despite some small cracks in the closed door, the problem recently has taken a new twist and has been compounded by those literary historians who are questioning not only the American canon but also theoretical approaches to American literature. And still the drama continues to be ignored. Although editors Louis J. Budd, Edwin H. Cady, and Carl L. Anderson have included folklore and photography as well as the predictable prose and poetry in *Toward a New American Literary History* (1980), they eschew the drama. Russell Reising's *The Unusable Past* (1986), Robert Weimann's *Structure and Society in Literary History* (1984), and the essays in *Reconstructing American Literary History* (1986), edited by Sacvan Bercovitch, all of which argue that aesthetic structures and social function are necessarily interrelated, and that hitherto "marginalized" texts must be included in American literary study, exclusively draw all their examples from prose and poetry.

Even turning to recent histories on the making of the profession offers little reassurance of a fundamental change in the attitude toward American drama. References, if any, provide slim pickings for the historian. Kermit Vanderbilt's *American Literature and the Academy: The Roots, Growth and the Maturity of a Profession* (1986) briefly mentions Arthur Hobson Quinn's critical and historical domination of the drama in the twenties (188). He also observes that Samuel Kettell omitted poet-dramatists from his *Specimens of American Poetry* because he knew that William Dunlap was writing a *History of American Theatre* (53). Otherwise, Vanderbilt has little to say about the status of drama or about its exclusion from the study of American literature. In *Professing Literature: An Institutional History* (1987), Gerald Graff, though he is troubled by what he terms the "field-coverage model" of departmental organization, that is, a division of expertise into literary periods and genres, and though he agrees with Terry Eagleton's call "to repair the disabling dislocation of literature 'from other cultural and social practices,'" does not consider that dramatic literature has itself been dislocated, even though the category of "genre" has not (11). In his chapter on national literature, "The Promise of American Literature Studies," though he is concerned with the dynamics of "patterned isolation," Graff considers only the status of poetry and prose.

Ironically, in the most recent disciplinary history, the problem of generic hegemony simply is erased as if it never existed and did not persist. David Shumway, whose *Creating American Civilization: A Genealogy of American Literature as an Academic Discipline* (1994) is, as he acknowledges, based on the information provided by Vanderbilt and the opening left by Graff, asserts that "members of the profession and the public at large normally think about 'American literature' as the novels, poems, plays, and some special works of nonfiction prose" and proceeds to describe the history of the discipline as if it did in fact include all four of the cited genres and did not exclude the drama (1).

To anyone who has even a passing familiarity with the rich diversity of American drama, the exclusion of an important and substantial body of material from so many possible perspectives is puzzling and distressing. In the understandable rush to incorporate hitherto overlooked forms, to re-dress the imbalance of race, class, and gender in American literature classes, the zealots have bumped drama farther out of the classroom and, as a long-term undesirable consequence, out of both American literature and cultural studies. As Theatre departments increasingly embrace performance theory, dramatic literature will get less attention. Institutional historians and critics, such as Graff, understandably and commendably concerned with the consequences of unexamined university structures, embedded compartmentalizations, and buried assumptions, are focused on issues

larger than the fate of one troubled facet. Yet, one way to take up Graff's
challenge to examine the conflicts and controversies within the academic
institution is to address the shuffling of American drama in and out of
departments and disciplines.

Genre and National Culture

The history of the bias against American drama suggests many reasons why
it has never been incorporated wholly into American literature. Some
generalizations from my survey lead to conclusions rooted in the related
dynamics of genre and national culture. Dion Boucicault, an early observer
of the American theatre, was one of the first to locate the problem in the
cultural diversity and lack of centrality that was and continues to be America's salient characteristic. "The American community," he wrote in 1890,
"differs essentially from every other . . . a ready made, polyglot population
has inflowed into the land . . . [but the] arts can find no residence here
where there is no central organ, which can be recognized as the brain of the
nation" (647). In 1907, a panelist in *The American Journal of Sociology* argued
that "in America we have no great art because we have a great commerce –
because we have a great individualistic form; and the building-up of democracy throws down all possibility of art; not because democracy is essentially
opposed to art, but because the artist sets out with the conviction which is
in the mind of every artist today, that he has to voice his own emotions –
that what he speaks for isn't the life of his time, isn't the life that has been
created through succeeding generations of conflict – but he aims to voice
his own notions – his own emotions" (Odenwald-Ungar 666).

Another of the early historians and critics of American drama, Thomas
H. Dickinson, saw the problem as being implicit in the genre when he
observed, in 1915 in *The Case of American Drama*, that "everything points to
the fact that America has not yet been discovered. America to-day is a great
brooding abstraction" (204). He concluded that America could not have a
national drama because the country was too large. Paul Green, a tireless
champion of a native American drama during the twenties and thirties,
later conceded that the country was probably too large to sustain a national
drama (109–29). These observers all believed that the size of the country
does not affect other genres, but that drama is addressed to a collective and
theatre to a communal experience. However, America continues to be a
culturally diverse country in flux whose citizens do not share cultural, moral,
political, or aesthetic assumptions on a large scale. As Francis Fergusson
observed in "Search for New Standards in the Theatre," though there had

been a moment in the twenties that promised a native drama, American drama best expresses a "strand" or a "province," but it does not reflect a common point of reference, such as the shared "social consciousness" the Group Theatre depended on, the "cultural villages" of the Federal Theatre, or the "group-mind" that Thornton Wilder found to be essential to drama (582). According to Travis Bogard, until the nation has what he has called a "central reflector," that is, a place that reflects the essence of the nation's cultural life, it cannot have a national drama ("Central Reflector" 42–65). On the other hand, given that America is pluralistic and culturally diverse, the possibility of a single voice is an unrealistic, nostalgic fantasy of a common culture.

As a consequence, much of the most representative and vital American drama, with few exceptions, has been regional, ethnic, or topical, thus it is inherently narrowly focused, culturally specific, or quickly dated. Yet critics have persisted in clinging to the idea of an integrated high-cultural norm because they persisted in believing in the necessity of homogeneity and a culturally elite core of playwrights. "Out of the three hundred and forty years of American theatre history," observes Joseph Golden, "one curious and continuing dilemma emerges: the United States never seemed to associate a developing civilization with a living theatre. . . . Like a stifling shroud, the 'American tradition' of dramatic composition – this ubiquitous sludge of melodramatic half-truths and badly-inflated passions – had one obvious effect: it preserved the notion of an inferior theatre in America" (15–16, 141). As Stanley Kauffmann recently and restrainedly observed, America lacks the "homogeneous culture" that binds European writers to their audiences. America suffers from what he calls "community hunger. This is not a general American phenomenon; it is an American *theatrical* phenomenon. I think the problem of playwriting has deep roots in American attitudes towards the theatre . . . in terms of theatre *seriousness*, this is a young country" (Clurman and Kauffmann 30). This "fundamental lack of real community," Eric Bentley pointed out after World War II, meant that mass entertainment would triumph over the "communal imaginative experience"; "I suspect that there can be very little greatness in the theater," he concludes, "without what Walt Whitman called 'great audiences'" (Bentley "American Theatre" 240).

Is American drama literature? Judged from certain elitist or Anglophiliac perspectives American drama may not be "great" literature, though many plays would stand up to even the most stringent elitist, formalist analysis, but it is literature nonetheless and a complex form of literature that should be studied in its full context. Critics supportive of serious consideration of

American drama have been aware of the discrimination for a long time. One of the earliest, Montrose J. Moses, setting forth in 1917 his list of plays neglected in favor of other genres, complained, for example, that Mercy Warren's *History of the American Revolution* was cited when her play, *The Group*, was not. His conclusion that "there has been almost a preconcerted action taken to blot out the existence of American Drama" rings true decades later ("Is There?" 505). C. W. E. Bigsby, painstakingly dissecting and refuting Robert Brustein's 1959 dismissal of American drama as "felonious intent," sidesteps the problem of early drama but does argue extensively for the literary merits of recent plays, concluding that "America has produced some of the very finest drama of the 20th century" ("Why" 3, 11).

One critic who would agree with Bigsby, if only on this point, is Harold Bloom, in whose recent list of 278 "must-reads" of twentieth-century American literature the following appear: Tony Kushner's *Angels in America*; David Mamet's *American Buffalo* and *Speed-the-Plow*; Arthur Miller's *Death of a Salesman*; Eugene O'Neill's *Lazarus Laughed, The Iceman Cometh*, and *Long Day's Journey into Night*; David Rabe's *Streamers*; a collection of Sam Shepard's work entitled *Seven Plays*; Tennessee Williams's *The Glass Menagerie* and *A Streetcar Named Desire*; and August Wilson's *Fences* and *Joe Turner's Come and Gone*. That this highly idiosyncratic list does include drama as literature marks it as a welcome departure from the American tradition of the narrow hegemonic canon; that it includes the complete plays of T. S. Eliot and has no work by women is but one indication of its traditional canonical nature. Given that this list is from the pen of a Yale critic who paradoxically marks himself as outside the academy – for him now no more than the site where the substantive aesthetic pleasures of reading have been slaughtered by feminists, Marxists, multiculturalists, and historicists wielding their finely ground axes of tendentious social agendas – it is unlikely that his list will have much effect or that the position of drama will be legitimated; within the canon, drama will remain fundamentally what it has always been, a bastard child.

Instead of continuing to discriminate against American drama because of a history of generic hegemony, it is time to consider the implications of the arguments for and against it as literature and as something less narrowly generic, perhaps as performative expression. American drama should be evaluated in relation to dramatic theory in general and to American literature and culture in particular. The very causes of its exclusion from the canon are problems worth investigation; these are not grounds for dismissal, but reasons for inquiry. Large-scale, serious work on American drama in this way is young, but the persistent historical attempts to dismiss dramatic literature suggest that such a critically contested genre must be fully evaluated in its cultural context. Models for the kind of work that needs to be done, work that moves away from a consensual and ideational model both of literature and of culture, can be found in such studies as *Melodrama Unveiled: American Theatre & Culture, 1800–1850* (1968) by David Grimsted; *Highbrow/Lowbrow: The Emergence of Cultural Hierarchy in America* (1988) by Lawrence W. Levine; *The American Stage* (1993) edited by Ron Engle and Tice L. Miller; *The Performance of Power: Theatrical Discourse and Politics* (1991) edited by Sue-Ellen Case and Janelle Reinelt; *Interpreting the Theatrical Past: Essays in the Historiography of Performance* (1989) edited by Thomas Postlewait and Bruce McConachie; and *Reframing Culture: The Case of the Vitagraph Quality Films* (1993) by William Uricchio and Roberta Pearson. A historically reconstructed sense of cultural production and reception, of the interplay between diverse subcultures and artistic expressions, of the binary oppositions between "high" and "low" cultures, informs these studies. Such work has been a long time coming even though the impulse lay with the very men who charted a different course for American drama. For instance, in 1916, Brander Matthews, one of the first American scholars to look seriously at the drama, observed that "of all the varied and manifold kinds of theatrical entertainment negro-minstrelsy is the only one absolutely native to these States, and the only one which could not have come into existence anywhere else in the civilized world," and suggested that the decline of the form would be an ideal subject for a Ph.D. dissertation (*A Book* 219). How different the course of American drama might have been had academics, including Matthews himself, pursued all the implications of his assertion.

American drama needs to be reassessed not only as literature but also as cultural artifact; it has embraced every conceivable subject in a wide diversity of styles. This needed reassessment should not just be limited to an examination of an aesthetic problem of canonical "correctness," or one of expanding the canon, and certainly not one locked in dated proscriptions, but a matter of enlarging the documentary record of the American literary past by reconsidering what constitutes drama and by re-placing drama in its larger cultural and social framework. American drama should be considered as a collection of complex cultural artifacts, as assemblages of conflicting voices and discourses such as those debating essential American characteristics, the university curriculum, and the function of a realist agenda.

3

No Corner in Her Own House

What Is American About American Drama?

W HAT HAS BEEN UNDERSTOOD to be "American" drama and what was understood to be the "Americanness" of American drama? Despite the enormous numbers of plays, pageants, burlesques, theatrical entertainments, and minstrel shows that have enlivened the American stage from the beginning, the traditionally constituted canon of American drama, a very small body of plays, proves to be a perpetually shifting conflation of American essentialism, moral and didactic purpose, and largely realistic dramaturgy written in English (with modest leeway for regional dialects) and is anything but an accurate reflector of what was transpiring in either dramatic literature or theatrical production. What the canon does reflect is an ideological and aesthetic consistency in interpretive values, although, obviously, some of the valued playwrights and plays and subgenres have changed as cultural and educational values and goals have shifted. The American dramatic canon also should be understood to be, for the most part, a product of the twentieth century; before Eugene O'Neill was heralded as America's first serious playwright, the critics largely were apologetic about the state of American drama as literature. And, of course, a canon was not a necessity until American drama became the object of academic study.

In the recent assessment of Marc Robinson, who in *The Other American Drama* (1994) strongly voices his resentment of the dramatis personae in the traditional American canon, the twentieth-century American dramatic canon begins with Eugene O'Neill and continues as a straight line through his "heirs," including Clifford Odets, Arthur Miller, Lillian Hellman, William Saroyan, William Inge, Sidney Kingsley, Robert Sherwood, and

August Wilson, an unwavering tradition marked by "overwhelming pre-
dictability," "wet nostalgia," "point-making social dramas," "overheated
historical verse plays," and "drawing-room doodles with champagne chit-
chat" and informed by the nineteenth-century legacy of plot-based melodramas (1). Though many historians of American drama might disagree
with Robinson's testy characterization of the canon, they would probably
concur on most of the playwrights he includes. One need only look at the
title of C. W. E. Bigsby's second volume of *A Critical Introduction to
Twentieth-Century American Drama* (1984), "Williams/Miller/Albee," to get
a good idea of the narrow, single-author construction of his canon.

But the canonized play list, in and of itself, is not the problem; it is
merely a symptom of a pervasive disease. Nor, in fact, is the debatable
status of American drama as literature the problem, and to focus exclusively
on either the canon or the status would be reductive and redirective. I
understand the dominating impulse to create lists and categories as an
exclusionary tactic to locate power and, consequently, control in a narrowly
defined professional and disciplinary domain, a domain governed for the
most part by a small academic constituency. But this generalization is also
reductive and simplistic. The present state of what accurately should be
called "an Americanist drama," a drama that participates in and is authorized by the long-standing dominant paradigm of what constitutes an essential "American" identity, is the consequence of a complex and shifting
interplay between political, social, aesthetic, pedagogical, and economic
practices too slippery to be defined easily. The very scope of an "Americanist drama" is the first problem in tracing canon formation. It is possible,
however, to consider one consequence, the exclusion of an enormous body
of plays, and to ask what was at stake in the creation of an American
dramatic canon, who was engaged in the creation of the canon, how the
canon was created, and of what larger cultural issues might the canon be
symptomatic.

There is a second problem in tracking the creation of an American
dramatic canon, namely, the historically prevailing idea that, unlike the
novel or the poem, which are deemed to have had early indigenous exist-
ences, American drama has evolved slowly, progressively, and organically in
large measure because American drama has been considered to be inferior
to European drama. The "un-Americanness" of American drama, whether
it was in imitation of French, English, or German models, was, of course,
a complaint that sounded for years. Warren Barton Blake's lament for *The
Independent* in 1912 is characteristic: He saw American drama as flawed by
crudity, sentimentality, creaky machinery, and "denaturalized importa-

tions" (507). As a consequence of this kind of persistent complaint, the history of American dramatic literature is shadowed by the continually recycled and reformulated idea that we haven't had it in the past, that we don't have it yet, but that it is coming and that it is getting better. The thematic problem of what is American about American drama, therefore, is inextricably linked with the formalist problem, the consideration of aesthetic criteria to the exclusion of any other.

The third factor in tracking the building of the canon is that the concern for a thematic indigenousness in the drama was inextricably bound up in the early stages with the desire for a national drama, not merely a native one, and in the later stages with a cultural determination to forge a seamless and collective past. For example, the erratic eruptions and unsatisfactory nature of early dramatic literature led Arthur Hobson Quinn in 1919 to assert that "our native drama, even though it antedated the novel and the short story, has practically no history until the latter half of the eighteenth century" (CHAL 215). Of course, Quinn, like other anxious historians before and after him, was erasing unacceptable work from the narrative. From a vantage point more than ninety years earlier, in 1827, in a review of William Dunlap's *The Father of an Only Child* and J. N. Barker's *Marmion* and *Superstition*, James Kirk Paulding calculated that to date there were sixty American plays but lamented that the country still suffered from "the absence of that wholesome, manly and vigorous taste, which may be said always to mark the best periods in the history of every civilized country" (343). Troubled by this lack of masculine civilization, the growth of which was being hampered by improbable melodrama and a penchant for imitating the "worst specimens of the high German school," Paulding addressed the lack of a "National Drama," by which he meant "not merely a class of dramatic productions written by Americans, but one appealing directly to national feelings" (345). For Paulding, a national literature's work was "administering to the just pride of national character, inspiring a feeling for national glory, and inculcating a love of country" (339). Critics, literary historians, and compilers of anthologies would ring changes on this nativist, patriotic, even propagandistic note for decades to come and the distinction between a native and a national drama would be used as one criterion to find fault with American drama. For instance, Arthur Hornblow, in *The Theatre in America* (1919), was careful to note that "up to the 1830s, America had no national drama" because before that time the plays had been "desultory" and had nothing "characteristic" or "vital enough" to qualify (50).

The Dominant Paradigm

I want to begin with the thematic paradigm that has, until recently, dominated not only American drama but also all of American literature. In "America in Theory," the first chapter in *Reading America*, Denis Donoghue describes the theory of America that, he explains, "is still predominant in American Studies: it supposes an ego psychology which is in turn predicated upon a national typology" (12). He lists the traditional attributions that set "the American experience" apart: "to the Frontier, or to New England Puritanism and covenant theology, to democracy, Transcendentalism, slavery, the divisions of North and South, utopian sentiment, the Indians, Unitarianism, immigration, the idea of America as a Redeemer Nation, or to what Reinhold Niebuhr has called 'the ironic incongruity between our illusions and the realities which we experience'" (5).

One basis for the typology Donoghue describes is Frederick Jackson Turner's by now infamous and largely discredited "frontier thesis," which he originally set forth in 1893 in a report to the American Historical Association. Of the location for the essential struggle of America, Turner wrote: "American social development has been continually beginning over again on the frontier. This perennial rebirth, this fluidity of American life, this expansion westward with its new opportunities, its continuous touch with the simplicity of primitive society, furnish the forces dominating the American character. The true point of view in the history of this nation is not the Atlantic Coast, it is the Great West . . . the meeting point between savagery and civilization" (200). Describing the essence of the American character who finds himself on that frontier, Turner wrote in praise of that "coarseness and strength combined with acuteness and inquisitiveness; that practical, inventive turn of mind, quick to find expedients; that masterful grip of material things, lacking in the artistic but powerful to effect great ends; that restless, nervous energy; that dominant individualism, working for good and for evil, and withal that buoyancy and exuberance which comes with freedom" (226–27).

Historians of the drama embraced this paradigm eagerly for two reasons. The insistence on an essential masculine and vigorous "Americanness" in the drama was one early strategy to authorize drama as worthwhile in the face of those who were dismissing it as European, feminine, and sentimental, and simultaneously to sidestep the troubling issue of its doubtful aesthetic qualities. This move would have long-range consequences; for instance, later it could be invoked to dismiss the extensive Workers' Theatre movement. The acceptance of a narrowly defined program for American drama allowed critics to simplify the criteria for judgment. Thus, Thomas Dickinson in *The Case of American Drama* (1915) could propose two tests of American drama: Is it natural and is it socially constructive? Arthur Hobson Quinn used this approach in 1923 when arguments about work derivative from or imitative of a European model threatened the body of dramatic material marked as "native." To those who questioned the composite whole, Quinn argued that it was "American to the core." Insisting that the drama was too varied to be simply classified, Quinn nonetheless argued that

> there is one prevailing characteristic which shines through its greatest representatives, whether they be social comedies like *The Contrast* or *The New York Idea* or romantic tragedies like *Brutus* or *The Gladiator* or *The Hairy Ape*. This characteristic is the celebration of a human being in his conflict with oppression, political, economic, or social, in his revolt against the crushing power of fate or circumstances, in his effort to preserve at all cost, his most precious asset, his rights and privileges as an individual. Of course drama has always staged the conflict between a hero and opposing events and forces, but it has remained for the nation which was founded in the attempt of the Puritans, the Huguenot, the Quaker, the Catholic, to preserve his freedom of conscience, and which has insisted through three centuries upon the preservation of individual rights, to represent in its playwriting a distinctly democratic attitude and atmosphere. One can easily strain too far, but the very language in which the framers of the Declaration of Independence expressed the ideals of American democracy provides a set of phrases which express the development of dramatic themes in our playwriting – "life, liberty, and the pursuit of happiness." ("Modern" 656–57)

Because drama depends on conflict and because aspiration without resistance goes nowhere dramaturgically, it is easy to understand how and why the masculine paradigm still continues to dominate the American stage. It will become clear from a review of the historians, critics, reviewers, and anthologizers that there was a widespread assumption that American drama ought to have a defined cultural mission of either spreading a hegemonic American ideology or questioning the contentious aspects of nativist assumptions. Drama at its best was understood to be purposefully instrumental in creating and reshaping attitudes, beliefs, and stereotypes. Not only was drama a medium for the dissemination of approved ideology, but certain plays become both artifacts of that ideology and also ubiquitous statements of an essential Americanness. By extension, many critics have appropriated this nationalist essentialism as a way of valuing a playwright and, as a further consequence, in their criticism thematic and ideological concerns frequently displace analyses of language and dramaturgy. It might be added that this thematizing was also a way for critics to avoid the fraught aesthetic issues and to claim a higher level of valuation. For instance, Doris Auerbach sets up Sam Shepard as a "mythmaker" when she claims him as a national spokesman: "Sam Shepard's subject is simply this – America. The America about us, the American dream that has been betrayed, the American hero whose quest has been betrayed, the American land which has become unproductive, sterile, and the American family which no longer nurtures its children – these are Shepard's themes" (1). Critics have used the same tactic to laud Lanford Wilson: Robert Asahina suggests that Wilson "represents a distinctly American tradition" (231), Ross Wetzsteon calls him "America's poet of loss and endurance" (43), and Frank Rich has praised him as "one of the few artists of our theatre who can truly make America sing" (C15). The question is: Whose song is being sung?

Throughout the history of American drama's critical reception, any deviation from the approved model would be excluded, castigated, or, at best, marginalized and positioned as an anomaly by the dominant critical voices. Thus, with few exceptions, the goal of the twentieth-century anthologizers would seem to have been to deliberately force commonality and turn a blind eye on the always evident disjunctions. Almost all anthologies fail to represent the diverse nature of theatrical practices and dramatic texts from the earliest college exercises, minstrel shows, vaudeville, and burlesque, to later imitations and adaptations of European work, sentimental melodramas, and patriotic grandstanding, all of which, to a significant degree, defied the very hegemony the historians struggled to create. This failure certainly ought now to raise the question of the existence of a single entity called American drama. For instance, the Workers' Theatre movement, which Harry Goldman and Mel Gordon have shown to span six decades, and which also challenged the dominant capitalist theories and dramaturgical practices, virtually is unrepresented in anthologies. Even though the histories concur on the broad outline – that is, that there was a linear and progressive development of American drama from melodrama to realism – the uniformity is a fragile construct. Although it is a center that does not hold, the highest critical accolade, "American" as opposed to "modern," continues to be employed by critics to authorize the playwright under study. An exception is Marc Robinson, who in *The Other American Drama* (1994) finds an alternative dramatic tradition, a tradition not driven by plot or marked by shared thematic concerns ("American" identity) or by subgeneric forms (realism, melodrama), in the works of Gertrude Stein, Tennessee Williams, Sam Shepard, Maria Irene Fornes, Adrienne Kennedy, and Richard Foreman, all of whom rediscovered "the essential elements of dramatic form – language, gesture, presence" (3).

Robert Spiller, in "The Cycle and the Roots: National Identity in American Literature," determined not only that there was such a thing as "an American national character" but also the time of its creation: "about the time of the American Revolution – that is, between 1763 and 1789" (3). While arguing on the one hand that there is no *one* thing but a thing in flux, Spiller begged both sides of the question. Essentially, he suggested that there are two Americas: one evolved from the Eurocentric spectrum, the French, German, Italian, Spanish, Scandinavian, and British cultures, which had by the seventeenth century reached "a degree of stability based on language, social structure, and relatively static geographical limits," and another, the "new" component of heterogeneous, multiethnic, constantly migrating and immigrating peoples that Spiller did not categorize by race or country of origin (5). What is accepted as the dominant culture is that established by the "stable" group; its drama became "American."

Spiller's simple bifurcation of American culture allows for a hegemonic base that flies in the face of fact and creates a chronological and, by implication, hierarchical priority over a heterogeneous "aftermath." Where does this leave an indigenous drama? By Spiller's reasoning, it is a long time coming. Arguing that American culture can be broken down into four stages of development, Spiller assigned a specific literary genre to each one. The first stage, "a period of exploration and settlement," finds expression in "narrative and descriptive journals and letters"; the second stage, the "embryonic" community, produces "newspapers, broadsides, and magazines, lectures and sermons, book-stores and libraries"; in the third stage, one that demands the "'leisure arts,'" the new society, being "still too crude to produce its own form of literary expression," is reduced to importation and imitation, the latter being a sorry solution because "the new material is twisted and turned to fit into [the familiar forms], like a farmer's broad-toed foot being pressed into a ballroom slipper" (8–9). Into this slot, Spiller put Royall Tyler's *The Contrast* (1787), citing it as "the first truly American play" because, despite its derivative form and style, it had "a central American theme – the contrast between the pseudosophistication of provincial society and the crude honesty of the native American Jonathan" (11). In making this claim, Spiller chose to deemphasize the significant fact that the city–country conflict was just as central to the Sheridan and Goldsmith plays on which *The Contrast* was modeled and that there was little that was "honest" about the manufacturing of national role models. Like Frances Trollope's "hard, greasy paw" at the dinner table, the image of the "broad-toed foot" bespeaks a disjunction between the spirit of democracy and its embodiment, to say nothing of its expression in drama. For Spiller, it was only in the fourth stage that "a new literature steps out with its new experience wrapped about it in natural folds" (8–9). The fourth stage, late in coming, "did not appear before 1850–55, on the eve of our greatest national crisis, the Civil War" and on its drama, Spiller was silent (12). To have addressed the drama of this period, Spiller would have had to confront G. L. Aiken's widely performed *Uncle Tom's Cabin; or, Life Among the Lowly* (1852), John Brougham's burlesque, "Original, Aboriginal, Erratic, Oper-atic, Semi-civilized and Demi-savage Extravaganza of *Pocahontas, or the Gentle Savage*" (1855), or William Gilman Simms's melodrama of the pre-lude to the war with Mexico, *Michael Bonham, or the Fall of Bexar* (1852).

When he backtracked to test his thesis, Spiller found that the idea of a "westward movement of Old World culture across a new continent" held only until multiethnicity reared up to be recognized. Of the three groups he identified – immigrants, blacks "who were brought to this country under special circumstances," and Jews – Spiller included only Jews in his expan-sionist model, even though they "rarely become absorbed into any alien culture" (15). To have included the drama in a multiethnically driven para-digm, Spiller would have had to accept the minstrel show and Yiddish theatre as part of the American dramatic output.

I have spent time on Spiller's reading of the development of a national identity because, although written in 1976, it reflects the prevailing tenacity of a dominant paradigm for the "American" experience, even if slightly modified by the idea of an "organic" progression, and it demonstrates the degree to which exclusion of the drama was necessary to maintain that dominant paradigm. But one need only look at Arthur Hobson Quinn's first volume of *A History of the American Drama* (1923), which covers hundreds of theatrical performances and plays from 1598 to the Civil War, to get a sense of the massiveness of Spiller's exclusion and the narrowness of his paradigm. In fact, Spiller was only perpetuating an already established predisposition to exclude drama as a genre that could carry the weight of a national literature. For instance, in "The Materials for an American Litera-ture: A Critical Problem of the Early Nineteenth Century," W. E. Sedg-wick traces the nationalist impulse from its revival in 1815 through the century as anxious critics dismissed efforts by novelists, poets, and essayists to wring epic grandeur from the likeliest subjects: American history, the American landscape, and the contemporary scene. Early literary histories also point to the exclusion of drama from the wide objective. In *A Literary History of America* (1901), Barrett Wendell tartly observes that "among other abortive phases of literary activity during the period of the Hartford Wits, was an effort to create a native American drama. In fact, up to the present time, the American theatre has produced no more permanent work than that of John Howard Payne, who is remembered only as the author of 'Home, Sweet Home'" (157–58).

Anthologizing American Drama

In part because anthologies of American literature reflected a commitment to the dominant exclusionary mode, anthologies of American drama, though collections of the shunned genre, also clung to the paradigm. From the start, most anthologists and literary critics, fired by a sense of urgency over establishing an Anglo-American cultural hegemony, an urgency that would grow into the advocacy of nationalistic progressivism, conflated a sense of American essentialism with the moral and didactic purpose they felt should be the primary function of the drama. A cursory survey of anthologies even might suggest that those were the limits of the genre. Anthologizers faced an additional problem, the fraught one of American drama's debatable literary merits. Shadowing the anthologizers were evaluations such as those made by Moses Coit Tyler, who in *The Literary History of the American Revolution* (1897) placed dramatic compositions after minor literary *facetiae* in the "eighth class" of a possible nine categories of writings. Nearly all the writings in dramatic form, Tyler contended, were "tentative, crude, dull, coarse, and provincial" and could only be commended for their "unshrinking realism" (210).

Tracking American drama through anthologies of American drama is a useful exercise in monitoring the continuing process of canon development, from the early stages of delimiting both the national and aesthetic criteria to the later manifestations of reluctant and minimal pluralism or aggressive revisionism beginning in the 1960s. Furthermore, because an anthology itself is understood to embody an authority and, as a consequence, implies institutional approval, dramatic literature accrues value simply by being anthologized. Finally, it should be noted that the anthologizing groundwork was being laid during the 1920s and 1930s, the period Gary Gerstle in *Working-class Americanism* (1989) has characterized as having a national obsession with Americanism, an Americanism marked by nationalistic, democratic, progressive, and traditionalist rhetoric. Given that the first such anthology was Arthur Hobson Quinn's *Representative American Plays*

(1917), the history of the American drama anthology begins at a much later date than that of the poetry anthology, for instance. Alan C. Golding, in setting forth the stages of development for American poetry anthologies, begins his study in 1793 with Elihu Hubbard Smith's *American Poems, Selected and Original*. For Golding, Smith was motivated by preservationism and Federalism, the earliest manifestation of a programmatic literary nationalism which would be felt strongly in the nineteenth century. The same "moral edge" which marked early nineteenth-century nationalism, the redemption of Puritan poetry by Samuel Kettell in 1829 for *Specimens of American Poetry*, the conviction that fine literature should be socially edifying and spiritually inspirational, and the dominance of the New England Brahminist's adherence to the romantic and transhistorical tradition, all had been played out and were established values in American poetry anthologies before the first anthology of American drama was published, and as a consequence, necessarily informed the taste of those who had to look back to the previous century and retrieve canonizable plays. Therefore, what happened to poetry anthologies in stages – stages described by Golding as "preservation, nationalism and historicizing, the belief in transhistorical excellence, revisionism as a reaction to the established canon" (330) – happened to drama anthologies in a retrospective rush of reclamation in the twentieth century.

Reviewing forty-three representative, standard anthologies of American drama compiled between 1917 and 1986 affords enlightenment about what constituted "Americanness" and reflects the various strategies editors have used to rationalize a collection of plays and their shared unease about the status of American drama. Many anthologizers forgo any introductory material at all; those who do, include an introduction rife with abstractions. Beginning with Arthur Hobson Quinn's *Representative American Plays* (1917) and Montrose Moses's three-volume *Representative Plays by American Dramatists* (1918), in general the editors, on the one hand, show a consistent acceptance of the fact of an "American" drama and, on the other, demonstrate remarkable inconsistency as to what constitutes the "Americanness" of American drama. Neither aspect is as easy a formulation as the uninvestigated assertion would seem to indicate. The first strategy, after all, was one of naming and claiming, of differentiating "American" drama from "English" drama. For instance, in *Representative Plays by American Dramatists*, Moses said of the thirty plays in the three volumes covering 1765 to 1911 that they were selected because of their "distinct American flavour" and because they treat "American subjects," none of which are explicitly defined. Moses marks the beginning of American drama as that point in

1765 when American writers ceased to be Englishmen, when they began to look for ways to express national characteristics. For Moses, this means, in the earlier plays, a focus on the war with England and on Indians and, in the later plays, the creation of vehicles for the acting style which dominated from 1830 throughout the 1850s, "which in its most excessive expression resulted in the American minstrel" (II 1). Moses begins his collection with *The Prince of Parthia* (1765) by Thomas Godfrey, includes topical historical plays such as Hugh Henry Brackenridge's *The Battle of Bunker's Hill* (1776) and R. T. Conrad's *Jack Cade* (1835), and a few thematically "foreign" plays such as J. H. Payne's *Brutus* (1818) and George Henry Boker's *Francesca da Rimini* (1855). It might seem odd that Moses opens this collection with *The Prince of Parthia*, because a few years later in an article, "American Plays of Our Forefathers" (1922), he claims a political satire, *Androborus: a Biographical Farce* (1714), written by Governor Hunter of the Colony of New York, as the beginning of American playwriting. But, though printed, *Androborus* was never acted and *The Prince of Parthia* was. Therefore, it is clear that for Moses the critical determining factor was production, not publication. This need for an "authentically located" production surfaces in *Representative Plays by American Dramatists* when Moses includes Robert Rogers' *Ponteach* and Mercy Warren's *The Group* despite lacking positive proof of production. Although Moses is vague about what constitutes the standard for Americanness, it is implied in such descriptive formulations as "distinct American flavour" and "American subjects"; his inclusion of plays like Nathaniel Willis's *Tortesa, the Usurer* and John Howard Payne's *Brutus*, which though undeniably American are "departures" from an American atmosphere, provides a more telling account by reverse inference. For example, Moses takes special pains to position Steele MacKaye's *Paul Kauver* as "farthest away from American life, inasmuch as it deals with Nihilism" (I 2).

Arthur Hobson Quinn was equally vague in his introduction to *Representative American Plays* (1917), a collection that underwent many revisions, citing only undefined "native themes" and undefined "intrinsic excellence" as criteria for inclusion. In the preface to *A History of the American Drama from the Beginning to the Civil War* (1923), Quinn was careful to point to the difficulty inherent in the term "American Drama," because while it presupposes "native origin," early stage history is too "interwoven" to permit the term. Admitting writers such as Boucicault for his contribution to the "progress" of American drama and excluding others such as Burton and Brougham whose works were "foreign in spirit," Quinn sets up a thematic criterion for inclusion: "It is the nature of the play and the circumstances of its production that determine the nationality of drama and not the accident of birth" (*Beginning* xii–xiii). That American drama would be written in English is an unstated given for Quinn, as it was for all anthologizers to follow. Quinn set up his collection in *Representative American Plays* to demonstrate the "development" of American drama, taking care to point out the "firsts" along the way. Because *The Prince of Parthia* is "the first play written by an American to be performed in America by a professional company of actors," it opens the collection and becomes, for many anthologizers to follow, America's "first" play (*Beginning* 3).

The urgency of claiming *The Prince of Parthia* as the "first" American play should not be ignored. Quinn's relief that the dramatic works that preceded it – college plays such as *The Masque of Alfred* (1761) and Major Robert Rogers's *Ponteach, or the Savages of America* (1766) – could not, for various reasons, stake the claim, is connected to the nativist insistence that colors his history: "It is in a real sense fortunate that none of these dramas disputes with *The Prince of Parthia* the honor of being the first American play. It is not only the relative superiority of Godfrey's play both as a piece of literature and as an acting drama that makes it fitting that the honor of priority should belong to it. It was a product of the dramatic impulses of the time, deliberately written not only for the stage but also for the company that performed it" (*Beginning* 30). Later attempts to elevate the status of *Ponteach* to America's first tragedy met with resistance on similar grounds; in "An American Drama of the 18th Century" in *The Dial* in 1915, William Cairns firmly placed the play as primarily a historical document and dismissed it as negligible in terms of its literary merits.

Clearly Quinn felt frustrated in his quest to build a solid corpus of respectable American drama, regretting the foreign-influenced excesses of romance and melodrama and praising the native impulse to portray the "aboriginal natives," "the heroic episodes of conflicts with man and nature," and the comic "types of character" (*Beginning* 392). For instance, of Julia Ward Howe's *Leonora or The World's Own* (1857), he wrote that it "represents the movement in the late fifties which, under the encouragement of managers like the elder Wallack and Laura Keene, brought into the theatre pieces of significant dramatic literature. Unfortunately, this movement was checked by the Civil War, and by the system of travelling companies for which Boucicault was responsible" (*Beginning* 387). Quinn felt that the move to realism and naturalism signaled an "advance" for American drama because it manifested a truthfulness of portraiture and an impulse to humanitarian social reform. He had in mind a broad range of plays, including Steele MacKaye's *Hazel Kirke* (1880), James A. Herne's *Margaret Fleming* (1890), and those in the folk drama movement such as Lula Vollmer's *Sun-Up* (1924) and Paul Green's one-act plays on Negro life, *Lonesome Road* (1926).

The anthologists' insistence on an American subject, that is, on native themes also usually aligned with moral uplift and patriotic didacticism, soon overrode all other concerns. Quinn himself, in a discussion of American plays of the romantic period (1825–1840), notes that the significance of the vast body of romantic plays "has been obscured by its foreign setting, and to the canon of dramatic art that demands national themes, a canon that has never been applied except to America" (*Beginning* 267). Quinn explains the social and American political relationship between these romantic plays and the variety of foreign revolutionary situations they dramatize. But, in general, he suggests that they have become as obscure as the 190 plays about American history written between 1825 and 1860, many of which did not survive. By 1860, according to Quinn, the romantic tragedies, the verse dramas, the "foreign" and unrealistic plays – in short, most of what constituted American drama to that point – were displaced by the rising tide of realism and the contiguous interest in national and local types embodied in social and domestic drama (*Beginning* 391).

The narrow criteria of valuation were laid down early and would not be seriously challenged for decades to follow. Anthologies of American drama would not be the place to look for truly representative or popular plays; they would not include the many adaptations Dunlap made of August von Kotzebue's plays, or Boucicault's from French and Irish theatre, or John Howard Payne's *Claire, or the Maid of Milan* (1823), or Penn Smith's *The Triumph of Plattsburg* (1830). For Thomas Dickinson, as for many other critics, the Americanness of the drama lay in its narrowly "nativist" thematic concerns. In *The Case of American Drama* (1915), he set forth four primary unsolved problems he felt should be the themes for future drama: the Indian and the White; the pioneer, in other words, the "American"; village neighborliness, which was for him Americanism in its simplest form; and the city, the site of uncertainty, the "hot furnace" of the melting pot (*Case* 204–13). The "native themes" approach endured for decades. It was echoed, for instance, by Bennett Cerf and Van H. Cartmell in *Sixteen Famous American Plays* (1941), a collection of commercial successes that covers Sidney Howard's *They Knew What They Wanted* through to Howard Lindsay and Russel Crouse's *Life with Father*. The most recent of the thematic collections, Stanley Richards's *America on Stage* (1976), which begins with Arthur Miller's *The Crucible* and ends with Irwin Shaw's *Bury the Dead*, is built on the thematic assumption that if America is known by its wars, then theatre is "an invaluable adjunct of history" (ix).

Recapitulating a naive sociological approach to drama in *Nineteenth-Century American Plays* (1967), Myron Matlaw finds Americanness in "distinct characteristics" which he accepts as being replicated in equally distinct American stage types that gained prominence in the first half of the century. Matlaw assumes, quite erroneously, that the stage types were modeled mechanistically after some social types and does not question the proposition to consider the other possibility: that the stage type itself helped shape society because it deliberately was intended to serve as a model of sanctioned "American" behavior for new citizens. Robert Allan Gates uses a similarly naive sociological approach in *18th- and 19th-Century Drama* (1984) by marking the appearance in early America of plays "that had distinctive American qualities which reflected the changing American scene" (1). Richard Nelson, editor of *Strictly Dishonorable and Other Lost American Plays* (1986), shares this assurance that "there is something unique to the American character that allows profound innocence and cold ruthlessness to inhabit the same being" (v). In every instance, the working assumption is that there are indigenous social types which are merely mirrored on stage, an assumption that sociologists later also insisted on when they looked at the drama.

What these anthologizers do not suggest is the possibility that the creation of stage types mediated between a state of immigrant uncertainty and a too boundless potential, that it set forth circumscribed models of productive citizenry for new Americans just as it established limited roles for those already in the country, such as African Americans and Native American Indians. Before the institution of technologically transmitted mass culture (radio, movies, television) the theatre was a prominent and powerful site for the distribution and reification of dramatized images of America. Premodern stage conventions (from epic heroism to purported realism and naturalism) only reinforced the idea of mirror images. Stage typing set up narrow horizons of expectation and sharply segregated racial and ethnic groups, ran counter to any impulse toward a melting-pot egalitarianism, and constituted and consolidated constituencies for moral aims and political purposes. The creation of stage types – usually comic, sentimental, or heroic – was a dramaturgical strategy of presenting Americans to themselves, to fix emerging Americans by highlighting a transformational potential within permissible limits and forms but disallowing radical nonconformity and inconsistency.

Subjected to the speculative and categorizing gaze of the twentieth-century anthologizers, American nineteenth-century and later drama was presented to readers as a mirror of life rather than the imaginary reflection of an unreal world its authors had created. There was nothing new in this approach; from the beginning of national formation conservative voices were making strong appeals to homogeneity, continuity, and national character, *the* American experience, and in so doing were flying into the winds of warring or suppressed ideologies and cultural pluralism. This confusion of dramatic imagining with empirical reality led to a self-duplicating discourse. In a diffuse society, the fixed dramatic stereotypes (the Yankee Jonathan, the Zip Coon, the Mose, the B'Hoy, etc.) offered an easy, essentially comic, assurance of a stabilized people and a model for immigrant patterning and assimilation. The touchstone implicit in such modeling was Walt Whitman's nonexistent "divine average."

Certainly such characters were widely popular. In "The American on Stage" (1879), Brander Matthews described the extent to which the survival of a play depended on the staging of American types, particularly those typed by region, such as the southern colonel Mulberry Sellers, the eastern judge Bardwell Slote, Rip Van Winkle of the Hudson, Davy Crockett of the West, Mose of New York, Kit the Arkansas Traveler, and the simple Massachusetts farmer Solon Shingle. Despite the regional differences, all the characters were comic and were presented, as Matthews describes, "with the rigor and vigor of a photograph." The result, he complains, is the equivalent of the *commedia dell'arte*, "mechanical and lacks the freedom of art" (333). In later years, the comic impulse was associated implicitly with an American optimism deemed an essential attribute of the country and a necessary characteristic of the best American drama. In 1927, Brander Matthews accounted for this devotion to comic types by observing that "your American cannot as some other races can, – for instance, the Scandinavian, – enjoy serious contemplation of social evils or maladjustments" ("Forty" 16). The attitude prevailed at midcentury. For instance, in their foreword to *Sixteen Famous American Plays* (1941), Bennett Cerf and Van Cartmell described their two criteria: "native themes" and "a preponderance of comedy" because "American theatre has reached its greatest form of development in that medium." Although Barrett Clark and William Davenport included O'Neill's *The Hairy Ape* in *Nine Modern American Plays* (1951), they noted that "the dark mood is not typically American" and pointed to other plays in the selection, such as Robert Sherwood's *Abe Lincoln in Illinois* and William Wister Haines's *Command Decision*, as "combinations of realistic presentations and reaffirmations of American faith" (ix). One of the baldest and ugliest statements linking an Americanist affirmative spirit with "good" drama must be this remark from Ludwig Lewisohn in 1932, that "the failure of the Guild to develop dramatic artists and the failure of John Howard Lawson and Arthur Richman and of Elmer Rice, the most gifted of the group, to develop creatively is due in large part to that moral nihilism of assimilatory Jewry which, blending with the American moral nihilism of what may be drastically but not impertinently called the 'gin age,' has blighted so many talents" (400–401). The insistence on both realism and lightness of spirit perhaps can be traced back to William Dean Howells's assertion in *Criticism and Fiction* (1894) that the more smiling aspects of life are the more American. Certainly Thomas Dickinson in *The Case of American Drama* (1915) believed that the "temper of the pioneer spirit," the quality that kept the village together, was "laconic optimism," an optimism he felt ought to inform and suffuse American drama (219).

Anthology editors who took the aesthetic, formalist, or intellectual route were as vague as their nationalist brethren about their terms and criteria for the inclusion of plays. For instance, Allan Gates Halline attempted to give an "adequate picture of the development of American drama" in *American Plays* (1935) by focusing on its kinship to philosophy and literature as opposed to its theatrical origins. Halline also used Norman Foerster's thematic categories, the Puritan tradition, the frontier spirit, romanticism, and realism, which he had set forth in "Factors in American Literary History" (1928). Presumably, Halline felt that by modeling his approach on Foerster's he was forging a link between "real" literature and the marginalized drama. The results largely were predictable because the anthology of seventeen plays progresses from Royall Tyler's *The Contrast* to Paul Green's *The Field God*. Richard Cordell displayed a similar defensive posture in his introduction to *Twentieth-Century Plays, American: Eight Representative Selections* (1947) when he wrote that one site for the beginning of "honorable" American drama "commensurate" with the European was Maurice Browne's Little Theatre in Chicago (vi). The desire to authorize and legitimize drama, "the poor relation in the family of American literary art," also drives Jordan Y. Miller's collection, *American Dramatic Literature* (1961), which, he claims, meets the demands of good literature and consequently is suitable to be used as a college text. That Miller includes Mary Chase's *Harvey* undermines his argument. Miller also discounts all early American drama, beginning his collection in 1918 because, he argues, that was the moment at which "playmakers" became "playwrights" (ix).

Some anthologizers eschewed any attempt to privilege the drama or rationalize its literary merits and merely stressed popularity, a more honest, if no better defined, criterion. Barrett H. Clark placed popularity over the writer's distinction or reputation when choosing plays such as Lillian Mortimer's *No Mother to Guide Her*, John Augustus Stone's *Metamora*, Benjamin Woolf's *The Mighty Dollar*, and Julia Ward Howe's *Hippolytus* for inclusion in *Favorite American Plays of the Nineteenth Century* (1943). Richard Moody claimed that the plays in *Dramas from the American Theatre 1762–1909* (1966), such as Royall Tyler's *The Contrast*, Robert Montgomery Bird's *The Gladiator*, William Dean Howells's *A Letter of Introduction*, and Clyde Fitch's *The City*, had no literary merit (without establishing what the criteria would be for literary merit) but were illustrative of the theatrical variety the public desired in a "non-literary drama."

Those who organized their anthologies with an eye to the cultural work of the drama were clearly conflicted in their aims. Arthur Hobson Quinn in his introduction to *Contemporary American Plays* (1923) operated from a guiding principle of explicit cultural didacticism and hegemony; his selection included Rachel Crothers's *Nice People*, Jesse Lynch Williams's *Why Marry?*, Gilbert Emery's *The Hero*, and George S. Kaufman and Marc Connelly's *To the Ladies!* By way of explanation, Quinn included a reprint of his article in *Scribner's Magazine* (July 1922) in which he argued that "there is no vehicle so powerful and so competent to carry the meaning of America to our assimilated and our unassimilated population as the drama" (xii). Although two chapters about drama were written for the three-volume *Cambridge History of American Literature*, these chapters (and any reference to drama) were deleted from the abridged version. Noting this, Montrose Moses acquiesced to the omission because, as he conceded in *Representative American Dramas* (1929), American drama as yet had no one towering figure. However, he also argued that American drama should be of interest because of the social diversity of topics and the experiment with style.

In her introduction to an anthology of essays, *Ethnic Theatre in the United States* (1983), Maxine Schwartz Seller observes that the theatre has served as a cultural institution of social, political, and educational importance for immigrant groups in two ways. First, the theatre kept alive traditions and customs of the homeland. (In fact, the difference between native drama and cultural imports was felt so strongly by Norman Hapgood that in 1901 he designated the classics being acted in German at Irving Place as "Our Only High Class Theatre" compared to the cheap stock work and theatrical amusements being pushed by the dominating syndicated theatres.) Second, the theatre was an active agent in the process of Americanization. Statistics presented in *The American Journal of Sociology* in 1919 point to the sense of urgency behind the need to "Americanize" aliens, especially the war industry's workers aged between twenty and thirty-five: 46 million persons of foreign birth and foreign origin; 5 million non-English speakers; 2 million illiterates; 3 million of military age (Hill 612). According to Seller, however, the theatre was primarily a source of entertainment to counterbalance the dreary, labor-intensive reality of the immigrants' lives. Such theatres catered largely to the foreign-born (the native-born having been assimilated) and fell into decline after 1925, being displaced in large measure by technological advances such as radio and, later, television. Seller notes a resurgence in ethnic theatre in the United States in the sixties and seventies, owing in large measure to the dominance of cultural pluralism over the melting pot. Within the already separated category of American drama, ethnic theatre, like the theatre of blacks or women, is usually ghettoized.

Although most general anthologies were offered as repositories of characteristic, if not the "best," work available in the genre, some were described by their compilers as, if not oppositional, at least alternative. But the rhetoric was stronger than the collections. For instance, Barrett Clark and Kenyon Nicholson made such an argument for their *The American Scene* (1930), in which they sought to "express a sufficient number of groups in America to capture a *divergence* from national standardization" (vi). The claim is greater than the realization because the thirty-four plays, though regional in focus and dialect, for the most part were written by such established writers as Edna Ferber, Susan Glaspell, Theodore Dreiser, Paul Green, and Michael Gold. Similarly, Barrett Clark and William H. Davenport assembled their *Nine Modern American Plays* (1951) with an eye to representing "a composite picture of the American way," arguing that America was widely diversified and contained different moral and political ideologies. The selection of plays, however, does little to bear out this assertion; Lynn Riggs's *Green Grow the Lilacs*, Tennessee Williams's *The Glass Menagerie*, and Maxwell Anderson's *High Tor* may focus on minority groups or issues but are far from being outside national standards. In claiming Elmer Rice's *Street Scene* and Moss Hart and George S. Kaufman's *You Can't Take It with You* as "universal, and typical, and basically American," the editors speak more as census takers than as spokespersons for either oppositional or alternative views.

In general, the old rule, that is, that there were no firm rules for inclusion, held sway. Clive Barnes has no stated theory of selection for *50 Best Plays of the American Theatre* (1969) other than that American drama, which like many other critics he believes really came into its own with O'Neill, has "vitality." Barnes's four-volume anthology moves from *The Contrast* to *Fiddler on the Roof* and positions Lillian Hellman as the first female playwright in the American canon. Lee A. Jacobus wrote that his selection in *The Longman Anthology of American Drama* (1982), comprising mostly melodramas and tragicomedies from *The Contrast* to *The Sunshine Boys*, represents an American world view dominated by "hopefulness, the sense of the possible, and the ideals of equality and law" (1).

The Cultural Location of American Drama

Long before the first anthology, however, the critical groundwork for a troubled reception of American drama was being done in the magazines and journals as well as in general literary histories. The most revealing sources for the debate over the cultural positioning of early drama are the magazines and journals; from time to time, theatre had its own journals, but theatre news was placed as frequently with sports and crime. From a cultural perspective this unholy alliance makes sense because, as Richard Butsch has pointed out, until the 1890s when American theatre was legitimated and feminized, it was a "male club" where rowdy behavior and prostitution prevailed (374). Lyon Richardson credits *The New-England Magazine of Knowledge and Pleasure* (1758) with being "the first American magazine to contain major examples of three types of eighteenth-century literature heretofore disregarded: dramatic prose, the moral epistle written for young children, and the moralistic story of humanitarian cast" (138). The play in question was *The Toy-Shop*, the dialogue of a fop out shopping. A more significant presence was William Dunlap's play, *The Father: or, American Shandyism*, which was serialized in three issues of *The Massachusetts Magazine* in 1789. According to Frank Mott, Dunlap was also the unidentified author of "The Theatrical Register," which ran for a year and a half until April 1796 in the *New-York Magazine* and "comprised the most important body of dramatic criticism in an eighteenth-century magazine" (I 56). Because the establishment and operation of theatre was opposed largely for religious reasons, there was a paucity of drama coverage in the first magazines, but during the early nationalist movement a special, albeit short-lived, class of periodicals dedicated to theatrical revues arose: these included the *Thespian Oracle* (1798), *Theatrical Censor* (1805), *Thespian Mirror* (1805), and *Mirror of Taste and Dramatic Censor*, which survived a full season in 1810–1811 (I 165–66). Some general magazines and newspapers published dramatic criticism, but the major thrust of public opinion was against theatres on moral grounds and, according to Neal Edgar, the only plays printed in magazines between 1810 and 1820 were British (33). Dramatic criticism between 1825 and 1850, the time when New York had become the theatrical center, when American dramatists had no copyright protection, and when the stage was dominated by foreign plays, was, Mott notes, left to the general periodicals and newspapers (I 427–29).

During this period, however, the first book about American theatre was published. In his anecdotal *History of the American Theatre* (1833), William Dunlap was concerned primarily with defending the reputation of actors and upholding the image of theatre as inextricably connected to a highly civilized state characterized by the triumph of morality and religion over barbarism. Presumably he was spurred by the proliferation of disparaging remarks about the behavior of American audiences that salted so many European reports, including Frances Trollope's *Domestic Manners of the Americans* (1832). An expatriated Englishman, Dunlap tried to make distinctions that would preserve the moral art form from contamination by its acolytes and devotees, the immoral artists and the immoral parts of the audience (those alluring vices displayed in the boxes). Sporadically in his defense of American theatre, however, Dunlap took on the question of the goals of American drama. Arguing that American drama ought to emulate the German and French models (as opposed to the degraded English ones) and that American theatre ought to be under government control and free of commercial aims, Dunlap called for the "powerful engine" of theatre "to instruct, to inspire love of country, virtue, religion, and morality [and] teaching and improving the public" (I 134–35). Dunlap's insistence that drama should be didactic and socially useful, that truth and morality were interchangeable, anticipated his theory of mimetic and idealistic art, which he set forth in the following year in *History of the Rise and Progress of the Arts of Design in the United States* (1834). Given his views, it is hardly surprising that Dunlap favored the elegant correctness of Thomas Sully over the "unfinished" paintings of Gilbert Stuart.

Although Dunlap noted approvingly that "the commencement of the American drama as united with the American theatre" occurred with the production of Royall Tyler's *The Contrast* (April 16, 1786), he later lamented that Tyler and other writers "seem to have thought that a Yankee character, a Jonathan, stamped the piece as American, forgetting that a clown is not the type of the nation he belongs to" (I 136, 162). Calling for a break from the English model (and apparently blinding himself to the American practice of slavery), Dunlap suggested that a "more severe and manly character, induced by our republican institutions," would better serve as an image of a "self-governed" country "which is destined to look back to the annals of long past ages for a record that ever a slave or master polluted her soil" (I 162–63). A champion of the German drama, Dunlap nonetheless ranked Shakespeare above all other playwrights, and in his own career as playwright mainly produced sentimental comedies and numerous revisions of English plays with new titles. Dunlap's call for heroic "manliness" anticipates the recurring and continued concern for a "virile" drama and for playwriting as a "masculine" enterprise that runs through the history of American drama.

Beyond the familiar moral arguments and vaguely defined patristic and nationalistic aims, Dunlap had little that was specific to offer about the substance or form of the desired American drama beyond repeatedly invoking the German and French models. The one American author he cited approvingly, and to whom the history was dedicated, was James Fenimore Cooper, whose novels were commended for being "fascinating" and "instructive," unlike "much of the trash of the stage" (II 363). Cooper himself, in *Notions of the Americans* (1828), had written dismissively of American drama:

> Of dramatic writers there are none, or next to none. The remarks I have made in respect to novels apply with double force to this species of American composition. A witty and successful American comedy could only proceed from extraordinary talent. There would be less difficulty, certainly, with a tragedy; but still, there is rather too much foreign competition, and too much domestic employment in other pursuits, to invite genius to so doubtful an enterprise. The very baldness of ordinary American life is in deadly hostility to scenic representation. The character must be supported solely by its intrinsic power. The judge, the footman, the clown, the lawyer, the belle, or the beau can receive no great assistance from dress Melo-dramas, except the scene be laid in the woods, are out of the question. It would be necessary to seek the great clock, which is to strike the portentous twelve blows, in the nearest church; a vaulted passage would degenerate into a cellar; and, as for ghosts, the country was discovered since their visitations ceased. The smallest departure from the incidents of ordinary life would do violence to every man's experience; and, as already mentioned, the passions which belong to human nature must be delineated, in America, subject to the influence of that despot – common sense. (150–51)

Margaret Fuller, in "American Literature" (1852), moves cautiously toward a definition of "American" in literature, rejecting imitations of European thought by American writers and arguing that before we could have a native literature, "an original idea must animate this nation." The imitators merely are colonists, "useful schoolmasters to our people in a transition state" (122). Calling for the completion of the "fusion of races," she envisions a literature predicated on "moral and intellectual dignity," which in turn is supported by a country that has been totally explored, "studded with towns, broken by the plow, netted together by railways and telegraph lines" (124). After lengthy considerations of poetry and prose, she ultimately has remarkably little to say about the drama. Rejecting "the heroisms of Rolla, and the sentimentalism and stale morality" of the Keans in *Town and Country*, Fuller suggests that a new nation needs something other than closet drama:

> A considerable portion of the hope and energy of this country still turns towards the drama, that greatest achievement when wrought to perfection of human power. For ourselves, we believe the day of the regular drama to be past; and, though we recognize the need of some kind of spectacle and dramatic representation to be absolutely coincident with an animated state of the public mind, we have thought that the opera, ballet, pantomime, and briefer, more elastic forms, like the *vaudeville* of the French theatre, or the *proverb* of the social party, would take the place of elaborate tragedy and comedy. (134)

Insisting that, at the present, "the only efficient instrument for the general education of the people" was being done by the journals, Fuller concludes: "The existence is foreshown of those forces which are to animate an American literature, that faith, those hopes are not yet alive which shall usher it into a *homogeneous or fully organized state of being*" [my emphasis] (142).

The position of the drama at this time, 1850–1865, is embodied by its continued location in the journals, very few of which were devoted solely to the drama. Lucile Gafford has documented the Transcendentalists' interest in the drama, an interest that proves to be an exception to more general standards of taste. For instance, Mott notes that "*Figaro!* was chiefly theatrical, but it ranges itself also with the comics"; and, by the same token, the humorous periodicals almost always took an interest in the theatres. Sports magazines such as *Spirit of the Times* and the *New York Clipper* also gave a lot of attention to theatres. Given these associations with low-culture activities, it is no wonder that the clerical ban on theatres persisted (Mott II 198–200). It did not improve matters that the *National Police Gazette* covered the rowdier theatres and the burlesque or that the *New York Illustrated Times* and Chicago's *Sporting and Theatrical Journal* considered theatre to be an amusement similar to sport (Mott III 198). In 1879, an article in the *New York Mirror* summarized the situation with the argument

that "the dramatic profession of this country was for many years degraded by having its affairs treated in the professedly theatrical papers side by side with prize fights, cocking matches, baseball, and other sports" (Mott III 198). By 1889, the popularity of theatre with ticket buyers was indisputable, but the drama's literary status was seen as threatened. "Is the divorce of literature and the stage complete?" queried Charles Warner in the *Critic*. "How long is it since a play has been written and accepted and played which has any so-called literary quality, or is an addition to literature?" (Mott IV 255). Despite the promise for higher drama being held out by the successes of James A. Herne and Bronson Howard, the serious theatre had two new competitors: the "new" burlesque, that is, the burlesque of legs and tights as opposed to the older variety of travesties and satires, and the great traveling vaudeville circuits and spectacles, notably *Ben-Hur*, which had drawn an audience of over 25,000 by its hundredth performance and had instilled a desire for massive, realistic spectacles in the audiences (Mott IV 258–60).

So pervasive were the diverse popular entertainments on the American stage, and so anxious was he for a worthy literature that in *Curiosities of the American Stage* (1891), Laurence Hutton, former drama critic at the *New York Mail* and at the time a literary editor at *Harper's Magazine*, dismissed as "curiosities" virtually every form of theatre work – a rich and varied panoply including Indian drama, Revolutionary and war drama, frontier drama, American character drama, "New York" drama, society drama, Negro drama, and the burlesque. Citing critical unanimity of opinion about the problem, he began with the pronouncement that "the American play is yet to be written" (3). Lamenting the lack of a "standard" let alone an "immortal" American play, Hutton called for a "greatness" resting on the foundation of "purely and entirely American scenes" (6). Disallowing a wide range of possibilities from the "alien" pen of Boucicault through the derivative scenes of *Uncle Tom's Cabin* to *The Contrast*, Hutton relentlessly cleared the way for an enduring drama to match the distinctive and creditable body of American poetry and prose. The playwrights themselves anticipated a future American drama, probably one grounded in realism, portraying American characters in American locales. The collected opinions of Augustin Daly, Edward Harrigan, John Grosvenor Wilson, Steele MacKaye, Bronson Howard, and William Gillette in *Harper's Weekly* (1889) show them to have been relieved that the theatre no longer had a moral stigma attached to it, conscious of a cosmopolitan sensibility in most American drama, and interested in the possibility of an American school of drama. Augustin Daly and Bronson Howard both argued that there really was no such thing as an American drama, simply plays written in English by Americans on a broad range of subjects, set in a wide variety of locations.

After the establishment of culturally respectable middle-class drama in the 1890s, writers after the turn of the century still sought to identify the defining characteristics of Americanness in literature. For instance, resisting the appellation "bourgeois" because it smacked of a European feudalism that she found tastelessly inappropriate to an "Anglo-Saxon" and "honest republic," Winifred Webb nonetheless embraced the essential idea of middle-class identity as apropos (122). In "The Spirit of American Literature" (1906), she rejected the "yearning for liberty," the "sensuousness," the "lasciviousness," the "morbid selfconsciousness," and other "ruins" of older cultures that have fed their "hungry art," and suggested that a nation in which all the citizens are politically equal and socially middle-class needed a vigilante literature that would "warn" us of "impurities" in the "main stream that is widening so rapidly" and "make us valiant for the defense of its borders." She sounds like a Jeffersonian landowner threatened by the urban immigrant. If the mission of American literature, then, was to preach "with moral force," or what amounts to good manners in Webb's catalogue – a warning against "vulgarity," "snobbishness," and "materialism" – what place was there for drama? None, given that drama, being about conflict, thrives on contestation and resistance. In fact, Webb found the true voice of hegemonic concern being expressed by magazine writers and newspaper editors rather than by "our so-called artists" (123–24).

One might expect a less narrow perspective from Kenneth Macgowan, who was both a critic for the *New York Globe* and producer of six of Eugene O'Neill's plays. The influential author of *The Theatre of Tomorrow* (1921), with Herman Rosse, *Masks and Demons* (1923), and, with Robert Edmond Jones, *Continental Stagecraft* (1922), Macgowan was responsible for the first New York production of Strindberg's *Ghost Sonata* (1924). Drawing on his knowledge of world theatre, Macgowan, in *Footlights Across America* (1929), his published report of his fourteen-thousand-mile tour of amateur theatres, was able to take the long view and state that the "amateur theatrical system" was the site of nationwide resistance to the professional theatre, which began "unobtrusively committing suicide" on the road about 1913 (3–4). Because theatre, for Macgowan, was a "mob-art" and drama was "psychic catharsis," he argued that both should have a mission far greater than mere leisure for amateurs (6). Seizing on the proliferation of "local" (the term he preferred to regional) theatres (most of which were in the Northeast), springing out of decentralized, noncommercial activity, as proof of a connectedness with "the reality of life," Macgowan analyzed the split as an ideological dialectic: "The product of local necessity . . . it savors of the democracy of Thomas Jefferson as surely as Broadway is a dramatization of federalism and centralization" (20).

But Macgowan, too, had a hegemonic goal. Although such local drama would speak first of local characters and local conditions, it would, if it "proves to have universal qualities, either of truth or of art," become the basis for a national art in a national theatre (22). The new voices for the new national theatre would come from four sources: "the men of professional or Broadway caliber who have come from Baker at Harvard and Yale," the writers of folk drama "who have been bred more often in universities than in the little theatres," the playwrights who have started their own ventures, and the people who participate in local theatre (207). What is not clear from Macgowan's prediction is how the four voices are to be reconciled into one "native" voice nor how the academic, elitist voice, the imitative voice of the writer who hangs out with workers, will pass as authentic. That the majority of the "local" drama would still be the product of educated people did not prevent Macgowan from claiming a basic authenticity for this new drama: "The United States is not homogeneous, more than that, it is rich in life far removed from sophistication" (208). This looking into the drama as if it were a multifaceted mirror of society was part of an American tradition. For instance, Charles Klein, in a self-serving and self-congratulatory article for *The Arena* in 1907, asserted that "the drama is the concrete reflection of the mental attitude of a race toward the religion and philosophy of its period. This link is felt rather than seen, for it is reflected in whatever is psychological or metaphysical in drama" (492). Compounding Klein's assertion, his article was followed by one by B. O. Flower praising Klein's work both as accurate social studies and as a civilizing power.

One of the few dissenting voices of this period belonged to the irreverent Percy Hammond who, of "Thespis, the male Cinderella of the arts" (22), wrote in 1927 that "the drama is the least dependable of the evidences of a nation's character, baseball, the cinema, the comic supplements, stud poker, the rotogravures of society in the Sunday newspapers, political conventions, bootlegging, and the U.S. Senate are more explanatory than it is possible for any play to be. . . . To art it is what chewing gum is to food or cosmetics to complexions" (120–21). For historians of the drama to agree to Hammond's thesis, they would have to accept the minstrel show as indigenous American drama. Of course many, including William Dean Howells, did point to the popular form of entertainment as the only truly "native" form but stopped far short of incorporating it into the literary canon. A few later historians have been more receptive to wider criteria. For instance, Ralph

G. Allen, writing in 1971, argues against the academic tradition that has
pressed for privileging hybridized forms and themes, mere variants on Old
World patterns, as "American." "To begin with," he writes, "there is no
native American form of drama – in the sense of a realized literary style
uniquely reflective of the spirit of the New World" (273). America's "first"
professionally produced play, Godfrey's *The Prince of Parthia*, he dismisses
as "an unimaginative imitation of the exotic baroque melodramas" popular
in late-eighteenth-century London. Furthermore, he contends, the only
thing native about Royall Tyler's *The Contrast* (1787), often heralded as
America's first comedy written by an American citizen, is its New York
setting. What America has instead, he says, if it would but put aside a
sentimental attitude to and elitist contempt for proletarian art, is the sub-
or nonliterary burlesque show. Born of the crossing of the minstrel show
with the honky-tonk, burlesque, the most popular of all theatrical entertainment from 1900 to 1930, is quintessentially American, he suggests,
because it is amoral, undignified, and undisciplined. "In addressing itself to
all these temporary, anti-social child-like inclinations, this most American
of all entertainments dramatizes the wish-fulfillment of a society that
thinks of itself as classless" (283). (Allen did not add, as he might have, that
the sexism and racism of all three forms, minstrel show, honky-tonk, and
burlesque, were also "American.") But such a free-wheeling irreverence for
authority, often enacted by farcical assaults on doctor, lawyer, policeman,
or businessman, clearly would not fit into the establishment's project,
reified by the legitimate, commercial theatres, of aggrandizing a hierarchical, capitalist system supported by the professional class.

Allen's is a minority opinion, and in fact there was a continued rejection
in American "official" theatrical culture of any oppositional voice that might
deliver a rowdy raspberry of disapproval from the subordinated or marginalized groups. To open the canon would be to admit popular work that
was ridiculing both the conventions and pretensions of "high" drama, such
as John Brougham's "*Columbus el Filibusters*, a New and Audaciously Original, Historico-plagiaristic, Ante-national, Pre-patriotic, and Omni-local
Confusion of Circumstances" (1857). The received history of American
drama for the most part presents a hegemonic front of decorous spectacle
and the appearance of realism to hide genuine conflict and subversive
anxiety within the increasingly corporate, capitalist society. Emblematic of
the move to consolidate the body of American drama within narrowly
defined thematic, nationalistic, high literary, and moralistic terms was the
celebration of the one hundred and fiftieth anniversary of Godfrey's *The
Prince of Parthia* as the "first" American play in the *Masque of American*

Drama, produced by the Zelosophic and Philomathean Societies of the University of Pennsylvania in May 1917 under the sponsorship of the Drama League of America. Written by Albert Trombly of the Romance languages faculty and interspersed with scenes from the authorized canon of American drama (*The Prince of Parthia, Gladiator, Francesca da Rimini, Rip Van Winkle*, and *Scarecrow*), the pageant celebrated the triumph of drama over the vicissitudes of war and commercialism as it progressed toward becoming an art. The personification of American drama as a beleaguered hero triumphing over political and popular obstacles was a strategy designed to affirm its hard-won cultural status as high art, a status it never was accorded despite the concerted efforts of the Drama League.

An Agency of Legitimation: the Drama League

One way to think of American drama is that it was going to be what the Drama League said it was. At a critical moment in the cry to reform American theatre, the Drama League was an openly self-conscious force that represented the consolidation of power among men of the universities, club women, and "little theatre" practitioners who determined that they alone must control the future course of production and evaluation. The Drama League should be understood as part of an ongoing educational movement that gathered force in the 1890s as a consequence of compulsory schooling, the rise in enrollments, the increase in library readerships, and an expanding middle class with a decided inclination to self-improvement. This wide-scale educational movement flowered with the growth of such cultural clubs as the Chautauqua Literary and Scientific Circle, the Browning Clubs, and Bellamy Societies, all of which increased the demand for "good" books. Interest in dramatic literature supplied by play publishers such as Samuel French, whose catalogue in 1910 listed six hundred new plays, was fueled by lists of plays and information on current productions circulated by such organizations as the American Drama Society (founded in 1909), the MacDowell Club (1910), and the Drama League (founded in 1910) (Kozelka 606).

Although the Drama League was not the first organization to tackle the tyranny of commercial theatre, it was the most successful and the most extensively represented in the community at large. In "The New Revolt Against Broadway," John Corbin described earlier attempts by the People's Institute of New York to bring Lower East Side residents to good plays and by the MacDowell Club to assess plays by bulletin. One advantage the Drama League had over these localized efforts is that it was also a national

organization originating in the union of sixty-three drama societies with a
total membership of ten thousand and growing to a hundred thousand by
1915. Taking on both the Scylla of public opinion and the Charybdis of
commercialism, the Drama League, officially founded in Chicago by a
women's club in 1910, grew to have a vast network of local chapters in place
to sanction productions and distribute plays throughout the United States
and Canada. The founders, in the words of their leader, Mrs. A. Starr Best,
"realized acutely that it was in large part the decadence of the audience
which was to blame for the conditions in the theatre world to-day, and that
we should never have clean, wholesome, clever, worthwhile drama until we
secured an educated, awakened audience which should support and demand it" (*Drama* n.p.).

Another significant factor in the extensive power of the Drama League
was that it brought influential civic-minded women together with influential, professionally academic men. The separation of high-cultural activities
from the American aristocracy and the assumption of the duties of discrimination and preservation by a new professional class was a fairly recent
phenomenon coextensive with the burgeoning commercial and academic
expansion of the arts. In "The Conduct of Life" (1895), one essay in "The
Art of Living" series for *Scribner's Magazine*, Robert Grant had called for
the "large minority" to be responsible for "the great educational and artistic
enterprizes." Charging that the "shallow worldlings," the "four hundred" of
New York aristocracy, those who ought to represent the "most highly
evolved civilization," had abandoned their civic mission for French amoral-
ity and "splendid inane social fripperies," Grant insisted that the hope lay
in "our clergymen, our lawyers, our doctors, our architects, our merchants,
our teachers, some of our editors, our bankers, our scientists, our scholars,
and our philanthropists" (588–90).

If the newly professionalized professoriate was beginning to exercise
control over the evaluation of culture not just within the colleges and
universities, women, who had control over their domestic spheres as con-
sumers in the choice of cultural events, were beginning to inhabit more
public spaces where their influence was marked. Therefore, organizations
such as the Drama League represented a powerful coalition and a new
cultural force, especially for the respectability and marketability of the
drama. The appropriation of masculine authority was, in fact, deliberate
and calculated; the affluent founder, Mrs. A. Starr Best, believed that the
"ignominy" of being a "woman's movement" was overcome by securing
prominent men to serve on the board and as speakers (K. Blair 150).
Though the men were the figureheads, the women did the work. Clayton

Hamilton, who did not miss the significance of the women's power, pointed to the "historical truth" that contemporary theatre, unlike Renaissance theatre, was written for women and that "the destiny of our drama has lain for a long time in the hands of women . . . in fact, the theatre is to-day the one great public institution in which 'votes for women' is the rule" ("Organizing" 163–64). As a consequence of the harnessing of the local power of women and the professional power of men, training American audiences through education and art was directed by an institutional agency; less than a school but more than a club, the Drama League was an interventionist agent, a mediator of cultural values blurring the boundaries between higher education and social organization. This consolidation of powerful cultural agencies proved to be quite effective though of limited duration.

Historian Karen Blair in *The Torchbearers* (1994) documents the phenomenal growth rate of the Drama League: Within a year and a half of the founding, the Drama League had 20,000 members; 80,000 by 1913; and 100,000 affiliated members in 114 centers by 1915. Both the rapid growth and the success of the Drama League, Blair suggests, can be attributed to its connections to other organizations, such as the five hundred Chautauquas and teachers' institutes that publicized the League. Although under the ostensible presidency of Mrs. A. Starr Best, the Drama League in fact had powerful alliances with the academic and noncommercial theatre world in such officers as Percival Chubb, Percy MacKaye, and Louis Anspacher. The creation of the Drama League coincided with the beginning of and was instrumental in the development of the Little Theatre movement in the United States, marked by its early chronicler, Constance D'Arcy Mackay, as starting in 1911–1912. By 1917 there were more than fifty Little Theatres firmly established across the country, some specializing in American work and all committed to intimate productions, a high standard of acting, and "good" drama. As part of both the educational and Little Theatre movements, the Drama League's influence should not be underestimated. Because of the work of the League and the needs of the burgeoning Little Theatre market, a demand for plays by Americans increased and was met by responsive publishers. Carter and Ogden noted in 1938 that the distributors of scripts estimated the number of amateur groups at three hundred thousand (11). Mrs. Best had seen that "nothing can so improve our national dramatic taste as the reading of a printed play" and had joined forces with Doubleday, Page & Company to publish the Drama League Series (*Drama* n.p.). One of the plays salvaged by both the bulletin and publication was Charles Kenyon's *Kindling*, selected because "it is distinctly

American, possesses a vital theme, is remarkably strong and virile and well constructed, and is decidedly one of the best of American plays." Clayton Hamilton reported that the successful run in Chicago of Louis Parker's *Disraeli* was largely due to the Drama League's endorsement ("Organizing" 165). By 1925, Thomas Edwards of Samuel French, recalling how such plays were unavailable fifteen years previously, credited the League with stimulating the three markets for plays: clubs, schools, and "art theatres."

Perhaps more important, however, was the League's involvement in directing the course of the canon, an enterprise undertaken through a system of rapidly published and widely distributed bulletins designed to guide the audience to the worthy plays. Sounding like both a fastidious consumer and a frugal housekeeper, Mrs. Best described the winnowing process as saving the theatregoer from the "annoyance of experimenting for himself on unknown and often worthless plays. Last year [1913] in Chicago there were 150 plays – 100 of these were musical comedies and, therefore, not noticed by the League. Of the other fifty, sixteen were approved by the League as worthy and bulletined. This will show a saving of attendance on thirty-four worthless plays, or more than two-thirds of all productions." Working from a speak-no-evil ethos, Mrs. Best was proud of the League's fairness, boasting that "it works only in support, never against, and is utterly altruistic and uncommercial" (*Drama* n.p.). An early essay in praise of the League's work describes this unique system of bulletins used to validate all that was supposedly sound, valuable, and worthy in dramatic art: "The purpose of the League is to educate a public by showing what is good and why it is good, not by telling it what is bad" (Peck 113). The remorseless attention to every aspect of theatrical production and the evaluative controls exercised by the Drama League were laid out by Richard Burton, then the president, in an article for *The Nation* in 1914.

This code of silence regarding negative opinions initially proved to be a powerful strategy for directing taste but ultimately proved to be the bane of frustrated reviewers. In 1917, a peeved Philadelphian submitting a Producing Centre Report complained that "of the musical comedy and the moving pictures we are not permitted to speak – although some day the League must take under its charge all dramatic effort, even a critique of the amateur. . . . We should exercise care lest we find ourselves disapproving the kind of drama the people like. . . ; it is an uncomfortable thought to remember that we have declined to bulletin all the 'long runs' and have favored all the failures" (Anon. "Producing" 418–19).

The Drama League, setting itself up as, in the words of its first president, "a great civic force," did its work through committees and "departments" and conscientiously covered every venue for play reading, publication, and production including the "Drama League Monthly" and "The Drama Quarterly." For instance, George Pierce Baker at Harvard headed the study of drama. The Junior department organized the work of children's clubs. There were also a Teacher's department, a department of Plays for Amateur Acting, a Lecture Bureau, a Library department out of the Newberry Library, which supplied book lists, and a Publication department headed by Barrett Clark. As evidenced by the Drama League's many play lists, the overriding concern was for edification through literary excellence, particularly for plays based on historical, allegorical, and biblical themes. Mindful that drama had its origins in religious expression and in the high seriousness of tragedy, the League's primary responsibility was to promote the drama as an indispensable educational tool for the creation of an ethical national citizenry. In this way, a naturalized response to drama was yoked to a naturalized sense of citizenship.

The Playgoing committee was charged with "the surveillance of contemporary plays" and with "keeping track of all good productions." If the committee deemed a production worthy, a one-page bulletin was sent to press immediately and was in the mail within twenty-four hours after the performance, "going to every member of the League throughout the country, urging support of the play." Claiming that "the indorsement of the League is disinterested," Peck notes that "the effect of these bulletins in increasing box-office receipts has been demonstrated again and again" (136–37). According to *The Nation*, "it is hard to dissociate the movement from these bulletins. Its success is bound up with them" (Wernaer 310). The 250 bulletins issued between 1910 and 1916 had to be paid for, of course, but the Drama League was as well connected to commercial allies as to those in education. In Pittsburgh, for instance, the corporate sponsor was Kaufmann's, a large department store in whose auditorium schoolchildren presented plays, and which also took out advertisements in the bulletin for its book department, which sold plays. Repeatedly the message in the bulletins was a warning against "the Perversion of Public Opinion," which "could not distinguish between the gold of drama and the tin of clap-trap." Nothing less than the salvation of both the drama and the theatre depended on the progressive "conversion of the Public Taste" to an appreciation of "the conditions of human life that makes for greater beauty, more rational living, and deeper ethical conviction" (Kenyon "Education" 1). The League was dedicated to the idea of drama "as something to be written, as something to be read, as something to be acted" (ibid. 1).

Though the Drama League surveyed all contemporary drama, the members also had a specific commitment to developing American drama. In the president's report of 1917, the year in which the Drama League devoted itself to the study of American drama, Percival Chubb looked less to the past than to the future, stating that "the task which awaits us in connection with American Drama is not so much that of surveying a comparatively unproductive past, as that of instigating the creation of whatever may be called (perhaps mistakenly) distinctive American Drama" (378). The demand for and interest in American drama flourished under the Drama League's auspices; it encouraged the study of printed plays, published collections of plays, and offered prizes for new plays. Ten of the twenty two-hour lectures offered in the 1923–1924 season were on American drama; approved works included Clyde Fitch's *The Truth, The Girl with the Green Eyes, The City*; Langdon Mitchell's *The New York Idea*; Louis Anspacher's *The Unchastened Woman*; Alice Brown's *Children of the Earth*; Augustus Thomas's *The Witching Hour* and *The Copperhead*; William Vaughn Moody's *The Great Divide*; Charles Kenyon's *Kindling*; George Hazelton's and J. H. Benrimo's *The Yellow Jacket*; and Owen Davis's *Icebound*. Mrs. A. Starr Best herself was the author of study course number 30, the *Brief Survey Course on American Drama* (1926), which was based on the anthologies compiled by Arthur Quinn, Montrose J. Moses, and Thomas Dickinson. It duplicated many of the plays in the season's lecture series and placed great value on "native material." That the course included John Howard Lawson's innovative *Processional* and *Roger Bloomer* as well as the more predictable *Fashion* by Cora Mowatt and *The Scarecrow* by Percy MacKaye suggests something of the wide range of approved texts, a range that would not be found in similar courses today.

But the Drama League, drawing the wagons in ever smaller circles around standards increasingly being called into question by its fractious membership, never rose fully to the opportunities for expanding its influence. Internal divisiveness, economic strains, World War I, the depression, the increasing attraction of filmgoing and the concomitant decline in participation in amateur dramatics, and the increased regional strength of local chapters of the Drama League, all resulted in a diminished national influence. Percival Chubb, president of the organization in 1916, had declared war on the movies and called for "more effective propaganda" for the drama, had argued that drama had to be "democratized" through amateur and folk productions, and had urged the Drama League to work with "Big Business" in order to get plays into smaller cities ("Mission" 1–2). A year later, he described the division within the Drama League as one between the "good-taste uplifters calling for a higher tradition of the stage, expressive, like architecture and music, of the better soul of the people, versus those interested in drama as a form of national culture" ("Task" 274). But the fissures widened and, as Applebee notes, with the declaration of war in 1917, "the Drama League dropped its literary emphasis and provided a play on food conservation" (67). The nation now had more compelling issues to contend with than those of taste. Though the national organization was disbanded by a vote in 1931, local centers such as the New York Drama League continued to function. Despite its extensive involvement in the preservation, study, publication, and production of American drama, most histories of American drama, focused as they usually are on individual playwrights or movements, ignore the essential activities of the Drama League, which demands more than the passing tribute of a sigh.

The Trope of Organic Evolution

The critical evaluations of American drama show it to have been in a state of perpetual decline or emergence or adolescence or invalidism or near death. Whatever the perilous state, the dominant trope was organic. Arthur Hobson Quinn, seeking to establish hope about the possibility for an American drama of distinction, worth, and note, sums up his survey of progressively bettering "types" of drama from 1756 to 1860 by pointing to "the evidence of organic growth" (CHAL 233). Decline was a common trope for critics and historians almost from the beginning: "Decline of the Modern Drama" in *New England Magazine* (February 1835), "The Decline of the Drama" in *Brother Jonathan* (July 1842), "Decline of the Drama" in *The Prompter's Whistle* (September 1850), "The Decline of the Drama" in *Spirit of the Times* (November 1858), and "The Decline of the Drama" in *The North American Review* (September 1877). Infantile, miserable, morbid, disintegrating, decadent, and languishing, the American drama in these accounts seems never to have been fully "adult," "healthy," or "alive." As a further irony, in many modern instances critics look back to a Golden Age in comparison to which they denounce contemporary drama. For instance, Brooks Atkinson in "No Time for American Drama" complains about the theatre season of 1965–1966 in comparison to the exuberant and vital offerings of the four previous decades. Confusing musicals and plays produced in America with drama by American playwrights, Atkinson fusses that even the best of the year's selection, Dale Wasserman's *Man of La Mancha* and Peter Weiss's *The Persecution and Assassination of Marat as Performed by the Inmates of the Asylum of Charenton under the Direction of the*

Marquis de Sade, were only "all theatre" (17). Ironically, Robert Brustein, who complained so vigorously about American playwrights in 1965, recalls things differently in 1992: "The new American play – once the proud staple of the commercial theatre in the 1930s, 40s, and 50s – has virtually disappeared from producer's agendas. . . . Everybody remembers a golden time when the American theatre could boast a succession of dramatists renowned throughout the world, beginning with O'Neill, and continuing through Odets, Hellman, Miller, Williams, and Albee" ("Reinventing" 246, 252).

A few examples must suffice to demonstrate that this pervasive and unpersuasive rhetorical metaphor has always haunted American dramatic history. If drama was only "miserable" and "languishing" for Walt Whitman in 1847, by 1886 drama was dead and ought to stay that way as far as William Dean Howells was concerned. For Brander Matthews in 1888, the drama was only "on the verge" of dying. The drama was dawning for John Corbin in 1907, in infancy for Walter Eaton in 1908, insurgent for Thomas Dickinson in 1917, in adolescence for Edward Goodman in 1910, just developing into "dramatic journalism" for William Archer in 1920, in decline for George Jean Nathan in 1921, moribund for Virgil Geddes in 1931, on the brink of death for Louis Kronenberger in 1935, coming of age for Allan Halline in 1949, dying for Samuel Barron in 1935, dying for Paul Green in 1943, at ebb for Eric Bentley in *The Kenyon Review* in the spring of 1945 but fully dead for Eric Bentley in *Partisan Review* in the same spring, dead for Vivian Mercier in 1948, in decline for Helen Lawrenson in 1960, and in transition for Henry Popkin in 1962. The reasons for the perilous state of the drama, either in its infancy or its dotage, were as many as the critics who espoused them, but the promise of a healthy and mature drama remains the same, tantalizingly out of reach on an ever receding horizon of expectation.

"Perhaps the theatrical drama will never revive," Howells speculated in 1886. "We have noted some signs of renewed respiration, but we should not think it quite cataclysmic if, after a few gasps, it ceased to breathe again" (*Editor's Study* 31). In "The Dramatic Outlook in America" (1888) in *Studies of the Stage* (1894), Brander Matthews noted dryly that though the drama was understood to be in decline at the moment, it had always been "on the verge of dying" and yet "it still lives." After proving the vital tenacity of drama on the stage, Matthews concluded that "we are thus led to declare that the decline of the drama can only mean that the dramatic is no longer the leading department of literature" as it had been for two centuries (39–42). Of course, that enterprise was not helped by writers such as

Bronson Howard, the first American to devote himself entirely to playwriting as a career and the founder of the American Dramatists Club (now the Dramatists Guild), who had written to Matthews that the "divorce" of drama from literature should be "absolute and final. . . . I have felt this so strongly, at times, as to warmly deny that I was a 'literary man,' insisting on being a 'dramatist'" (Moody *Dramas* 567). Noting that newspapers and Sir Walter Scott's expansion of the novel drew off the talented writers, Matthews took hope in the revision of the copyright laws. Applauding the consequent disappearance of French plays from the American stage, Matthews looked to not only Great Britain but also America for signs of "improvement." Arguing that because the "Americans are a quicker people than the British and of a more artistic temperament" and that "the American novelist now surpasses his rival across the Atlantic," Matthews placed his hope in a new American drama that would forego the previous "rude farce and crude melodrama" (*Studies* 65–66). Because Americans have the essential qualities of the dramatist – invention, ingenuity, and a sense of humor – Matthews continued, they could, with the proper training, learn "the trade." Matthews had little use for drama considered merely as literature: "a play is something to be played and what is kindly called a 'drama for the closet' is a contradiction in terms; it is a play intended not to be played" (*Studies* 73). He also had no doubt that "the drama is the highest form of literary endeavor" (74) and linked its flourishing in America with "the future of our institutions" both of which would be dependent "on the enlightened common-sense of the American people" (76). However, Matthews was still anticipating an American drama in 1927 when he addressed the National Institute of Social Sciences, asking only for "another dozen years" for the playwrights and "another generation" for the audience (18).

John Corbin, in "The Dawn of American Drama" (1907), invoked Edmund Clarence Stedman's lament from twenty-two years previous: "'The time has come for poetry in any form that shall be *dramatic*. . . . I think that our future efforts will result in dramatic verse, and even in actual dramas for both the closet and the stage'" (632). Corbin prophesied that dawn was breaking and pointed to what he termed the "anti-syndicate" of independent theatre managers (634). Although crediting the syndicate and the commercial managers with raising the calling of both actor and playwright to lucrative stability and with familiarizing American audiences with the best of European drama, Corbin charged that the "radically false and factitious" dramas of the Victorian era were not sufficient. "Our national indifference to dramatic art, even our native puritanism, has not been more ruinously conservative than these managers whose sole purpose is avowedly commercial" (633–34). "As for plays from the Continent, two influences combined to invalidate them. The growth of native feeling in our audiences rendered the old method of false and specious adaptation powerless; and with the growth of realism and the literary sense abroad, the plays themselves were becoming more and more difficult to transpose into terms of American life. . . . The new order of dramatists – Ibsen, Sudermann, Hauptmann, Capus, Brieux, Donnay, Lavedan and others – were on the whole impossible, at once because of their greater intellectuality, their more local and individual presentation of life, and the gloominess or unmorality of their themes" (635). Corbin's strong valuation of a needed national moral consciousness led him to single out the muckraking dramas inspired by Ida Tarbell's *History of Standard Oil* as the beginning of the new American drama. While hailing Charles Klein's *The District Attorney* and *The Daughters of Men* as pioneering albeit flawed plays about industrial corruption and the conflict between labor and capital, Corbin singled out George Broadhurst's *The Man of the Hour* as preparing the way for American drama. The critical distinction between the writers was not clearly articulated, however; Klein was faulted for the false and factitious morality of happy endings, and Broadhurst was credited with making a "drama" even though "superficially the play resembles melodrama" (638).

In "Our Infant Industry" (1908), Walter Eaton noted that though Mrs. Mowatt's *Fashion* (1845) was "perhaps the first native drama of any considerable merit," it had passed without influence. The beginning of the drama of ideas was marked by W. Vaughn Moody's *The Great Divide* (1906). But for Eaton, American drama's great white hope was Percy MacKaye because he had "the grace of culture and of lyric speech." Eaton concluded that the most important thing was to "avoid realism – we need to plunge through it to deeper truths" (25–26). In 1910, Edward Goodman characterized American drama as a capricious and blundering child just evolving into consciousness caught between the undesirable state of being didactic and the mature state of being presentative.

For Florence Kiper, writing "from the feminist viewpoint," American drama in 1914 still lacked social relevance and seriousness about one of the most pressing questions of the time, the feminist question. "One must frankly confess at the outset that it is by the unconscious rather than the conscious method that the American dramatists are revealing themselves in regard to the woman movement. We have at present no Ibsens, Shaws, Bjornsons, Strindbergs, Brieuxs. . . . Yet the woman movement is undoubtedly, if perhaps the class-consciousness in the labour struggle be excepted, the one most important tendency of the century" (921). Anticipating the arrival of "big American playwrights" in the coming decade, Kiper charged American audiences to exchange "shows" for the "thesis play," for "until the American audience ceases to demand only cant and provincialism, prudishness and sentimentality, America can produce no dramatists of import" (922). Kiper's concerns mirror those of the Drama League; the calls for a literary drama were contemporaneous with and, of necessity, linked to the drive for a "better" theatre and more educated audience. That the organized efforts of leagues and clubs, to say nothing of the persistent complaints of critics, had little demonstrable effect on either dramatic literature or theatrical production is attested to by the continued laments for an improved American drama.

For Thomas Dickinson, writing in 1917, the theatre was still "insurgent." Examining all the extant venues for developing American drama – circuit theatres, subsidized theatres, workshops, laboratories, children's theatres, and the Little Theatre movement – Dickinson saw no contradiction in proclaiming that all those forms were "against professionalism" and in bemoaning the fact that good plays had yet to emerge. Lamely, he concluded that "the watched pot of a national literature doesn't boil" (224). From the later vantage point of 1949, John Gassner claimed 1917 as the transitional year before which there was no quality, only quantity. Even this moment was qualified for Gassner, who wrote that because there was nothing comparable to Frank Norris's *The Pit* or Theodore Dreiser's *Sister Carrie*, "American drama still stood many rungs below achievements in the novel and was still some distance qualifying as literature" (vii). In 1918, Clayton Hamilton voiced his opinion that though the best plays were of foreign authorship, if America won the war, a "genuinely worthy" drama would arise (289).

William Archer, writing in 1920, reflected that though it was now "possible to speak without absurdity of an Anglo-American drama," it had been "going to the dogs" in 1899 and had only just arrived at a "journalist level." But, he hastily cautioned, "there is nothing discouraging in the fact that the average of literary or technical merit in contemporary drama is not high: *At no period and in no country has popular drama shown a high average of merit*" (77–78). For George Jean Nathan in 1921, the blame was "Herman Kraus', who had come over in the steerage from Buzlau, Leon Przkwzi's, who had come over as a stoker's chambermaid from Novograd Volynsk, and Giacomo Spumenti's, who hailed from Boscotrecasi" (256). According to Nathan, when the war put an end to immigration, American dramatic fare improved. For Virgil Geddes in 1931, drama needed to be reborn. Calling for stages accurately to be renamed "drama-houses," Geddes fretted about "the subterfuge of too much theatre scenery" getting in the way of the real business of drama and about the uncivilized exposure of emotion that characterized the current theatre (7). In the same year, insisting that "nothing can be wrong with the theatre where no Theatre exists. And America has as yet no Theatre," Harold Clurman charged the playwright who selfishly had become "an independent literary artist" with abandoning the collaborative enterprise of theatrical production and causing literature to dominate the theatre (5–6).

Louis Kronenberger in 1935 felt that skilled workmanship never passed into art, that Broadway was "backward and banal in its commercialism" (49), that realism spelled doom, that the good writers went to Hollywood, and that in the playwrights there was a "want of adultness, of audacity, of integrity" (51). Allan Halline's concern is with dramatic theory as espoused by American dramatists, an index of growth because they moved from William Dean Howells's "disappointing" principle of "fidelity" to Arthur Miller's affirmation of the tragedy of the common man (1). Samuel Barron, who believed that the technologically flexible movies would be the salvation of the drama, blamed Freud and Marx because they "gave the theatre new things to say, but they have not given the theatre the power to say them. Where O'Neill has failed despite Freud, Odets must fail despite Marx" (116).

In "The Dying American Theatre" (1943), Paul Green faulted "the little traders in the temple" writing for the stage. Eric Bentley had the same aggrieved attitude toward commercialism, holding up the current success, *Oklahoma!*, as the example of all that had gone wrong in American theatre. In the 1945 *Partisan Review* article, Bentley charges that *all* drama, from American to German to English to Irish, has been dead since 1933 because of fascism in Europe and "minor experiments in social drama and poetic drama" in America; "the most one can say is that the theatre at present fulfills the first precondition of renascence. It is dead" (251). In *The Kenyon Review*, Bentley also considers European and American drama under the same aegis. As far as Bentley is concerned, the move to "entertainment" or "theatricalism" in the arts, fueled by industrialism, capitalism, and the democratic movement, signals the death of a fine art like drama, which has been relegated to the colleges. "The dramatist," insists Bentley, "is a poet in verse or prose who transmits his work through gesturing elocutionists" (180).

Charging that the drama was dead, Vivian Mercier, searching for "the guilty ones who brought the drama to its present state of stagnation," concludes that "Expressionism thus completed the degradation of the actor's art that Realism had begun." Looking back to America's Golden Age of drama, Mercier locates it between 1920 and 1940 (375). In 1960, Helen Lawrenson, deploring an unchallenged theatre wallowing in undeserved superlatives, blamed the genial mediocrity of the critics for "killing [the theatre] with kindness" (94), citing Walter Kerr's pedestrian solicitude and Brooks Atkinson's unmemorable gentleness as examples of the lack of a needed "intolerant talent" (97). Henry Popkin argued that a "curious corner" had been turned in 1962 because "in Europe, American plays rule the roost," an attitude, he confessed, that "gives the American critic pause." In trying to account for this European valuation, Popkin points to the "inexhaustible American energy" as a possibility because he still finds too much triviality and inarticulate incomprehension in American drama (568).

As a general rule, the critics, sensitive always to the shortcomings of the present-day writers who are forever being compared unflatteringly to their European antecedents or sometimes even to their American predecessors, anxiously scanned the theatrical horizon looking for the savior who must be on the verge of emerging to redeem American drama from its provincialism, crudeness, lack of poetry, and so on. Like anxious parents anticipating a toddler's first word or step, the American critics worried about which play could be considered genuinely "American" and which could be, if not literature, at least a respectable entrant in the literary arena. Jack Vaughn, for instance, in a history of early American playwrights, describes realism as a reforming achievement, an antidote to the mindless farce that was melodrama. This evolutionary, organicist trope may account for the prevalence of the word "vital" in all positive descriptions of American drama; it is an adjective that turns up repeatedly in historical, critical, and sociological accounts and one that locates the drama within a biological rather than a mechanistic sphere. Norman Foerster noted in *Toward Standards* (1928) that "'intensity,' along with its synonym 'vitality,' is now in the forefront of our critical terminology" (173). But an evolutionary process, especially one grounded in what are understood to be primitive or rudimentary forms (namely, minstrel shows or melodrama), presumes a developmental growth and a linear progression toward an improved, advanced, or mature state as if there were some perfect and realizable final state of American drama, an ideal form that could universally be acclaimed unequivocally as "literature." It should be noted that the history of American theatre, as distinct from the drama, has also been controlled by the organic metaphors of growth and illness. In her brief study of the narrative strategies used to describe American theatre economics, Margaret Knapp observes that this phenomenon is linked to a quantitative assessment of ticket sales rather than a qualitative one of productions. Recently, Thomas Postlewait has warned against the "developmental terms of evolution and revolution," showing how such historical practices are linked to the equally pervasive and equally flawed insistence on periodization, both of which participate in an erasure of what ought to be the object of inquiry, namely the "growths, diversions, anomalies, ruptures, disjunctions, and discontinuities" in which a truer history lies ("Criteria" 318).

The Differentiating Impulse: Separation from Europe

Most critics, anthologizers, and literary or theatre historians of the nineteenth and twentieth centuries understood that one important advance in the development of an indigenous if not a superior dramatic literature was the necessary separation from European models and influence. What moment marked the transition from European dominance of the American stage to the American takeover? That depended on who was passing judgment and by what criteria. In 1894, Paul Leicester Ford, taking sharp exception to assertions that the "beginning" of American drama was in America, challenged Dunlap's positioning of Tyler's *The Contrast* as "'the first successful play written by an American and the first of native plays to be acted.'" Charging carelessness on the part of previous literary historians, Ford cites *Eastward Hoe* written in 1605 by George Chapman, Ben Jonson, and John Marston with uniting America and the drama "by the introduction of a scene in praise of Virginia, which is so laudatory and inaccurate as to suggest some more interested reason for its writing than the dramatic value of its dialogue. The proposed colony thus puffed was already the fashionable project of the day" (673). The article, broadening the horizon of what was understood as early American drama, is a careful exercise in differentiation and categorizing. Throughout, Ford also points to the unabashedly political agendas of dramas about America, from Aphra Behn's *The Widow Ranter; or, Bacon in Virginia* (1690), about the insurrection in Virginia, through Le Blanc de Villaneuve's *Le Pere Indian* (1753), about the parental sacrifice of a Choctaw, to Dunlap himself and his *The Father; or, American Shandyism* (1789). Dunlap's play, rewritten and printed as *The Father of an Only Child*, was for Ford the first successful play written by an American-born professional playwright and acted by a professional company. Like so many critics to follow, Ford anticipated a greatness ahead, a Golden Age to come, but unlike so many critics to follow for whom Americanness would be the apotheosis of a native drama, Ford looked to the day when that "master hand" would produce an American drama "which shall be something more than national" (687).

For Robert Grau, writing in 1912 in *Lippincott's Magazine*, the break from Europe was much later and was marked by an entirely different achievement, the moment of financial triumph for a theatre manager with an American play in 1879. "It was [Bartley] Campbell who first broke the hoodoo attached to the American playwright. This was accomplished with *The Galley Slave*. Even though Campbell, previously a journalist, earned only a few hundred dollars, the manager made nearly a quarter of a million and American plays finally were in demand at the box office." So successful was the shift, Grau claims, that "for the first time in American theatrical history, plays by foreign authors are in the great minority in the announcements of our playhouses, ninety per cent of the plays offered for the first time being by native writers" (617–18). Though Grau's assessment was based on the profitability of productions of plays not high or literary drama, but popular entertainments such as *Ben Hur*, *The Lion and the Mouse*, and a vaudeville sketch, *The Chorus Lady*, the national shift had been made. However, although the drama may have been accepted as "American," the greater problem, the acceptance of the drama as literature, was far from an accomplished fact. Part of the problem, at least as far as James Tupper was concerned, was what was meant by "literary." In *The Dial* in 1914, he pointed to the consequences for the drama of the tendency to equate "literary" with "poetic," namely, that literary drama was conceived of as "only that which is decked out in the flowing robes of blank verse" (56).

In 1914 Sheldon Cheney marked differently the desirability of a mystified "poetic" aspect in the shift to a distinctively American drama. For him, there were two significant forms of modern drama in America and Europe, the "aesthetic drama" represented by Gordon Craig and Max Reinhardt and the "school of sincerity" or "psychologic drama" exemplified by John Galsworthy and George Bernard Shaw, a form that appealed primarily to the emotions and the intellect. Noting that American dramatists had "contributed practically nothing" to the sensuous, impressionistic, and poetic theatre, he argued that "the American dramatist has made notable progress only in the field of the psychologic drama" ("Sincerity" 498–99). Yet even after he had located a site of strength, Cheney hurriedly qualified his enthusiasm and judged that, compared with their English counterparts, the dominant American dramatists, Percy MacKaye, Eugene Walter, and Augustus Thomas, were still "failures" and that America still must wait for "a body of drama close to the people, reflecting the life of the times, touched by imaginative beauty, and emotionally appealing in a sincere way"

("Sincerity" 500). Though he kept citing "sincerity" as the valuative touch-stone, Cheney returned to the lack of poetry as the chief fault of American drama. He was, however, vague about what he meant; it is "a poetic element, a literary distinction, a pervading beauty that cannot be defined, and yet is always sensed by the reader or spectator" ("Sincerity" 501). Searching for the "sincere" playwright of the future, Cheney suggested that among Edward Sheldon, Joseph Medill Patterson, or Charles Kenyon audiences might find the coming "man of wide vision, the poet who is yet the perfect technician" America needed before it could claim to have great drama ("Sincerity" 512). Cheney's mystification of and insistence upon the missing element as a "poetic" essence anticipates the later New Critical yoking of literary value to high poetic expression.

Anticipation, expectation, and high anxiety came to welcome closure in the second decade of the twentieth century, the moment at which an acceptable American drama was understood by the critics to have "begun." Richard Cordell marked "some time between 1910 and 1916" as the begin-ning of the "new," that is the "honorable" American drama, the drama that had at last shed the shackles of "exoticism" and "romanticism" that so marred nineteenth-century drama (vi). This new American drama, at last able to stand with pride beside its European contemporaries, could be found in the Little Theatre in Chicago, in O'Neill's plays, and in the Provincetown Players, the Washington Square Players, or the Neighbor-hood Players. Ludwig Lewisohn is even more precise: "The American theatre may be said to have originated with that group of players who, under the leadership of Maurice Browne and Ellen Van Volkenburg founded the Little Theatre of Chicago and produced *The Trojan Women* of Euripides in February, 1913" (389). Barnard Hewitt places the moment later, noting that "American drama did not become completely 'American'" until it attained "full maturity" in the twenties with O'Neill, Rice, Sherwood, and Howard (3).

For Barrett Clark, as for most modern critics, a quite specific date, December 20, 1920, marked the moment at which a respectable American drama was born. On that day, Eugene O'Neill's *Beyond the Horizon*, which would win the Pulitzer prize the following year, opened at a special matinee at the Morosco Theatre. Travis Bogard, O'Neill's chronicler, observes that "it was a signal, the first important view of the American drama" (*Contour* 117). That American drama needed a savior had been a common idea for some time; James Metcalfe, for instance, had voiced this urgent need for a single figure in a review of the New York season in 1895, stating that "such a genius will surely appear to save the American stage from its present degradation and to establish a high standard for the whole country" (285). As Thomas Postlewait has observed: "The assumption in almost all studies is that American drama, in an historical progression from its earliest days, finally grew up (became mature, achieved wholeness, attained seriousness) between 1890 and 1920." Further, he points out that O'Neill came to represent the fulfillment of a "manifest destiny," noting that Alan S. Downer characterized the drama from 1860 to 1920 as "waiting for O'Neill" ("Melodrama" 6). Before O'Neill, the critics had picked up and discarded various writers; in 1910, for instance, Clayton Hamilton, morosely surveying the lean pickings of the younger playwrights, only reluctantly allowed Augustus Thomas into the exalted rank of American "dramatist" ("a play-wright who also teaches"), consigning all others to being merely entertain-ers or "playwrights" (250–51). Brander Matthews pointed to the "yeoman's service" of Clyde Fitch and Augustus Thomas as a tentative beginning ("Forty" 15).

So great was the impact of O'Neill on the American theatre and so anxious were the critics to locate one purely American playwright of whom they could be proud, that the waters parted for O'Neill almost from the start of his career. Some claims were more modest than others. According to Jay Hubbell and John Beaty in *An Introduction to Drama* (1929), though William Vaughn Moody's *The Great Divide* (1906) was the first American play of real importance, "O'Neill is the only American playwright who is generally accepted as a great dramatist" (525–26). Less measured, and dizzy with relief, Arthur Hobson Quinn wrote of O'Neill in 1924 that "he is too great a dramatist to be classified or to be placed in a school of playwrights. He, like Napoleon, is himself an ancestor" ("Modern" 7). Given that this judgment was made on the basis of four plays – *The Emperor Jones* and *The Hairy Ape*, both heavily indebted to the European expressionist movement about which O'Neill learned through Kenneth Macgowan, and *Beyond the Horizon* and *Anna Christie*, domestic dramas that owe much to O'Neill's extensive interest in Ibsen – Quinn's isolating claim is an index of the urgency for a native and nativist playwright.

O'Neill would continue to be evoked as the transitional playwright bringing American drama into respectability. For Heinrich Straumann, in his explanation of the rise of American drama, O'Neill was the first Ameri-can playwright to couple the material issues of social problems, realized in pragmatism and determinism and always active in American drama, with the spiritual forces hitherto present only in poetry and prose. For V. F. Calverton, O'Neill was an unequivocally American playwright because "there is no return to English drama for inspiration" (*Liberation* 35). John

Gassner's appraisal of O'Neill in *Masters of the Drama* (1954), that he combined American and European characteristics, is more representative and indicative of the necessity for a European component to legitimate American drama: "In him Europe and America interbred, the one providing the chromosomes of thought and experiment, the other the genes of grappling vitality" (640). Robert Spiller in *The Cycle of American Literature* (1955) notes that "with *The Emperor Jones* America found that it had its first major playwright, as well as a free theatre movement similar to that of Europe" and that this success lay in the movement away from the binding forms of romantic comedy and melodrama to realism and expressionism (249–50). Walter Fuller Taylor echoes Spiller in *The Story of American Letters* (1956), in which he nominates O'Neill as the "first American dramatist of major literary stature . . . in whose plays the drama achieved the artistic maturity already attained by the American novel" (379). Of course, one playwright was not quite enough; as Montrose Moses put it in a 1924 lament for *The North American Review*, "we need a Preacher of the Power of Theatre . . . we need someone like Emerson . . . to invest the theatre with a soul" (82). O'Neill has continued to dominate the American dramatic canon; in a recent survey of research and criticism, Jackson Bryer and Ruth Alvarez discovered that there was more material on O'Neill than on all the other American playwrights of the twenties and thirties combined.

In 1930, Barrett Clark proclaimed that American drama finally was "adult," and that it was O'Neill who had changed playwriting from a trade to an art (*Hour* 13–22). From the further stabilized vantage point of 1932, Clark could boast that "the American drama written during the past decade was on the whole better than that of any other country during the same period" ("Second Decade" 1). The thirties were another matter, however. The exodus to Hollywood and the financial depression marked a period of dramatic "retardation" for Clark. Seven years later in another appraisal of "our grownup American drama," Clark shifted his focus from the "regular" theatre to the "rebel groups" of the Left, groups whose serious work on social and political problems marked a new nationalism and another new beginning for American drama. For Clark plays like Elmer Rice's *We the People*, Albert Maltz's *Black Pit*, and George Sklar and Paul Peters's *Stevedore*, "reflect clearly a state of mind that our native playwrights, at least, have since almost the beginning of our national history either not understood or not deemed suitable for dramatic use" ("Most American" 339).

Despite the general sense that with O'Neill and those who followed American drama was at last respectable, and despite the very obvious connections to European modernist movements, critics and historians from the 1920s through the 1970s continued to cling to the exceptionalist idea. Arthur Hobson Quinn's conclusion to his history of American drama (1936) sets the requirement when he insists on a distinction between the American and European drama, characterizing the best American drama as being dedicated to realism of character and being located in the dramatization of emotions rather than ideas. Above all else, however, the best American dramatists are dedicated to the noble, social mission; "where a European dramatist would paint the satisfaction of passion as sacred," the American playwright "knows that self-respect and generosity of soul establish character more surely than desertion of duty and satisfaction of passion" (*Present* II 280).

Thirty-five years later, Francis Hodge, tracing the European influences on American theatre in 1971, cited Barrett Clark's contention that there was no entity separable from English, French, or German theatre until after World War I. "Before that point," he had written, "there was little to distinguish theatre in America from provincial theatre in England, except for dialect comedies – such as the plays involving the stage Yankee; the minstrel variety entertainment; local coloring in the settings of some plays; some peculiarities of style in American-born actors; and a small body of plays that seemed to be dealing with adjustments in American society" (3–4). After World War I, Hodge explained, American drama fell under the influence of European and Russian "intellectualism" (9). The biggest impact was on stagecraft, but Hodge suggested that a new critical, evaluative spirit moved American playwrights to reassess the American theatre as the site of entertaining and patriotic sentiment. But for Hodge it was the depression that finally unleashed genuine native voices; the "outpouring of American drama that for the first time dealt with the present realities: the dark cruelties and inequities of everyday life. America had ugly sores and boils just as Europe had, and here was a drama of 'social significance,' oftentimes documentary in style, to discuss them and torture over them" (12). Hodge begged the issue here; it isn't clear how this drama of disease, influenced by European thought and dramaturgy, was any more "American" than the earlier plays resisting European "voices" if not forms. A cultural elitism was implicit in Hodge's judgment. He compounded his oddly skewed argument with the contradictory conclusion that by throwing off "the European forces that have shackled it since the 18th century," the new American drama, moving away from "commitment drama" . . . "may be more Artaudian in design than Brechtian" (18).

Travis Bogard in "The Central Reflector" (1977), though clearly hegemonically based in the Greek model of the *polis*, takes a more cautious approach to the indigenousness of American drama, stating that

> to find the moment when there appeared an unequivocally American drama is impossible. The individualistic, informal theatre of the nineteenth century was, to be sure, congenial to the nation at large, but it produced no playwrights whose work clearly reflected the dominant concerns of the nation. . . . Until a nation has created a city of such wealth and prominence that it is like a city-state, an urban centre that holds in its confines a cross-section of the nation's population, a city that is a magnet for the cultural life of the country and that reflects the essence of that life in such a way as to define it and give it artistic and social formulation – until such a city is achieved there will be no national drama. (43–44)

The need to differentiate American drama from European drama, to insist on American essentialism, drove many critics to extreme exercises in rationalizing. For instance, arguing that essential nationalistic traits exist and endure despite political and economic change, Donald V. McGranahan and Ivor Wayne in 1948 set out to prove the inherent differences between the German and American character as manifested in forty-five of the most popular plays in each country in 1927, a period they determine was both prosperous and democratic in both. This earnest and naive attempt to document national character is now interesting to historians of American drama, in part because it demonstrates how much the drama was regarded as a mirror of social behaviors rather than as an index of aesthetic taste. After exhaustive and lengthy comparisons of themes, the authors reached eleven conclusions, among them being that American plays dwell on private problems, especially the difficulties of achieving love and virtue, that can be solved; that the hero is an ordinary person whose personal ambitions and satisfactions are sanctioned just as his personal crimes and sins are forgiven; that the moralistic American orientation stresses educational reform of attitude or character in a society open to persuasion; that, unlike the German who rebels against authority and society, the American rebels "in the name of his personal right to happiness" (453–55). The implication that American drama is narrow, solipsistic, domestic, and assimilative reiterates disciplinary judgments made against American drama and participates in the widely held assumption that American dramatic texts are less imaginative or literary than descriptive and journalistic.

The "scientific" search for demonstrable indices of a mystified essence should be understood as an ideological paradox and not as a workable theoretical or methodological analytical tool. Despite the obvious reductivist flaws of such an approach, the marking of drama by national characteristics rather than by participation in aesthetic movements that transcend nations, such as modernism, or in political concerns, such as critiquing totalitarianism, has persisted to the present day. In a recent review of Tony Kushner's *Slavs!* and Tom Stoppard's *Hapgood* for *The New Republic*, Robert Brustein offered the following "comparative generalizations": "American drama, with some notable exceptions, is often crude, untidy, undisciplined, overwritten, but pulsing with subterranean power, on the model of Eugene O'Neill. British drama, with some notable exceptions, is often polished, civilized, witty, technically ingenious, but rather undernourished emotionally, on the model of Noel Coward" (31). Brustein's explicit charge, that American drama is emotional, and his implicit charge that, as a consequence, American drama suffers in comparison with British drama, points to another long-standing concern about American drama, its "masculine" properties.

American Drama as a Masculine Science

About 1915 Brander Matthews and others began authorizing the writing of drama as masculine and scientific, vital and dynamic. The rhetoric of masculinity and vitality was a communicative strategy designed to discount others as enfeebled; science was equated with objectivity and the search for truth, and left any unscientific enterprise behind in the dust of a benighted romantic solipsism pejoratively associated with femininity and untempered emotions. Books such as M. L. Malevinsky's *The Science of Playwriting* (1925) and journals such as *The American Playwright* (1912–1915), an offshoot of the American School of Playwriting, are examples not only of the upsurge in a market of readers and theatregoers stimulated by agencies such as the Drama League but also of the urge to make a "science" of the art. The insistence on vitality and masculinity can be tied to the larger objectives of the new American literary professionals; David Shumway has pointed to "the pervasive sexism" of the *Cambridge History of American Literature*, quoting the editors' intention to go beyond the "purely aesthetic" and to "enlarge the spirit of American literary criticism and render it more energetic and masculine" (92). Elizabeth Renker, in her brief history of American literature studies, explains that the "rising American university culture . . . enshrined 'science' as both its goal and its domain, and the rhetorical and institutional masculinity of science exerted pressure on 'fields' of knowledge to 'defeminize' themselves in order to be adequate to the university culture's demands" (347). This insistent masculinizing also can be tied to other professions and could account for why men involved in drama and theatre had particular reason to be exceptionally anxious. In "Institutionalizing Masculinity: The Law as a Masculine Profession" (1990), Michael Grossberg examines the strenuous efforts by American lawyers in the first decades of the nineteenth century to insist on the masculinity of their profession by setting it against literary pursuits such as the writing of poetry or fiction; if lawyers were manly activists dedicated to the practical and utilitarian, men of letters were little more than effete, idle, and impassioned visionaries.

The history of the drama and theatre in America in particular necessitated participation in this forceful strategy of scientizing and masculinizing; both the literature and the site have been gendered, degendered, and regendered as well as virilized and feminized, causing an unstable and uneasy relationship with the culture at large as well as with its institutions of high-cultural valorization. As Herbert Brown detailed in a survey of the didactic sensibility in eighteenth-century American drama, "sentimentality reigned triumphant on the English stage from 1760 to 1800, the period of the beginnings of our native professional drama" (47). Sentiment, and by extension a feminine association, may have dominated the American stage of the eighteenth century, but boisterousness and rowdiness prevailed in the early nineteenth, at which time, Richard Butsch claims, it was a "masculine space" where the "manly" virtues were preferred over romance until these in turn were displaced by the sensation melodramas of the 1860s and 1870s for a newly respectable and feminized audience (378–79). Butsch argues that as a consequence of this change, the commentators blamed women for the perceived decline of American drama between the 1890s and the 1920s, citing Walter Prichard Eaton's claim that drama was altered for the worse by the demands of female patrons for melodramatic romances (Butsch 397).

That sentiment and moralizing were understood to "gratify feminine fancy" thus increased the sense of urgency for the critics such as Matthews who wanted to legitimate American drama as both a respectable and a masculine profession. Of course, by focusing only on drama's romantic antecedents, Matthews was sidestepping the more complicated fact of American drama's intense engagement in social and political issues; in a study of American drama from 1782 to 1812, Josef Aaron Elfinbein details the thematic obsession with American "problems" such as Catholics, Jews, Indians, Masonry, the Whiskey Rebellion, popular education, and abolition. Despite the contradiction inherent in the historical record, the connection of drama to the "feminine" and the "foreign" persisted; in *The Rise of American Civilization* (1934), Charles and Mary Beard diminished and denigrated early modern American drama with a misogynistic and xenophobic blow:

> [women] ruled with a rod of iron huge principalities in the dramatic realm – calling for precious things, mild emotions, nothing raucous . . . themes of little men and little women. . . . Not without appeal to women as well as to trade psychology were the many sentimental dramas dealing with Jews, Irish, Germans, and other racial stocks in the American Babel and the numerous plots built on "social climbing" in a volatile world. (807–08)

In fact, Henry Arthur Jones, in "The Aims and Duties of a National Theatre" (1911), had stressed the nation's need for drama and had laid the groundwork for its masculine provenance:

> There is one thing to note about dramatic literature. It is essentially creative, essentially masculine – more so than any other kind of literature. It must, therefore, have something of brutality in it, however much this may be disguised or concealed. . . . You cannot have a great literature, especially a great dramatic literature, unless it is forged of this alloy, hu... an body and spirit. Young ladies' literature soon dies. Indeed it never lives. (*Foundations* 79)

"Greatness" was thus locked to masculinity.

Matthews was willing to concede that a woman could be a good actress because she is "called upon only to embody and to interpret characters conceived by man with the aid of his wider and deeper knowledge of life," but he noted that when a woman attempted to write in a form other than the narrowly domestic novel of conduct, "when she seeks to go outside her complete inexperience of existence she soon makes us aware of the gaps in her equipment" (*A Book* 117). Not only could women not handle "largeness in topic," but also they were incapable of "strictness in treatment. . . . And here we come close to the most obvious explanation for the dearth of female dramatists – in the relative incapacity of women to build a plan, to make a single whole compounded of many parts, and yet dominated in every detail by but one purpose" (120). Likening the drama to "the sister art of architecture," Matthews explained that drama demanded "plan and proportion," values unattainable by women who

have not yet revealed themselves as architects, altho they have won a
warm welcome as decorators – a subordinate art. . . . In other words,
women seem to be less often dowered than men with what Tyndall called
"scientific imagination," with the ability to put together a whole in which
the several parts are never permitted to distend a disproportionate space.
This scientific imagination is essential to the playwright; and the novelist
is fortunate if he also possess it, altho it is not essential to him. (121–22)

Matthews concludes that "women are likely to have only a definitely limited
knowledge of life" and are also "deficient in the faculty of construction. The
first of these disabilities may tend to disappear if ever the feminist movement shall achieve its ultimate victory; and the second may depart also
whenever women submit themselves to the severe discipline which has
compelled men to be more or less logical" (124–25).

Despite Matthews's assertions, many women did write many plays,
though the standard anthologies of American drama offer little evidence of
this and the canon long has been gendered male. The links in the chain that
stretches from Godfrey to Tyler to O'Neill to Williams to Miller to Albee
to Shepard and Mamet are all male. Harold Bloom in *Esquire* (September
1994) allows nine male playwrights and some of their plays into his canonized list. This gendering is not just the work of literary critics at large; recent
historians of the drama, though certainly obliged to obey the facts of a
dominant male presence, have done little to redress the historical imbalance. C. W. E. Bigsby's three-volume history, *A Critical Introduction to
Twentieth-Century American Drama* (1985), one volume of which is devoted
entirely to Williams, Miller, and Albee, devotes only two complete chapters
to women; one is on Lillian Hellman, the other is on women's theatre. It
could be argued that one way to exclude the taint of the feminine from the
dramatic canon has been by limiting the visible number of women playwrights. In forty-five anthologies of American drama compiled between
1918 and 1986, from Quinn and Moses to Jacobus and Gassner, eleven
collections had no plays by women at all and fourteen included only one.
Of the 740 plays anthologized, only 90 were by women and many of those
were one-acts and/or from the regional theatre movement of the twenties
and thirties. The only volume in which there is equal representation,
Spontaneous Combustion: Eight New Plays (1972), was edited by a woman,
the playwright Rochelle Owens.

The self-serving insistence on playwriting as a masculine and scientifically
based art was connected to another factor in the artificial constitution of a
nativist drama: "virility." The "folk" playwriting movement, which began

with Frederick Koch's creation of the Dakota Playmakers at the University of North Dakota in 1910 and his subsequent move to the University of North Carolina in 1918, culminated in the development of Paul Green and the Carolina Playmakers, the first such theatre "to be dedicated to the creation of a native drama" (Carter and Ogden 14). The plays, written and performed by university students, were offered as accurate representations of "primitive" and "picturesque" Americans, not, as Quinn notes, from "decadent" parts of New England or Pennsylvania but from the West, the mountain regions of the Carolinas, of Georgia and Kentucky where the "virility" of the people, the essential American frontier attribute, had been preserved (*Present* II 240). Thus a white man, Paul Green, became both the modern spokesman for American essentialism and the voice of the Negro with the one-act plays in *Lonesome Road* (1926) and longer works such as *In Abraham's Bosom* (1926) and *The Field God* (1927).

The "virility" of the dramatic canon, evidenced, for instance, by texts such as McGraw-Hill's *The American Tradition in Literature*, eighth edition, in which playwrights are represented by Royall Tyler, Eugene O'Neill, Tennessee Williams, Arthur Miller, Sam Shepard, and August Wilson, is part of the larger problem Emory Elliott points to in "New Literary History: Past and Present." Of Perry Miller's preface to the second edition of the *Literary History of the United States* edited by Spiller et al. (1953), Elliott writes, "the belief that [American literature] has also 'been on the whole an optimistic literature made virile by criticism of the actual compared with the ideal' perhaps helps to account for the fact that there was only one female among the fifty-five contributors who participated in this search for virility" ("New Literary History" 614).

The "folk" movement also satisfied other felt needs for a respectable nativist drama in that it was deemed to be both "poetic" and "picturesque." For Montrose Moses writing in 1931 that "there is no more significant date in American letters than the year of the publication of *Uncle Remus*" (1882), the folk drama shared in the sincerity, dignity, and sympathetic realism ("Cobwebs" 82). Marc Connelly's *The Green Pastures* (1930) was, for Moses, a comparable landmark. Moses believed that, far from limiting American drama as "provincial," the folk plays connected American playwriting to work being done by the Manchester, Birmingham, and Dublin groups, to the "universality in the poetic glamour of folklore" ("Cobwebs" 87). In the final analysis, however, the folk movement did not further the cause of American drama as literature. In his introductory comments to Lula Vollmer's *Sun-Up* in *Representative Plays* (1953), Arthur Hobson Quinn observed that the subjects of her plays were those "who have retained the primitive culture of their ancestors, and whose emotions have remained in that inarticulate but unsophisticated state which allows them free expression and make them therefore well suited for the drama" (1017). The yoking of uncensored expression, emotionalism, and inarticulacy cemented the fate of American drama as unliterary.

Nervous and defensive in the face of the New Critics, John Gassner, writing in 1952, noted that though American drama had "ceased to be provincial" in 1918–1920, "it still remains to be proved that a vital American drama could arise from the New Critics' specifications" ("Answer" 59). The concern over the New Critics points once again to the problem of legitimizing American drama, which, because it was understood to address the emotions in colloquial speech, had little chance of recognition by the New Critics. The conventional understanding of drama was expressed in the words of Chester Calder, that drama's "primary appeal is to the emotions, and that dramatist who would succeed with the largest number of people should study the psychology of the crowd. Humanity in the mass demands simplicity of story and treatment" (53). Thus, by this reasoning, drama lacked intellectual content, sophistication, and complexity, all the attributes valued by critics. As William Cain explains, "the explication of texts was meant to be an exacting discipline, one that eliminated subjective responses and gave criticism an 'objective' basis and the 'professional' austerity of the sciences" (82). Of one thing about American drama, however, Gassner was sure, that "there *is* a cultural context – a rough, bouncing democratic one. . . . Our drama made an impression on the world for more than a quarter of a century largely because it was masculine, buoyant, hard-driving and uninhibited" ("Answer" 61).

Geographical Determination

In tracking the shaping of the American literary canon, Paul Lauter has argued that "a central problem with American literature, or so some seemed to feel, was its 'feminization.' Joseph Hergesheimer, a then-popular if rapidly dated novelist, had attacked 'The Feminine Nuisance in American Literature' in a *Yale Review* article of 1921. Literature in the United States, he claimed, 'is being strangled with a petticoat,' written primarily for women, 'without a grain of masculine sand.'" Hergesheimer's hero clearly had to be marked by one outstanding quality, "'vitality'" (*Canons* 32). This call for masculine vitality, Lauter demonstrates, grew louder by the end of the decade, at which point "professors and male novelists" rejected narrow gentility for a "strenuous nationalism" that was beyond the domestic sphere;

"America needed the grand encounters with nature of Melville or even Thoreau, the magical abnormalities of Ahab, the deeper possibilities for corruption Twain and even James in their different ways established" (34). Of course, such essential American masculine vitality can be dramatized and staged but the vastness of the land on which that masculine vitality expended itself, the expansive geographical site, posed a problem for the drama especially if it was going to follow James Kirk Paulding's early insistence that the land was the location for manly, vigorous, and national feeling.

The land itself would seem to be an inescapable thematic concern, certainly in the late nineteenth century when canon formation was solidifying with the professionalization of academics who produced the histories and textbooks. The insistence on the formative force of the land was part of the culture as a whole. In "Environmentalism," Wilson D. Wallis demonstrates that "geographic determinism," the molding influence of the land on the man, his character and pursuits, was accepted as a fact by late-nineteenth- and early-twentieth-century geographers and historians (562). In *Frontier: American Literature and the American West* (1965), Edwin Fussell has documented the literary alliance to the West that was forged during the American Renaissance. Therefore, by 1855 the frontier was a psychological if not a literal reality in American literature. In *Virgin Land: The American West as Symbol and Myth* (1950), Henry Nash Smith has shown how eighteenth-century literary conventions shaped the West variously as a vast commercial empire, a contested natural refuge, and a rich agrarian utopia, and how the stereotypes of the West influenced American writing. Long after the West had been reunderstood, the nostalgic landscape persisted as part of the material used by conservative historians of the 1940s and 1950s to define a hegemonic tradition. As a consequence, one factor for determining the essential "Americanness" of American literature was a close connection to the land, which did not escape the notice of those struggling to create an acceptable American drama. For instance, Thomas Dickinson in *The Case of American Drama* (1915) wrote, "so let the drama achieve the expression of the larger America through the province" (204). "If we could drop everything that is meant by the term 'American' and retain the meaning of 'pioneer,' we should have lost nothing" (208) because the "typical American spirit lies rather more near to the heart of the village than to the heart of the city" (210). William Cody's efforts as Buffalo Bill to bring the Wild West into an eastern outdoor arena stadium or elaborate pageants like *An Historical Pageant of Illinois*, performed in Evanston, or even the restaging of American battles on historic sites, could not satisfy the need to embody and dramatize vastness on a scale commensurate with the desire to locate "Americanness" in the land.

But the Americanness of American literature was determined not only by a narrow thematic criterion but also by a generic one, namely, the belief that only the novel could best capture the westering American male's relationship to the land. For instance, in assessing the "divorce" between American drama and the American novel, which is the failure of the former and the success of the latter, Clayton Hamilton, in *Problems of the Playwright* (1917), pointed to the "sanity" and "honesty" of American novelists, men like Hawthorne, Twain, James, and Harte who, he claimed, were "planted in the soil" (293). He argued that whereas "American literature has discovered America," American drama has not because "there isn't any soil in Times Square." Hamilton ventured the judgment that "our drama is metropolitan, and therefore un-American; for what do they know of America who only know Broadway?" (293). "New York is not America: New York is not even – as has been said before – American . . . we should look to the provinces" (298). Charles and Mary Beard offered a variation in their similar analysis in *The Rise of American Civilization* (1934): "Had the railway developed without a correlative growth in steam navigation, it is conceivable that the course of dramatic art in the United States would have been more nationalist" (795). Because New York was the port of entry and because the star system was a profitable enterprise, they argued, foreign imports dominated American drama and pushed "American issues and psychology" aside (796). By this reductive thinking, drama is an urban form and the novel belongs to the land, which, by extension, equals the nation. As a consequence, assessments such as David Mogen's are the common and predictable matter of American literary history: "Cooper's paradisaical wilderness is perhaps the most evocative and pervasive symbol of modern American literature, informing all our tales of Nature destroyed to advance dubious ends, all our ironic visions of the vanishing American Dream" (330). So too, Lionel Trilling's assertion in "Manners, Morals, and the Novel," in *The Liberal Imagination* (1953): "American writers of genius have not turned their minds to society. The reality they sought was only tangential to society" and the novel leaned toward the abstract (206). If the American novel was indeed, as Trilling contended, grounded in ideas, in symbolism, in democratic abstractions, and if, too, the subject of that novel was the isolated individual whose elusive identity is located in a sense of deprivation, a "crisis both private and impersonal," as Marius Bewley described it in 1959 in *The Eccentric Design* (18), then the novel is at a great remove from the drama, which necessarily represents manners and society in confined, domestic spaces. Nor can the drama in any immediate or literal way participate in the "symbolic landscapes" of the New England village, the Main Street of Middle America, and the California suburban sprawl that D. W. Meinig claims "impinge upon the very essence of what we mean by 'American'" (172).

This relentless domination of landscape is not the exclusive property of American literature and no doubt gathers authority by being reiterated in other disciplines no less blind to thematic diversity and stylistic richness. Elizabeth Johns reviews the similar thrust in the mid-twentieth-century metanarratives of American art history. As Johns explains, one of the most influential studies of landscape painting was Barbara Novak's *American Painting of the Nineteenth Century: Realism, Idealism, and the American Experience* (1969), in which she argued that landscape painting was the definitive accomplishment of the century. American art historians would continue to insist, even in the face of Abstract Expressionism, that there existed a through line from the realistic landscape to Abstract Expressionism because of a continuity not stylistic but thematic, an insistence on spatial emptiness and a sense of alienation. So reasoned, even the psychological, if not the stylistic, roots of much Abstract Expressionism lay in nineteenth-century American landscape.

Whatever the reality of artistic diversity of expression may be, the land remains a pervasive trope and a dominating criterion for assessing Americanness. Travis Bogard accounts for it in the drama this way: "The American has always thought of himself as an Antaeus, deriving his strength from his contact with the earth. . . . His roots are geographic, not historic" ("Central" 45). If it is true that Americans are deeply autochthonic, then it is no wonder that Miller's *Death of a Salesman* and Sam Shepard's *Buried Child*, both of which locate their dramatic tensions in an American heritage of pioneering and mastering the soil, have been acclaimed as artifacts of an "essential" Americanness. Furthermore, one possible way to account for David Mamet's popularity as a playwright is the way in which he addresses what appears to be the crucial issue of "land." In a study of Mamet's "Mimetics," Matthew Roudané has argued "that the majority of his plays' action occurs *outside* of what has grown into a certain narrowness of play space for American playwrights and their valorized classics, the home, is central to Mamet's vision" (7). Documenting the pervasiveness of the idea of Nature as "a divine and secular force within our writers and culture" (14) in historiographic studies as well as the distinctive absence of the same in contemporary studies of the drama, Roudané places Mamet's work in "a mythologized context of the American view of Nature" (25).

The same mythologizing impulse characterizes the work of Sam Shepard, whose "pathology" David Wyatt finds "distinctively American." Citing Charles Olson's beginning to *Call Me Ishmael* (1947) – "I take SPACE to be the central fact to man born in America from Folsom cave to now. I spell it large because it comes large here" – Wyatt yokes Shepard to a Melvillean and Lawrentian phallic destiny manifested in "continual westering" (356). The emphasis on Melville is not misplaced, because it links Shepard to the masculinist essence of canonized American literature and accounts in large measure for Shepard's success. Nor is it difficult to yoke Shepard's tortured male protagonists to D. H. Lawrence's menaced, doomed, and disintegrating "white psyche." Paul Lauter argued in 1994 that the distinctively masculine "'Melville' was constructed in the twenties as part of an ideological conflict which linked advocates of high modernism and of traditional high cultural values – often connected to the academy – against a social and cultural 'other,' generally, if ambiguously, portrayed as feminine, genteel, exotic, dark, foreign, and numerous" (6). And, as will become clear in Chapter 4, on education, Melville was for F. O. Matthiessen, whose *American Renaissance* (1941) fixed the canon, the American Shakespeare.

Certainly much canonized American drama participates in the dominant paradigm of masculine westering and valorizing of nature, but unlike fiction or poetry which rely solely on language to convey images, the drama is usually pictorial as well and the translation of scenic grandeur to a literal stage set is clumsy and reductive at best. The realistic or naturalistic stage set is hard-pressed to replicate what David Lowenthal has called the "cult of bigness," which peaked at the turn of the century, or Gertrude Stein's description that "what makes America what it is" is a sense of "more space where nobody is than where anybody is" (65–68). The enshrinement of vast size, of scenic expanse, of insignificance in a howling wilderness cannot be visualized easily within the proscenium arch. Can an American dramatist convincingly become a Whitmanesque poet barding America's "geography and natural life" or flooding himself with "the vast oceanic tides"?

Americanness located in the land has less to do with a specifically masculine paradigm than it does with a sense of connection with the physical environment; but it is still widely exclusionary because it hardly accounts for extensive immigrant experience of cities or farms, the restrictive conditions of slavery, the domestic confinement of women, or the institutional circumstances of industrial employment, issues explored extensively in American drama. So perhaps the autochthonic paradigm is the wrong paradigm because it is both narrow and thematic. Perhaps we should consider instead a generic paradigm for determining Americanness: the desire to perform, the desire to engage in dialogic practices onstage in public, to particularize and localize and dramatize (for whatever hegemonic or subversive goals) the experience of being in a diversely populated and once geographically expanding country. By this measure, an expanded sense of what is "American" would no longer be the exclusive property of westering white men. Furthermore, the dramatic and performative impulses and expressions, from minstrelsy to Mardi Gras, rather than a hegemonic, nativist thematic paradigm become the valuative touchstones by which the Americanness of American drama, whether located in the city or the country, whether realistic or abstract in form, could be measured.

4

Did She Jump or Was She Pushed?

American Drama in the University Curriculum

WHAT IS THE CULTURAL VALUE of American drama and how does that valuation correlate to the place of American drama in the nation's university curriculum? To begin an answer that informs my study and critique of the curricular placement of American drama, I suggest the relevance of an approach that analyzes comparatively drama's material relations with other forms of cultural enterprise. In his sociological study of art, literature, and aesthetics, *The Field of Production* (1993), Pierre Bourdieu, basing his assessment on late-nineteenth-century French culture, establishes a cultural hierarchy predicated on two valuations, economic and symbolic. Using an economic valuation, Bourdieu ascertains that drama was above the novel and poetry because it secured large profits, provided by a bourgeois and relatively restricted audience, for very few theatres. On the other hand, this credit was countered by the discredit that accrued as audiences grew. Nonetheless, he argues, "the theatre, which directly experiences the immediate sanction of the bourgeois public, with its values and conformisms, can earn the institutionalized consecration of academics and official honours, as well as money" (51). Not only is Bourdieu writing about French theatre, he is also equating theatre and drama, which, in American culture and curriculum, are largely separate institutions. Nonetheless, Bourdieu's demonstration of the factors involved in arriving at cultural value are pertinent to the problematic position of American drama in its social and academic contexts; because dramatic literature is the basis for theatrical performance it suffers the taint of economic success (when it is successful) but in American culture, and certainly in academe, reaps few of the benefits.

Perhaps more useful, however, is Bourdieu's analysis of the academic world, *Homo Academicus* (1988), in which he draws up a table demonstrating the "poles" of power represented by the faculties. In Bourdieu's first formulation, law and medicine belong to "society" whereas science belongs to "science" and the humanities to a middle ground (73). In his second formulation, Bourdieu sets up a spectrum of "theoretical and pure" sciences – physics, applied maths, chemistry – at one end and an equally "theoretical and pure" arts and social sciences – philosophy, history, philology – at the other. Caught in the middle of this are the "practical, applied, empirical, impure" disciplines, those with "scientific pretensions" such as economics, psychology, and sociology (122). By applying Bourdieu's categorization, I get the following: The study of dramatic literature, because it assumes an understanding of performance, is not "theoretically pure," but because performance studies has no "scientific pretensions," the drama, though "impure," cannot be classified as a social science. Let me rephrase the proposition in an American context. According to Samuel Haber in *The Quest for Authority and Honor in the American Professions, 1750–1900*, in the early struggle to legitimate disciplinary fields in the new American universities of the 1880s and 1890s, science and the "practical arts," because they were understood to be "utilitarian," were in greater favor than the increasingly diminished classical studies in which the drama was prominent. "American" was itself not yet fully legitimated as a course of study, and the vernacular drama was located more in extracurricular student activities than in the classroom. If American drama has no "place," it has no "power" and, as a consequence, has little cultural value in the curriculum.

Evidence is not hard to find. For instance, with the growing prestige of criticism, the problem of the critical capital of American drama surfaces in Claudia Johnson's contribution to the *Columbia Literary History of the United States* (1988) in which she positions early American plays as "popular culture texts" of "scant literary interest" that, because they often dramatized political events, "seemed to blur the line between art and life." Therefore, the theatre, not the drama, is the site of "liveliness and artistic merit." Finally, the early American drama, according to Johnson, does not harbor sufficient theoretical complexity to allow critics fullest exploitation of their talents:

> The critic to do a new critical or poststructuralist literary study of the dramas of early America has not yet appeared, nor is ever likely to appear, given the character of the plays. The kinds of literary scholarship that they inevitably do generate with some regularity are bibliographies, the-

matic studies of frequently recurring character types – the Indian, the frontiersman, the spunky heroine, George Washington – and considerations of particular dramatists as prologue to the realists of twentieth-century America. (324)

Thus it is, by this formulation, that the critics' particular interests determine the standing of a literary genre, drive the canon, and determine the curriculum; lacking "complexity" and skirting too closely to realism and political propaganda, early American drama is not a rich enough lode for two specific types of criticism, the New Critical and the poststructuralist varieties that have dominated the arena in recent decades. As a result, the subject has received less critical and professional recognition and it has also been devalued in the hierarchy of literary genres and texts that are taught, studied, and valued in American university English departments.

Two recent studies of English departments conducted by Bettina J. Huber for the Modern Languages Association prove the extent of the problem for American drama. The first study of 571 departments, which included an analysis of works considered to be important to selected upper-division literature courses in 1989–1990, reveals that no playwright is understood to be particularly important or essential to the study of American literature between 1800 and 1865, but, given the "incubational" status of early American drama, this is hardly surprising. The second study of 527 departments, which included an analysis of authors read in lower-division American literature survey courses in 1990–1991, reveals that playwrights are not among the forty-two most frequently studied authors (from Hawthorne to Alice Walker) and only four white male playwrights (Miller, O'Neill, Williams, and Shepard) are among the thirty-one authors mentioned by no more than two respondents. As Huber claims that "the uniformity of the responses is striking," it can be assumed that the minimal presence of American drama of any kind, let alone a representative range, is standard (45). It should be safe to hazard a guess that much of this exclusion can be attributed to the minimal presence of drama in anthologies on which survey courses are constructed and to argue that an unexamined curriculum is not worth teaching.

The problem of American drama in the American higher educational curriculum needs to be understood not just as the problem of drama in the curriculum, but also as the problem of the minimal cultural capital of drama in American literary studies and, as well, of the creation and justification of disciplinary fields and hierarchies within universities. The first problem, that of American literature as an academic discipline, recently has been dealt with by David Shumway in *Creating American Civilization: A Genealogy of American Literature as an Academic Discipline* (1994), in which he argues that the *Cambridge History of American Literature* established "the legitimacy of American literature as an academic subject" (93). Given that Arthur Hobson Quinn and Montrose Moses had contributed chapters on American drama and that the *Cambridge History* also includes chapters on French, German, Yiddish, and "Amerind" drama, it might seem that the drama should have entered the curriculum as part of American literature. It was not to be that easy. The advocates of American literature as a respectable subject had to fight hard to establish a disciplinary area, and American literature as an acceptable "field" did not come into its own until after World War II when it surged into the university on the tidal wave of patriotism. The development of professional journals and organizations followed with the creation of *American Quarterly* in 1949 and the American Studies Association in 1951. If those who professed American literary studies had to battle the entrenched prestige of English studies, those wishing to profess American drama had to fight harder. In fact, in Shumway's recounting of the move from marginality to security of American literature as a discipline, poetry and prose dominate; drama is but a shadowy presence both in the canon and in the discipline.

The model for the new disciplinary area, of course, was English. Howard Mumford Jones, in "Arms of the Anglo-Saxons," attributed the thick Anglophilism of American literary study to three foundational scholars, Moses Coit Tyler, Charles F. Richardson, and Barrett Wendell, all of whom exhibited New England parochialism and insisted on an Arnoldian valuation of high culture. As Shumway notes, the English literary canon was dominated by Chaucer, Shakespeare, Spenser, and Milton; the interest in the Renaissance stage notwithstanding, Shakespeare was understood to be a poet. Shumway credits F. O. Matthiessen's *American Renaissance* as fixing the American canon: Emerson, who, in Matthiessen's phrase, was "the cow from which the rest drew their milk," Thoreau, Hawthorne, Whitman, and Melville were the great writers (xii). Shumway notes that Melville "is for Matthiessen, quite literally, the Shakespeare of our Renaissance" (252). The importance of Matthiessen should not be underestimated; according to Sacvan Bercovitch in *Rites of Assent*, with *American Renaissance* Matthiessen not only created the canon, he also set the terms for discussing American literature. That heroic tragedy on a mythic scale became the stuff of American novels rather than the stage has some bearing on the fate of American drama as, too, does the fact that many American playwrights drank a stiffer and more proletarian brew than Emersonian milk. But more of an impediment was the inescapable link of the drama to the stage.

Although a narrative of the troubled history of American drama and its academic place could certainly be structured by focusing on tensions and conflicts such as the predictable binarism of theatrical performance and dramatic literature as well as the parallel split of the study of drama into Theatre and English departments, the divisive tension between performance and text was not at all new to evaluations of dramatic literature, of course; it only was exacerbated and reified rather than challenged and rectified when drama entered the higher education curriculum. In fact, in the struggle to legitimate areas of study and to claim materials to be studied, the dramatic text was a critical component to Theatre departments. If it could be authoritatively argued that a play was only a script to be performed, the playwright and, by extension, the literary critic had less authority and consequently less power than the theatre historian or the director. By this reasoning, Theatre departments could strengthen their claim to the whole area of study, a claim that in turn would be undermined by departments of English reluctant to lose the seminal figure of Shakespeare but just as reluctant to take on the undesirable baggage of American drama. It should be noted that at least one theatre historian has formulated a very different narrative of the place of drama in general in the American university. Ron Vince, in "Theatre History as an Academic Discipline," argues that English departments have so much appropriated drama as their responsibility that Theatre departments have been left with almost only practical training. But, however one reconstructs the disciplinary battles and as damaging as this binarism has been, the problem of the competing claims of text and performance is more complex.

For Richard Schechner the problem is culturally constituted. In *Performance Theory* (1988) he argues that

> those cultures which emphasize the dyad drama-script de-emphasize theater-performance; and vice-versa. Generally, among the world's cultures an emphasis on drama-script has occurred only occasionally: ancient Greek drama, the Sanskrit drama of India, various Chinese and Japanese traditions, the modern drama of Europe and its cultural extensions from the Renaissance on. Even among these, only "modern drama" since the late nineteenth century has so privileged the written text as to almost exclude theater-performance altogether. (73)

Given Schechner's formulation that the theatre-performance dyad involves a far greater number of people (performers and audience) than the drama-script dyad (only author and teacher), it becomes clear that the tight, small focus is easier to control and authorize. Schechner also points to another issue pertinent to establishing a sharp difference between drama and theatre in the academy, namely that of the dominance of "the Cambridge thesis" about the origins of drama. In America, Francis Fergusson's *The Idea of a Theater* (1949) consolidated this flawed and codified theory of the cultural evolution of theatre, which narrowly locked theatrical expression into a Dionysian "primal ritual." The consequence of this approach, which Schechner complains is still being taught, is a separation of ritual and entertainment instead of the more likely "dynamic braiding" of the two (1–6). It could be said, therefore, that to argue for the drama as literary text is to argue for an anomalous blip in a cultural matrix.

However one might refocus attention and expand the horizons or conditions of the dramatic event, and despite arguments such as Martin Esslin's that "*all* dramatic performance is basically iconic," some sort of text still remains at the core of most, if not all, structured performances (*Field* 43). Una Chaudhuri argues that "most dramatic events have a text of some sort, susceptible to some form of reproduction in the future" and that the presence of the text "makes for a tension between two temporalities (the performative present and the compositional past) and two ontologies (theatrical presence and fictional absence). . . . Thus the drama is born of temporal disjunction; it flourishes as a deeply fissured discourse, and both its meaning and its pleasure derive from this feature. . . . Transgression is the practice, the logic, and the experience of drama" (51). It is possible to argue, therefore, that it is the indubitable transgressiveness and not the debatable textuality of drama that challenges the traditional, dominant, and narrow categories marking most literary study. Precisely because of the transgressiveness, the elusiveness, and the slipperiness of drama, to say nothing of its incubational status for film, the critics and historians have, for the most part, sidestepped or excluded the dramatic forms that resist easy categorizing and have embraced those more easily named by reductive, simple labels such as the "pure" examples of realism or melodrama.

While not neglecting the problems that result from the conflict between drama and theatre, I also focus on the discourse of legitimation, appropriation, and exclusion that arose from the struggle over constructing disciplinary fields. I do so because some of the ways in which American academics were reconfiguring educational enterprises and disciplines separated them from their European antecedents and, as a consequence, what happens to the drama can be marked as peculiarly "American." I suggest that the problem of American drama is not just one of a simple conflict between drama and theatre but is, at the very least, the consequence of a multiplicity of interests competing for aspects and uses of the drama but never for the whole art form. For instance, the manager-dominated commercial theatres run purely as a business enterprise and, later, Broadway productions, must be addressed in a consideration of the colonizing of the genre. Although the distaste for the manager-run system was culturally pervasive, the resistance to drama as a business largely came from two quarters: academic departments and the semiprofessional, experimental theatre movement. But here another split occurs: For the most part, academics would be interested only in "high" drama and the Little Theatres in "poetic" drama. In setting up parameters of difference, the academics and the artisans attempted to legitimate their enterprises by appropriating a discourse of nationalist and democratic interest. As a consequence, the writing of plays variously was understood to be an "art," a "craft," or a "science" and the writers as "dramatists," "playwrights," or "playmakers." Both academics and Little Theatre proponents tried to establish systems of inequality, subordination, and qualified inclusion with respect to each other, and both attempted to exclude or deny commercial theatre. The debate over legitimation was complicated further by the variety of sites in which plays were produced (community, university, or commercial) and by the range of capabilities (amateur, student, or professional) of the playwrights and producers. But the idea of difference is a fragile one and needs to be understood in relational terms; the commercial theatre had its trade journals just as academics had their scholarly journals and the experimental theatres had their arts and crafts magazines. In each venue the nature and value of drama was reconfigured to suit the specific ends of the discipline or cultural enterprise; each configuration represented an essentialist and separatist impulse that has had the undesirable consequence of fragmenting approaches to the drama so that, in the academic versions of its several venues, drama is now relegated to a marginalized borderland in higher education except for the relative success of strongly vocational theatre practice programs in acting, management, and technical aspects at a very few universities.

In *Tradition and Reform in the Teaching of English: A History* (1974), Arthur N. Applebee links the recognition of English as an accepted subject in high schools with the Social Darwinism of Albion Small, the head of America's first sociology department at the University of Chicago, a link that would have a profound impact on the position of drama in both high school and college curricula. Applebee says that when Small, addressing the National Education Association in 1896, argued that schools needed to be the site of "'the amelioration or reform of society,'" he provided "a philosophical justification for crusaders" in the cause of progressive social change (47). In tracing the consequences of the resultant shift in focus from an analytic approach to literary studies to an emphasis on the ideas or values embodied in a work, Applebee observes that "the methodological advances which received the greatest attention and fullest development were in the teaching of drama. Two forces converged in drama during the years before World War I, one from an academic stress on oral presentation, the other from a progressive concern with self-expression; they elevated drama to a position it has never had since" (61). And because interest in oral expression and rhetoric have waned, the drama is left only with the association with self-expression which is understood to be emotional, amateurish, and childish.

Applebee continues with the assertion that "the central figure in the academic justification of drama was Hiram Corson of Cornell University. His works, especially *The Aims of Literary Study* (1894), were cited by virtually every writer concerned with drama in education – Carpenter, Baker, and Scott; Chubb and Hall acknowledged their debt to him. Corson's principal concern was to free literary study from the excessive factualism which diverted attention from the ethical value of the works studied. His cure was oral reading, not as performance or entertainment but as a means to a disciplined knowledge of the text" (61). "Literature, more especially poetic and dramatic literature," Corson wrote, "is the expression in letters of the spiritual, cooperating with the intellectual, man, the former being the primary, dominant coefficient" (*Aims* 24). Arguing against a Gradgrindian scientific valuation of philology and for an "organic" and "natural" expressiveness that would carry a reader to the essentialized truth of God, Corson equated poetic and dramatic literature by stressing their emotional and spiritual content. But in an increasingly secularized academy in which oration also figured less and less, this early connection of drama with emotion and hence, emoting, would have grave consequences when efforts were made to introduce it into the higher education curriculum.

Literature itself, of course, was a contested subject needing legitimation as an academic subject, especially given the increasing prominence of science. Two essays by Harvard's New Humanist Irving Babbitt, "Literature and the College" and "Literature and the Doctor's Degree" (1908), describe arts and letters as threatened by the Germanic model of the university as a scientific laboratory that variously characterized the study of arts and literature as dilettantism, play, entertainment, passive, sentimental, aesthetic, emotional, and feminine. "The man who took literature too seriously would be suspected of effeminacy. The really virile thing is to be an electrical engineer. One already sees the time when the typical teacher of literature will be some young dilettante who will interpret Keats and Shelley to a class of girls" ("Doctor's" 134–35). This taint of gender and attendant emotionalism would have to be striven against by academics like Babbitt who would turn to the masculinizing sciences to authorize literary study; it was a formative cultural and professional object lesson for the men who would determine the fate of American drama.

Drama in Early American Textbooks

Gerald Graff, in his history of the discipline, *Professing Literature*, rejects consideration of rhetoric as central to the development of literature studies and, in so doing, reenacts the dominant paradigm of American literary study in this century, which lops off one limb on which drama so precariously was perched beside the equally vulnerable field of composition, a coupling that would have consequences for both following the 1960s. According to the 1948 National Council of Teachers of English survey, "American literature in the mid-nineteenth century was associated with English literature and with oratory, both of which usually fell within the department of 'Belles-Lettres'" (W. Crane 4). The position of American drama proves to be unique because, unlike poetry or the novel, the drama could fall into either category, literature or oratory, and in fact, since many texts devoted to the study of oration and elocution drew heavily on dramatic literature, it was inevitable that drama should be compromised from the start. Two other factors had an adverse impact on the future of American drama in the curriculum. The compilers of the survey assert that "the two important developments in American literature in this early period were the production of a textbook, more or less adequate for collegiate use, devoted solely to American literature and the production of a first-rate scholarly work covering a limited part of the subject" (W. Crane 7). The two works cited as marking the beginning of American literature as an independent college course are John Seely Hart's *A Manual of American Literature: A Text-Book for Schools and Colleges* (1872) and Moses Coit Tyler's *A History of American Literature During the Colonial Time, 1607–1765* (1878). Although Hart covered a vast range of writers by type – poets, science writers, political economists, theologians, magazinists, journalists, novelists, tellers of tales, humorists, and legal writers – he did not include dramatists. And although Tyler was an early proponent of a non-belletristic approach, he made no mention of drama, which for him began in America with *Ponteach* in 1766.

Even when Tyler included drama in *The Literary History of the American Revolution, 1763–1783* (1897), he was dismissive of it as "tentative" and "crude," admitting only two dramatic poems, Hugh Henry Brackenridge's "The Battle of Bunker Hill" (1776) and "The Death of General Montgomery at the Siege of Quebec" (1777), into the status of serious literature (210).

In "Anthologies of American Literature before 1861," Fred Lewis Pattee described eighty-two anthologies of which only two included drama, *Boston Prize Poems and Other Specimens of Dramatic Poetry* (1824) and *The Class Book of American Literature* (1826). But if drama was neglected in anthologies for adults, it was more richly represented in instructional collections aimed at the young, especially as a means for "naturalizing" behavior and for "civilizing" the young citizenry. But even in these texts, other genres are modified to look like partial dramatic texts or drama is presented in an attenuated form. These transformed texts were important because they set up patterns of appropriating dramatic literature to teach children reading, oration, elocution, and heightened language (but not drama), patterns that would have a negative effect when dramatic literature was finally admitted to the higher education curriculum.

For instance, Lindley Murray's *Introduction to the English Reader* (1845) comprises selections of prose and poetry as examples of narrative, didactic pieces, description, and dialogue, all set up as if they were playscripts but without context, set, or action. H. Mandeville's *A Course of Reading for Common Schools* (1846) boasts of a "fulness [sic] of sentential illustration" (4) and insists on reading as a vocal (versus silent) process. Mandeville used very little from dramatic literature; there is an exchange between Cassio and Iago but the passage is not contextualized in any way. The reader is not told that the passage is from a play, who the author is, what the context for the dialogue is, or what action is involved; the passage stands simply as a free-floating piece of dialogue. P. A. Fitzgerald's *The Exhibition Speaker* (1856) offers sample texts for "exhibition days," stressing primarily the voice but also focusing on gesture and descriptions of the stage. The examples are categorized as "dramatic," "scenes from Shakespeare," "senatorial," and "comic." By "dramatic," Fitzgerald means farce, romance, comedy, or domestic drama and gives directions on how to play the parts for maximum "elocutionary display." McGuffey's *New High School Reader* (1857) sets forth exercises in prose and poetry, a few of which are drawn from the plays of Shakespeare. For example, a scene between Hamlet and Rosencrantz and Guildenstern is offered as prose, one between Hamlet and Marcellus and Bernardo as poetry. Lines from *The Merchant of Venice* are presented without attribution of the play, the speaker, or the context. The mercy speech between Isabella and Angelo identifies the speakers but not the play or situation. In J. C. Zachos's *The New American Speaker* (1857), a collection of oratorical and dramatic pieces, soliloquies and dialogues for use in schools, academies, and colleges, the teacher of elocution ultimately is concerned with movements and breathing. For Zachos, "dramatic" means heightened and emotional language, nothing more. Epes Sargent's *The Intermediate Standard Reader* (1859), which contains pieces for declamation in schools and colleges, was written for teachers of elocution and was designed to make a sharp distinction between readers and speakers. Relying for the most part on altered passages from Shakespeare, Sargent emphasized inflection and gesture. *Stepping Stones to Literature: A Reader for Fifth Grades* (1897) by Sarah Lewis Arnold and Charles B. Gilbert, containing all American literature of the "better" variety, its aim to stimulate good oral reading with attention to carriage and quality of voice, dedicated to teaching discrimination and taste and arguing that "the reading lesson should be primarily a literature lesson" (xii), contains no drama. Marietta Knight's *Dramatic Reader for Grammar Grades* (1910), which might be expected to contain plays, was designed to help children become more "natural" and less "artificial" when they read aloud. But the text contains no plays. Instead, the author constructed dialogues based on such literary works as Poe's "The Gold Bug" and Sir Walter Scott's *Kenilworth*. Knight explained that "these dialogues are not 'plays;' they are not intended for action, but for reading" (3).

The rationale for these diverse appropriations of the drama for purposes other than the teaching of dramatic literature can be found in John Nietz's *Old Textbooks* (1961). Nietz begins his history with the earliest American primers, primarily religious in subject matter, and traces their development to 1900. The content of 1,370 such readers was classified by topic by R. R. Robinson in 1930 as either prose or poetry. Nietz observes that "even though the more or less purely religious concepts largely disappeared in readers shortly after 1850, references to morals and conduct continued much longer. However, the individualistic rather than social virtues were emphasized throughout" (56).

Citing an unpublished study of the advanced readers from 1785 to 1900 by Vincent Davis, Nietz notes that the percentage of the literary content, though literature consistently was regarded as a "powerful agent for the teaching of political, social, moral, and religious lessons," fluctuated from decade to decade. "For example, the readers that emphasized the didactic did not include as much good literature as those aiming to present mainly selections of superior literary value. The readers from 1860 to 1900 consistently included a higher percentage of excellent literature than the readers of the first half of the nineteenth century. Prefatory statements in the readers after 1860 definitely indicated that the authors aimed to emphasize literature rather than history or science" (59–60). "Nearly all the readers until just before 1900," Nietz explains, "emphasized the mastery of effective oral reading or elocution . . . it was often the prime objective in the advanced readers" (61).

In *The Evolution of American Secondary School Textbooks*, Nietz explains that because public speaking was considered important in a growing democracy, rhetoric, with an emphasis on correctness and elegance of style and diction, was taught in most American academies after 1800, and that until 1825 the rhetoric texts were written in England. The first rhetoric textbook to gain popularity in America, *Lectures on Rhetoric and Belles Lettres*, was written by Hugh Blair in 1783 at the University of Edinburgh. Drama was one of several kinds of writing Blair used to illustrate the best principles and practices. According to Nietz, "not only were the Blair books the most commonly used rhetorics in America for many decades, they set the pattern for most other authors of rhetorics for many decades. . . . English and Scottish culture were considered so superior during the 18th and early 19th centuries that even American schools believed rhetorics written in England to be better than any produced here" (*Evolution* 15–16). An 1824 abridged version of Blair includes a chapter on the drama, but introduces the genre as a "favorite amusement" of all "civilized nations" and is riddled with concerns for the "decency" of plays (215).

According to Nietz, the "so-called English subjects" came into their own in secondary schools in 1870 because most colleges began to require credit in rhetoric for admission and though all rhetoric textbooks before 1830 gave oratory considerable attention, after 1830 about one-third failed to give it space (*Evolution* 19). Nietz argues that the teaching of literature in American secondary schools developed in four stages: classical readers, often called *Speakers*, composed of extracts from great writings deemed suitable for elocutionary presentation; literary histories, which were primarily biographies with brief comments about their work; whole classic works; and anthologies. According to Nietz, nearly all of the American literature textbooks published before 1900 were written by college professors or presidents, while after 1900 more than one-third were written by high school teachers of English. Examples from three of the American written general literature books show the troubled state of drama. In James Robert Boyd's *Elements of Rhetoric and Literary Criticism* (1844), American literature is represented only by poetry. There was no drama in Henry Beers's *A Century of American Literature* (1878), and George Cathcart's *Literary Reader* (1874) represents American writers as poets, historians, scientists, and novelists. One of the most widely used texts in America, Shaw and Backus's *Shaw's New History of English Literature* (1884), includes history, essays, humor, belles lettres, poetry, and song, but no drama. A sharp dismissal of Dryden's writing for the stage as "degrading his talent for the service of an immoral public" accounts for this omission (179). One of the later revisions in 1897 offers this on the rise of the novel: "prose fiction is, in fact, the expansion of the drama. In the growth and variations of the novel may be found the reasons why the drama has never recovered its ancient ascendancy" (196). It is hardly surprising to learn that textbooks that dealt with English writers only were used more commonly than those with American writers only or those that combined the treatment. In fact, the study of English literature did not become a widely accepted subject in American secondary schools until after 1870. American literature was not taught as a separate subject until the late 1880s and then only in about one-third as many high schools as English literature was. Apparently, no acceptable textbook dealing with American literature alone appeared before 1872 and that was John S. Hart's *A Manual of American Literature*, from which the drama was absent.

By the end of the nineteenth century, American literature had won the right to its own textbooks, but the presence of the drama was negligible, according to Nietz, getting the least space, approximately 8 percent (42). Clearly even that space was given grudgingly and the sentiments expressed were damaging. Henry A. Beers, in *Outline Sketch of American Literature* (1887), swept aside Royall Tyler as merely a wit and a journalist and asserted that "there is, in fact, no American dramatic literature worth speaking of; not a single American play of even the second rank, unless we except a few graceful parlor comedies, like Mr. Howells's *Elevator* and *Sleeping-Car*" (79). Similar valuative assertions without benefit of explanation were expressed by Albert Smyth in *American Literature* (1889): "The list of American dramas is brief and uninteresting. Compositions like *Metamora* (J. A. Stone) and *The Gladiator* (R. M. Bird) have no place in literature" (61).

American Drama and Higher Education

In tracing the development of modern language study in higher education in America, Wallace Douglas locates 1883–1884 as the end of classical liberal studies because it was the year in which Harvard switched to an elective system, the year in which "letters" were set up in opposition to "scholarship," cultivation against pedantry (45–46). According to Douglas, those professing English and suffering from the patronizing dismissiveness of philosophers and classicists, needed to counter the imputation of inferiority by proving English to be a discipline. They turned to what Douglas calls a "spiritualized" claim on character-forming and on disseminating the best of human thought in order to produce the perfect man (52–53). The desire to maintain a political agenda and to insist on a moral goal marked many of the rationales produced by the founders of higher education in America. William Rainey Harper, the first president of the University of Chicago, for instance, posited a reciprocal relationship between education and government while describing the university as a prophet engaged in priestly service. Whatever the merits of this claim, the enrollments increased and, as a welcome consequence, departments and fields within departments also grew. That the expanded curriculum and the creation of "subjects" allowed the universities simply to serve both God and Mammon is evidence for Douglas that there were no principles controlling the creation of "whimsically specialized courses" (59). Furthermore, as Bernard Beckerman observes, because theatre was an extra- and semicurricular activity in colleges and universities it was not until 1925, with the creation of its own department, that it could claim legitimacy.

It is not too much to claim, therefore, that the place of drama in American literature studies, now entrenched as aesthetic and belletristic on the eve of twentieth-century professionalism, was already in jeopardy. In "The Relation of Drama to Literature," an address to the MLA in 1897, Brander Matthews, two years before he was named by Columbia as the first professor of dramatic literature, set up drama and oratory as the two oral arts, on the same plane and needing to be judged by the same standards, for "to measure a drama by literature alone is like trying to criticize a painting by a photograph alone." Matthews drew a distinction between success, which depended on playability, and survival, which depended on literary quality. But because the drama of "lofty poetic pretense," closet drama, was unactable anyway, the drama was "the most difficult of all the arts" (230). Montrose J. Moses, in his contribution to the *Cambridge History of American Literature* (1921), noted that though Matthews did a great deal to popularize the philosophy of the theatre, it was to be regretted that he had never written a book on American drama. Moses, marking Matthews's lack of success as a playwright with *Margery's Lovers* (1878), *Decision of the Court* (1893), and, with Bronson Howard, *Peter Stuyvesant* (1899), observed that "Professor Matthews, as an American dramatist, has scarcely exhibited the qualities or won the fame which belonged to him as a professor of Dramatic Literature" (CHAL 274). It would be speculative and malicious folly to attribute Matthews's views on the genre to his failure as a playwright, nonetheless, his views did not alter. In *The Development of the Drama* (1903), Matthews reiterated his insistence that the stage was "less rhetorical, less lyric, less epic, more purely dramatic . . . less poetic" than literature (342). Matthews separated the study of drama from the study of literature; in *An Introduction to the Study of American Literature* (1896), Matthews focused exclusively on poetry and prose and marked only the increasing ascendancy of fiction over the once dominant poetry. Matthews's position that drama was not coincident with literature was echoed and applauded by Henry Arthur Jones in a lecture at Yale University in 1906, "Literature and the Modern Drama," in which he insisted that "the greatest examples of drama are poetic drama" but that neither Americans nor contemporary Englishmen could hope to produce by labor what came "naturally" to the Elizabethans (*Foundations* 61). By this reasoning, England could have a dramatic literary heritage but America did not, and as a consequence Shakespeare was assured a haven in an academic curriculum. By severing drama from literature, Matthews cut the philological umbilical cord to the higher reaches of the academy.

But drama, though it lacked a legitimate or clearly defined position in a literary curriculum, had secured a permanent place in university life long before it was recognized as a fit subject for study. Certainly the feelings of President Timothy Dwight of Yale capture the early antipathy toward the theatre; in his posthumously published "Essays on the Stage" (1824), he warned that to indulge in playgoing "means nothing more or less than the loss of that most valuable treasure, the immortal soul" (Angoff 372). But the dramatic impulse would not be stopped by moralizers. Paul Leicester Ford, writing for *The New England Magazine* in 1894, made this argument: "No matter how severely public opinion, the government, the clergy, and the press might view the drama, the schools and colleges . . . were natural centers in which . . . the instinctive craving for drama would manifest itself. At a time when there was no theatre in New England, when no professional company could act there, . . . the Harvard boys were acting plays. . . . Indeed, we can broadly claim that the forces of youth and college education broke down the laws and prejudices against the theatre" (683). Though they may have broken down some social prejudices, they hardly overcame them. In an assessment of the theatre in 1918, William Lyon Phelps expressed his disgust at the "so-called Dramatic Societies that produce musical burlesques and farces" and that had no place in his history or in any institution of learning (85). The acceptance of drama into the curriculum would depend on factors other than students' extracurricular activities, activities that did little to smooth the path of academic acceptance.

In *The "Types Approach" to Literature* (1945), Irvin Ehrenpreis described the division of the study of literature in the newly formed university English departments of the 1880s and 1890s into three phases of literary discipline: author, period, and "species of literature," of which the two "most enduring types courses were on the drama and on fiction." He noted that "the drama was pre-eminent partly because it is intrinsically the most individual of the types, possessing the most peculiar traditions, and partly because Shakespeare was a dramatist" (66). In fact, in Ehrenpreis's study of eight major American universities, the drama, as a "type," figures prominently and even, at Harvard, expanded significantly under George Pierce Baker and Barrett Wendell. At the University of Chicago, until 1905, drama was the most popular "types" course in the English department. For instance, at Princeton, by 1911, half of the undergraduate courses were in "types" and most of these were in the drama. Though by 1931 the drama was receiving less emphasis at Princeton, it still represented at least one-third of the courses. In all the universities in Ehrenpreis's study, the drama was, at both the undergraduate and graduate levels, the most frequently studied "type" of literature. But, Ehrenpreis, citing the rise of condemnations of the use of genre studies, especially in the extended debate between Irving Babbitt (for the defense of genre) and Joel Elias Spingarn (on the assault), observed that "the doctrine of genres was beginning to be a favorite piece of shatter-practice for iconoclastic scholars" just as its effect on teaching was becoming apparent (55). Between 1895 and 1915, textbooks, in the form of series of genre studies, appeared to address the need and as a consequence became part of the curriculum.

The fate of the drama as part of an academic curriculum also was tied up in the new professionalisms. The movement that, according to one historian, emerged and matured between 1870 and 1900, marked the freeing of education from church control and, consequently, "all subjects – however dependent on professional practice or applied arts – [were] raised to the status of theoretical study" (Bledstein 291). In Bledstein's narrative, between 1865 and 1875 the beginnings of the "age of the university," the concern for cohesive nationalism after the Civil War, gave rise to a middle-class unease seeking assurance in "the accepted authority of an elite of merit" (322–33). When the academy was the site of new authority, it became the site of professionalizing study, a matter of establishing fields, disciplines, departments, methodologies, graduate programs, national professional organizations, and journals. The valorizing of one area of study often meant the devalorizing of another. For instance, James Berlin, in *Rhetoric and Reality: Writing Instruction in American Colleges, 1900–1985*, describes the convergence of the complex set of forces, from the desire to increase the status of English department members to the new college entrance exams, which culminated in the decentering of rhetoric and the enthroning of the poetic text, a shift with corollary consequences for the drama, yoked as it was to the teaching of rhetoric and oratory.

Throughout 1894, *The Dial* ran eighteen articles on the teaching of English in the more important American colleges and universities, including not only the major eastern institutions but also state-supported schools and those built on private philanthropy. As Gerald Graff points out in *Professing Literature*, this series was one sign of "a reaction against the narrower Germanic methods" then dominating American universities and "the most revealing indicator of the ideological divisions marking the new profession" (100). Given that the primary battle lines were drawn between linguistics and philology within English departments (with some rattling at the gates by rhetoric), as a consequence the drama was hardly a matter of major concern at this stage. Nonetheless, the drama was part of the curriculum. Of course Shakespeare's plays dominated and were treated as literature, although at the University of Illinois students were "never allowed to forget that Shakespeare wrote primarily for the stage and not the closet" (Dodge "Illinois" 261). The only qualifying remark about the drama was that at Yale, "the decadence" of drama between 1603 and 1660 was given "special reference" (Cook "Yale" 69). Some schools were offering courses in American literature but there was no mention of American drama, although F. A. March, describing the English curriculum at Lafayette College, noted that "the best work is done when the author selected is an American. Students find their own life and thought depicted in the American authors. The language is their own" (296).

The most interesting report for a study of drama in the curriculum was from Charles Mills Gayley at the University of California because it points to a possible reason for excluding drama from critical examination early in the formation of the English curriculum. Dramatic criticism and the theory of art were included in a course on poetics, but the course on the problems of literary criticism focused on the function of literary types other than the drama. Gayley faults the "sentimental, the formally stylistic, or the second-hand-historical fashion" of teaching English for the "uncertainty of aim which instruction in English is frequently approached." This lack of a system however, Gayley assured his readers, was being remedied by "literary science," a science that was "not yet organic, but dynamic," a science that would take the teaching of English literature beyond the current limits of aesthetics, philology, versification, and rhetoric (31–32). Presumably, therefore, Gayley's "literary science" was not suited to drama, a genre that, by his definition, was more suited to the "uncertain" approach he characterized as sentimental, formal, and historical.

In sum, as far as *The Dial* was concerned, the American experience "establishes beyond question the claims of English as a proper subject of university instruction" ("English at the Universities" 325). The drama, however, was a long way from being settled in the English curriculum. Although Brander Matthews, appointed professor of literature at Columbia in 1892, moved to a chair of dramatic literature in 1902, the first such position in the United States, it was the troubled relationship between George Pierce Baker and Harvard and Baker's subsequent move to Yale in 1925 that had the greater impact on the location of American drama in the university curriculum. In the battle for the disciplinary configuration of drama, which would escalate with the formation of Theatre departments, both Matthews and Baker were instrumental in focusing study away from the text and onto performance. Those struggling to get serious recognition of the drama and theatre invoked the work of both pioneers in the field as models for introducing new approaches. Brander Matthews (1852–1929) taught at Columbia until 1924 and, although he was a professor of literature, he was adamant that a play was meant primarily for performance. A playwright himself, he also firmly believed that the only valid test of drama was in performance, an idea he propounded in *The Development of the Drama* (1903) and *A Study of the Drama* (1910).

A great deal was at stake in getting drama, let alone American playwriting, into the curriculum in colleges and universities. An important article, "American Professors of Dramatic Literature," in 1911 by Montrose J. Moses, who had just published *The American Dramatist*, points to a host of connected concerns from the accurate reconstruction of staging to the creation of libraries for the drama. What is interesting about Moses's piece is his implication that the general public's acceptance of and the academic legitimation of American drama both would have to come from American university professors, who themselves had to be freed from the public image of the dry-as-dust scholar. Drama and theatre and the study and practice of both had to be presented as vital enterprises as important to the public interest as to the academy. Moses points to Mrs. Phoebe Hearst's gift of a Greek amphitheater at Berkeley as placing the drama in two spheres, academic and public, simultaneously. His article describes the work done by Brander Matthews at Columbia and George Pierce Baker at Harvard and refers in passing to Phelps of Yale, Burton of Minnesota, F. W. Chandler of the University of Cincinnati, Tucker of the Brooklyn Polytechnic, and Gayley of the University of California. Matthews's acquisition of a reconstructed interior of the Fortune Theatre, in which Shakespeare was said to have acted, represented to Moses "scholarship revivified, for analysis should always be followed by synthesis. . . . This objective dealing with the theater is a new phase of collegiate work. A literary discussion of the drama is different from actual dramaturgical considerations. While there have always been courses in the Greek drama, and on Shakespeare and his related craftsmen, it is only since 1892 that a more strictly theatrical consideration has begun to develop" ("Professors" 814). Moses also applauded Matthews's determination to deal only with "permanent examples of dramatic art," concurring that "the college should not be offered opportunities in the study of contemporary drama" (814). For Moses, though he was a little troubled by Baker's theoretical and didactic stance, Baker's results at Harvard were the "most encouraging" because he had developed a course in playwriting in the English department. Moses fretted that "the public libraries have not yet given the drama the specialized position accorded it by the university" but anticipated that the future of American drama lay with the "collegiate playwright" (815–16). Thus, although the study of dramatic literature, an art, should concentrate on the canonized classics in the "permanent" record, the writing of new American plays, plays as craft work to be performed not studied, would also be under the supervision of English professors. Also, the writing of drama was not going to be left to the amateurs, at least not without academic supervision.

This cozy, closed situation did not last long, however, and in the discourse of legitimation wars soon to ensue, those advocating the priority of performance over textual analysis targeted Matthews as the focus of effeteness, dullness, and unmasculine attitudes in the unenlightened academy. For instance, in a review of Matthews's *A Book About the Theatre* (1916), the editors of *Theatre Arts Magazine*, a vehicle for promoting the experimental stagecraft movement, charged Matthews with dogmatism, aridity, and with laboring over the unimportant; "we recommend this book to the old women of the theatre – and of the universities" ("Theatre Bookshelf" 43). Others unhappy with the new importance being given to the inclusion of material theatre history within the study of dramatic literature included Joel Elias Spingarn, an aesthetic formalist and Renaissance scholar at Columbia, who vehemently voiced his objections in "Dramatic Criticism and the Theatre" (1913). Exercised about "a collection of theatrical antiquities in the

American University, bric-a-brac which is called 'The Dramatic Museum,'"
Spingarn gathered his evidence from Aristotle to Croce to prove that this
was "dead material" with only the most peripheral bearing on critical issues
of interpretation (52). In fact, he contended, such museums should be
offered as a "literary 'chamber of horrors,' a permanent symbol of the false
theories which have encumbered the dramatic criticism of our time" (92).
It is difficult to assess the damage done by Spingarn's assault, but it is worth
noting that at the same moment the study of drama is legitimated within
the professoriate, there is also a serious, public, internal rift over the "literary" versus "theatrical" modes of study and research. Robert Spiller believed
that Spingarn supplied the "rationale and method for the analytical criticism of Eliot and the critics of the thirties and forties" (*Literary History*
1155). Marvin Carlson suggests that the unbridgeable animosity between
Spingarn and Matthews and their subsequent followers caused an essential
split in American dramatic theory that had long-term consequences in that
"their many disciples nourished opposing critical camps in American dramatic theory for many years thereafter" (313).

Damaging though the divisiveness that weakened a unified presence for
drama was, even more important to the location of drama in higher education was George Pierce Baker (1866–1935). Not only was Baker responsible
for instituting playwriting as a fit subject for higher education, he also
argued for the drama as the subject of theatre not literature, stressed the
primacy of production over writing, and saw to it that the profession was
masculinized. Under the disciplinary aegis of English, Baker taught contemporary drama at Radcliffe in 1897 and at Harvard in 1900, but it was not
until 1903 that he initiated a course in playwriting at Radcliffe and then
offered it at Harvard. What began inauspiciously enough grew into a
milestone. As Giles Gray describes it, "In 1905, the year [Baker] was
elevated to a full professorship, he offered for the first time his English 47,
which was destined to be 'the most celebrated academic course in America'"
(428). Although English 47 has become renowned among literary historians, especially O'Neill scholars, it was unique in its time. Kenneth
Macgowan, in a retrospective survey of educational theatre, pointed to how
precarious was the place of Baker's course in academe as compared to
Macgowan's present, the year 1957, at which time close to four hundred
universities and colleges offered theatre majors. Macgowan also noted that
although the course was offered to graduates, Eugene O'Neill, who had
been thrown out of Princeton as a freshman, was a student in the class, that
Harvard never thought much of Baker, and that "despite many loose-
minded historians of the theatre, his famous 47 Workshop, which he

started in 1912–13, was always extra-curricular" ("Educational" 85). It is
ironic that the playwright usually heralded as America's "greatest" was only
marginally the product of the institutional machinery set in motion to
contain, train, and produce American playwrights; Travis Bogard notes
that of the work O'Neill did for Baker, "what has survived is dreadful –
without question the worst writing he ever did" (*Contour* 49).

Samuel Eliot Morison's history of Harvard certainly bears out
Macgowan's assertion that the theatre really occupied an extracurricular
place in academe. "As early as 1758," he writes, "we find evidence of plays
being performed by the undergraduates in college hall: Addison's *Cato* and
The Roman Father; *The Recruiting Officer*; *The Orphan*; a scene from Ter-
ence before the Overseers' Visiting Committee (1762); and, in 1765, 'Scholars punished at college for acting over the great and last day in a very
shocking manner, personating the Devil, etc.'" (91–92). Although undergraduate theatricals continued to be popular through the First World War,
and although serious plays were produced by the French, German, Italian,
and Spanish language societies as well as by students of classics and English
departments, and although the Harvard Dramatic Club was founded in
1908, it was not until Baker's 47 Workshop in 1912 that a significant
advance, the merger of theory and practice at a graduate level, was achieved.
Baker's need to move from an English department to Theatre, however,
was seminal in the displacement of dramatic literature. Nor was his the only
such experience. Clifford Hamar points to Thomas Dickinson's trials as
being similar, noting that "with his series of textbooks entitled *Chief Contemporary Dramatists*, Dickinson may have done more than any other single
teacher to encourage the growth of college courses devoted to the study of
living playwrights" (573). But between 1909 and 1916 Dickinson could not
prevail against his colleagues in the English department at Wisconsin and
finally redirected his efforts to the off-campus Wisconsin Dramatic Society.

American Drama and Social Education

Articles published in *English Journal* between 1912 and 1915 reflect the
prevailing uncertain attitude about the place of both American literature
and drama in the curriculum. Nellie A. Stephenson, concerned with the
neglect of American literature, surveyed college catalogues and discovered
that in 1915 at best only one elective in American literature was offered. She
argued for the inclusion of American literature because of its "cultural
value" and "distinctly ethical value" but suggested that the texts be novels,
diaries, and essays (569). While remaining vague on specific points, Henry

Burd argued for drama as a genre as an essential but separate part of a literature curriculum, noting that American literature had its own category. J. Milnor Dorey, extolling the virtues of taking part in the production of a play, argued for "dramatics" in the curriculum, claiming that "a systematic course in dramatics will develop in the pupil resourcefulness, or knowledge of human life, and altruism" (427). William Lyon Phelps was blunter, noting in 1918 that though courses on contemporary drama were now a regular part of the curriculum in most American universities, "the object of these courses is not to train playwrights, *but to train audiences*" (84). In 1903, James Hackett had published a call for a "Dramatic University," where actors could be as professionalized as lawyers and physicians were (973).

One way in which the theatre and drama were legitimated as academic disciplines and culturally refined pursuits was by the creation of scholarly journals. This enterprise complemented the rising number of popular magazines devoted to theatre, such as *The Play* (1905), *On Dit* (1906), *The Dramatist* (1909), *The Drama* (1911), *The American Playwright* (1912), *Theatre Arts Magazine* (1916), *Critic* (1919), *American Theatre* (1920), and *The Drama Yearbook* (1924). For instance, the distinctly popularizing mission of *The Theatre* was explained by the editor, Arthur Hornblow, in the inaugural issue of May 1901: to present to the public the "sister worlds of the Drama and Music" not only to the small class already interested but also to win favor with the general public by relying on *"lavish illustration"* [my emphasis]. The theatre, as imaged by this popular magazine as the location of unsurpassed spectacle and dignified beauty, was for the eye. Shifting drama toward visual art and away from its earlier location with oratory as an aural art further distanced the drama from consideration as a literary text. Furthermore, the imagery is decidedly upper-class; the actors pictured in *The Theatre* are dressed as wealthy gentlemen and ladies with a classical air. The illustrations are very much in keeping with the stated editorial policy of encouraging that which "elevates the tone of the stage" and of adding "to the dignity of the profession of the artiste" (1). The high cultural value is insisted upon in this transfiguration: not actor but artist, not honky-tonk performer but aristocrat. Another important aspect of the transvaluating effort was the feminizing discourse of describing productions. Repeatedly words such as "daintiness," "exquisite," "delicious," "pretty," "pretty sentiment," "picturesque," and "refined" are used. From this perspective, drama and theatre became a matter of postures, manners, and good behavior, not of literary merit or performative vitality.

This insistence on the dignity of drama and the presentation of drama as a high art characterized *The Drama*. The magazine published the full text of a play in every issue, but few of those plays were by Americans. The first American play to be published in *The Drama* was *Cowards* in 1917. The playwright, Robert Lovett, was both a graduate of Harvard and an English professor at the University of Chicago. Lovett's academic credentials legitimated his play, making it the equal of the European texts usually published in the magazine. Not coincidentally, American drama as a separate course was offered for the first time in 1917 by Arthur Hobson Quinn at the University of Pennsylvania. On a different social level entirely, the drama was being put to other educational uses that also account for important counterdirections in the disciplining of American drama as an educational institution.

In the early 1900s, Emma Sheridan Fry, a student of both Steele MacKaye and David Belasco, was invited by Alice Minnie Herts to join the Educational Alliance on New York's Lower East Side, an organization dedicated to "Americanizing" Polish and Russian immigrants. There, she developed "educational dramatics," a "science" whereby "the spontaneous functioning of the Dramatic Instinct may be regulated to Educational purpose" (Fry vi). Codified as a system of "laws" by Emma Sheridan Fry in 1913 and directed at teachers, club leaders, and amateur players, educational dramatics stressed "living" rather than "acting," was tested out at the Children's Educational Theatre between 1903 and 1909, and drew the attention and approval of a number of cultural leaders, including William Dean Howells, Samuel Clemens, and Charles W. Eliot. Later, Fry was the dramatic director of the Educational Dramatic League, "designed to lift the level of amateur dramatics" and, through carefully selected plays, to teach correct English, diction, bearing, vocabulary, patriotism, and morals (Tukesbury 346). Traveling widely, Fry pitched various versions of educational dramatics to diverse schools and agencies, including the War Department in 1918, arguing for what her chronicler calls prototypes of "sociodrama and roleplaying" (Tukesbury 347). Fry's educational dramatics was player-based rather than audience-based; it positioned the dramatic instinct as "the agent of the subconscious mind," so it was focused on "real-life" situations, was expressed through a body divided into "zones," was expressed spontaneously, and was dedicated to allowing the "Centre" to swing open the "sense-gates" to "Environment's call." One long-range consequence of the "educational dramatics" movement was the poisoning of the academic well; drama, at the moment of scholarly legitimation and disciplinary appropriation, was being contaminated by connections not only with amateurs but also with children and emotions rather than adults and ideas, with "real life" rather than imagination, with the environment rather than texts, with education rather than research, and with democratic not elitist aims. This association of drama with educational aims that produce prejudicial adverse responses in college and university literature departments turns up later in revisionist approaches to the curriculum in the 1950s and 1960s, especially after the 1966 seminar at Dartmouth on teaching English.

Issues of legitimation and appropriation were being played out in other recently founded professional journals of the developing disciplines. In a report by the National Council of Teachers of English published in *The English Journal* in 1915, drama in general, if not American drama in particular, was considered to be about as important to the preparation of high school teachers as American literature, though drama figures last in a list of courses needing to be added to the college English curriculum. Articles in the 1919 run of the *Quarterly Journal of Speech*, which range from silly skits to eloquent rationales, reflect the diversity of the arguments. In the May issue there appeared a little play, *The Princess's Choice*, written for a high school class in public speaking to inculcate good habits in elocution. In the play, royalty selects Lord Good English but has to deal with other characters such as Slang and Mumbling. In the October issue, a high school teacher argued for dramatics because students could be self-expressive, could develop poise, and would learn to work like a team. Thus dramatics covered all developmental needs: artistic, physical, and social. The stakes were explicitly higher for Beatrice Humiston, for whom the theatre as an educational institution was vital not only because it provided relaxation for "the industrial classes, because it educated in ethics," and because it was an avenue of self-expression for the young, but also because the theatre could "cultivate artistic appreciation in a nation, as well as to develop an understanding of history, language, good speech, of ideals. The theater ought to be our most efficacious civilizing and nationalizing agent" (127). Gertrude Johnson, bemoaning the fact that statistics showed that dramatics "remain the most utterly extra curricular step-child, a thing to be conscientiously censored," called for "dramatic activity" to assume its "proper place" in the educational curriculum, that is, "in the hands of the department of Public Speaking" (161–62). The one thing these diverse arguments do share in common is the insistence that drama in education served the formation of a cultivated, moral citizenry.

The "dramatics" approach led to journals like *Dramatics: An Educational Journal for Directors, Teachers, and Students of Dramatic Arts*, founded in 1929 and popular through the 1950s, and to the increased focus on production rather than on the literary analysis of plays, and the continued, as well as the expanded, employment of theatre arts professionals in schools. In her account of American theatre's decentralization away from the dominance of Broadway production, Felicia Londré notes that "one early impetus was the introduction of dramatic literature courses into the college curriculum" (528). For the status of drama as serious literature, the move to dramatics was a damaging one. Increasingly, in such venues as *Educational Theatre Journal*, "dramatics" was yoked to psychology and sociology, as a "science" of emotional aestheticizing (Henry 8). Claims to science, however, would not be enough to offset the emotional, aesthetic, and feminine aura clinging to drama nor to its location on the boundary with other performing arts such as dance.

In Mortimer J. Adler's *Paideia Program* (1984), by way of Robert Hutchins's Great Books program – itself the offspring of the progressive movement, which does include the drama, even some American drama – drama is not connected to emotion but it is classified with the nonverbal arts. Elementary students are urged to read Robert Sherwood and Thornton Wilder; high school students are directed to Arthur Miller and Eugene O'Neill. The thinness of the selection aside, the interesting aspect of Adler's program is how the drama is perceived. Although language, literature, and the fine arts are needed to acquire "organized knowledge," drama is classified with music and the visual arts and is needed to enlarge understanding of ideas and values. Moreover, this understanding is acquired through "involvement in artistic activities" (8). For Adler, drama is, like dance, a "symbolic art" because it requires the student to engage in "interpretation and expression" (142–43).

George Pierce Baker: Harvard English 47 to Yale Drama 37

Although the Carnegie Institute of Technology created in 1914 the first department of drama with a degree in theatre arts combining theatre history and practice, the most influential department was Yale's Department of Drama established in 1925 and headed by Baker, newly moved from Harvard's English department (see Figure 4). Writing from the perspective of 1957, Kenneth Macgowan credited Baker's reputation with leading "more imaginative universities than Harvard into the establishment of curriculums in the theatre" ("Educational" 86). Stressing the degree to which theatre depended on its academic location for survival and economic viability, Macgowan noted that "not one commercial theatre has been built since the depression of 1929, but the universities and colleges have constructed at least 50" (86). Furthermore, he continued, "the 80 more or less 'legitimate'

Photograph by Pach

GEORGE PIERCE BAKER

Professor of Dramatic Literature at Harvard University. The man who broke the pedantic prejudice against teaching the modern drama. He has done much to bring the University and the Theatre together. He founded a course to instruct aspiring dramatists in the technique of the stage

Figure 4. George Pierce Baker. (From Percy MacKaye, "George Pierce Baker," *American Magazine* 73, Dec. 1911, p. 180.)

theatres of New York have shrunk to less than 30. The 5,000 theatres of the Road are now hardly 50. The 400 stock companies are gone. You all know too well that the heart of the living stage today is the educational theatre and, to a lesser degree, the community theatre" (87).

By the late 1930s and early 1940s, theatre had broken from both English and Speech departments into its own academic department. In Mary Anderson's *Drama in Education,* reports on the formation of Drama departments at English universities in the 1960s reveal how American universities were held up as models for the pioneering break toward "adult" autonomy for academics in theatre studies. The language reflects the uncomfortable relationship Drama had with English: The separation was understood to be an "escape," the site of departure was seen as a "parent." Furthermore, the academic theatre and the professional theatre, according to James Butler, had by the 1950s consolidated their relationship with such programs as Stanford University's Artists in Residence program in 1944. So extensive had the practice become that the May 1950 issue of *Theatre Arts* had a report devoted to the situation. One consequence of this new partnering was the hiring of theatre professionals, regardless of their academic qualifications, to teach in colleges and universities.

The increasing professionalization of Theatre departments and the double location of dramatic literature in English and Theatre can be traced to the influence of George Pierce Baker and the move from Harvard to Yale. According to Wisner Payne Kinne, as early as his freshman year at Harvard, George Pierce Baker was "more interested in acting than in what was acted, in the whole emotional appeal of the theatre than in the literary appeal of any particular drama. Indeed, he did not think of drama as literature" (16). Drama at Harvard originally had been connected to the teaching of elocution, but Henry Dixon Jones shifted the emphasis to an elective cultural subject and worked to legitimate theatre's literary and artistic spheres. When Jones failed in his bid to create a chair of elocution and drama, he left the university, leaving a place for Baker. Baker carried the belief that a play was a script for an actor and not a text for a reader with him into his classes in English 14, a study of English drama that had been offered first by Barrett Wendell. Initially Baker's concern was for English drama, and as a consequence, he accepted D. C. Heath's invitation in 1900 to contribute to the Belles-Lettres Series. By 1905 Baker had firmly established himself as one of the leading authorities on dramatic literature and created a literary foundation for the popular study of drama outside the university which would blossom before World War I under the leadership of the Drama League.

Kinne summarizes Baker's position from 1890s lectures: that there was no American drama, that the fault lay with the public and the playwrights, and that there had to be a demand for art as well as entertainment (68). After 1900, because Baker knew that the future of American drama was linked with universities and schools, not only did Baker acquire a theatre collection for Harvard by 1902 but also began to win support for the idea that a dramatic collection was an essential part of a national university's library (74). Despite Baker's commitment to acquiring play texts for the library, his pedagogical interest increasingly was focused on production. Kinne describes Baker's teaching playwriting at Radcliffe in 1903 and at Harvard in 1905–1906, under the rubric of English Composition, as a method for marking generic distinction. In order to expose his students to the irreconcilable difference between literature and drama, Baker had them reduce stories to scenarios to prove that the essence of drama was action and the essence of fiction was narrative. For Baker, Shakespeare was the exemplar of this difference, especially because he wrote for a nearly illiterate audience. Made Professor of Dramatic Literature in 1910 and able to take his theory to mature writers, Baker divided the theatre in half: a theatre of entertainment for the masses and a theatre of art for the cultured (138). That his stand provoked criticism is demonstrated in an article by Percy MacKaye for *The American Magazine* (1911). Because Baker represented both "dramatic craftsmanship in the university" and "university training in the theatre," "it is not strange that he has been called by the ultra-theatrical 'academic' and by the ultra-scholastic, 'sensational' " (181). Increasingly, Baker moved away from argumentation, his raison d'être at Harvard, and from dramatic literature to an interest in performance. According to Kinne, the turning point was marked by his self-designation as "Pageant master" in 1910, an obsession that would stay with him and culminate in his own effort, *The Pilgrim Spirit* (1921). As David Glassberg documents in *American Historical Pageantry* (1990), Baker's carefully researched dramatic story was lost in the spectacular lighting effects and Baker's effort became little more than an object lesson in the rise of the technology leading to the dominance of film.

Part of Baker's project at Harvard was the 47 Workshop, the place where plays written in the courses in dramatic technique at Harvard and Radcliffe could be tried out and in which amateurishness could be avoided. A collection of student work, published as *Plays of the 47 Workshop* (1918), was presented not as a contribution to American literature but as experimental work that, as the editors of *The Quarterly Journal of Speech Education* noted, "should be on the shelves of every dramatic club and little theatre library"

(Baker "47" 185). Established as a "laboratory" for dramatists and stage directors on the Abbey Theatre model, the 47 Workshop was itself a model for the Theatre Workshop of New York, the Playshop in Chicago, and the Vassar Workshop. That such "shops" had one foot in academe and the other in the community signals a move away from "fine art" toward "high craft," toward a large but informed audience, not just an academic one, and toward an experimental rather than a commercial theatre. The increasing movement away from what Harvard perceived as his immediate academic responsibilities toward the supplemental productions and his insistence on having a theatre, marked the beginning of Baker's break with that university.

Dramatic Technique, Baker's collection of essays originally delivered in 1913 before the Lowell Institute, Boston, contains the essence of his approach to the legitimation of performative value. For Baker, drama, that is, plays to be performed, was distinct from "closet drama," which was drama "intended primarily to be read" (1). (There was nothing new about Baker's distinction; English critics were making similar arguments.) Furthermore, Baker insisted that the drama was more greatly separated from the novel or short story than most would wish to acknowledge, offering, by way of proof, the fact that most dramatizations of fiction were failures, as were most novelizations of plays. To this he accredited the fact that, though the novel is highly personal, "the best drama is impersonal" (7). Rejecting the conflict model of drama as espoused by Ferdinand Bruntière and William Archer, Baker argues that "accurately conveyed emotion is the great fundamental in all good drama" (46). *Dramatic Technique* lives up to its title; Baker moves from proportion to characterization to dialogue, comparing drafts with finished texts, never troubling about the thematic content or social relevance of the finished play. As for language, Baker cautions against confusing style with concise, clear expression, calls for dialogue that is "emotionally significant," and advises against speech influenced by "the dramatic theories of the *litterati*" (314, 337). Repeatedly, Baker's concern is for the emotional impact on an audience, a condition that only could be tested in a theatre. A meticulous description of Baker's course noted that the three required texts for Baker's class were by Alfred Hennequin, William Thompson Price, and William Archer (McLaws 460).

In 1924 Baker left Harvard for Yale, which had promised him not only a department of drama but also the theatre that Harvard had denied him. Of the twelve courses offered in New Haven in the first semester, five were the courses Baker had offered at Harvard, three were in stage lighting, and the remainder, in costume and scene design, were extensions of fine arts courses. To dedicate his new theatre, Baker chose Boyd Smith's *The Patri-arch* over Eugene O'Neill's *Lazarus Laughed*. Yale Drama 37 had won over Harvard English 47. The three important consequences of Baker's shift from Harvard to Yale were: The students were all men, production took precedence over playwriting, and drama became aligned with theatre instead of English. Shortly after the move, in order to consolidate his theoretical position Baker proclaimed the necessity of having a theatre in every college and university.

In "The Theatre and the University" (1925), Baker created a chronology of the study of drama from the "timorous" inclusion of Shakespeare to the drama of the Restoration and the eighteenth century to the "inevitable" contemporary English drama to a demand by American students to learn how to write plays themselves – but, significantly, not for a course in which to study previous American drama. Dismissing "historical" courses that study "characterization" and "beauty of prose or verse," "matters which could as well be illustrated by the reading of some poems or of most novels," Baker pushed his preference for the theatrical art to a call for physical theatre as a necessary laboratory for students (99). As for the drama, it "has a strange history," occasionally being "a great spiritual force" and as infrequently, when "genius has touched it, drama has become literature" (105). There was no mistaking Baker's firm argument that the business of university Theatre departments was to teach the theatrical arts, including playwriting. Within this system, a work of American drama might become literature but only by random, unpredictable, and divine intervention.

Not everyone was sanguine about the future of American dramatic writing as it was managed by the professoriate. In "The Old Professor of English: An Autopsy," Fred Lewis Pattee, one of the champions of American literary independence, fussed that "never has there been a generation so thoroughly read in the drama and so painstakingly schooled in dramatic technique, and never has there been a period when the whole world has been so barren of original dramatic creation" (195). Complaining that the consequences were no more than "moving-picture melodrama and the slap-stick movie comedy," Pattee urged colleges to "ditch Shakspere [sic]" and give courses in "that small clear stream of living drama" (196). Silent on which playwrights were swimming in that favored stream, Pattee blamed the "old Teutonic curriculum" which focused on philology at the expense of the "esthetic beauty" being cultivated in college-trained poets, fiction writers, essayists, and critics (225).

For Baker, the theatre at Yale, endowed by Edward Harkness, was the last step in recognizing dramatic production as an "educational force" and as "Fine Art" (Baker "University" 105). Behind Baker's long struggle there was more at stake than just securing academic respectability and a disciplinary location or even economic advantages for a community of theatre practitioners. For many, the consequences of war created a sense of nationalist urgency. Fred Lewis Pattee, for instance, presented his *Century Readings for a Course in American Literature* (1924) as "a handbook on Americanism" for the years between 1607 and 1914: "Americanism should be made prominent in our school curriculum as a guard against the rising spirit of experimental lawlessness which has followed the great war" (v). In a sweeping cleansing of the fragile dramatic canon, Pattee deemed only parts of only two plays to be suitable for his enterprise: the last act of Godfrey's *The Prince of Parthia* and some acts of Royall Tyler's *The Contrast*. Even though Pattee had noted with some approval the "living drama" and even though he was a founding Americanist with a strong nationalist agenda, he did not see the study of American drama as particularly significant in the great enterprise.

Baker's Legacies

While the push had been on to get Baker his theatre, Walter Eaton had claimed, in one of the earliest issues of *Theatre Arts Magazine* (January 1919), that nothing less than "national reconstruction" after the war depended on having a national theatre. At first, Eaton toyed with the notion that the American disrespect for theatre, compared to German and Russian dedication, was only "racial," but then determined that what was needed was a nationwide community dramatic movement: "A national art consciousness, a national art unity, is the result, because the whole nation shares in the new national works of art, judges them, talks about them, is moved by them, at the same time and while they are yet fresh and vital. Such a condition is at present utterly impossible in America; and to the fact that it has so long been impossible I believe we can trace no little of our national indifference to vital drama, and our lack of a living relation to the theatre." America must, he concluded, "bend every effort to arrange for *simultaneous production* [my emphasis] of new, important, vital American plays, or plays of general interest and value, in as many, and as widely separated, communities as possible" ("Reconstruction" 12). To the modern ear, this call for simultaneous productions sounds like a call for movie theatres, especially given the astonishing implicit assumption in Eaton's utopian vision that all theatrical productions would be uniform, to say nothing of good, and thus effective in stimulating a reconstructed American nationalism predicated on communal values.

Given how much Eaton felt was at stake, it is no wonder that he so valued Baker. "More than any other one man in America," he wrote in 1919, Baker "has been responsible for the changed academic attitude toward the theatre." Until Baker, "the study of past drama led to philology, not play writing" ("Professor Baker" 478). By way of ocular proof, in 1925 Stanley McCandless drew up a map for *Theatre Arts Monthly* showing Baker's influence in the United States, designating the locations of all the teachers, directors, writers, critics, producers, and managers of little theatres who had come under his tutelage (see Figure 5). The new attitude toward theatre had consequences for the drama. In his brief history of the development of Yale's Department of Drama, Dixon Morton outlined the shift that had occurred at Harvard precisely because drama was not allowed to be a department: The shift was from, first, a course in the history of drama to, second, a course in playwriting to, finally, a workshop for production. By the time Baker was ensconced at Yale, the importance of the playwright was being balanced, if not overshadowed, by the importance of the producer, the designer, the costumer, and so on. The literary history "in detail" was left to the English curriculum, which, because it was offered as an undergraduate course, was not open to women (257).

The drama as text was not lost, of course. In fact, the expansion of public involvement in private and collective reading practices and in production as well as its place in academic study, whether within departments of drama or of literature, had a significant economic impact on the publishing industry. The extensive drama bookshop ads from stores all over the country in the professional journals testify to the extent of business. A survey of publishers and librarians in *The Drama* in 1921 documented the newly thriving industry's advances just within the decade. Houghton Mifflin, arguing that it required "a more sophisticated, more trained mind and imagination" to read plays than novels, boasted that for the first time a play, John Drinkwater's *Abraham Lincoln*, was the best-selling nonfiction work in the United States. Noting that the readership for plays was growing because of college courses, their "pioneer volume," Thomas H. Dickinson's *Chief Contemporary Dramatists*, was selling well. Little, Brown & Company revealed that it didn't pay any attention to drama until 1915, but that since that time the firm had had success with Montrose Moses's *The American Dramatist*, "the first book to deal comprehensively with the work of American dramatists," and with Margaret G. Mayorga's *Representative One-Act Plays by American Authors*, all of the plays in which previously had been

THE LEGEND OF THE MAP

The map above and the following list aim to show the widespread influence of Professor Baker's work at Harvard in our dramatic life. Neither map nor list can claim a final correctness or completeness but they have been compiled from the most authentic available sources. No attempt has been made to record the term of service in school or theatre because the chief intention of the map is to indicate the area of the influence. If the map were of the world instead of the United States, Shanghai, where Shen Hung has started a Little Theatre; Honolulu, where Mrs. F. R. Day and Mrs. F. H. Burnham have been active; Amsterdam, where the plays of Herman Roelvink are produced, and Paris, where Ralph Roeder has been Copeau's assistant stage manager, would be included. Map sketched by Stanley Russell McCandless.

ARKANSAS
TEACHER, J. R. Williams, U. of Ark.

ARIZONA
DIRECTOR, H. K. Behn, Phoenix Little Theatre ('22-'23).

CALIFORNIA
WRITERS, Winifred Hawkridge Dixon, *The Florist Shop;* Agnes Johnston Dazey and Vianna Knowlton, Hollywood.
TEACHERS AND DIRECTORS, Sam Hume, Irving Pichel and F. E. Glass at U. of Cal.

COLORADO
PLAYWRIGHT AND PRODUCER, Lute H. Johnston, Denver.

ILLINOIS
DIRECTOR AND TEACHER, Alexander Dean, Northwestern.
LITTLE THEATRE, Abby Merchant, Mark Reed, and J. A. Crafton, formerly of the Prairie Theatre; Mrs. C. B. Chorpenning, Hull House.
TEACHER, H. H. Hildebrand, U. of Ill.

INDIANA
TEACHER, Maurice D. Watkins, U. of Ind.; C. C. Mather, Culver Military Institute.

IOWA
TEACHER, W. B. Sowers, U. of Ia.

KANSAS
DIRECTOR AND TEACHER, J. A. Crafton, U. of Kan., see Vt. & Ill.

KENTUCKY
PLAYWRIGHT, Cleves Kinkead, *Common Clay.*

MASSACHUSETTS
(In Boston)
PLAYWRIGHTS, Florence Lincoln, *End of the Bridge;* Frederick L. Day, *Makers of Light;* Edward Massey, *Plots and Playwrights;* Eleanor Holmes Hinckley, *High Tide;* Josephine Preston Peabody, *The Piper;* Doris F. Halman, *Set the Stage for Eight;* T. P. Robinson, *The Skylark, Brook;* Katherine Searle, *Roderick's Career.*
CRITICS, W. E. Harris; William Brewster.

TEACHERS, Robert E. Rogers M.I.T.; Esther W. Bates, Boston U.; Alice H. Spaulding, Brookline High School.
DIRECTORS, Edward Massey, Boston Stage Guild; Angela Morris, Boston Theatre Guild, J. W. D. Seymour, Harvard Dramatic Club, Ruth Delano, Radcliffe Idlers; Virginia Tanner, Esther W. Bates, pageant directors.
ACTOR, John Collier.

(In State)
TEACHERS, Nannie L. Snydor, Arlington High School; E. B. Watson, Dartmouth; A. H. Gilmer, Tufts College; Katherine Clugston, House-in-the-Pines School, Norton; Violet B. Robinson, Wheaton College.
TEACHER AND DIRECTOR, Sam Eliot, Smith Workshop; F. E. Glass, formerly at Amherst, see Cal.
LITTLE THEATRE, Edward Mas-

continued

Figure 5. A map of these United States showing the influence of the work of George Pierce Baker (1890–1924). (Map by Stanley McCandless, *Theatre Arts Monthly* 9, Feb. 1925, pp. 106–08.)

sey, Playhouse on the Moors, see Boston.

MINNESOTA
DIRECTOR AND TEACHER, J. A. Crafton, formerly at Carleton College.

MISSOURI
LITTLE THEATRE AND CRITIC, R. P. Noble, Kansas City.

MONTANA
DIRECTORS, at U. of Mont. at various times, Alexander Dean, Roger Williams, J. M. Brown, Esther M. Bates, George Cronyn.

NEW HAMPSHIRE
PLAYWRIGHTS, Henry Carleton, *Up the Line;* William F. Manley, *The Crow's Nest,* Madison.

NEW YORK
(In New York City)
PLAYWRIGHTS, Kenneth Andrews, *The Year of the Tiger;* Philip Barry, *You and I, The Youngest;* Lewis Beach, *The Square Peg, The Goose Hangs High;* Frederick Ballard, *Believe Me, Xantippe;* Roscoe Brink, *Catskill Dutch;* Rachel Butler, *Mama's Affair;* Edward Dulaney Dunn, adapted *The Claw;* Rachel Field, *Three Pills in a Bottle;* Dorothy Kuhns Heywood, *Nancy Ann;* Sidney Howard, *Swords, They Knew What They Wanted;* Abby Merchant, *The New Englander;* Herman Hagedorn, *The Heart of Youth;* Eugene O'Neill; Percy MacKaye, *The Scarecrow,* etc.; Edward Knobloch, *Kismet;* Edward Sheldon,

Romance; Leila Taylor, co-author, *Voltaire;* Carola Bell Williams, *The Fairy Four Leaf;* J. V. A. Weaver, *Love 'Em and Leave 'Em;* Jules Eckert Goodman, *The Man Who Came Back;* Hubert Osborne, *Shore Leave.*

CRITICS, Robert C. Benchley, Heywood Broun, Van Wyck Brooks, David Carb, Walter Prichard Eaton, Kenneth Macgowan, Percival Reniers.

ACTORS, Mary Morris, Dorothy Sands, Ruth Chorpenning, Walton Butterfield, Albert Ward, George Abbott, Osgood Perkins, Kathleen Middleton, Ethel Woodworth.

DESIGNERS, Robert Edmond Jones, Lee Simonson, Donald Mitchell Oenslager, Rollo Wayne.

MANAGERS, Theresa Helburn, Kenneth Macgowan, Maurice Wertheim.

PRODUCERS, Winthrop Ames, Robert Edmond Jones, Agnes Morgan.

(In State)
TEACHERS, Rudolph W. Chamberlain, Syracuse U.

TEACHER AND LITTLE THEATRE, Gertrude Buck (died 1923), Vassar Workshop.

NORTH CAROLINA
TEACHER AND LITTLE THEATRE, Frederick H. Koch, Director of North Carolina Playmakers.

PLAYWRIGHT, Thomas Clayton Wolfe, *Welcome to Our City.*

NORTH DAKOTA
LITTLE THEATRE AND TEACHER, Frederick H. Koch, formerly at U. of North Dakota, see N. C.

OHIO
TEACHER AND PLAYWRIGHT, Percy MacKaye, see New York, Miami U., Oxford.

PENNSYLVANIA
TEACHER AND LITTLE THEATRE, Hubert Osborne, Director of Dramatics, Carnegie Institute, see N.Y.C.

TEACHER, Leon Pearson; Haverford College.

TEXAS
LITTLE THEATRE, Alexander Dean, Dallas, see Ill.

VERMONT
DIRECTOR AND TEACHER, Alice Spaulding, Rollo Wayne, D. M. Oenslager, J. A. Crafton, Middlebury.

VIRGINIA
LITTLE THEATRE, sometime directors, Richmond Little Theatre, Louise Burleigh, and A. P. Archer.

WASHINGTON, D. C.
TEACHER, W. N. Morse, formerly instructor of drama, Georgetown U.

WASHINGTON
TEACHER, Mrs. A. H. Ernst, U. of Wash., Seattle.

WEST VIRGINIA
LITTLE THEATRE, Percival F. Reniers, formerly director, Charleston.

WISCONSIN
TEACHER, A. R. Thompson, U. of Wis.

produced in Little Theatres. Librarians reported a similar growth, the secretary of the American Library Association claiming that the increase in the reading of plays was one of the "outstanding and significant features of library circulation during the last several years." He credited university courses such as that taught by Thomas Crosby at Brown and a popular course in public speaking at the University of Illinois as well as the work done by Little Theatres and the Drama League ("Books" *The Drama* 284–87).

Despite this growth in the market, there were still problems for dramatic literature as a complaint in *The Drama* (January 1921) revealed. Committing the journal to providing a "dignified medium" for the publication of plays, an editor noted that the writer of the one-act play had virtually no outlet for his work (Hinckley 139). Both *The Drama* and the *Theatre Arts Magazine* consciously set themselves up against the academic journals as well as trade journals. In "What We Stand For" in the first issue of *Theatre Arts Magazine* (May 1917), the editors positioned themselves as champions of the experimental groups, of new professionalism, of dedicated amateurism, and of "the development of a new body of poetic drama: poetic in content, but not seeking to escape contact with the world of to-day;

musical in expression, but not in the borrowed meters and measures of a dead past" (149).

In February 1927, at a national conference at Yale on the development of American theatre, Lee Simonson spoke of his belief in little groups and community theatres as the future source of indigenous American drama. This attitude was Baker's legacy; as Kinne observes, "from the mid-century viewpoint, it may seem that the renaissance which marked the twenties was decorative rather than literary, more productive of stage craft than of great plays" (Kinne 292). Baker's students, such as Stewart Chaney, Maurice Gnesin, and Elia Kazan, became designers, directors, and producers or, like Alistair Cooke, went into broadcasting. Not all of Baker's students met with success. As Kinne observes, "undoubtedly some of G.P.B.'s most effective teaching was achieved with such 'cures' of the itch to write plays as he administered to John Mason Brown, Heywood Broun, and Thomas Wolfe" (228).

The deliberate exclusion of women from Baker's long-range plans must be accounted a failing aspect of his legacy, for even though his most promising writers were women, Baker, around 1910, "became impatient that the preponderant interest in what he cared so much about was feminine" (Kinne 154). Most of his audience when he spoke publicly was female, specifically club women. In fact, Baker turned to a women's club, the MacDowell Club of New York, to fund a fellowship in playwriting at Harvard, "'for a student in dramatic composition, not in the history of drama'" (Kinne 155). That John Frederick Ballard, one of the first masters of arts, won the Craig prize and had a Broadway success with *Believe Me, Xantippe!*, proved to Baker that he would be instrumental in producing male playwrights for an American theatre that would be academic and educational rather than commercial and professional or amateurish and female. And amateurism was on the rise. An article in *The Drama* in 1917 heralded the "dramatic wave," the "universal desire for self-expression," which was "now breaking all over the country"; "so many magazines and dramatic associations are now offering prizes for the best one-act plays, that a new dramatic literature is swiftly being created in this country" (Hubbard 625–26). Baker needed to separate his students from this undifferentiated outpouring of self-expression. According to Kinne, the main forces of growth in the American theatre from 1913 to 1925 were from plays by three of Bakers's students: John Frederick Ballard, Edward Sheldon, and the team of Arnold Bennett and Edward Knoblock (179). This conscious effort to establish playwriting as a masculine as well as an academic enterprise clearly is linked to related fears about the intrusive and threatening presence of women in the teaching profession. This fear has been amply documented; one example will suffice. In a lengthy diatribe in the *Educational Review* in 1914, "The Woman Peril in American Education," F. E. Chadwick, protective of the American masculine energy needed to build, command, manufacture, fight, steer, and tunnel, insisted that the women who had taught boys had an "unconsciously destructive influence" and already had produced a "feminized manhood, emotional, illogical, non-combative against public evil" (115).

American Drama in the Curriculum

American drama, for all that it was the straggling ugly duckling of American literature, sometimes was included in the struggle to gain a significant place for American literature in the curriculum. It is not surprising that drama would figure prominently in Arthur Hobson Quinn's efforts to establish American literature as a subject for graduate study; in his survey of seventeen institutions in 1922, he found that "so far as forms of literature are concerned, the drama and the novel, especially the former, have been emphasized" ("American" 13). However, he observed an imbalance in the *Cambridge History of American Literature*, namely, that the bibliography of American theatre is "vast" while that of the drama is "scant," but he saw the greatest hindrance to graduate study in American dramatic literature in the lack of library resources. Quinn noted that the courses at Pennsylvania and Chicago owed their inspiration to the existence of special libraries and hoped that the Wendell Collection of American Plays at Harvard would have a similar impact. In his summation, Quinn lamented that "the present situation in the field of American drama is an example to university libraries and English departments. Due to an almost universal disregard of what had been accomplished in the field of American playwriting, universities had remained quiescent, while private collectors acquired material which now has reached almost prohibitive prices" ("American" 14–15). Even less sanguine, Ferner Nuhn, in his survey "Teaching American Literature in American Colleges" (1928), observed that American literature received only as much attention as Scandinavian literature and that though one-third of the courses in History departments were devoted to America, only one in twenty-five were in English departments. As for American drama, he complained, not even O'Neill was included in Ohio State University's contemporary drama class.

In 1936 Howard Mumford Jones described American literature as "the orphan child of the curriculum" though he insisted that "I do not read my

American literature narrowly. Though the older books confined literature to *belles lettres* (and that within a small compass), the newer treatment of the subject ranges more widely; it includes materials by the pioneers, it includes folk song and ballad; it includes the drama . . ." (386). William Crane and the compilers of *American Literature in the College Curriculum* (1948) point to the fact that by this time virtually every university and college was offering courses in American literature. In the survey courses none of the dominating thirty-seven authors, from Emerson to Cather, was primarily a playwright, but modern drama was the most frequently offered course that included American writers. Forty-three percent gave half the course time to American plays and 33 percent allotted one-third. "Aesthetic appreciation" was the most common method of approach. While this emphasis on drama might appear surprising given its troubled history in the curriculum, it must be placed in perspective; the most frequently offered elective course devoted entirely to American literature was the American novel (W. Crane 27–29). The compilers predicted a future condition, a "fluid state" of interdepartmentalism, because the most noticeable trend in the teaching of American literature from 1938 to 1948 was the creation of American studies programs. American drama, however, would not be rescued by American studies. As David Shumway points out in *Creating American Civilization* (1994), although "American studies took as its object American culture . . . [they] did not radically transform the academic field of American literature. Rather, they contributed to the course of development that the field was already bound to take" (217). And though the literature itself might have been placed in a larger context, the focus remained largely on the established literature.

In October 1949, George R. Kernodle, then at the State University of Iowa, raising the issue of integrating theory and practice in theatre studies in *Educational Theatre Journal*, initiated a discussion that recurred in the journal for years to follow. Blaming Harvard for its unsupportive attitude toward Baker and noting that "our dramatic arts departments have mostly arisen because of the appalling lack of interest in the English departments," Kernodle pointed to Yale mediaevalist Karl Young's indifference to practice and to his privileging of theory as symptomatic (82). Given that drama was now the provenance of Theatre departments, Kernodle was anxious that it should be treated correctly, that is, "as an art of performance" (85). Kernodle's first move was to align the study of theatre with the study of science, especially medicine, and with masculinity as "a subject worthy of man's study." Calling on the laboratory model, Kernodle wanted to generate principles that could be tested in practice. Kernodle's second strategical maneuver was to shield theatre from the undermining "long-standing prejudice against the sensuality of the arts and the high prestige of anything that can be called abstract and intellectual" (83). Certainly, "we must combat the neo-intellectuals who respect a play only for words, which can be studied on the printed page, or ideas which can be analyzed philosophically" (81). Kernodle's piece was only the first in the extended discussion that continued into the mid-1950s and that drew responses from Edwin Burr Pettet, William W. Melnitz, Norman Philbrick, and Samuel Selden.

Edwin Burr Pettet of Carleton College responded in 1949 about the dislocation of drama from the liberal arts curriculum. His take on the decline of drama was that it had been decimated by disciplinary divisions within the college. He located the moment of separation in the 1920s when liberal arts colleges added Speech and/or Drama departments and theatre lost its identity as an essential component of academic study in the liberal arts because "the English department whirlpool sucked in" Shakespeare and English dramatic literature, the Romance languages took Pirandello, Racine, et al., and Classics took the Greeks (109). As a consequence, "either because of an assumption that all dramatic literature was forever lost to them or because of a lack of scholarship and the ability to teach content courses, many theatre teachers set up curriculums featuring Scenic Design, Make-up, Radio Workshop, etc." (110). In Pettet's version, the hapless, disempowered drama teacher who might be left in the English department was generally "down-the-nosed" by his colleagues and was pushed into practical crafts courses and forced into mere play production, itself tainted by the push for box office popularity (110).

In 1951, William W. Melnitz joined the discussion with an article extolling the virtues of Max Herrmann's *Theaterwissenschaft* (Science of the Theatre Arts), which had first been given as lectures in 1900 and which later had flourished in Berlin, Cologne, and Munich with simultaneous publications in 1949 by his disciple, Hans Knudsun, and Carl Niessen and Artur Kutscher. According to Herrmann, within *Theaterwissenschaft* drama is considered only as "the subject for performance" and "the essential goal of all scientific endeavor applied to the theatre's past is 'reconstruction'" (135–36). Knudsun, Niessen, and Kutscher had their intradisciplinary differences, but, as Melnitz points out, they agreed that "the sun around which *Theaterwissenschaft* revolves is the theatre, and not the drama, which must be viewed as literature, inherently and historically" (137). Melnitz's stated objective was to make *Theaterwissenschaft* "not strange" to his readers, pointing to the writings of stage designers such as Simonson, Jones, and Bel Geddes as commendably precise (141). Praising the "thoroughness of the scholarly approach that measures the ultimate value of studies in the science of Theatre Arts," Melnitz cites two of "the best American books in our field," George C. D. Odell's *Shakespeare from Betterton to Irving* and H. M. Hillebrand's *Edmund Kean* (140–41).

While Norman Philbrick's outline for a graduate program in drama in 1953 is directed largely at the theatre practitioner rather than the scholar in dramatic literature, his proposed curriculum addresses the split between theatre and drama that marked higher education. He takes sharp exception to Melnitz's argument that drama and theatre are so different that they cannot be part of the same discipline: "The alarming aspect of this discipline is that the theatre is the core of it, and not the drama, which Mr. Melnitz notes, is to be 'viewed as literature, inherently and historically.' He says that the stress must be on *theatre* in the study of drama. I insist that drama should not be sacrificed for the sake of the theatre. Composition written for contemplation in the study is a fragile thing which cannot bear the brunt of translation to the theatre. *Drama* contains the heart of the dramatist, his mind, his intention, his belief, his sense of values, his judgment of man" (96–97). Arguing that the current practice of separating completely "academic discipline and artistic accomplishment" is "patently absurd," Philbrick deplored the relegation of the study of drama to the English department, "where they assume, oftentimes erroneously, that drama is unmasked and its iambs are numbered" (93–95). In summation, Philbrick called for a reintegrative graduate program in which "the principles and mechanics of theatre and drama can be correlated with the philosophical, historical, and sociological disciplines" (98).

But Philbrick's proposal only elicited a distressed response from Samuel Selden a year later. In "Academic Shadows on the American Theatre," Selden voiced his concern that while Philbrick's outline "is extremely articulate about the scholarly side," it was "quite vague about the creative" (103–104). Selden worried that although American theatre had yet to have a Golden Age, "one might refer to the drama of the vigorous 1920's as having an argent glow" (97). Troubled by what he saw as a decline in quantity as well as quality, Selden argued that "serious drama – not just tragedies but also comedies of thought and the warmth of the human heart – have mostly vanished from the American scene" (97). For this he blamed the universities because they shaped the skills and mind of the theatre apprentice, a man, according to Selden, now so "ridden by the incubus of conformity – conformity to ideas of sacrosanct 'authorities' that his primary attention was no longer focused on *feeling*" (100–102). Selden's insistence on the primacy of an emotional theatre clearly was linked to his assertion that American playwrights "have seldom concerned themselves very long with international or even national matters. The principal interest in drama has always been, and will always be, in individuals – individuals in family groups, individuals in small sections of society" (99). Ultimately, Selden's concern was for the playwright, not the historian or critic of drama, and, intentionally invoking Benedetto Croce and inadvertently echoing Hiram Corson and George Pierce Baker, Selden insisted that the American play-wright should be intuitive, not rational, and should see only with "the eye of innocence" (103).

The extended debate in *Educational Theatre Journal* did not resolve the academic fate of drama, let alone American drama, and only thirty years after Walter Eaton's heralding Baker's 47 Workshop as the birthplace of American drama, Kenneth Macgowan could ask, "What has happened to the hundreds of students who took the courses that followed English 47? Why have so few of them seen their plays on Broadway? And why have so few of their plays been produced by the universities?" ("Educational" 87). The leading contemporary dramatists such as Miller, Williams, Anderson, and Inge, though educated at universities, were not products of playwriting courses. Macgowan blamed not the writers for being lured away by radio, television, and film but the universities for reproducing rather than produc-ing new plays and for placing too much emphasis on the history and literature of drama in graduate courses than on theatrical practice. In an address to the American Educational Theatre Association, Alan S. Downer took exception to Macgowan's position, at the same time dryly observing that though it ought to be a symbol of how the liberal arts and the creative arts were drawing closer, the fact that he was, within the space of six hours, also addressing the Modern Language Association, only made him more aware of the separateness of the two academic worlds. Reading drama, analyzing drama, and "most of all writing drama," were for Downer "the disciplines which seem to me proper for an academy of liberal arts." Theatrical production could provide "the opportunity for personal expres-sion," but historical context, esthetic study of dramatic literature, and philosophic value were essential for the academic "secure platform." Downer gave an Arnoldian shudder at the thought that "the best that has been thought and said" would be dropped in order to perform an untested new play. Better, he suggested, in educational theatre that the main stage largely be given to canonized works and a "workshop stage" be the site for student experimentation ("Pedant" 97–98).

Taking a similar line about the responsibility of universities to turn out America's new playwrights and arguing for academic training, John Gassner, in "The Meaning and Scope of Playwriting Study," suggested that America could have better playwrights than it had had to date if playwriting were reimagined as a humanistic study instead of a professional discipline, in other words, that it be understood as one of the liberal arts. Thus repositioned, "it need never be the barely tolerated stepchild of the graduate faculty, regarded as a narrow and frequently barren craft-speciality or relegated to the rumpus-room of the academic mansion as a sub-standard and rather trivial avocation" (170). Pointing an accusatory finger at America's "would-be" playwrights as "too uninformed and too limited in mental range for a sustained career on any level of distinction," Gassner reasoned that America's playwrights had been the "crude est" [sic] and "most vigorous" of the century (170). True genius can withstand the leveling effects of a traditional education, Gassner argued, adding that there was the additional benefit of producing wide literary capabilities that, by implication, would be advantageous for American literature in general: "Among American playwrights alone who have books of fiction and nonfiction to their credit one could list such known writers as Sherwood Anderson, Behrman, Rice, Williams, and Miller. There are also playwrights who became more successful as writers of fiction than as writers for the stage; Irwin Shaw is the best known among these" (171).

In a paper for the Symposium on the Responsibility of the Universities to the Theatre in 1951 at the University of Bristol, site of Britain's first Department of Drama established in 1947, Sawyer Falk, describing Drama departments in American universities, observed that given the report of the Oxford Drama Commission and Granville-Barker's lecture "Drama in Education" presented at Princeton, "it would seem that any account of drama departments in American universities would have to be a justification if not an actual apologia" (8). The Oxford Commission had embraced Granville-Barker's charge that the student of drama was in danger of losing himself to "devotional" involvement in performance if he were engaging in a production instead of maintaining a "detached," scholarly engagement with the text. By repeatedly asserting that drama was the simplest of the arts and that even though the lessons to be learned from drama could now go beyond the old rhetorical exercises, Granville-Barker observed that the elements of drama, concise writing, clear speaking, and appreciative listening found their place in early education (32). Arguing that drama is a respectable academic subject, Falk insisted on two principles: that there were legitimate relations to the cultural purpose of a university and that "the acted-out play on stage before an audience is the basic dynamics of such a study" (8). In pursuing his theme, that drama was not taught for vocational ends in American universities, Falk pointed to the essential division of study into "content" (literature, history, and criticism) and "performance," which he analogized to the working of calculus problems in a math class. As to the second principle, he observed that the primary emphasis on production, a priority he traced back to Brander Matthews and George Pierce Baker, led to the focus on the creative, rather than the literary or scholarly, aspects of study.

In the same symposium and agreeing with Falk that "if drama is regarded as literature, then a play comes to be regarded as a book, a thing to be read not seen," Nevill Coghill, in "The Study of Drama at a University," argued for a lesser status, that is, a Department rather than a Faculty of Drama (43). He reasoned that "the drama, even more than a literature, depends for its understanding on intuitive power and must involve a greater number of subjective judgments not amenable to the discipline of thought in any convincing way. Dramatic utterance is more dominated by style and quality than by philosophic reasoning . . . the drama is a less rigorous intellectual training than literature. Secondly, compared to literature and above all to history, the drama is discontinuous" because it appears and disappears in bursts, that is, in Greece, Rome, medieval Christendom, Renaissance Europe, and modern times and is too "patchy" and "spasmodic." In conclusion, Coghill argued that a Department of Drama could be envisaged as "ancillary" to literary studies (47).

Troubles plagued the production side as well. In an effort to track the progress of American drama as it was represented by play production in American universities, beginning in 1950 *Educational Theatre Journal* ran a series of reports on play selection. These reports serve as another index of the troubled locus of American drama in higher education and the response of theatre and drama professionals to the perceived lack of cultural value for their subject. Although, not surprisingly, Shakespeare emerges as the most produced playwright until, for the first time, in the 1963–1964 season, an American playwright, Edward Albee, headed the list. However, the 1961 survey, reported on by Thomas Shank, reveals that the most produced plays were American, which causes Shank to charge university play selection with being "provincial." This charge is a little severe because, in fact, the list shows that among the most produced playwrights are Anouilh, Giraudoux, and Shaw; what Shank means by "provincial" is that a little over half the plays are American. But this idea that to produce a substantive number of American plays in an American university, without examining what was transpiring in, for instance, a German or French university, was "provincial" persisted and smacked of rank Europhilic elitism. In Alan A. Stambusky's five-year report for 1966, he noted that "in terms of production of plays by country, the United States continues to dominate the field, with more plays and total number of productions of plays by native writers than by any other country" (Stambusky "Production" 123). In fact, the taste for American drama was so pervasive, Stambusky lamented, that "the apparent overall apathy towards the production of foreign plays is deplorable" (Stambusky "America First" 136).

The Taint of Emotion

Of all the problems standing in the way of American drama being fit into the higher-education curriculum – the early extracurricular status of performance, the increasing devaluation of oratory and rhetoric, the slipperiness of the genre, the problematic cultural capital of American drama and theatre, the thick Anglophilianism of American literary study, the territorial struggle with Theatre departments, the thematic prevalence of politics at the expense of "poetry" – the most insurmountable would seem to have been the taint of emotion coloring drama in general and American drama in particular. This emotionalism, inevitably linked to the histrionic and the "feminine," was also linked to childhood if not also childishness. A history of "dramatic action" in the British elementary and secondary school systems, Gavin Bolton's *Drama as Education* (1984), demonstrates that drama in education had long been tainted with what Bolton calls "the legacy of preciousness" and with "child-centeredness and self-expression" (6–9). As for the primary focus of drama in education, Bolton complains that the influential Brian Way, an associate of the equally influential Peter Slade, had taken teachers away from dramatic context and that in the 1950s and 1960s they had stressed speech and mime over text. Bolton's concern is relevant to the situation of American drama in education because it recalls Emma Sheridan Fry's "Educational Dramatics" and because it turns up in revisionist approaches to the curriculum. The old assertions that drama is a simple form directed at the most basic and unsophisticated responses fed into the new rationales and allowed James Moffatt, in *Teaching the Universe of Discourse* (1968), to place drama not only at the center but also at the first level of his pedagogical structure for elementary and high schools: "Drama is the most accessible form of literature for young and uneducated people. It is made up of action. . . . Drama is primitive" (63–64).

This stage in the development of American drama in the curriculum was conditioned by the contact with British educators in the fifties that culminated in the month-long seminar in 1966 at Dartmouth College on the teaching of English. According to Applebee,

> the aspect of British programs which surprised most Americans, both at Dartmouth and during the study of British schools, was the emphasis on drama. . . . In a sense the dramatic response is the antithesis of the analytic, content-oriented teaching of English against which the British were in the process of reacting. At the same time, drama is the embodiment of the role playing and experiment which are part of the British pedagogy of growth. To take part in a drama is to take on at least for a moment new linguistic, social, and personal roles, and to do so with all the protection of self that the acknowledged "playing" in drama affords. . . . Concern with a literary heritage played virtually no role, being dismissed as irrelevant or redefined as a "legacy of past satisfactions." (230–31)

In *Drama in the English Classroom* (1966), one of the papers presented at the Dartmouth conference, Douglas Barnes of the University of Leeds insists not only on the separation of the "non-dramatic activity," that is, literary study, from "dramatic interpretation" but also from the theatre, that is, an audience (9). "Dramatic interpretation" is symbolic, nonverbal, imaginative, emotional, attitudinal, primal, and preliterary. This probably has had more serious consequences for the teaching of writing in the American academy than for the teaching of drama; nonetheless drama continues to be associated not with rational expression but with solipsistic emoting. Recently, for instance, the English theatre critic Benedict Nightingale complained of the American stage that there are "just too many diaper dramas" (133). Martin Esslin concurs, observing that in America one "goes to the more 'serious' plays above all to be immersed in a steambath of *emotion*, and not to be made to think" ("Dead!" 27). These comments, of course, are part of the ongoing discourse about American drama I have documented in Chapter 1 on generic hegemony.

What is clear even from this cursory review of the multiple positions of dramatic literature is that it often, far more than any other literary genre, inhabits a borderland between the scholarly and the creative disciplines and, as well, between academic and public enterprises, between professional and amateur performance, between emotional and scientific expression. The borderlines are blurred, and it is impossible to locate absolutely the value of American drama as cultural capital except to suggest that it has very little institutional or disciplinary power. What is certain is that just as the study of literature had less prestige than the study of hard sciences in universities, dramatic literature in general, with the notable exception of Shakespeare, and American literature in particular, carried and continues to carry less intellectual weight in English departments relative to other genres and less prominence in Theatre departments that must separate themselves from philology by emphasizing performance. An American play, freighted with the multiple flaws of being dramatic and performative, of being American, of being debatably "masculine," and of being the vehicle for childish self-expression and emotion, clearly was doomed to a hardscrabble existence in higher education from the start. To the extent to which high-cultural legitimation and canon creation and conservation were understood to be the work of education, especially higher education, the fate of American dramatic literature exemplifies the struggle to legitimate hierarchies and consolidate power along disciplinary and departmental lines, and the alarming degree to which a rich body of literary and cultural material can be shunted aside when it does not seem to serve narrowly conceived ideological ends.

5

Caught in the Close Embrace

Sociology and Realism

In "AMERICAN DRAMA VERSUS LITERATURE" (1938), Walter Prichard Eaton tackled the vexed issue of American drama's literary value by beginning with Homer E. Woodbridge's assessment of Quinn's *Representative American Plays* (1923) as "'depressing.'" To Woodbridge's conclusion that "to get up much interest in the American theater before O'Neill one must consider it from the historical or sociological point of view," Eaton quite sensibly asked, "Well, why not? Is it not perhaps true that in our study of the drama, certainly our academic study, we have put an emphasis on the literary side which neither the nature of the drama nor the function of the theater wholly warrants, and dismissed as unworthy of study much which, properly considered, is interesting and important? . . . Literary charm is an accident, or overtone, of drama, not its end. The end of drama is the emotional excitation of an audience in a theater" ("Drama" 81–82). If, Eaton asked, literary permanence depends on "romantic timelessness of theme" and on "a heightened speech which transcends its own hour," how could the "realistic plays characteristic of our generation" survive (83)? Of course, in many literary histories and the canon such plays have not survived, and as a consequence a vital link between charged historical incidents and their dramatization has been obscured.

The very qualities that made modern drama powerful, its journalistic thrust and conversational vernacular, Eaton argued, ironically were the same characteristics that made it vulnerable: "The better [realistic plays] met the exacting test of realism, the slighter were their survival chances; . . . its vital appeal and its great creative dignity was its newly found technical ability to comment seriously on the contemporary scene, to be

159

a weapon, consciously employed, of social criticism, and even of reform"
(83). If American drama could not be expected to endure as literature
because it lacked thematic universals and rhetorical energy, then it also
could not be judged later by any ordinary academic or literary standards.
Eaton concluded that "it can only be estimated fairly by taking, in Professor Woodbridge's phrase, 'the historical or sociological point of view,'
and also, I fear the theatrical point of view – something which, alas, too
many academic critics are incapable of doing" (86). By way of demonstration, Eaton went after one of the plays in Quinn's collection, *Rip
Van Winkle*, Dion Boucicault's vehicle for the actor Joseph Jefferson. Eaton dismissed the minimal plot and banal dialogue but stressed the fact
that "from 1865 until after 1900, Jefferson played Rip in every city in the
land; to see him was part of the education of every American child. . . .
From the point of view of American cultural history, this play can hardly
be ignored" (88).

To strengthen his argument about the need to approach American
drama from a sociocultural rather than a literary perspective, Eaton put
aside the traditional idea of a printed text and took up Negro minstrels,
about which he remarked, "In any serious study of the drama as a literary
art, the minstrels have, I'm sure, no recognition." Arguing for their importance as a critical conditioning experience for American theatre audiences,
Eaton noted that "for at least two decades the Negro minstrels were
undoubtedly the most widely popular form of entertainment in America"
(90). Both of Eaton's claims, that "they were based on a realistic observation
of Negro life" and that "there was no hint of literary creation about them,
no likeness to the classic repertoire," should be sharply contested and
carefully contextualized; but what matters here are Eaton's broad parameters, his sociohistorical grounding for the study of American drama, his
concern for the dramatizations of Negroes and Indians, and his insistence
on intertextuality. If Eaton's criteria were to be followed, they would set up
a new paradigm for valuing and studying American drama. By way of
example, Eaton argued that John Augustus Stone's *Metamora* ought to be
read with an awareness of its parodic version, John Brougham's *Pocahontas*,
as well as with a knowledge of the tempering influence the parody had had
on Dion Boucicault's *The Octoroon*. Eaton also suggested a triangulation
among the Negro minstrel shows, *Uncle Tom's Cabin*, and *The Octoroon* as
a subject for study.

In his summation, Eaton challenged the literary approach to American
drama and argued that plays could not be appreciated unless they were
considered in their

social, historical, and above all their theatrical setting. Hence it is that the study of drama solely, or chiefly, from the printed text and the literary point of view not only results in failure to understand many interesting and important examples of playmaking, but actually sometimes in distortion of the real progression and direction of dramatic art. . . . In America the future was not with Boker's *Francesca*, which has definite literary merits, but with *Mose the Fireman*, the Negro minstrels, and *Yankee Hill*. In fact, to study the history of drama from a collection of the literary highlights of various periods may very easily result in missing almost completely the true line of evolution, and never seeing the sources of even the master works themselves. (96–97)

Eaton concluded with an explicit statement of what had been implicit in his entire essay, namely that "literature" educates the audience, is written in heightened language, and transcends temporal reality, whereas native American "drama" entertains its audience, is written in the colloquial vernacular, and stimulates an emotional response through verisimilitude. According to his judgmental reasoning, literature has a self-sustaining life that can be enhanced by critical reception, but the drama automatically dies unless selectively salvaged by compartmentalization in sociocultural studies.

Emergent Sociology

The problem of Eaton's insistence on the primacy of emotion as the desired effect of drama aside, the next question must be, why didn't the sociocultural studies approach advocated by Eaton displace the dismissive tyranny of literary criticism? A partial answer may lie in the way in which drama and theatre were approached by sociologists. One place to look is at the drama reviews of Melvin J. Vincent for the *Journal of Applied Sociology* from 1924 to 1957. But to understand why a sociologist was reviewing not theatrical productions but plays as literature for an academic sociology journal, one has to go back to the beginnings of sociology as an academic discipline in American universities. In a recent and substantive history of the discipline, *The Origins of American Social Science* (1991), Dorothy Ross traces the development of American social sciences from their origins in the movement away from religion, metaphysical speculation, and moral philosophy toward independent, secular natural science, a movement that was also committed to a progressive politics of American exceptionalism. The split between science and speculation conditioned the split between science and literature. (That this split was also gendered had implications for the drama, which I discuss in Chapter 4.) Of the social scientists' insistence on establishing which principles of the social order were true, Ross writes, "Realism helped to set American social science on a deliberately 'masculine' course. Disdaining romantic fantasy, realism abandoned the subjective authorial voice for the objective things in themselves. In the gendered language of Victorian culture, hard facts and hard science were masculine, and sentiment, idealism, and the imaginative constructions of literature were feminine" (59). The implication was that the political authority of social scientists was based on their disinterested objectivity and was directed toward improving social conditions.

Sociology, a new discipline, struggled to legitimate itself by insisting that it was both a hard science with a scientific methodology as well as a constructive social philosophy of human welfare. Wolf Lepenies in *Between Literature and Science: The Rise of Sociology* (1985) traces the way in which the field legitimated itself by distinguishing itself from the literary arts and by identifying with the sciences. This did not preclude the study of the arts, however; in fact, it was imperative that sociologists prove the all-embracing scope of their discipline in order to claim authority. As a developing field, sociology was competing for recognition and territory with other disciplines, notably psychology and political science, but there was also a struggle within the emergent discipline among several factions proposing variant methodologies. One way in which sociologists authorized their discipline was by gradually abandoning evolutionary social theory, that is, the precepts of Spencerian and Darwinian evolutionary biology, and by taking up instead the argument that culture was determined by superorganic phenomena such as public opinion, education, and ceremonies. This opened the way for domination by the other strain of sociological thinking, which existed before 1900, the "humanist-reformist Social Science" body, as Hamilton Cravens describes it (8). According to Cravens, although sociologists in the 1890s looked to the individual physiological psychology posited by William James in *The Principles of Psychology* (1890), they shifted their attention to the social group and broke with psychology in 1909 to argue for the complete autonomy of the discipline and for a cultural rather than a psychological or naturalistic approach. By the 1920s, empirical sociologists, dependent on statistics, marked an even greater separation from the earlier commitment to a philosophical and theoretical approach.

Albion Small, the founder of America's first department of sociology at the University of Chicago in 1893 and of the first journal of the new discipline, *The American Journal of Sociology*, in 1895, embodied several of the strains of early sociology: the strong ethical bent of a moral philosopher concerned with gradual reformist social action predicated on comprehensive structures and a codified understanding of what he called the six "human interests" – health, wealth, sociability, knowledge, beauty, and righteousness. Concerned with conflicts of interest and classes in human society, Small, as he explained in *An Introduction to the Study of Society* (1894), aligned himself more closely with German scientific historians than with Lester F. Ward, whose monist and social psychological theories of sociology developed from Comte. Small's conflict model was drawn in large measure from the Austrian Gustav Ratzenhofer, who emphasized the creation of a nation-state out of common goals. Small amplified upon this idea in *General Sociology* (1905) and postulated that "natural life is conflict, but it is conflict converging toward minimum conflict and maximum cooperation and sociability," an idea compatible with Small's Christianity and his reformist goals (371). Two of Small's chroniclers, Vernon Dibble and George Christakes, note that Small's moderate political progressivism died around the time of the New Deal and that his attempt to synthesize a detached scientific methodology with an impassioned ethics to achieve a Spencerian "equilibrium of a perfect society" also broke down.

His ultimate failure notwithstanding, Small had a profound impact on the discipline he had articulated and professionalized as well as on the ways in which Americans looked at themselves. In his editorial debut in *The American Journal of Sociology* (July 1895), Small wrote that in an age in which "human association is more obtrusive and relatively more influential than in any previous epoch . . . perception of subjection to human devices or of advantage to be won by personal combinations becomes decisive." The ranchman, the miner, the manufacturer, and the mill operative "learn to disregard the fixed factors in human relations, and instead to watch other players in the game of life as exclusively as opponents at the chessboard or rival teams on the gridiron or diamond. Through influences such as these it comes about that the fact of human association becomes a most intimate reality" ("Era" 1–2). Small, desirous of introducing "discipline" into this "social self-consciousness" and of remaining "true to life," insisted that "the aim of science should be to show the meaning of familiar things" and not to obscure the familiar "under an impenetrable disguise of artificial expression" ("Era" 14). His characterization of social interactions as the "antithesis of individuals" stimulating each other "through the medium of conflicting wants" resulting in "self-assertion" by the individuals and the creation of a "system of dominance" strikingly parallels most dramatic situations.

In *An Introduction to the Study of Society* (1894), Albion Small and his co-author, George E. Vincent, the vice-chancellor of the Chautauqua

System of Education, had argued for the building of theatres as one culminating act of advanced social progress, supplanting evolution with "specifically educational agencies in the community" (157). They mapped the progression from schoolhouse tableaux through amateur dramatic association to professional theatre as paralleling similar moves in the creation of public libraries, art galleries, and colleges. For Small and Vincent, theatre was the form that satisfied many of the six "human interests" on which Small based his theory of progressive social cohesion because theatre was a "form of sociability," was a "means of increasing knowledge," was "conducive to aesthetic cultivation," and was a way to teach "ethical lessons" (176). This idea of social desirability would persist. For instance, in "The Rise of Amateur Drama" (1917), the sentiments of a professor at Teachers' College, Fargo, North Dakota, an agricultural college, reveal how far from literature and how near to progressive sociology the drama had come: "The real purpose is to use the drama, and all that goes with the drama, as a sociological force in getting people together and acquainted with each other, so that they may find out the hidden life forces of Nature itself" (Hubbard 628). Attentive to their reformist intentions, Small and Vincent also stressed the need to stimulate an individual's social consciousness, to remind him perpetually that "every social act is consciously performed," so that he might disrupt passive acceptance of authority and modify it for a positive influence (329–30).

Melvin J. Vincent: The Sociologist Reviews Drama

Although Small had laid out the theoretical path for a sociological approach to drama, plays were not reviewed nor was drama, either as literature or as performance, considered in *The American Journal of Sociology*. Indeed, with three exceptions – "The Fine Arts as a Dynamic Factor in Society" (March 1907); "The Folkway of Art: An Analysis of the Social Theories of Art" (September 1938); and "The Relationship of Literature and Art" (1954) – the arts in general were ignored in *The American Journal of Sociology*. The sustained practice of reviewing dramatic texts as sociological texts was begun in 1924 by Melvin J. Vincent, who announced his goals in "Fiction, Drama, and Sociology" in the *Journal of Applied Sociology* in which he also briefly reviewed Laurence Stallings's *Plumes*, Hatcher Hughes's *Hell-Bent Fer Heaven*, and Lewis Beach's *The Goose Hangs High*. Given that Vincent, a specialist in industrial sociology, would be virtually the journal's sole reviewer of American drama for the next thirty-three years, concluding with a review of Eugene O'Neill's *Long Day's Journey into Night* in July/August 1957, his premises about the function of his own discipline in analyzing the value of drama are worth noting. Furthermore, Vincent demonstrated a remarkable consistency: A survey of his reviews proves that his attitudes and principles remained unaltered by time, changes in the drama, or even sociology, for that matter. Of the seventy-seven reviews, all but five were on American drama and all the reviews were of published texts, not of theatrical productions. At least in the *Journal of Applied Sociology* (which became *Sociology and Social Research* in 1927 when it merged with the *Bulletin of Social Research*), American dramatic texts were being treated as works of literature rather than of performance albeit for specifically socio-logical ends. But why would a sociologist concern himself at all with the form?

Vincent argued that the ultimate aim of the social scientist was to perceive the drama of life more exactly than by simple observation in order to improve the social order and to rebuild a defective society. Where better to turn for a close analysis, he asked, than to the arts? "Art has been held by its followers to this regenerative task, and sociology has recognized this by acclaiming that which is true art to be a definite factor in social progress. Particularly, in the field of fiction and in that of drama the sociologists may well look to see what materials of human experiences have already been gathered" ("Fiction" 124). Vincent cites Shaw on drama as "the most effec-tive means of moral propagandism" but seems not to recognize any contra-diction when he goes on to insist that "the serious purposes of dramatists reveal the true function of a socialized theatre," which is objectively to mirror troubled social conditions ("Fiction" 125). In all the reviews that followed, Vincent equated everything from modest social satire to leftist propaganda with scientific scrutiny and reformist purposiveness. He never distinguished between art and reality and never supposed that a play could have been written only to amuse, for commercial gain, or as an end in itself. Thus, in his first attempt, he praises *Hell-Bent Fer Heaven* because "it gives a superb picture of the effects of isolation on both the individual and the group mind" ("Fiction" 127) and *The Goose Hangs High* for its "effective portraiture of home life as it probably exists in a multitude of Middle-West families" ("Fiction" 128).

"Social Drama Notes," which were almost always the work of Vincent, appeared for the first time in the January/February 1925 issue of the *Journal of Applied Sociology*, which itself first appeared out of the University of Southern California's year-old sociology department in September 1916. Though there was no stated rationale for the inclusion of reviews of dramatic literature, other categories, such as "Social Fiction Notes," "Social

Work Notes," "Social Book Notes," and "Social Poetry Notes," suggest the broadly ambitious scope of the journal as well as the editorial move to appropriate all the art forms for sociological scrutiny. ("Social Photoplay Notes" began to appear, though only sporadically, after January/February 1941 and shifted to "Motion Picture Notes" in September/October 1952 and back again to "Photoplay" in March/April 1956 – suggesting the uneasy distinction between drama and film still being worked through. In fact, there is no technical or generic distinction between the forms in the reviews.)

In a note to the introduction of "Social Poetry Notes" in the fall of 1925, Vincent observes that "since poetry is so closely related to the human feelings, and social poetry to the social feelings, the study of social poetry takes on an interest to psychiatric studies with their analyses of the feelings and emotions, of conflicts and complexes. For the same reason the study of social fiction and social drama has definite scientific and sociological significance" ("Poetry" 94). (It should be noted that "Social Poetry Notes" did not survive, although all the other "Notes" did.) The only other general statement on drama was in January/February 1926 when Vincent, praising the establishment of "a genuine Repertory Theatre in Boston, the first of its kind in America," noted that "the importance of the drama as an educational force and the sociological significance of it in the field social control, especially, ought to be considerably enhanced by the establishment of such theatres throughout the country. We have been much stirred by the evil that bad drama can create but too little concerned with the constructive results which may emanate from good drama" ("Drama" 294). This statement is important because it is clear that Vincent, though he reviewed published texts rather than productions of plays, nevertheless imagined the work of the drama to be done in the theatre.

Vincent placed power in dramatic literature to stimulate readers' thoughts but greater power in theatrical production to stir audiences to action. In "The Influence of Drama upon Human Attitudes" (1932), Vincent equated "attitude" with "that trend of conscious thought which has a tendency to lead one on to real activity, especially if the social situation seems to demand action" (142). Instead of looking for the harmful effects of theatre on spectators, which, he correctly observed, was the usual approach, he looked for "the delivery of constructive ideas" (144). Unfortunately for Vincent, whose disappointment in his findings is evident, his respondents, more often than not, had *not* been moved by a dramatic hero, had *not* been made aware of a social problem, did *not* alter their activities, and did *not* improve their morals. Determined, nonetheless, to salvage hope from ashes, Vincent concluded his investigation with the following: "Not that any one would expect a modern audience to emerge from the theatre prepared to act, but in the course of time, the reflection of the ideas may result in the formation of a definitely molded attitude which will furnish the motor power for action in the real world" (151). Vincent's tenaciously optimistic insistence on the efficacious effect of drama on its audience was, of course, connected to his brand of sociology. The editor of *Sociology and Research*, Emory S. Bogardus, a student of Albion Small's at the University of Chicago, explained the journal's theoretical base in his farewell article of July 1961, citing Lester F. Ward as the inspiration: "By applied sociology Ward meant the development of ideas by research which could be put into operation for effecting desired social change. His emphasis on telic or purposeful attitudes as a frame of reference for sociology had a dynamic appeal. According to him sociology is primarily interested in social function rather than social structure" (455–56).

In fact, in defining and placing sociology in 1895 for the first issue of the first journal of sociology, *The American Journal of Sociology*, Ward had traced the inception of sociology to Auguste Comte's altruism. For Ward, sociology was to the philosophy of history as physics was to natural science and as biology was to natural history, that is, a qualitative and quantitative improvement. Eschewing Spencerian stasis for Comtean dynamism, Ward elevated sociology from the same plane as political economy and economics to a loftier position of "the calm contemplation of the central problem of determining the facts, the laws, and the principles of human association. . . . Sociology is an advanced study, the last and latest in the entire curriculum. It should be mainly postgraduate. It involves high powers of generalization, and, what is more, it absolutely requires a broad basis of induction. It is largely a philosophy, and in these days philosophy no longer rests on assumptions but on facts" (25).

That Ward had written the fine arts out of consideration as a "dynamic" force seemed not to interfere with Bogardus's and Vincent's commitment to appropriating drama precisely for that end. In an exchange on the subject in *The American Journal of Sociology* in 1907, the participants resisted Ward's contention, expressed in his *Dynamic Sociology* (1883), that the aesthetic faculties and the fine arts had no part in the improvement of society: "'their study belongs entirely to the department of social statistics, and this brief notice is merely intended to fix their true position and exhibit their negative character'" (Odenwald-Ungar 656–57). Art, for Ward, was "nonprogressive" because it served no useful purpose, it did not raise the moral tone of society, it added no new truth, it did not make men more comfortable, better, or wiser. While it might be considered as a socializing agency, it was not a necessity. Ward was taken to task for this view by the respondents, one of whom cited Russia as an example of a country roused from torpor and awakened to a sense of action mostly by "art in its highest manifestation, the drama" (Odenwald-Ungar 661). The incensed president of the American Society of Dramatic Art retorted that "the theatre and drama are merely a mirror of life which exists, and if you have anything to say against them at all, you are also speaking against the life which it reflects. . . . I only wish there could be founded for this work of the theatre a dramatic science as well as a dramatic art" (Odenwald-Ungar 669, 671). In fact, in that same year, 1907, at least one playwright, Charles Klein, author of *The Lion and the Mouse* and *The Daughters of Men,* and one of his supporters, B. O. Flower, labored in *The Arena* to demonstrate the many ways in which theatre and drama could be "the handmaid of progress" by fostering culture, stimulating an interest in history, and dramatizing the redemption of men by spiritual idealism (Flower 498).

Ward notwithstanding, Vincent aggressively proposed progressive readings of the plays he reviewed. To accommodate his assumptions, of course, most of the plays he reviewed, especially in the twenties and thirties, tended to be socially concerned, even leftist plays, about black, poor, and struggling Americans, for example, William H. Wells's *Brotherhood* (1925) about striking union seamen, *Plays of Negro Life* edited by Alain Locke and Montgomery Gregory (1927), Maxwell Anderson and Harold Hickerman's *Gods of the Lightning* (1928) about the Sacco-Vanzetti case, Mordaunt Shairp's study of homosexuality, *The Green Bay Tree* (1933), and John Wexley's dramatization of the Scottsboro case, *They Shall Not Die* (1934).

Vincent's reviews, demonstrating a concern for two things, reportorial accuracy and responsible persuasiveness, also reveal the values Vincent repeatedly privileged: the sincerity of the playwright (as opposed to his dramaturgical skill), the truth and realism of the play as mirror of a troubled society, and the implicit moral or reformist purpose of the play. His values, in fact, were similar to those espoused by Arthur Hobson Quinn in *A History of the American Drama.* Occasionally Vincent allowed himself to make a judgment on the dramaturgy, perhaps remarking that a play was a good melodrama or noting that a character was carefully drawn, but for the most part he stuck to the business of contextualizing the play for sociologists. Of Marc Connelly's *The Green Pastures,* Vincent observed "the play is rendered sociologically important because of its marked implication of the phenomenon of cultural diffusion" ("Drama" 1930, 595). Repeatedly, Vincent recommended plays for their "truth to life" qualities and their focus on troubling social issues. In fact,

Vincent had a tendency to praise a play for being like a case history. For example, of George Kelly's *Craig's Wife* he wrote, "Mr. Kelly has thus created very successfully the picture of a woman, unusual in literature, but by no means uncommon in life. The play is worthy of study and attention by those who are interested in the social process and in types of family life" ("Drama" 1926, 397). Ultimately, the moral thrust of the play mattered most. For example, in his enthusiastic review of *Susan and God* by Rachel Crothers, Vincent wrote that the comedy was "essentially worth-while" and "valuable for the moral that it suggests – that human service and good will are after all the test of good religious motivation" ("Drama" 1938, 497). It should come as no surprise that Vincent's approach often produced forced interpretations. He recommended *Life with Father* because it revealed "some intriguing case materials for sociological scansion" ("Drama" 1940, 98) and *A Streetcar Named Desire* because the play, "a case history of social decadence," also "serves as a good exposition of the dramatist acting as a sincere case investigator and reporter of the personality disorganization of one of his clients" ("Drama" 1948, 906).

It is obvious from the summary of Vincent's work that the primary problem with this early sociological approach is that it suggested that there is an unmediated equation and direct correlation between the social world of the text and the social world in the text. From this perspective, the text is nothing more than a clear mirror of the world offstage. But sociologists were not alone in calling for a sociological approach to literature. For instance, V. F. Calverton in *The Newer Spirit: A Sociological Criticism of Literature* (1925) called for "scientific" readings, charging that American criticism was "a series of shallow rationalizations, a puffery of the inessential, a confused scribbling about morality, a blathery defense of slapstick emotionalism, a projection of a *new* approach that antedates Goethe, onslaughts on the business man's psychology, sedate apologies for traditions, archeological remnants of deceased social epochs, denunciations of psychological and historical esthetics, vain retreats to Horace and Aristotle, all subsidized by a wealth of allusion and imagery but a paucity of insight and analysis" (152). Calverton insisted that literature was a product of sociology, that genre was conditioned by hierarchy, that aesthetics mirrored society, and that literature should be read through the lens of the rising proletariat.

Breaking the Mirror

The sociological approach to drama persisted through the 1930s. In "Is Art the Product of Its Age?" in *Social Forces* (1935), John Mueller heralded the natural science movement for rescuing the arts from "romanticism and Kantian metaphysics" and giving it a "material function associated with the physical universe" (368). A few years later in "The Folkway of Art," Mueller expanded this argument, calling for attention to the social forces, as opposed to the individual authorial or aesthetic factors, forming a work of art. In critiquing the current theories of aesthetic culture, however, Mueller invoked the drama to resist the simple and reductive idea of the stage as a mirror, contending that so "much drama runs counter to the moral and other standards of the group . . . that the censor has to be invoked. Instead of a mirror of life, art turns out, just as frequently to be its contradiction" (229). In *Society: A Textbook of Sociology* (1937), R. M. MacIver argued that social conflict, the conflict between an individual and the code, was the subject of drama; by way of demonstration, he used *Antigone* and *Hamlet* as models to elucidate O'Neill's *The Emperor Jones*.

Despite the social focus of Mueller's and MacIver's approach to drama, neither claimed the simple stage-as-mirror-of-life approach that so characterized Melvin J. Vincent's reviews. In fact, it is possible to point to a shifting relationship between drama and sociology. A clue to this change, at least as far as *Sociology and Social Research* was concerned, lies in a farewell by the editor, Emory S. Bogardus, "Forty-Five Years as an Editor," in July 1961. Observing that the journal had been marked by "a shift from qualitative to quantitative research, and a related change from an interest in general concepts to specific ones supported by empirical research," Bogardus's overview of the shift into new systems of sociological thought points to the concomitant declining interest in dramatic literature but the increased interest in theatrical productions (454). Apart from Vincent's regular reviews of individual plays, *Sociology and Social Research* devoted little space to either drama or theatre. In 1934, there was an article on the characteristics of an academic theatre audience and a similar effort in 1956 correlating socioeconomic backgrounds and theatrical preference, neither of which contain any surprises. In 1958, James Barnett bemoaned the sporadic and unsystematic research in the sociology of art in the United States. Citing John Mueller's *The American Symphony Orchestra: A Social History of Musical Taste* (1951), Barnett listed the possible areas for sociological research: art as a process, including "serious theatre," artists' social origins and style of life, works of art other than literature that had been scrutinized, styles and content, performance, and the audience (402). But with the exception of an essay in 1968 on the American juvenile delinquency novel, concern for the arts and creative expression all but vanished from the journal. The most recent and only article of relevance to the relationship between drama and sociology to appear in *Sociology and Social Research* was "Death as Theater: A Dramaturgical Analysis of the American Funeral" in 1976, a study that reflects the profound shift in sociology's interest in drama. Informed by the theories of Erving Goffman and even more so by those of Kenneth Burke, the authors were careful to reiterate their position that "we take dramaturgy to be a metaphor, perspective, and strategy for viewing life, not for life itself" (Turner and Edgley 390).

Realism as Salvation: Social Pragmatism

The early sociological approach to American drama clearly was linked to American pragmatism, a specific historical and cultural set of philosophically informed social practices that was characterized by a rejection of metaphysics and authorized by institutionalized education and by the scientifically grounded emerging disciplines of sociology and psychology. The insistence on improving life for man in this world, especially the social and moral conditions, can be traced to America's revolutionary antecedents, in entrepreneurship sanctioned by moralizing philanthropy, in the belief in reform through education, and in the ideal of communities built on negotiated compromise. This unromanticized and pragmatic attitude was compatible with the realist's agenda and was understood by some to be the salvation of the troubled and problematic drama. Vernon Lewis Parrington in *The Beginnings of Critical Realism in America, 1860–1920* claimed that "the new realism was a native growth, sprung from the soil, unconcerned with European technique," and though originally "primitive" had been supplemented by the "sociological school," which in turn marked a needed departure from romanticism (238). Benjamin Spencer, in *The Quest for Nationality*, discussed the inevitability that early American writers placed their hope for a national literature in the expression of a distinctive sociopolitical ideal because realism would provide a powerful counteragent to alien modes of expression and thought, citing dramatist J. N. Barker's plea that his "plain-palated homebred" drama not be expected to "lisp the language of Shakespeare" (61). In 1827, James Paulding had complained of the "lofty, noisy, measured and sonorous dialogue" which pointed to the fact that American plays were not "properly naturalized" (342).

The impulse to make drama "real" started early. Travis Bogard in "Art and Politics," notes, "As early as 1891, the author Hamlin Garland, impressed by the serious realism of the plays of James A. Herne, attempted to found a new kind of theatre," the aims of which would be "'to encourage truth and progress in American Dramatic Art, . . . to secure and maintain a stage whereon the best and most unconventional studies of modern life, and distinctly American life, may get a proper hearing'" (25–26). Faced with the charge that plays written before 1870 were marred by unacceptable melodrama, bombast, and sentiment, in 1922, Montrose Moses, in a revisionist's reclamatory move, argued in support of P. I. Reed's pamphlet, "The Realistic Presentation of American Characters in Native American Plays Prior to Eighteen Seventy," that Mrs. Warren's *The Group* (1775), Jonathan Sewall's *A Cure for the Spleen* (1775), Hugh Henry Brackenridge's *The Battle of Bunker's-Hill* (1776), and John Leacock's *The Fall of British Tyranny* (1776) although polemical also were worthy examples of "correct portraiture and powerful, relentless caricature" ("Forefathers" 796). Although he wished to claim "social atmosphere" as the determining factor in valuing these native plays, Moses was also very careful to distance them from any claim to literary merit, describing them as "entertainments" (793) and "unliterary scripts" (798).

Jürgen Wolter explains the formative rise of realism between 1790 and 1860 as a consequence of the shift in the conception of morality from a religious to a social context; nationalism and realism replaced universalism and idealism, and historical accuracy became an essential component of the reformist stage (11). What emerges in discussions of this kind is a debate about the necessity to yoke natural American speech with realistic American social situations. In 1906 Henry Arthur Jones had insisted that American drama would be literature only when it was written in "the colloquial American language," which was a better instrument than English for a "purely realistic class of play," a class that would be dedicated to accurately depicting life on American streets, drawing rooms, and prairies (60). Between 1860 and 1915, there was an increasing call for faithful representation of the lives of ordinary people, but for some critics, such as Alfred Hennequin, this heralded the death of drama (20). Of approximately this same period, Warner Berthoff has little to say on the drama in *The Ferment of Realism: American Literature, 1884–1919* (1965) because it did not "effectively emerge from the mass of popular entertainment" until Eugene O'Neill and Elmer Rice (xi–xii).

Though critical opinions differ about the merits of realism, the sentiments expressed in the *Columbia Literary History of the United States* (1988) are those of most modern histories of American drama, that the most significant literary development in drama from the Civil War to 1900 was realism, specifically, the move away from melodrama. American drama gained only incrementally in stature as a consequence of this "advance," however; the emotional excesses of melodrama were understood to have been replaced only by the simplistic literalism and journalism of realism. And, until recently, few historians have troubled themselves over what was, and continues to be, the multiplicity of dramatic expressions that have been gathered under the reductive rubric of realism. The entrenched narrative formula of the "growth" of drama from melodrama to realism has been so pervasively persuasive that Bruce McConachie in "New Historicism and American Theater History" (1991) argues that "any reconstruction of American theater history must question the dominance of stage realism in the United States during the present century" (270).

William Dean Howells and Realism

An examination of American dramatic realism should begin, as Arthur Hobson Quinn begins it in *A History of American Drama*, with William Dean Howells. "One of the common errors in the discussion of American drama," Quinn begins, "is to assume its divorce from the main current of our literature" (*Civil War* 66). Pointing to writers such as Mark Twain and Bret Harte who also wrote plays, Quinn singles Howells out because of both his own dramatic achievements and his influence on others. In fact, Quinn claims that Howells's creative work, published in *Atlantic Monthly*, *Harper's Weekly*, and *Harper's Magazine*, surpassed his critical articles in importance because not only were they inherently American in atmosphere and form, they also "taught manners and social values to thousands who played in them or saw them on the amateur stage" (81). Calling Howells a "master playwright," Quinn notes that the "fact that the one-act plays of Howells were acted chiefly by amateurs has obscured their significance" (67). Perhaps the amateur status of Howells's actors could account for his absence as playwright from major literary histories of American literature. In Spiller et al.'s *Literary History of the United States* (1978), Howells is described as a crusader for realism, but only novels and his reviews are discussed. The same oversight exists in the *Columbia Literary History of the United States*, which marks Howells as an influential disseminator and promoter of realism in theory and practice but only insofar as he was a literary and critical essayist, novelist, and short story writer.

As editor of *The Atlantic Monthly* and contributor to *Harper's Magazine*, William Dean Howells between 1866 and 1920 also exercised an enormous influence over the developing theoretical interest in realism, an influence thoroughly documented by Brenda Murphy in *A Realist in the American Theatre* (1992). According to Murphy, "between 1880 and 1916, Howells's realistic viewpoint on drama and theatre was a constant presence in American culture" and Arthur Hobson Quinn's *History of the American Drama from the Civil War to the Present Day*, "for fifty years the standard history of American drama, established Howells's version of evolutionary realism as the central element in American dramatic history between the 1870's and the 1930's" (1). In a series of missives from the "Editor's Study" in *Harper's Magazine* between July 1886 and August 1889, Howells considered what he perceived as the dismal condition of American drama or, more precisely, "the abject trash" the theatre managers put on in "these days of a material theatre but no drama." Looking to the past, Howells wrote that "our one original contribution and addition to histrionic art was Negro minstrelsy, which, primitive, simple, elemental, was out of our own soil, and had the characteristics that distinguish autochthonic concepts." Looking at the present, Howells praised Edward Harrigan's depiction of a New York Irishman, which Howells valued as the beginning of "true American comedy" with the added advantage of being "decenter than Shakespeare." Theatre was only an amusement but the novel was the "consoling refuge" in which the "real drama" could be found (July 1886, 30–31). In his "Editor's Study" series, Howells amplified his appraisal of Harrigan in July 1889, claiming that Harrigan was "working on the lines of a natural and scientific development of drama from local origins" but that all other stage types such as "the Darky" and "the Yankee" were no more than "American masks." For Howells, character was the essence of a real play, "the timeless work," and "a charming piece of dramatic art," and only in the "prolongation of sketches," such as those written by Denman Thompson in *The Old Homestead*, would America have a "right beginning" for the drama (July 1889, 201–3).

This insistence on native character as opposed to caricature continued to be Howells's theme. By June 1890, Howells was exercising restrained optimism because, although American drama was "retarded in its development," still held back by "too much of the old Miller Coupler and Buffer pattern," Bronson Howard's *Shenandoah* proved to Howells that fresh characters and local color, "the simple" and "the natural" could be guiding criteria (June 1890, 259–60). His last words from the "Editor's Study," in August 1891, reiterated his modest hope and targeted a second cause for American drama's unclean state: "The drama has been trying to climb out of [the pit]," he wrote, and even though the theatre is still "coarse," even "shameless," he thought it had "some impulses to purge and live cleanly." The "nascent reform" which began when playwrights turned to "real life" had gotten stuck in the "inevitable" mix of the romantic and the realistic. Howells equated romance with miracles and complained that romance was the "ancestral monkey" swinging in a tree in the forest, whereas realism was the man on the flying trapeze (August 1891, 329–30).

It was not only Howells's theoretical views on realism that had an impact; Walter Meserve argues that Howells's thirty-six plays, in particular the social comedies, were significant forces in the rise of realism. Meserve also admits that Howells was attracted by the high potential financial rewards of theatrical success as well as the enormous accomplishment such success for an editor and novelist would mean, given the failure of Henry James, Mark Twain, Bret Harte, Hamlin Garland, Joseph Kirkland, Joaquin Miller, and Thomas Bailey Aldrich. Meserve halves Howells's career: Comedies written mainly in the 1880s and serious plays, after 1893. That Howells's plays were not theatrical successes Meserve attributes to the demand for full-length rather than one-act plays, to his critics not being fully appreciative, to his weakness for farce, and to "a desire to dramatize the commonplace" (Meserve, ed., *Howells* xv–xxxiii). Although Howells's influence on realism is not disputed, the qualified nature of Howells's accomplishments as a playwright and the place of drama in the canon were marked from an early date; in 1887, Henry Beers wrote that "Howells is almost the only successful American dramatist, and this in the field of parlor comedy" (*Outline* 278). Clearly, at the very least, Howells's contribution to amateur theatricals, especially insofar as they offered models for a rising middle class or satirized artificial behavior, and insofar as their performance by amateurs suggests a "boundary crossing" between the formal, professional stage and home theatricals, ought to be reconsidered from a cultural studies perspective if not also from a literary one.

Muckraking Journalism

The other major influence in amplifying the drama's engagement with realism was the "muckraking" journalism movement, a connection that, in the minds of the critics, would take drama even further away from "high" literature. A concern that was voiced early on in the construction of American drama as literature and that has prevailed was the undermining of literary status by topicality and too close an association with journalism. William Winter in 1889 pointed out that "the plays of both Dryden and T. B. De Walden, one an English genius, the other an American scribbler, have been forgotten because they were local, ephemeral, and temporary. . . . There is the same difference – or a kindred one – between sterling plays and incidental plays that there is between literature and journalism. The one is permanent, the other evanescent" (101).

In 1916 Harold de Wolf Fuller located the beginnings of a serious American drama in the muckraking impulse of Ida Tarbell, "the mother of dramatic realism in this country" because "it was undoubtedly the muckraking spirit which begot the first serious attempt to bring the American stage into close contact with life" (307). Fuller's reference was to Ida Tarbell's study of John D. Rockefeller's monopoly, *History of the Standard Oil Company* which was serialized in *McClure's Magazine* (1902–1904) and reprinted as a book in 1904. Two consequences of Tarbell's effort were the publication of nearly two thousand muckraking articles in popular magazines between 1903 and 1912 and the creation of an American school of realistic drama under the leadership of Charles Klein (Bloomfield 169). Harold de Wolf Fuller credited Charles Klein's *The Lion and the Mouse* (1905), a thinly veiled adaptation of Tarbell's history, with breaking from the American tradition of melodrama, comic opera, and farce. Fuller believed that along with Eugene Walter and Edward Sheldon, Klein started a fashion "freer from foreign influence than might be supposed" because "an American play, to be realistic, must partake of the nature of an exposure," which, in turn, is connected to reform. Such plays still fall short of literary greatness and are only works of "mechanical realism" because they lack "outstanding characters" of the kind Shakespeare dramatized (308). Later critics agreed with Fuller's judgment about the lack of literary merits in Klein's play but pointed to the importance of *The Lion and the Mouse*, which had the longest continuous run of any American play to that time. According to Maxwell Bloomfield, the success marked a turning point in American drama to say nothing of Klein's career: "Between 1905 and 1917 a school of popular 'realists' flourished in the American theater as a counterpart to the journalists of exposure" because "virtually every exposure made by the journalists found an echo in the theater" (173–74). From municipal corruption to juvenile delinquency to miscegenation to tenement house conditions, the muckraking playwrights followed the journalists who covered a panoply of social ills. Bloomfield notes that the reformist zealotry had its costs; the dramatists became so absorbed in details and with faithful reproductions of the reporters' stories that by 1912 the plays dwindled into little more than mechanical still lives empty of psychological insight. The response within the world of theatre and drama, according to Bloomfield, was the creation of "art theatres" and "little theatres" where psychological realism would supplant the cruder realism of exposure. The consequence was a perceived separation into two dramatic modes: realistic exposés and aestheticized psychology, neither of which was substantive enough to merit sustained literary critical attention. Montrose J. Moses approved of the suffusion of a "journalistic sense" into American drama at an early stage insofar as it gave playwrights such as Bronson Howard a needed sense of reality; but he also complained that "it has stayed in the theatre and has deprived it, in its later exponents, of a logical completeness of ideas. It has in most cases kept our drama external" (CHAL 279).

Other critics were less enthusiastic about Klein and muckraking drama. Arthur Hobson Quinn acknowledged that Klein's "theatrically effective" plays were among the most successful of the first decade, but found them locked into a melodramatic practice and not up to the "test of analysis" (*Civil War* 105). On Klein and the muckraking playwrights, C. W. E. Bigsby was silent. Despite the remarkable profusion of muckraking plays and their connections with the novel and essay, many general literary historians also were silent on the subject. In fact, the neglect is pervasive enough that a reader might never know that the drama had participated forcefully, let alone at all, in what was one of the major facets of realism at the turn of the century. For instance, in his long discussion of muckraking as the satirical attacks on business and politics, "The Rise of Realism, 1871–1891," Robert Falk attends only to fiction. Similarly, both Louis Filler's *The Muckrakers* (1968) and Edward Cassady's "Muckraking in the Gilded Age" (1941) consider only the essays and novels.

But the drama was a major means of exposing and attacking corruption, and to whatever degree it has been thought of as being "melodramatic," it also was realistic. Monroe Lippman and Lois Gottlieb both have documented the large number of plays frankly skeptical or openly satiric of big business, which form a throughline from the muckraking movement of the turn of the century through the "dramas of attack" of the late 1920s and the 1930s and which were arguably distinctively "American" plays: Mead's *Wall Street, or Ten Minutes Before Three* (1819), *Wall Street as It Is Now* (1826), and two farces on President Jackson's 1833 decision that federal funds would no longer be deposited in the Bank of the United States, *The Removal of the Deposits* (1834) and *Removing the Deposits* (1835); the first act of Dion Boucicault's *The Poor of New York* (1857); Augustin Daly's *The Big Bonanza* (1875); Bronson Howard's *The Banker's Daughter* (1878), *Baron Rudolph* (1881), *Young Mrs. Winthrop* (1882), and *The Henrietta* (1878); Augustus Thomas's *New Blood* (1894), a response to the Sherman antitrust laws passed by Congress in 1890, and *The Capitol* (1895); Channing Pollock's dramatization of Frank Norris's *The Pit* (1904); Charles Klein's *The Lion and the Mouse* (1905); Upton Sinclair's *Prince Hagen* (1909), *The Second Story Man* (1909); Clyde Fitch's *The City* (1909); Charles Klein's *The Money Makers* (1914); Kaufman and Connelly's *Beggar on Horseback* (1924); Brooks and Lister's assault on corrupt American business practices in Mexican mining, *Spread Eagle* (1927); Eugene O'Neill's *Marco Millions* (1938); John Howard Lawson's exposé of unethical American business tycoons starting a war in the Far East in *The International* (1928); George O'Neil's trilogy *American Dream* (1933); and Sidney Kingsley's *Ten Million Ghosts* (1936). As Monroe Lippman points out, although American playwrights turned their attention to World War II, after the war they refocused again on big business: Garson Kanin's *Born Yesterday* (1946); Arthur Miller's *All My Sons* (1947); Sigmund Miller's *One Bright Day* (1952); and Howard Teichmann and George S. Kaufman's *The Solid Gold Cadillac* (1953).

Such work was not really anomalous because, in fact, from the beginning of the republic, American drama was a powerful vehicle of civic expression deriving its inspiration from current events. The specific, temporal, and immediate engagement of American drama in American political life is an essential part of the American dramatic tradition. Norman Philbrick in his introduction to *Trumpets Sounding: Propaganda Plays of the American Revolution* notes that from 1773 to 1783 at least thirteen "pamphlet plays" were printed in the colonies, early examples of the political press and convergence of dramatic genre with newspaper form. Philbrick finds a strong resemblance to two kinds of newspaper writing, the factual story and the feature article, and links them to the "Living Newspapers" of the 1930s. He also points out that because staging of plays was prohibited during the Revolutionary period, dramatic literature could be circulated only through print; thus, muckraking drama in its earliest manifestations was more the creature of print, if not "literature," than the stage.

Some critics were appreciative of American playwrights' engagement in political affairs. For instance, in 1920 William Archer claimed for American drama "a general relevance to life," which he heralded as its "chief merit; the typical American dramatist is sensitively in touch with reality as he finds it in the newspapers" and his "vivacious comments" in "competent dramatic form" are "a perfectly legitimate form of art." He hastened to qualify even this modest praise, noting that this "dramatic journalist" was not an Ibsen, a Hauptmann, or a Shaw any more than he was a "searching psychologist nor a profound sociologist," though he was in command of his "craft." Superior examples of this kind of play for Archer included Montague Glass's *Potash and Perlmutter* (1913), George M. Cohan's *Get-Rich-Quick Wallingford* (1910), Medill Patterson's *The Fourth Estate* (1909), and Edward Sheldon's *The Boss* (1911), works that "would leave Aristotle gasping," but that were "racy of the soil, and that is to my thinking a very high encomium" (79). But if Archer valued this feisty "dramatic journalist," not all approved of Archer. Of Archer's effect on dramatic criticism, R. S. Crane charged that it had not recovered from the shock it was administered by *The Old Drama and the New*, in which Archer insisted on a purity of form, a faithful imitation of life freed from poetry and lyricism, and a progression to the logic of realism (R. Crane 234).

The Close Embrace of Realism

"Drama by its nature," writes Jovan Hristič, "is a nonrealistic genre. It is hardly accidental that the idea of 'realism,' when applied to drama, has come to have pejorative connotations" (315) but not when applied to the novel, "certainly the genre in which the ideals of realism are best and most adequately realized" (311). The novel, he reasons, "does not require that universal and transcendental plane on which conflicts and events are projected in the drama, the drama is always focused on something which is beyond and above life" (314). As a consequence, when psychological drama is yoked to classical tragedy, as in O'Neill's *Mourning Becomes Electra*, the result is mere pathology. Directing his discussion at all of realistic dramaturgy, not just American, Hristič tells us that "Balzac is great, while Ibsen remains only a great second-rate writer" (312). Wary of individual successes because they become clichés, Hristič notes that the Pirandellian theatre-within-the-theatre, the Brechtian epic theatre, and the theatre of the absurd cannot serve as models: "To be created, a great dramatic form demands a method of observation of man which is directly contrary to our own. That is why, no matter how many efforts are made to break with realism, it is characteristic that modern drama returns to realism" (316). By way of evidence, he offers Beckett's *Not I*, Albee's *All Over*, and Pinter's *Old Times* as "psychological realism," which is to say, "the novel on the stage" (317).

These operative assumptions about realism have long haunted the drama but, given American drama's close ties with journalism, seem to have been a particular problem for American drama. The general critical metanarrative suggests that the closer American drama gets to "life," that is, the social and political problems unique to America, the closer it gets to "greatness" but that the more realistic it becomes, the farther it gets from poetry and that the farther it gets from poetry, the farther it gets from literature. Or, to put it less paradoxically and more judgmentally, the problem lies in attempts at the representation of "pure" realism; the mimetic contract assures the audience that it can accept the stage as a slice of the real world, it interprets the world for the reader, it insists on a narrow referentiality, an absolute authority, and empties the text by reproducing only surfaces. As a consequence, a critic like

David Denby can compare drama unfavorably with film: "For moviegoers like myself, the theater seems caught in a gigantic double bind. The closer it comes to realistic representation, the more it betrays how inadequate it is next to the cinema; the further away from representation it moves, the more it loses contact with what interests us in the world and becomes preoccupied with the means of its own existence" (50).

A review of some of the assessments about the troubled relationship between realism and American drama points to both the ongoing nature of the debate and the lack of critical consensus. Montrose Moses in "A Hopeful Note on the Theatre" (1932) wrote that though it ought to be self-evident that the American outlook on drama has ceased to be provincial, "the American playwright has been accused of a slavish dependence on realism, on a reportorial sense which makes him more concerned with sequence of events than with logical progression of thought," characteristics manifested in Belasco's stagecraft and George Kelly's writing (534). But for Moses realism was simply one example of American drama's internationalism, of the fact that it was participating in the same movements as Europe. Furthermore, he pointed out – citing the first French history of American drama, by Léonie Villard, that acclaimed the vitality of American drama – Europe had become interested in American drama.

In *Major American Writers* (1935), Howard Mumford Jones and Ernest Leisy expressed their dissatisfaction with dramatic realism: "When the American stage was reborn after its long immersion in false and theatrical romanticism, it became too accusatory." Fussing that the new playwrights who preferred the problem play had made the theatre serious, they charged that "in its sociological career the theater but echoed the magazines which excoriated the conditions of modern industrial society" (20). John Anderson's complaint in *The American Theatre* (1938) is similar: "It is journalistic, and it is a trait which, curiously enough, goes through the American theatre from the earliest days of the newspapers to the present. Its effect on playwriting in America is apparent . . . [both in themes and method there] is too much second hand material – dated, as 'dead as yesterday's paper'" (99). In *Revolution in American Drama* (1947), Edmond Gagey felt much the same, that "it is the fate of drama to become more rapidly dated than other literary types" (267). Theophilus Lewis writing in 1954 in support of ideas in the drama, realized how difficult they were to dramatize and tried to make a distinction between a "permanent" drama and the "dynamic" or "topical" drama of ideas. He felt that plays such as *Uncle Tom's Cabin* or *They Shall Not Die* could have an immediate sociopolitical effect but that such plays were also "a short cut to obscurity" (631).

In *Masters of the Drama* (1954), John Gassner observed that the uncommercial, socially critical and militant dramatists of the 1920s and 1930s "were immature and some were sociologists rather than artists. . . . The emphasis they placed on economic motivation and upon 'dialectical materialism' tended to become literal, stereotyped and even naive" (665). Of the drama of the 1930s and 1940s, Gassner reiterated this judgment in *Theatre at the Crossroads* (1960). Alert to the dangers of what he called "social drama," he charged that its proponents were likely "to confuse art with sociology and drama with preachment" and that as a consequence dramatic art was debilitated (39). He felt that there had been a risk of reportage at the expense of drama, that "to a considerable degree the strength of the American stage was equated with its realism and social awareness" (45). And from the perspective of 1960, seeing the threat to social drama from the right wing, he noted that "an essentially moralistic play such as Arthur Miller's *All My Sons*, a principled, well-built drama voted the best play of the year by the New York Drama Critics Circle, was banned for production abroad by our State Department in 1949" (45).

Francis Fergusson, in "Beyond the Close Embrace: Speculations on the American Stage" (1955), suggested that Ibsen and Chekhov had already exhausted the possibilities of realism, the "noncommittal medium," well before America's best practitioner, Clifford Odets, was born. Odets's *Golden Boy*, Fergusson argued, showed the playwright to be "the master of the most delicate, musical, and accurate realistic dialogue our stage has ever heard." Odets's achievement was, for Fergusson, the consequence of his involvement with the Group Theatre's project of the "close embrace," that is, a refined and deepened realism through which audience and artists would share the same intense feeling and understanding. "But this fine achievement revealed the limits of the whole Group Theatre's effort to build a realistic American theatre: its temporal limit, when the public sanctions of the New Deal's social idealism leaked away – the public mood which had enabled the Group to recruit an audience; its theoretical limit as it became evident that the 'close embrace,' though congenial to the candid young, is not enough to enable a playwright to reach maturity as an artist. Some more stable and general view of life, and of the art of representing it, is required" (195). Fergusson explored the possibility that Thornton Wilder might be the playwright who had such a vision and art but rejected him because he did not share Odets's interest in realism, because he was too remote and too cool, and because he learned nothing from American theatre and everything in Paris from Gertrude Stein, James Joyce, and André Obey. So what was left of realism in American drama?

Though Fergusson concedes that William Saroyan, Carson McCullers, and Tennessee Williams had a "lyric realism," he faulted their work for lack of "artistic, social, moral, or philosophic scruple" (201). In conclusion, Fergusson doubted that there would ever be a real American theatre: "Our plan of founding it is half-forgotten, unfinished business. Probably we should be wise to accept the pathetic realism of the present trend as foreground only, portentous though it seems; the expression of a mood which will pass" (203).

Of all the complaints about American realist drama, Mary McCarthy's attack, "The American Realist Playwrights" (1961), is the most virulent. Complaining of the "backwardness" of the drama compared to the novel, she points out that "the theatre feeds on the novel; never vice versa; think of the hundreds of dramatizations of novels, and then try to think of a book that was 'novelized' from a play. There is not even a word for it" (209). Worse, according to McCarthy, is that realism in general pejoratively is associated with journalism and photography and that the criterion for dramatic realism in particular is drawn from journalism. Attempts to write well by playwrights such as Arthur Miller, she argues, are no more than pretentiousness; American realist playwrights produce only "petty or color-less" heroes, "drab" settings, "lame" language, and "ugliness" of form (216). On the other hand, she concedes that "the realist drama at its highest is an implacable exposé" (219). In her evaluation of the American realist play-wrights, O'Neill is deemed "clumsy," Miller is found to have "an evident hatred of and contempt for reality," and Williams is valued for his ear for colloquial speech (227). Finally, it would seem to be the "sadism" of realism that most bothers McCarthy, the confrontation of an audience with unre-lieved social ugliness, a confrontation that was acceptable to her only as long as it was justified with moral, reformist intentions. Now, however, realism is too close to "pornography" (228).

Susan Sontag in *Against Interpretation* (1966) complains about a lack of the avant-garde: "Most American novelists and playwrights are really either journalists or gentlemen sociologists and psychologists. They are writing the literary equivalent of program music. And so rudimentary, uninspired, and stagnant has been the sense of what might be done with *form* in fiction and drama that even when the content isn't simply information, news, it is peculiarly visible, handier, more exposed" (11).

Despite the plethora of complaints, by and large realism continues to have a tyrannous and iron grip on most historians of American drama and is understood to represent an "advance." The last chapter in Jack Vaughn's *Early American Dramatists* (1981) is entitled "Realism Achieved," and in it he argues that this achievement marks a welcome "reform" of American theatre (153). Another recent manifestation of the phenomenon is Gerald Berkowitz's critical history, *American Drama of the Twentieth Century* (1992), in which he argues that realism was the "natural voice of American drama" (2) and that realism "was far more useful and natural to the American drama" than the other experiments of the teens and twenties (43). Not only does he push the organicist approach, he also erases much dramatic literature that does not fit the paradigm. For instance, there is no mention of Maria Irene Fornes, of Gertrude Stein, of Joan Schenkar, or of Adrienne Kennedy. John Guare gets one paragraph for *The House of Blue Leaves*, Ntozake Shange gets one sentence for *for colored girls who have considered suicide/when the rainbow is enuf*, and Megan Terry is referred to as "anti-textual." All minorities are ghettoized in one chapter. Women get one chapter but only three women, all arguably realists, Wendy Wasserstein, Beth Henley, and Marsha Norman are considered.

Widening the Close Embrace

That much American drama was and continues to be judged by its relation to realism is a measure of the stranglehold realism had and still has on critical thinking. However not every historian and critic concurs with such a limited scope of understanding. In "Theatre Without Walls," an appraisal of American drama from 1945 to 1962, Gerald Weales states that of all the playwrights of this period "Tennessee Williams and Arthur Miller alone have any claim to the laurels of the major dramatist" (140). Weales values both writers for their interest in psychology, an interest that could align them with their lesser colleagues too narrowly devoted to introspection, but that is tempered and enriched by social concerns which in turn bring them closer to the "world of large ideas." That both Williams and Miller engage in experimental dramaturgy further strengthens their claim to greatness because, according to Weales, even though new methods of production and staging have "made great holes in the restrictive walls of realism, only a very few American playwrights have dared to break through, to go out and up" (143).

William Demastes, in *Beyond Naturalism: A New Realism in American Theatre* (1988), has addressed some of the fraught issues that have arisen around the concept of "realism" and traces the current "sense of stylistic and formal tyranny" to Eric Bentley's 1946 phrase "the triumph of realism" (Demastes 1). For Demastes, the fundamental problem is the confusion of realism, that is, scientific empiricism, with naturalism, that is, philosophical determinism and Darwinian materialism. This confusion, Demastes argues, lies at the heart of a critical rejection of plays that depart from the narrowness of naturalism, plays that variously have been described as "new realist," "super-realist," and "hyper-realist," as "bad drama" (7). Certainly such reductive thinking worried John Gassner in "Social Realism and Imaginative Theatre" (1962) in which he located two distinct schools of realism: the predominantly psychological realism of Group Theatre productions and the nonpsychological, propagandistic style of realism. There was, he argued, a significant difference between O'Neill's *Strange Interlude* and the Theatre Union's *Stevedore*. For Gassner, a realism that transcended mere literalism should be understood as "dynamic realism" (459–60). Brenda Murphy in *American Realism and American Drama, 1880–1940* (1987) also points to the dominance of the limited idea in histories of dramatic literature that realism meant only "the creation of a bourgeois milieu on the stage, the use of 'common speech' in the dialogue, and the avoidance of sensational melodramatic effects in the action." One way to correct this limited idea of mimesis, she argues, is to think of realism as far more complex and sophisticated, as "an informing worldview ('theoretic form'), which manifests itself in the patterned action of the play ('technical form')" (x) and which has evolved in American drama into new dramatic structures expressing "rhythms of life" hitherto unaccommodated by traditional generic forms of drama (177).

But however much Demastes, Gassner, and Murphy have argued for an expanded understanding of realism in American drama, the fact remains that the prevailing assumptions were laid down early, and it would seem in impervious stone, and produced, correctly or otherwise, an idea that realistic drama did indeed attempt to create the illusion that the action onstage mirrored the reality offstage. This insistence annoyed Gassner, who took pains to detail the vast range of experimental theatricalism of the 1920s and 1930s: "If nonrealistic stylization manifested so much variety and inventiveness during the period, why didn't it prevail? Why has the social theatre of the period been identified primarily with realism and why did American theatre continue to be predominantly realistic?" ("Social" 466). Gassner speculated that the efforts toward stylization were too crude and that although American playgoers insisted on realism in their drama, they insisted on theatricalism in their musicals.

Taking a different though no less critical stance toward the historical insistence on the centrality of realism in his introduction to *Performing Drama/Dramatizing Performance* (1991), Michael Vanden Heuvel argues that the expansionist mode of the "new realism" begs the real question of what is lost when critics continue to hold realism to be the "'source' or privileged form of drama." He argues that the "new realist" approach, one that addresses "altered or ironized dialogue, self-conscious theatricality, or expressionist staging," does so "at the expense of plenitude, comprehensiveness, and *différance*" and links this insistent linearity to the "genetic history" already in place "to describe the move from melodrama to realism in American theater" (16–17).

Resisting the Close Embrace

"Cast the realism aside – its consequences for women are deadly." This prescription from Sue-Ellen Case in "Toward a Butch-Femme Aesthetic" (1989) speaks to a renewed interest in fighting the tyranny of realism (287). In her call for a feminist mimesis, Elin Diamond concurs with Case: "Realism is more than an interpretation of reality passing as reality; it *produces* 'reality' by poisoning its spectator to recognize and verify its truths: this escritoire, this spirit lamp affirms the typicality, the universality of this and all bourgeois living rooms" (60).

The pressing need contemporary feminists feel to break away from the stranglehold of realism and to create a new aesthetics in part arises from the historical connection between women and realism in American literary history. Two examples must suffice. In an article entitled "The Interregnum in American Literature" in *The Dial* (May 1, 1910), Charles Moore, locating the weakness in American literature, took a stand against realism because it was didactic, dull, and addressed to women: "My last indictment of our late literature is that it has been edited for women, who have been its main readers. Women like the pretty realism which reproduces the everyday facts of their lives. With their practical instincts and craving for authority, they approve of didacticism, which seems to them plain good sense" (309). Joseph Mersand in "When Ladies Write Plays" in *The American Drama 1930–1940* (1941) argued that realism was a woman's speciality: "Women are realists in life and have carried over their skill into the theatre. They make good reporters for the stage. They rarely philosophize, their social consciousness is rarely apparent; they don't preach sermons; they don't raise you to the heights of aesthetic emotions. This is true even of the best women who write" (153). Further, he wrote, "Realistic plays relax. They strike home because they are home to you. . . . Why try to give people ideas when they don't want them?" (159–60).

Current feminist resistance to realism also is grounded in a suspicion of both a language and a rhetorical praxis that are fixed, rational, orderly, impersonal, and aimed toward climactic closure and the perpetuating of the illusion of a stable world, characteristics that are understood, rightly or wrongly, to belong to realism, which in turn and quite correctly, is understood to be the dominant form of discourse embedded in capitalism. Consequently, as Ann Kaplan has pointed out, feminist playwrights, like their sister filmmakers, have called for radical disruptions to subvert that dominant discourse. In her summary of the problem, "Realism, Narrative, and the Feminist Playwright – A Problem of Reception," Jeanie Forte points to the debate regarding playwriting, insisting that a realist play could not be also a feminist play because realism supports the dominant ideology by constructing the reader as subject within that ideology. "Classical realism," she concludes, "always a reinscription of the dominant order, could not be useful for feminists interested in the subversion of a patriarchal social system" (116).

In rejecting realism, feminist dramatists are reenacting battles previously fought in American theatre in such sites as the New Playwrights' Theatre's destabilizing assaults on Taylorism in the twenties, the Black Revolutionary Theatre's separatist repudiation of reformist movements in the late sixties, and the anti–Vietnam War response of the late seventies. The New Playwrights' Theatre stridently resisted traditional, bourgeois, realistic theatre in part by appropriating and hybridizing indigenous American forms such as burlesque and vaudeville in an expressionist mode. The Black Revolutionary Theatre movement, which strove to repudiate the hegemonic assertions of American realism, posited a radical alternative to a rigorously ordered structure and traditional verisimilitude. Spokesman William Oliver put it this way: "We must avoid standards that define drama by means of technical or conventional structures which do not make reference to both the rhetorical purposes of communication and to the sensuo-hypnotic communion of ecstatic arousal" (20). James Reston in "Coming to Terms" called for a nonrealistic dramatization of the effects of the Vietnam War: "The modern playwright becomes more important than the historian, for in no other war of our history was the private word more important than the public pronouncements. . . . With the Vietnam experience, the history is the subtext." Because Vietnam vets are tortured by internal conflicts that the voices of soothing denial threaten to drown out, the internal conflicts "are the stuff of the stage. . . . Its tools are beyond those of the historian and the journalist, for the stage is at home with the interior of things." Arguing that the theatre must recapture its confrontational function and citing such work as David Rabe's *Streamers* (1976) and Emily Mann's *Still Life* (1979), Reston insisted on a nonrealistic medium: "The theater is not at its best when it attempts to reproduce history or contemporary politics, but rather when it presents a *concept* of history against which the audience can test its own perceptions. The stage can humanize history and bring it alive, while professional historians and television are dehumanizing" (18). In light of this brief overview, it is not too much to say that whenever there has been trouble in the land, modern American playwrights, male or female, black or white, have turned to experimental dramaturgy as the only possible powerful site for exposing contradictions and illusionist hegemony.

Dramatic Discourse Versus Modern Management

Despite its significant ambition, the New Playwrights' Theatre usually is regarded as a disruptive hiccup in the historical metanarrative of the smooth progress of American drama toward realism, an unfortunate experiment that ended in failure, and one of many such movements that Douglas McDermott has called "theatre that nobody knows." Setting themselves up in conscious opposition to the Guild and the Provincetown theatres, which represented bourgeois commercialism, the New Playwrights' Theatre planned to be the voice of the real America, the progressive working class (Goldman and Gordon 170).

Two recent studies of the impact of modern technology on American culture, Cecilia Tichi's *Shifting Gears* (1987) and James Knapp's *Literary Modernism and the Transformation of Work* (1988), discuss the ways in which the "scientific management" movement redefined both workers' and artists' relationships with work, machinery, and the modernist project. Tichi argues that by the 1910s, the techniques and values embodied in Taylorist management theory and in machine technology, such as personal competence, effectiveness, immediacy, functionalism, minimalism, and social harmony under skilled leadership, were liberating forces for the artist, who now had a new identity as a "designer-engineer" (79). Even writers thematically hostile to "Taylorism," she argues, were stylistically influenced by the new "ethos of synchronized design, abundance, functionalism, its kinetics, its utilitarian motivation and method of spatial and temporal reformation" (90).

Knapp's concern is with how Taylor's appropriation of scientific inevitability authorized his system while undermining the engaged modernists' project. Even though modern art resisted theories like Taylor's "scientific management," he writes, it "ultimately became symptomatic of the very modernity it opposed. While modernist literature spoke loudly against the degradation of all kinds of work, it nevertheless tacitly accepted contemporary assumptions about the instrumentality of reason, and so reproduced within itself a social discourse which would deny to art any authority to address social and economic issues" (18).

Given the wealth of plays written about work and technology during the period under consideration in these studies, one might expect the drama to figure prominently in Tichi's and Knapp's discussions. Furthermore, because many plays vociferously and insistently resisted the ideology of uniform technology, one might expect some qualifying remarks about the American modernists' enthusiasm for machine technology. However, Tichi makes only a passing reference to Eugene O'Neill's *Dynamo* and Knapp considers no plays at all. This is a significant oversight because American drama of the early modernist period, especially the work done by "the revolting playwrights," plays an important part in the response to work and the new technologies. Although Eugene O'Neill and Elmer Rice are the best known of those who wrote against the prevailing enthusiasm for the "Efficiency Movement," the work of a small radical group, the New Playwrights' Theatre, commands attention because of its unique objectives.

The New Playwrights' Theatre, as C. W. E. Bigsby notes in the first volume of *A Critical Introduction to Twentieth-Century American Drama*, was "the first attempt to build a theatre on a social foundation in America" and was to have been a genuinely native theatre engaged in cultural exchange with a huge, active, working audience (194). "Unfortunately," Jordan Y. Miller and Winifred L. Frazer observe in their recent history, *American Drama Between the Wars*, "the New Playwrights' Theatre was ahead of its time" and it was "bedeviled" by the "avowed purpose of demonstrating social injustice at the expense of dramatic artistry" (100–01). Rosemarie K. Bank describes the general organizational thrust of historical accounts of the New Playwrights' Theatre as following the new mode of binarism, that is, of setting up an opposing term or concept: "Accounts of the New Playwrights' Theatre of the 1920's reflect such a strategy, since its history has been read in terms of two positionings: first, as an experimental theatre in opposition to commercial American theater values and practices, and, second, as an art theater whose largely 'expressionistic style' of dramaturgy and production prevented it from effectively presenting the sociopolitical values to which its founders . . . were dedicated" (324).

Organized in the spring of 1927 with the financial backing of the banker Otto Kahn, the New Playwrights' Theatre had only two full seasons, 1927–1928 and 1928–1929, when it was disbanded in the spring. The five directors, John Dos Passos, Mike Gold, Em Jo Basshe, John Howard Lawson, and Francis Faragoh, all wrote plays for their joint enterprise;

the plays produced were: John Howard Lawson's *Loud Speaker* (1927) and *The International* (1928); Em Jo Basshe's *Earth* (1927) and *The Centuries* (1927); Paul Sifton's *The Belt* (1927); Michael Gold's *Hoboken Blues* (1928); Upton Sinclair's *Singing Jailbirds* (1929); and John Dos Passos's *Airways, Inc.* (1929).

In the manifesto, "Toward a Revolutionary Theatre," John Dos Passos explained that "the revolutionary experimental futurist 'revolting' (or whatever you want to call it) theatre" wanted not only to break with present-day Broadway theatrical tradition run by "smart real estate men" but also to "draw its life and ideas from the conscious sections of the industrial and white collar working classes which are out to get control of the great flabby mass of capitalist society and mould it to their own purpose. In an ideal state it might be possible for a group to be alive and have no subversive political tendency. At present it is not possible." Dos Passos emphasized the need for huge scale; "the day of the frail artistic enterprise, keeping alive through its own exquisiteness, has passed. A play . . . has got to have bulk, toughness and violence to survive in the dense clanging traffic of twentieth century life" (20). According to John H. Wrenn, Dos Passos also had a national agenda, namely, the creation of an American theatre similar to the theatre of the socially critical Spanish playwright Jacinto Benavente y Martínez, whose *La malquerida (The Passion Flower)* had been produced in New York in 1920. Praising Benavente for his sense of "*lo castizo*, the essence of the local, of the regional," Dos Passos heralded the public, social, and communal theatre that reflected acutely the indigenous spirit of people in a neighborhood café rather than "'the empty shell of traditional observances'" (140).

The modernist focus on alienation in the workplace and the concomitant increased mechanization of the worker can be understood as a response to a change in the nature of work itself. Under the authority of the "scientific management" movement pioneered by Frederick Winslow Taylor, its principal spokesperson, work was transformed from a skilled, individual enterprise into a carefully controlled, scientifically authorized, and fiercely hierarchical "system" that sharply restricted the worker. Taylor argued that this change was necessary to save a country suffering from economic inefficiency and to replace "an antagonistic state of war to peace" (37). Taylor wished to impose an illusory state of ordered and productive harmony against the reality of both unpredictable individualism and rebellious collectivism. He challenged two basic American egalitarian principles in his manifestoes, "Shop Management" (1903) and "The Principles of Scientific Management" (1911), collected in *Scientific Management*. First, he wrote that "men are not born equal and any attempt to make them so is contrary to nature's laws and will fail" (90). Second, arguing that a competent man was not born but was made by "disciplining," Taylor called for a control of human beings by enforceable, standardized methods. Disallowing the intrusion of individual judgment, Taylor repeatedly insisted that "every single act of every workman can be reduced to a science" (64). The "system" would now take priority over the individual. The implementation of responsibility clearly had to shift from worker to management because the worker was lacking imagination and was "incapable" mentally (41). Taylor's simply dichotomized division of labor separated *homo sapiens* from *homo faber*, aligning the brain with management and the body with the worker, the premise being that the two, stimulated by the shared profit motive, would work in tandem "like a smoothly running machine" (120). In sum, Taylor reduced "scientific management" to five points: (1) "Science, not rule of thumb." (2) "Harmony, not discord." (3) "Cooperation, not individualism." (4) "Maximum output, in place of restricted output." (5) "The development of each man to his greatest efficiency and prosperity" (140).

The transformation of work under Taylor's "scientific management" intersected sharply with the transformation of art under the modernist aegis. As Knapp observes, "notions of human subjectivity became increasingly to be regarded as sites of uncertainty and conflict, by those setting out to formulate a 'modernist' program for the arts, as well as by proponents of the new scientific management" (4). The generalization that follows from this is that fragmentation and other dislocations of traditional literary forms became prominent features of many modernist responses to technological control and systematizing. While this may be true in the majority of instances, nonetheless, the New Playwrights' Theatre exposed a conscious effort, in the plays as well as in the organization, to, in Dos Passos's words, "create a real focus in American life. In method of presentation it will be something between the high mass in a Catholic church and Barnum and Bailey's circus, both of which are rituals stripped to their bare lines. Vigor and imagination must take the place of expensiveness and subtlety." Far from being unmediated and fragmentary chaos, the work of the New Playwrights' Theatre was both a carefully orchestrated assault on traditional forms and, more important, an attempt to establish a huge community predicated on the value of "sincere work" (20).

The classic charge against much modernist art is that it simply turned away from banalities such as everyday work and turned in on itself, avoiding conflict and contestation in an elitist self-absorption and sanctuary-seeking ivory-towerism. Certainly this charge cannot be leveled at the group of playwrights who resisted both Taylor's "scientific management" theory and any elitist aestheticized evasion of engagement in social issues. C. W. E. Bigsby, in fact, points to Michael Gold's concern that the futurist set for *Hoboken Blues* should never be esoteric, lest it "seem too purely modernistic, dangerously detached from the world it pictured" (*Critical* 195).

When the New Playwrights' Theatre was formed in 1927, the five founding dramatists had a complex agenda that could be described as an ill-defined, uneasy, and hybridized mix of Marxism, humanism, and modernism informed by a commitment to expressionism. Disgusted by the "diseased" commercial theatre that Dos Passos called "hokum," the politically left group turned to the Russian revolutionary theatre as a model but not as a template for what they hoped to accomplish in America. They dreamed of a proletarian, democratic theatre, incorporating all the arts and made for the laboring masses, a theatre that would attack "Interests" and "The System." Theirs was to be an assertive, assaultive presence characterized by inexhaustible experimentalism and innovative expression. Conceived of as a unifying agent, this theatre was also to be native and national as well as a subversive and counteractive force to what Dos Passos called the grinding engine of industrial life. It was a way to reorganize American workers and to awaken them to their potential existence as worker/actors in an undirected, egalitarian collective instead of as worker/spectators in a mediated, hierarchical structure.

In the light of Tichi's and Knapp's analyses of the modern artists' response to Taylor, there are three questions to ask. How did these playwrights, who took an explicitly oppositional stance to "scientific management," dramatize their resistance? Did their plays indeed reclaim the authority to address social, economic, and historical issues by appropriating modernist techniques based on the contemporary assumptions about the instrumentality of reason? Or were the plays merely symptomatic of the very ideas they opposed?

Inevitably and ironically, in describing their objectives the playwrights reveal the extent to which they were indoctrinated by the new discourse. For instance, Dos Passos in "Why Write for the Theatre Anyway?" wrote of the new theatre that it could "play an important part in creating the new myth that has got to replace the imperialist prosperity myth if the machinery of American life is ever to be gotten under social control" (xxi–xxii). In his introduction to Lawson's *Roger Bloomer*, Dos Passos wrote of "the welding of our cities into living organisms" and of his hope that they would "either come alive or be filled with robots instead of men" (v). In a passage that seems to smack of Taylorist efficiency, Dos Passos states that "what we have in America today is a great uncoordinated swirl of individual energy and mechanical skill, that if it could only be got in motion towards an end would produce something inconceivable" (vi–vii). But the appropriation of current technological discourse doesn't necessarily signal capitulation to "Taylorism." We need to look at the plays themselves for "symptoms."

The plays produced during the short life span of the New Playwrights' Theatre, from its inception in the spring of 1927 to its crash with the market in 1929, are less interesting thematically than they are dramaturgically. The playwrights did not share a sharply defined position (for instance, Michael Gold later would fault Dos Passos for not being ideologically correct), but their prose statements as well as their plays, taken collectively and crudely generalized, suggest a shared leftist stance tempered by an Americanist, humanist egalitarianism. Thematically, or more accurately, politically, the plays protest the dehumanizing and degrading of natural man by institutions such as racism, Christianity, industrialism, and capitalism, that is, the various modern "machines" that threaten and fragment organic, individual identity. The plays show greater imaginative and expressive range in their dramaturgical strategies, which are, for me, at least, the real site of resistance and of reclamation of authority.

A few examples drawn from statements of intention point to a concerted effort to destabilize "rational," that is, traditional, realistic, and bourgeois theatre. In an assessment of Dos Passos and Basshe in *Theory and Technique of Playwriting and Screenwriting*, John Howard Lawson explained that their plays' intentional lack of structural unity "reflects the uncertainty of the action" and fights against the "limitations of reality" and "prosaic neatness." Therefore, in Dos Passos's *The Garbage Man*, Lawson emphasizes, "Tom becomes free by an act of intuitive emotion" (289). Similarly, Dos Passos understood Lawson's *The International* to be an assault on mimetic, realistic theatre and as a "broad cartoon" "warping" stock figures (Wagner 73).

The stage directions to the plays also show the resistance to rational discourse. In *Earth*, Em Jo Basshe calls for "a whirling mass about the altar – words are indistinguishable. Cries, gestures, terrific sounds" (101). John Howard Lawson explained in the preface to *The International* that "it requires a full musical score along modernistic lines with special emphasis on broken rhythms, machine noises and chanting blues" (7). Later in the play, he describes a simultaneous cacophony of sounds: "louder roaring of guns, rapid music, and the buzz of an aeroplane" (194) and, at the end, huddled women, "laughing and screaming hysterically forming an actual tune" (220). Similarly, Paul Sifton in *The Belt* underlines the tension between man and machine: "The distant hum of The Belt seems to form a continuous curtain against which the Act is played. Talk is carried on in high, strained tones, rising frequently to sudden peaks of shouts and screeching" (9). The last act has an "interlude of revelry" with "jazz, laughter, cursing, argument, dancing, frank kissing and love-making, loud talk, quarrels, slapped faces, more jazz, more laughter, rising in a fierce, nervous, desperate gaiety throughout" (178).

Though Lawson, in particular, had a horror of proscriptive manifestos and defended the group's versatility and flexibility, nonetheless certain dramaturgical strategies recur in the documents he and others wrote about the theatre's aims: unifying the worker/actor with the worker/audience; importing the most vital techniques of the experimental European theatre such as expressionism and constructivism; and using nativist forms such as burlesque, folk tales and song, musical comedy, vaudeville, jazz, and Tin Pan Alley; in other words, eliminating the hierarchical distinctions among art forms by employing all and privileging none. The wide embrace of pluralistic flux speaks to the need to reflect a national consciousness, valorizes change, and, of course, resists any standardized methodology in a paradoxical intersection of serious thought with playful expression.

Clearly, the relentlessly imaginative and playful dramatic strategies challenge Taylorism: for example, the deliberately incoherent plot of John Howard Lawson's *Loud Speaker* (1927), the intentionally oblique distorted vision of Faragoh's *Pinwheel* (1927), the deliberate cacophony of factory noise and jazz in Paul Sifton's *The Belt* (1927), the jagged, inconsistent, broken rhythms and chanting in John Howard Lawson's *The International* (1928), and the delirium-induced dreams in Upton Sinclair's *Singing Jailbirds* (1929). The deliberately disturbing hybridization of poetic and discordant forms resulted in a disordered aesthetics that was diametrically opposed to prosaic, rational, scientific discourse. When Taylor insisted that "every single act of every workman can be reduced to a science" (64), the New Playwrights' Theatre retaliated with rebellious and unpredictable individualism. To Taylor's elitist rationale that "men are not born equal, and any attempt to make them so is contrary to nature's laws and will fail" (190), the New Playwrights' Theatre dramatized a humanized, egalitarian enterprise. To Taylor's argument for peace, the New Playwrights' Theatre answered with a battle cry; to his privileging of science over intuition, they offered unrestrained imagination; to his wish for harmony, they replied with dissonance and discord; to his call to develop men for maximum efficiency, they celebrated man's unmanageable creativity.

What did the New Playwrights' Theatre put up against Taylor's persuasive, rationalist discourse that seemed to effectively consign workers to a fixed place in the factory assembly line? They put up theatre itself and, in particular, an American worker's theatre enriched by folk and popular expression that resisted in content and form Taylor's systematized programs. Their serious theatre, wrapped in the mantle of play, provided a site for open exploration of history, culture, and work; was a place that embraced change and experiment; dismantled the production system by looking at the worker and the repressive means of production rather than at the end product; and showed workers not only the tyrannies that rendered them powerless but also the means to liberation. To return to Dos Passos's manifesto, "Toward a Revolutionary Theatre," is to be reminded that the New Playwrights' Theatre was as much concerned with creating an authentic American community, "an active working audience," as it was in producing plays free of "hokum" (20).

The New Playwrights' Theatre not only reintegrated *homo faber* with *homo sapiens*, it also included *homo ludens*, a necessary and integral aspect of the working man missing completely from Taylorist discourse. Whereas Taylor sharply dichotomized the worker and the manager on a body–brain axis, the New Playwrights' Theatre, from its inception, made a triangulated union of body, intelligence, and imagination that was realized both in the plays' themes and in their dramaturgical strategies. First, the theatre replaces the factory as the site of the struggle. Second, in productions that remove the fourth wall, the union between actor and audience signifies an implicit engagement in the dramatized rebellion and an explicit sharing in the state of being a worker. Third, the work is shown to be play and play is shown to be work, and both are shown to be communal and egalitarian efforts. Fourth, an aggressively open, even incoherent, kind of dramatic discourse displaces arguments about the instrumentality of reason. In fact, all the dramaturgical strategies argue for reclamation of the authority to address the issues.

That they failed politically, Dos Passos attributed to the reified, compartmentalized thinking that separated art from ideas, that is, Taylorism. In his postmortem "Did the New Playwrights Theatre Fail?" Dos Passos surveys the merits of the experimental productions and the demerits of an audience trained in conventional theatre and expecting realistic dramaturgy. "*Loud Speaker*, in spite of many crudities, was a fairly successful attempt to put a political farce into three dimensions, to break down the pictureframe stage and to turn a stream of satire on the audience vigorously and unashamedly. . . . *The Belt* was a success all along the line. It was a play that had something to say very much in the spirit of American workers; it said it simply and recklessly and the audience understood. . . . The form of farce-melodrama [of *The International*] it seems to me is one of the best for transmitting large-scale ideas to an audience . . . and everybody was trying to see it in terms of a three act problem play by Pinero" (13). Facing criticism from all sides, Dos Passos admitted that "the whole drift of American cultural life" was against the New Playwrights (Rosen 57).

Despite its innovations and undeniable pioneering impact on later, leftist American theatre, the New Playwrights' Theatre enterprise was and continues to be deemed a failure by contemporary critics, left and right (including Joseph Wood Krutch, John Mason Brown, Ben Blake, Arthur Hornblow), and later historians of the drama who have charged the writers with a vast catalogue of crimes, including being incoherent, careless, tiresome, experimental, noisy, boisterous, amateurish, incongruous, anti-illusionistic, unfinished, fantastic, dizzying, inconsistent, episodic, blatant, crude, plotless, unrealistic, and so forth. Of course, judged by these criteria, the New Playwrights' Theatre did not fail but, rather, succeeded in subversively challenging everything traditional bourgeois theatrical practice and rationalist thinking sanctioned. It did employ a native American idiom built on the multiple voices of jazz, vaudeville, circus, melodrama, and burlesque, what Lawson had termed "the real manners and modes of the theater" (Wagner 71). In a particularly astonishing assessment of the "failure," George Knox and Herbert Stahl, in a study of the New Playwrights' Theatre prompted by a special session at the American Studies Association in 1961, asserted that "in good drama the playwright's thought is an accurate formulation of thought already existent in the minds of the audience. He has to cater to a composite intelligence. . . . He cannot tell his audience what to think but what it *is* thinking" (148). Of course, had Dos Passos et al. followed this line, they would have been Taylorites addressing the managerial classes, arguing for the instrumentality of reason and employing realistic dramaturgical strategies. One could conclude that the New Playwrights' Theatre may have failed to institute political change but it did not resort to contemporary assumptions about the instrumentality of reason to make its argument; in fact, it did quite the opposite. Therefore, it was symptomatic not of the rationalist efficiency it opposed but, rather, of the imaginative creativity it championed.

The uses of dramatic representation by twentieth-century political and ideological movements show that if mimetic discourse is the appropriate instrument of power in an institution that seeks to verify its solidity and authority over time, a conservative, historically oriented model aligned with narrow domesticity and hegemonic nationalism, then those who resist must repudiate realism. Oppositional, revolutionary postures must stand at the periphery of the normative enclosures; if you step inside the circle, you risk transformation and assimilation. The move is similar to Augusto Boal's resistance to Aristotle's "coercive system" of tragedy in *Theater of the Oppressed* (1974), in which he argues that a powerful system of intimidation is designed to eliminate all that is not commonly accepted. Boal insists that to stimulate the spectator to transform his society, to engage in revolutionary action, we have to seek another poetics. To return to Dos Passos's interest in *lo castizo*, perhaps the real poetics of drama lies in the voices of Americans in all their local and regional variety. Such a poetics would bring us back to Walter Prichard Eaton's suggestion with which I began this exploration of realism, that we approach American drama from the historical or sociological point of view, a suggestion that, from a contemporary position, would also open the way for an analysis of the cultural work being done by the drama as well as a literary analysis of its pluralistic "voices."

6

Conclusion

Beyond Hegemony and Canonicity

THE PRIMARY PROBLEM of American drama seems to be located in the convergence of its two components, as if the union of "American" and "drama" were a coupling of the worst elements of both, carrying with it only the tainted characteristics and none of the approved qualities. In the hierarchized categories of genre, drama, too closely aligned with entertainment and with emotion, has been affixed in the cement shoes of high critical disdain and sunk to the murky bottom of academe; as well, in the long-standing competition between teachers and scholars of English and American literatures for control of the discipline, American is the lesser force. The fact that the most canonized figure in the discipline of English literary studies, Shakespeare, was primarily a dramatist does nothing to mitigate the sin of drama. But to accept this double damnation would be to arrive at a worrying conclusion: that the problem of American drama is the problem of cultural capital and that American drama has none because it is not "literature," nor is it wholly "American," nor does it belong in higher education, nor is it free from the stranglehold of realism. Yet all of these assertions, I have been arguing, are not true but are manufactured constructs, the products of a matrix of forces that has distorted and simplified nearly beyond recognition the rich and complicated history of American drama largely still buried under narrow canonicity, hegemonic New Criticism, theoretical indifference, and academic shortsightedness and only recently unearthed, dusted off, and looked at in the brighter light of culture and performance studies. In fact, one might argue that drama, theatre, and performance exist in such abundance and suffuse every human activity to such a degree that it is nothing more than willful folly to ignore their powerful, disruptive presence; or that, as Benjamin Bennett has argued, the form of drama is a uniquely revelatory locus of the sense of rupture, so much so that "its significance and dangerous disruptive power can be measured precisely by the extent to which literary theorists, as a rule, avoid setting it off as an object of concentrated study" (1). One might argue further that drama really cannot be regulated or disciplined and that the multiplicity of efforts to contain or erase its manifestations as literature are evidence of its complexity and resistant force and of the critics' uneasiness in the face of the challenge. But, as C. W. E. Bigsby asks in his assessment of the critics' avoidance of American drama as literature, "The Absent Voice: Drama and the Critic" (1988), "Can they, moreover, continue to regard the American theatre as socially and culturally marginal, peripheral to the concerns of the critic, whether that critic be committed to an exploration of the structure of language, the generation of character, the elaboration of plot, the nature of readership, or the aesthetic response to ideological fact?" (21). Obviously, those working in the field believe that they should not, but they still have to account for and contend with the phenomenon of the persistent resistance.

The distinction between modes of reading rather than kinds of discourse that Louise Rosenblatt develops in *The Reader, the Text, the Poem* also may help explain American drama's situation. She distinguishes between an "aesthetic" reading, that is, what is actively happening to the reader at the moment of reading, and an "efferent" reading, which is focused on the acquisition of information (25). Wendell V. Harris in *Interpretive Acts: In Search of Meaning* points out that if a genre is designated "literary," "its recognition leads one to expect that aesthetic as well as or instead of efferent reading is likely to be rewarded" (93). But to approach dramatic literature from only one of these two perspectives is to neglect the critical element; dramatic literature also addresses the imagination because, as I have argued earlier, it must be staged in the head. It demands a different kind of reading than poetry or prose, a reading that unifies language and image. But the critics stubbornly persist in separating the components of drama as if those components were discrete units rather than tightly integrated parts of a whole. Just as a study of dramatic literature must not erase the human agency necessary to its performance, so must not performance studies ignore the central authority of the text.

A case in point is Roman Ingarden, in whose *The Literary Work of Art* a dramatic work is "not a *purely* literary work" but "a *borderline case*" (322). Ingarden reasons that a play is split into two different texts: the main text itself and the "side text" or stage directions. Of the main text, Ingarden contends that it consists "exclusively of sentences that are 'really' *spoken* by the represented characters" and that "we should learn virtually everything that is essential for the given drama from the words that the characters speak" (208–9). Of course, Ingarden is wrong and any reader familiar with Eugene O'Neill's *Mourning Becomes Electra*, Arthur Miller's *Death of a Salesman*, or almost any play by George Bernard Shaw, to name but some obvious examples, knows how essentially inseparable the "side text" is from the whole. In "Behind the Clichés of Contemporary Theatre," John McGarth worries about the tyranny of the word: "But words are not the 'language' of theatre, and by exclusively attending to them we reduce, impoverish the event for academic convenience. The act of *creating theatre* has nothing to do with the making of dramatic literature: dramatic literature is what is sometimes left behind when theatre has been and gone" (260). I strongly disagree; dramatic literature both precedes the performance and remains after. The text is a constant that can be enriched or diminished but never replaced by performative interpretation. John Styan in *Drama, Stage and Audience* (1975) resists the idea that "the primary evidence of the play resides in the most stable element in the line of transmission, in the script itself. But the script is not the play" (6–7). Indeed it is not, but it is the literary form of the dramatic expression and as such merits attention.

Unproductive and dangerously divisive interdisciplinary quarrels to one side, the important question to ask is, What is to be done? Should the mutually crippling binarism of drama/theatre be allowed to continue? Should drama as a genre continue to be subjugated to the dismissive tyranny of other genres? Should American drama continue to be excluded from the American literary canon? Should American drama continue to be problematic in the curriculum? Should American drama be isolated in a xenophobic bell jar? Obviously I do not think so because all these perpetuate antiquated practices predicated on an equally antiquated paradigm and are, therefore, as intellectually bankrupt and as artificial as the construct of a homogeneous canon. Although I would continue to argue for the primacy of the literary text in the study of dramatic literature, I would also argue for an enriching and historically responsible integration of the study of dramatic literature with theatrical practices and performance theories. I think that arguably there are generic distinctions between dramatic literature and poetry, prose, song, and the like, but I think that the characteristics of the drama suffuse other literary forms to a greater degree than many would allow; how else has M. M. Bakhtin been able to appropriate and construct his carnivalesque theory of the novel or Kenneth Burke his dramatistics theory? Given that much of this book has been devoted to documenting the neglect and exclusion of dramatic literature from the canon and the class-room, I believe less in the value of expanding the canon than in making the neglect and exclusion themselves the subjects of investigation.

Finally, it is important to remember that American drama, of course, is not "American," even though what happened to it in academic and cultural institutions has been peculiarly American. American drama began by imitat-ing European models, expanded widely with waves of immigrants from all over the world, has participated in all the major movements, and has, con-versely, exerted its own influence on the drama of other countries and cul-tures, an influence too often overlooked in standard histories, even those that acknowledge hyphenated or hybridized Americans. The notion of a purely "American" literature was based on an idealized cultural nationalism that was appropriated by the burgeoning academy and refined by a proliferating, self-justifying professoriate intent on professionalizing themselves as the proponents of an elite culture. Now the dogs of multiculturalism are yapping up the tree of traditionalism and hyphenated American literatures are dis-placing the centrality of national and generic hegemony. What is to be done?

What is manifestly clear is that first the dominant paradigm needs to be broken. In *The Structure of Scientific Revolutions* (1962), Thomas Kuhn demonstrates the way in which the scientific community operates within a normative paradigm, a coherent tradition of research, the study of which prepares a student for "membership in the particular scientific community with which he will later practice." Joining "men whose research is based on shared paradigms," they, in turn, partake in the consensual continuation of the paradigm. The more esoteric the research, the more "mature" the field (11). The whole enterprise of "normal science" is staked on the survival and perpetuation of the paradigm and new theories are actively resisted, a resistance Kuhn claims is necessary so that in-depth work on a small part of nature can be carried forth. Awareness of anomalies can lead to a paradigm change, but the emergence of a new theory demands such a large-scale destruction that Kuhn compares it to a crisis "generally preceded by a period of pronounced professional insecurity" such as the shift from the Ptolemaic to the Copernican systems (67–68). Historically, Kuhn ar-gues, though scientists may lose their faith when confronted with the crisis, they do not renounce the paradigm nor do they treat the anomalies as "counter-instances" because "a scientific theory is declared invalid only if an alternate candidate is available to take its place" (77). The transition to a new paradigm is, for Kuhn, nothing less than a revolution based on an acceptance that the old paradigm was malfunctioning. Of course, more than the paradigm must change; the methodology and the field need to be redefined because the whole worldview has changed. Although Kuhn has expressed surprise at the enthusiasm with which those outside the unique provenance of science have embraced his thesis about tradition-bound periods punctuated by noncumulative breaks that, he points out, are borrowed from other fields such as literature and politics, nonetheless it remains one of the most clearly articulated descriptions of consensual cycling, perhaps the more compelling within literary study precisely because it does not focus on literature.

Although it is well known and often cited, I invoke Thomas Kuhn's parable of the scientific paradigm in order to draw an analogy with the stalemated situation of American drama, the canon, and disciplinary boundaries. I want to have recourse to Kuhn because he raises what for him is an important distinction between scientific insularity and the more contestable ground of the liberal arts. Arguing that, unlike science, literature studies is not dependent wholly on textbooks but can also turn to readings in original sources, Kuhn believes that the student is constantly aware of the immense variety of problems that have been dealt with and, more important, "he has constantly before him a number of competing and incommensurable solutions to these problems, solutions that he must ultimately evaluate for himself" (165). Would that Kuhn were right. But one need only look at the average classroom practice, read the average scholarly article, or listen to the average conference paper (my own not excepted) to know that ideas and ideologies are not presented in this forthright way for contestation, reexamination, and reevaluation.

While there are compelling reasons to reunify dramatic literature and theatrical practice, to redress imbalances in a curriculum, to reassess constrictive tendencies and open up the canon, to embrace cultural pluralism, and to reimagine aesthetic criteria, there are equally pressing matters at stake. We need to test the whole notion of sharply delineated generic parameters, to avoid thematized readings of texts, to reject speculative psychologizing either about the playwright or about the characters, and to abandon facile sociologizing about the ways in which plays reflect a society. Frankly, we need to alter completely the way we approach, teach, and write about drama and theatre. We must leave the impoverished and intellectually exhausted high ground of specialized and narrowly segregated disciplinary coverage, still predicated for the most part on aesthetics, and reenter what Raymond Williams in *Writing in Society* has described as the way of life as a whole through the analytical examination of the "really active society" of "conventions and institutions" (189).

Clearly what I am calling for is a broader, multi-, cross-, and interdisciplinary approach to "high" drama as well as to "low," to say nothing of a rejection of hierarchies of this kind save as subjects of investigation. The history of the cultural reception of American drama is inseparable from American economic, educational, political, and social institutions. On this point I have not trodden the winepress alone. Just as I am not the first to complain about the generic hegemony that has marginalized American drama for so long, I am also not the first to advocate investigating the relationship between cultural form and social process. I have, in the course of this book, mentioned work being done by scholars in theatre and drama that is both ambitious and conscientious about integrating the study of the art form with the study of social, economic, and political factors. Issues of traditional literary value and reputation must be considered as the consequences of institutional and, by extension, disciplinary struggles for power, authority, and hegemony. This does not displace or discount necessarily the formal, linguistic or aesthetic dimensions of a work nor the considerations of drama as a genre, but it opens the way for a more comprehensive assessment and simultaneously investigates the reasons for privileging certain aesthetic and linguistic configurations. What it certainly should do is open the way for intense examination and reformulation of what has come to be understood as normative criteria for judgment. As Barbara Herrnstein Smith so aptly describes current American critical theory, "Beguiled by the humanist's fantasy of transcendence, endurance, and universality, it has been unable to acknowledge the most fundamental character of literary value, which is its mutability and diversity" (14). American drama's future lies in paying critical attention to both its mutability and diversity.

Such work, of course, has been done by others in American literary studies as well though the needed "field" crossovers and blurring of disciplinary boundaries have not been made in many instances. In "The Integrity of Memory: Creating a New Literary History of the United States," Annette Kolodny calls for "dislodgings and reordered contexts," for an examination of works such as women's frontier narratives or chants of Native Americans that "defy our inherited categories of discourse and evaluation" (295–96). I have been arguing that American drama as a whole and virtually all unorthodox plays and dramatic works have been outside the canon and therefore excluded from thoughtful or extended consideration in American literary history. But breaking a paradigm requires more than an opening of the canon and the more accurate rewriting of the history. Kolodny expands her position by imagining an approach in which two corollary questions are asked: Why do certain texts "fail to gain power at their moment of composition," and why are some texts "resurrected at later periods and are seen to speak to historical moments not their own"? In this way, "attention is directed toward cultural contexts (which . . . rehistoricize the text) and to the material facts of literary production, distribution, and dissemination (which historicize the publishing industry and the reading public both)" (304–5).

What might this reimagining mean for the study of American drama? Clearly, at the very least, it means a reevaluation of dramatic literature, theatre history, and performance practices. It might begin by considering both drama as a genre and the generic distinctions within drama. For instance, Thomas Postlewait has argued that rather than dismissing melodrama as a "youthful" or "impoverished" stage in the organic development of American drama on its way to a "mature" realism, it be understood as a fully achieved form in its own right and as a form that continues to thrive in film and television as well as on the stage. In fact, he argues, it is "the most important, narrative form of modern times" ("Melodrama" 9). For the reconsideration of the genre itself, which for me is still of primary concern, it might mean return to any moment in the history of American drama to reassess its cultural patrimony, to reevaluate the dominant texts and authors, to resurrect the marginalized or even "invisible" voices, especially those of dissension and parody, and to reconstruct the academic discipline and the theatrical practice of the moment as conditioned by immediate political, social, aesthetic, and economic factors. The possibilities are limitless. By way of a very simple, preliminary example, one might return to Barrett Clark's essay "American Drama in Its Second Decade" in *The English Journal* (1932) or any comparable historical retrospective survey to ask why the author privileges certain texts. For instance, Clark lists his twelve best of the 1920–1930 decade: O'Neill's *Lazarus Laughed*, Lynn Riggs's *Lonesome West*, Leonard Ide's *Mrs. Tony Trentor*, J. H. Powel's *Brief Candle*, Burdette Kinne's *Fatted Calf*, Knowles Entrikin's *A Graceful Generation*, Martin Flavin's *Achilles Had a Heel*, Paul Green's *Potter's Field*, Zoe Akins's *Morning Glory*, Dawn Powell's *The Party*, Dan Totheroh's *Distant Drums*, and Frederick Schlick's *Man*, of which plays only O'Neill's *Lazarus Laughed* has endured and then only as an oddity in his career, not as part of the American canon. How were these plays received when they were first produced and printed? What aesthetic criteria were brought to bear? Did production precede publication? Who constituted both the theatre and reading audiences and where were they located? What constituted their "power"? How have these plays been evaluated since that decade? Also, in the same essay Clark singles out for approbation *Third Little Show, Mid-*

night, and *Arabesque*, the plays that constituted the commercial competition. Did these plays actually have more economic power by virtue of their popular success? How have they fared in the canon wars? If we can learn as much if not more from the texts that have been despised as from those that have been valorized, then both need an equal measure of consideration.

Second, the interdisciplinary gaps must be closed. Joyce Flynn, in "Melting Plots," pointing to the long-standing critical and historical practice of separating literature and performance, text and context, especially in considerations of the early drama, calls for more cultural histories: "The need is to combine an understanding of both *stage* and *drama* in research that goes beyond biographical or local minutiae and literary analysis respectively, that combines the particular and the pattern and goes on to suggest the implications of the theatrical event for our knowledge of the surrounding society" (418).

Third, new critical theories need to be brought to bear on the inquiry. Calling for an "interdisciplinary paradigm for scholarship," Bruce McConachie has suggested that the New Historicism offers a needed way to examine the construction of the dominant idea behind American theatre and drama studies, that of a "single, unified tradition bereft of major internal contradictions, a 'natural' evolution tending toward the realistic theatre of the twentieth century" (267). Specifically, he calls for three topics to be thoroughly investigated through a New Historicist methodology: "historical erasures and representations of race, ethnicity, class, and gender in the American theatre; context, narrativity, and explanation in constructions of the theatrical past; and the ideological limitations of the major movements of theatrical realism in America" (268). In a similar vein, Michael Vanden Heuvel, arguing for foregrounding drama's differences from literature, has urged that "progressive applications" of various forms of interdisciplinary theory be used in the teaching of drama as a means to avoid reducing texts "to purely linguistic structures" ("Textual" 159). In "Textual Harassment: Teaching Drama to Interrogate Reading" (1993), he suggests that "the material conditions and the ideological formations of the culture" that produce the drama would "help to reclaim literature and theatre from reading practices that stress literature's autonomy from the world and to reestablish the connections between literature and history, culture, and society" (162).

The contributors to the special issue of *Resources for American Literary Study* (Spring 1990) suggest a wide range of considerations, methodologies, and approaches. Carla Mulford calls for a rejection of the assumption that Puritan proscriptions tyrannized theatrical activity to the extent it has hitherto been assumed that it did, for an investigation into the nonelite groups, and for methodologies adapted from the newer theories of representation, social history, and cultural anthropology. For Brenda Murphy, the greatest need concerns issues of concept and intertext because "drama is perhaps more intricately enmeshed in intertextuality than fiction or poetry because earlier plays did not exist merely in the past, but in the present as theatrical events, even as new plays are being produced" ("Breaking" 30). Murphy points out that not only do American plays need to be understood in the ways in which they both participated in and departed from the dominant American paradigms and conventions, they also need to be compared to the European plays as partaking in a cosmopolitan interaction. Mark W. Estrin wants "varieties of the new critical discourse now largely ignored by dramatic literature scholars . . . gender and genre theory; semiotics (of the sort applied by Martin Esslin in *The Field of Drama*) and performance theory; notions of spectatorship, theatre space, and set design; and psychoanalytic and, especially, ideological contexts for these writers whose plays were produced in times of social and political ferment," as well as the effects of O'Neill's long shadow on his contemporaries (43). Thomas P. Adler points to the need to relate American drama to the rest of classic American literature, to focus on the way contemporary drama reflects and refracts sociopolitical issues, to consider the technical and stylistic relationship between drama and the other arts, to question what "postmodern" means in American drama, and to examine the metatheatrical impulses of modern American drama.

More recently, in *Theatre Journal* (December 1992), Joseph Roach has called for a reinterpretation and complication of the crisis in American drama and theatre, contextualizing it as part of a larger crisis, that of multiculturalism. Recalling that Alexander Drummond, Richard Moody, and Barnard Hewitt had "once debated and then rejected a broader, intercultural, performance-oriented conception of American drama in favor of the primacy of Anglo-American genres," Roach advocates "re-opening the debate with three objectives: 1.) to re-define the historical canon in line with current research in performance studies; 2.) to expand the definition of performance beyond predominantly literate cultures and traditions; 3.) to re-interpret American culture as a series of political boundaries both marked and contrasted by performances" (462).

It is clear that the redefinition and reinterpretation Roach calls for have yet to occur on the scale needed because the received devaluation is being perpetuated. The consequences can be found in the most recent historical accounts in the first two volumes of the new *Cambridge History of American*

Literature (1994). In his chapter on the drama from 1590 to 1820, Michael Gilmore catalogues the characteristics of the earliest American drama, characteristics that are, in his narrative, reasons for the drama's low status compared to that of the novel. Gilmore posits that American drama was irreducibly social, that theatres were sites of public disturbance, that drama was marked by extravagance, orality, temporality, overt politics, and collectivity, and that it was derivative. Drama receives scant attention in the second volume in a few pages from Michael Davitt Bell, who finds little reason to consider drama as literature. Although Bell notes the "extraordinary expansion" of theatrical activity in America between 1820 and 1840, he explains that "these developments in the American theater are at best incidental to the history of American literature and American literary vocation in the first half of the nineteenth century" and that "none of the American plays produced before 1850, however great their interest as documents of popular culture, has survived as literature" (44). As for what constitutes "literature," given that Bell charges the drama with being unsubtle, emotional, and spectacular and excludes minstrel shows, vaudeville, and burlesque as being "hardly literature," the only conclusion to be reached is that "literature" must be subtle, unemotional, and unspectacular. If these narrowly restrictive, rigidly rationalist, and antihistrionic criteria still prevail as the dominant mode of evaluation in American literary studies, of necessity drama will continue to be discredited, disregarded, and marginalized.

But suppose we invert the value system. Might it not be possible to understand those characteristics of early American drama and of later aggressively political and experimental drama not as weaknesses or flaws but as strengths and virtues? Might we not think of American drama as being interactive, as calling for participation, as celebrating its irreducible social engagement, as being multicultural? The move to multiculturalism marks a shift in American literary studies in general, and therefore should afford a place for drama. In a 1994 review of the work of Peter Carafiol, Philip Fisher, Gregory S. Jay, and José David Saldívar, Carolyn Porter heralds the new approach to American literature that is no longer "parochial or insulated or exceptional" and predicts at the very least an altered curriculum and a transformation of the disciplines occasioned by the dissolution of "the disciplinary and departmental lines that still separate American literary studies as a field from the Asian-, African-, and Native American scholarship that has vitally challenged and complicated both its traditional and its anti-traditional assumptions" (521). For many scholars working along these new lines, one way to erase the historical and geographical frames that bound American studies to national and nativist

concerns would be to acknowledge the permeability of "American" boundaries and to shift the center to the Caribbean, where cultural hybridity not
hegemony is the vital force. These are some of the fruitful branches growing
out of the stony rubbish of generic hegemony, elitist Anglophilia, cultural
xenophobia, and disciplinary myopia.

What could this mean for a study of American drama? It would address
and redress the problem both of "American" and of drama. It could mean
a total remapping, recentering or, better, decentering, and revaluation, an
acceptance and appreciation of all forms of dramatic literature, theatrical
production, and performative expression especially including those which
are not necessarily always author-centered, which are informed by a lively,
not artificially manufactured, folk sensibility, which are instances of cultural
hybridity, which are overtly political not aestheticized, which do celebrate
intense emotional expression and vivid spectacle, which yield willingly to
the seductive power of mimesis, which free, enrich, and extend our lives,
and which accept the spiritual world as a vital presence in the "real" world.
Given all the critical, historical, and theoretical shifting now shaking the
institution, perhaps American drama will finally gain its total, rightful, and
liberated audience.

References

Adler, Mortimer J. *The Paideia Program: An Educational Syllabus.* New York: Macmillan, 1984.

Adler, Thomas P. *American Drama, 1940–1960: A Critical History.* New York: Twayne, 1994.

"American Dramatic Scholarship, 1940–Present: The Contours and Some Items for an Agenda." *Resources for American Literary Study* 17 (1990): 51–61.

Alexander, Doris M. "Psychological Fate in *Mourning Becomes Electra.*" *PMLA* 68 (1953): 923–34.

Allen, Ralph G. "Our Native Theatre: Honky-tonk, Minstrel Show, Burlesque." *The American Theatre: A Sum of Its Parts.* New York: Samuel French, 1971. 273–86.

Anderson, John. *The American Theatre.* New York: Dial, 1938.

Anderson, Mary C. *Drama in the English Department.* Mimeographed survey. University of South Carolina, 1984.

Angoff, Charles. *A Literary History of the American People.* 2 vols. New York: Knopf, 1931.

Anonymous. "Producing Centre Reports to the Drama League at the Pittsburgh Convention." *Drama League Monthly* 2 (1917): 418–20.

"The Theatre Bookshelf." *Theatre Arts Magazine* 1 (November 1916): 43.

Applebee, Arthur N. *Tradition and Reform in the Teaching of English: A History.* Urbana, IL: NCTE, 1974.

Archer, William. "The Development of American Drama." *Harper's* 142 (1920): 75–86.

The Old Drama and the New. London: Heinemann, 1923.

Arnold, Sarah Lewis, and Charles B. Gilbert. *Stepping Stones to Literature: A Reader for Fifth Grades.* New York: Silver, Burdett, 1897.

Asahina, Robert. "*Angels Fall.*" *Hudson Review* 36 (1983): 231, 233, 235.

Atkinson, Brooks. "No Time for American Drama." *Critic* 25 (1967): 16–25.

Auerbach, Doris. *Sam Shepard, Arthur Kopit, and Off Broadway Theater*. Boston: Twayne, 1982.

Babbitt, Irving. "Literature and the College." *Literature and the American College*. 1908. Washington: National Humanities Institute, 1986. 118–33.

"Literature and the Doctor's Degree." *Literature and the American College*. 1908. Washington: National Humanities Institute, 1986. 134–50.

Baker, George Pierce. *Dramatic Technique*. New York: Houghton Mifflin, 1919.

"The 47 Workshop." *The Quarterly Journal of Speech Education* 5 (1919): 185–95.

"The Theatre and the University." *Theatre Arts Monthly* 9 (1925): 99–105.

Bank, Rosemarie K. "The Doubled Subject and the New Playwrights Theatre, 1927–1929." *Critical Theory and Performance*, ed. Janelle G. Reinelt and Joseph R. Roach. Ann Arbor: University of Michigan Press, 1992. 324–35.

Barish, Jonas. *The Anti-theatrical Prejudice*. Berkeley: University of California Press, 1981.

Barnes, Clive. *50 Best Plays of the American Theatre*. New York: Crown, 1969.

Barnes, Douglas. *Drama in the English Classroom*. Champaign, IL: National Council of the Teachers of English, 1986.

Barnett, James H. "Research Areas in the Sociology of Art." *Sociology and Social Research* 42 (1958): 401–05.

Barron, Samuel. "The Dying Theater." *Harper's* 172 (1935): 108–17.

Basshe, Em Jo. *Earth*. New York: Macauley, 1927.

Baym, Nina. "Early Histories of American Literature: A Chapter in the Institution of New England." *American Literary History* 1.3 (1989): 459–88.

Baym, Nina, et al., eds. *The Norton Anthology of American Literature*. 2 vols. New York: Norton, 1994.

Beard, Charles, and Mary Beard. *The Rise of American Civilization*. New York: Macmillan, 1934.

Beckerman, Bernard. "The University Accepts the Theatre: 1800–1925." *The American Theatre: A Sum of Its Parts*. New York: Samuel French, 1971. 339–56.

Beers, Henry A., ed. *A Century of American Literature*. New York: Henry Holt, 1878.

An Outline Sketch of American Literature. New York: Chautauqua, 1887.

Beiswanger, George. "Broadway Letter." *The Kenyon Review* III (1944): 318–20.

"Theatre Today: Symptoms and Surmises." *Journal of Aesthetics and Art Criticism* 3.9–10 (1944): 19–29.

Bell, Michael Davitt. "Beginnings of Professionalism." *The Cambridge History of American Literature, II: Prose Writing 1820–1865*, gen. ed. Sacvan Bercovitch. Cambridge: Cambridge University Press, 1995. 11–73.

Bellow, Saul. "Theater Chronicle." *Partisan Review* 21.3 (1954): 19–29.

Bennett, Benjamin. *Theater as Problem: Modern Drama and Its Place in Literature*. Ithaca, NY: Cornell University Press, 1990.

Bentley, Eric. "American Theatre, '47–'48: A Report." *Harper's Magazine* 196 (1948): 232–40.

"The Drama: An Extinct Species?" *Partisan Review* 21 (1954): 411–17.

"The Drama at Ebb." *The Kenyon Review* 7 (1945): 169–84.

"Drama Now." *Partisan Review* 12 (1945): 244–51.

The Playwright as Thinker. 1946. New York: Meridian, 1955.

"Theater Chronicle." *Partisan Review* 21.4 (1954): 416.

Bercovitch, Sacvan. "The Problem of Ideology in American Literary History." *Critical Inquiry* 12.4 (1986): 631–53.

Reconstructing American Literary History. Cambridge, MA: Harvard University Press, 1986.

Rites of Assent. New York: Routledge, 1993.

Berkowitz, Gerald M. *American Drama of the Twentieth Century.* New York: Longman, 1992.

Berlin, James A. *Rhetoric and Reality: Writing Instruction in American Colleges, 1900–1985.* Carbondale: Southern Illinois University Press, 1987.

Berthoff, Warner. *The Ferment of Realism: American Literature, 1884–1919.* 1965. New York: Cambridge University Press, 1981.

Literature Without Qualities: American Writing Since 1945. Berkeley: University of California Press, 1979.

Best, Mrs. A. Starr. *Brief Survey Course on American Drama.* Monograph 30. Chicago: Drama League of America, 1926.

The Drama League of America: Its Inception, Purposes, Wonderful Growth and Future. Garden City, NY: Doubleday, Page, 1914. n.p.

Bewley, Marius. *The Eccentric Design.* New York: Columbia University Press, 1959.

Bigsby, C. W. E. "The Absent Voice: Drama and the Critic." *Studies in American Drama, 1945-Present* 3 (1988): 9–21.

A Critical Introduction to Twentieth-Century American Drama. 3 vols. Cambridge: Cambridge University Press, 1982–1985.

"Drama as Cultural Sign: American Dramatic Criticism, 1945–1978." *American Quarterly* 30.3 (1978): 331–57.

"A View from East Anglia." *American Quarterly* 41 (1989): 128–32.

"Why American Drama Is Literature." *New Essays on American Drama*, ed. Gilbert Debusscher and Henry I. Schvey. Amsterdam: Rodopi, 1989. 3–12.

Black, Alexander. "Photography in Fiction: 'Miss Jerry,' the First Picture Play." *Scribner's Magazine* 18.3 (1895): 348–60.

Blackmur, R. P. "The Lion and the Honeycomb." *The Lion and the Honeycomb.* 1950. New York: Harcourt Brace, 1955. 176–97.

Blair, Hugh. *An Abridgement of Lectures on Rhetoric.* Boston: True & Greene, 1824.

Blair, Karen J. *The Torchbearers: Women and Their Amateur Arts Associations in America, 1890–1930.* Bloomington: Indiana University Press, 1994.

Blair, Walter. *The Literature of the United States.* Chicago: Scott, Foresman, 1949.

Blair, Walter, et al., eds. *The Literature of the United States.* Third edition. 2 vols. Glenview, IL: Scott, Foresman, 1966.

Blake, Warren Barton. "Our Un-American Stage." *The Independent* 72 (1912): 503–8.

Blankenship, Russell. *American Literature as an Expression of the National Mind.* Revised edition. 1931. New York: Henry Holt, 1949.

Blau, Herbert. "The American Dream in American Gothic: The Plays of Sam Shepard and Adrienne Kennedy." *Modern Drama* 27.4 (1984): 520–39.

Bledstein, Burton J. *The Culture of Professionalism.* New York: Norton, 1978.

Bloom, Harold. "The Twentieth-Century American Canon." *Esquire* 122.3 (1994): 118–21.

Bloomfield, Maxwell. "Muckracking and the American Stage: The Emergence of Realism, 1905–1917." *South Atlantic Quarterly* 66 (1967): 165–78.

Boal, Augusto. *Theater of the Oppressed,* trans. Charles A. McBride and Maria-Odilia Leal. 1974. London: Pluto, 1979.

Bogard, Travis. "Art and Politics." *The Revels History of Drama in English, Volume VIII, American Drama,* ed. Travis Bogard, Richard Moody, and Walter Meserve. New York: Barnes & Noble, 1977. 24–42.

"The Central Reflector." *The Revels History of Drama in English, Volume VIII, American Drama,* ed. Travis Bogard, Richard Moody, and Walter Meserve. New York: Barnes & Noble, 1977. 42–65.

Contour in Time: The Plays of Eugene O'Neill. New York: Oxford University Press, 1972.

Bogardus, Emory S. "Forty-five Years as an Editor." *Sociology and Social Research* 45 (1961): 455–61.

Bolton, Gavin. *Drama as Education: An Argument for Placing Drama at the Centre of the Curriculum.* Burnt Mill, Harlow, Essex: Longman, 1984.

Bonnet, Henri. "Dichotomy of Artistic Genres." *Theories of Literary Genres,* ed. Joseph P. Strelka. University Park: Pennsylvania State University Press, 1978. 3–15.

"Books." *The Drama* 11 (1921): 284–87, 294.

Bordman, Gerald. *The Oxford Companion to American Literature.* New York: Oxford University Press, 1984.

Boucicault, Dion. "The Future American Drama." *The Arena* 12 (1890): 641–52.

Bourdieu, Pierre. *The Field of Cultural Production,* trans. Randal Johnson. Oxford: Blackwell, 1993.

Homo Academicus, trans. Peter Collier. Stanford, CA: Stanford University Press, 1988.

Boyd, James Robert. *Elements of Rhetoric and Literary Criticism.* New York: Harper & Brothers, 1844.

Boynton, Percy H. "American Drama." *American Writers on American Literature,* ed. John Macy. New York: Horace Liveright, 1931. 476–87.

Literature and American Life. Boston: Ginn, 1936.

Bradley, Sculley, Richmond Croom Beatty, and E. Hudson Long, eds. *The American Tradition in Literature.* Fourth edition. New York: Norton, 1974.

Bradley, Sculley, Richmond Croom Beatty, and E. Hudson Long, eds. *The American Tradition in Literature.* 1956. Revised shorter edition in one volume. New York: Norton, 1962.

Brooks, Cleanth, and Robert Heilman. *Understanding Drama.* New York: Holt, 1945.

Brown, Herbert R. "Sensibility in Eighteenth-century American Drama." *American Literature* 4 (1932): 47–61.

Brustein, Robert. "Intellect Into Passion." *The New Republic,* January 30, 1995, 30–31.

"The New American Playwrights." *Modern Occasions*, ed. Philip Rahv. New York: Farrar, 1966. 123–38.

"Reinventing American Theater." *The South Atlantic Quarterly* 91 (1992): 243–56.

The Third Theatre. New York: Knopf, 1969.

"Why American Plays Are Not Literature." *American Drama and Its Critics*, ed. Alan S. Downer. 1959. Chicago: University of Chicago Press, 1965. 245–55.

Bryer, Jackson R., and Ruth M. Alvarez. "American Drama, 1918–1940: A Survey of Research and Criticism." *American Quarterly* 30.3 (1978): 298–330.

Budd, Louis J., Edwin H. Cady, and Carl Anderson, eds. *Toward a New American Literary History*. Durham, NC: Duke University Press, 1980.

Bullowa, Alma M. "The One-act Play in High School Dramatics." *Quarterly Journal of Speech* 5 (1919): 351–57.

Burd, Henry. "English Literature Courses in the Small College." *English Journal* 3 (1914): 99–108.

Burton, Richard. "The Drama League of America." *The Nation* 99 (1914): 668–69.

Butler, James H. "The University Theatre Begins to Come of Age: 1925–1969." *The American Theatre: A Sum of Its Parts*. New York: Samuel French, 1971. 357–78.

Butsch, Richard. "Bowery B'hoys and Matinee Ladies: The Re-gendering of Nineteenth-Century American Theater Audiences." *American Quarterly* 46.3 (1994): 374–405.

Cadden, Michael. "Rewriting Literary History." *American Quarterly* 41 (1989): 133–37.

Cain, William E. *The Crisis in Criticism: Theory, Literature, and Reform in English Studies*. Baltimore: Johns Hopkins University Press, 1984.

Cairns, William B. "An American Drama of the 18th Century." *The Dial* 59 (1915): 60–62.

Calder, Chester. "The Drama, an Art for Democracy." *The Drama*, February 1918, 53–68.

Calverton, V. F. *The Liberation of American Literature*. New York: Scribner, 1932.

The Newer Spirit: A Sociological Criticism of Literature. New York: Boni & Liveright, 1925.

Carafiol, Peter. *The American Ideal: Literary History as a Worldly Activity*. Oxford: Oxford University Press, 1991.

"The New Orthodoxy: Ideology and the Institution of American Literary History." *American Literature* 59.4 (1987): 626–38.

Carlson, Marvin. *Theories of the Theatre*. Ithaca, NY: Cornell University Press, 1984.

Carpenter, Charles A. "American Drama: A Bibliographical Essay." *American Studies International* 21.5 (1983): 3–52.

Carter, Everett. *The American Idea: The Literary Response to American Optimism*. Chapel Hill: University of North Carolina Press, 1977.

Carter, Jean, and Jess Ogden. *Everyman's Drama: A Study of the Noncommercial Theatre in the United States*. New York: American Association for Adult Education, 1938.

Case, Sue-Ellen. "Toward a Butch-Femme Aesthetic." *Making a Spectacle: Feminist*

Essays on Contemporary Women's Theatre ed. Lynda Hart. Ann Arbor: University of Michigan Press, 1989. 282–99.

Case, Sue-Ellen, and Janelle Reinelt, eds. *The Performance of Power: Theatrical Discourse and Politics*. Iowa City: University of Iowa Press, 1991.

Cassady, Edward E. "Muckraking in the Gilded Age." *American Literature* 13 (1941): 135–41.

Cathcart, George. *Literary Reader*. New York: American Book Company, 1874.

Cerf, Bennett, and Van H. Cartmell, eds. *Sixteen Famous American Plays*. New York: Modern Library, 1941.

Chadwick, F. E. "The Woman Peril in American Education." *Educational Review* 47 (1914): 109–19.

Chaudhuri, Una. "When's the Play? Time and the Theory of Drama." *Theater* 22 (1991): 48–51.

Cheney, Sheldon. "The American Playwright and the Drama of Sincerity." *The Forum* 51 (1914): 498–512.

"Editorial." *Theatre Arts Journal* 1.1 (1916): 48.

The New Movement in the Theatre. New York: Kennerley, 1914.

Christakes, George. *Albion W. Small*. Boston: Twayne, 1978.

Chubb, Percival. "The Large Mission of the Drama League: A Rallying Cry for the Convention." *Drama League Quarterly* 1.1 (1916): 1–2.

"The League's Larger Task." *Drama League Monthly* 1.7 (1917): 274.

"President's Report." *Drama League Monthly* 2.2 (1917): 375–80.

Clark, Barrett H. "American Drama in Its Second Decade." *The English Journal* 21 (1932): 1–11.

An Hour of American Drama. Philadelphia: J. B. Lippincott, 1930.

The Modern Drama. Chicago: ALA, 1927.

"Our Most American Drama: Recent Developments, 1930–39." *The English Journal* 28 (1939): 333–42.

Clark, Barrett H., ed. *Favorite American Plays of the Nineteenth Century*. Princeton: Princeton University Press, 1943.

Clark, Barrett H., and William H. Davenport, eds. *Nine Modern American Plays*. New York: Appleton, 1951.

Clark, Barrett H., and Kenyon Nicholson, eds. *The American Scene*. New York: D. Appleton, 1930.

Clark, Harry Hayden. *Transitions in American Literary History*. Durham, NC: Duke University Press, 1953.

Clurman, Harold. "Critique of the American Theatre." *The Drama Magazine* 21 (1931): 5–6, 12, 18.

Clurman, Harold, and Stanley Kauffmann. "Dialogue: Theatre in America." *Performing Arts Journal* 3.1 (1978): 20–34.

Coghill, Nevill. "The Study of Drama at a University." *The Universities and the Theatre*, ed. D. G. James. London: George Allen & Unwin, 1952. 40–50.

Cohn, Ruby. *Dialogue in American Drama*. Bloomington: Indiana University Press, 1971.

"Twentieth Century Drama." *Columbia Literary History of the United States*. New York: Columbia University Press, 1988. 1101–25.

Colacurcio, Michael. "Does American Literature Have a History?" *Early American Literature* 13 (1978): 110–31.

Cook, Albert S. "English at Yale University." *The Dial* 26 (1894): 69–71.

Cooper, James Fenimore. *Notions of the Americans*. 1. London: Henry Colburn, 1828.

Corbin, John. "The Dawn of the American Drama." *The Atlantic Monthly* 99 (1907): 637–44.

"The New Revolt Against Broadway." *Scribner's Magazine* 54.4 (1913): 516–23.

Cordell, Richard A., ed. *Twentieth Century Plays, American: Eight Representative Selections*. New York: Ronald Press, 1947.

Corson, Hiram. *The Aims of Literary Study*. 1894. New York: Macmillan, 1906.

Crane, R. S. "Varieties of Dramatic Criticism." *The Idea of the Humanities and Other Essays: Critical and Historical 2*. 1956. Chicago: University of Chicago Press, 1967. 215–35.

Crane, William G., chair. *American Literature in the College Curriculum*. Committee on the College Study of American Literature and Culture. Chicago: NCTE, 1948.

Cravens, Hamilton. "The Abandonment of Evolutionary Social Theory in America: The Impact of Academic Professionalization upon American Sociological Theory, 1890–1920." *American Studies* 12 (1971): 5–20.

Cunliffe, Marcus. *American Literature to 1900*. London: Barrie & Jenkins, 1973.

The Literature of the United States. Revised edition. Baltimore: Penguin, 1954.

Daly, Augustin, et al. "American Playwrights on the American Drama." *Harper's Weekly* 33 (1889): 98–101.

Dasgupta, Gautam, Michael Early, and Bonnie Marranca. "The American Playwright: A Life in the Theatre?" *Performing Arts Journal* 4.1, 2 (1980): 33–51.

Davies, Henry. "The Stage as a Moral Institution." *The Critic* 43.1 (1903): 24–28.

De Tocqueville, Alexis. *Democracy in America*, trans. Henry Reeve. London: Oxford University Press, 1946.

"Decline of the Modern Drama." *New England Magazine* 8 (1835): 105–7.

Demastes, William W. *Beyond Naturalism: A New Realism in American Theatre*. New York: Greenwood, 1988.

Denby, David. "Stranger in a Strange Land: A Moviegoer at the Theater." *The Atlantic Monthly* 225 (1985): 37–50.

De Voto, Bernard. "At the Cannon's Mouth." *Saturday Review of Literature* 15.23 (1937): 8.

Diamond, Elin. "Mimesis, Mimicry, and the 'True-Real'" *Modern Drama* 32 (1989): 58–72.

Dibble, Vernon K. *The Legacy of Albion Small*. Chicago: University of Chicago Press, 1975.

Dickinson, Thomas H. *The Case of American Drama*. Boston: Houghton Mifflin, 1915.

The Insurgent Theatre. New York: B. W. Huebsch, 1917.

Dickinson, Thomas H., ed. *Chief Contemporary Dramatists*. Boston: Houghton Mifflin, 1915.

Dodge, Daniel Kilham. "English at the University of Illinois." *The Dial* 26 (1894): 261–62.

Dolan, Jill. "Geographies of Learning: Theatre Studies, Performance, and the 'Performative'" *Theatre Journal* 45.4 (1993): 417–41.

Donoghue, Denis. *Reading America: Essays on American Literature*. New York: Knopf, 1987.

   The Third Voice: Modern British and American Verse Drama. Princeton: Princeton University Press, 1959.

Dorey, J. Milnor. "A School Course in Dramatics." *English Journal* 1 (1912): 425–30.

Dos Passos, John. "Did the New Playwrights Theatre Fail?" *New Masses* 5 (1929): 13.

   "Foreword to *Roger Bloomer*." *Roger Bloomer*. John Howard Lawson. New York: Thomas Seltzer, 1923. v–vii.

   "Toward a Revolutionary Theatre." *New Masses* 3 (1927): 20.

   "Why Write for the Theatre Anyway?" *Three Plays*. New York: Harcourt, Brace, 1934. xi–xxii.

Douglas, Wallace. "Accidental Institution: On the Origin of Modern Language Study." *Criticism in the University*, ed. Gerald Graff and Reginald Gibbons. Evanston, IL: Northwestern University Press, 1985. 35–61.

Downer, Alan S. "The Pedant and the Playmaker." *Educational Theatre Journal* 9 (1957): 96–98.

Downer, Alan S., ed. *American Drama and Its Critics: A Collection of Critical Essays*. Chicago: University of Chicago Press, 1965.

Dunlap, William. *History of the American Theatre*. 2 vols. 1833. New York: Burt Franklin, 1963.

Eaton, Walter P. "American Drama Versus Literature." *The Writer and His Craft*, ed. Robert M. Lovett. Ann Arbor: University of Michigan Press, 1954. 81–99.

   "The American Theatre and Reconstruction." *Theatre Arts Magazine* 3 (1919): 8–14.

   "Our Infant Industry." *The American Stage Today*. Boston: Small, Maynard, 1908. 6–26.

   "Professor Baker's Method of Making Playwrights." *The Bookman* 49 (1919): 478–80.

Edgar, Neal A. *A History and Bibliography of American Magazines, 1810–1820*. Metuchen, NJ: Scarecrow Press, 1975.

Edwards, Thomas R. "The Evolution of Play Publishing." *The Drama* 15.6 (1925): 121–22.

Ehrenpreis, Irvin. *The "Types Approach" to Literature*. New York: King's Crown, 1945.

Elfenbein, Josef Aaron. *American Drama 1782–1812 as an Index to Socio-political Thought*. Ph.D. diss. New York University, 1951.

Elliott, Emory. "New Literary History: Past and Present." *American Literature* 57.4 (1985): 611–21.

Elliott, Emory, gen. ed. *Columbia Literary History of the United States*. New York: Columbia University Press, 1988.

Engle, Ron, and Tice L. Miller, eds. *The American Stage*. Cambridge: Cambridge University Press, 1993.

"English at the Universities." *The Dial* 26 (1894): 325–26.

Esslin, Martin. "'Dead! and Never Called Me Mother!': The Missing Dimension in American Drama." *Studies in the Literary Imagination* 21.2 (1988): 23–33.

The Field of Drama. New York: Methuen, 1987.

Estrin, Mark W. "The American Drama 1900–1940: Areas of Recent Scholarly Achievement and Critical Neglect." *Resources for American Literary Study* 17 (1990): 35–50.

Falk, Robert P. "The Rise of Realism, 1871–1891." *Transitions in American Literary History*, ed. Harry Hayden Clark. Durham, NC: Duke University Press, 1953. 381–442.

Falk, Sawyer. "Drama Departments in American Universities." *The Universities and the Theatre*, ed. D. G. James. London: George Allen & Unwin, 1952. 8–22.

Fergusson, Francis. "Beyond the Close Embrace: Speculations on the American Stage." *Anchor Review* 1 (1955): 189–203.

The Idea of a Theater. Princeton: Princeton University Press, 1949.

"Search for New Standards in the Theatre." *Kenyon Review* 17 (1955): 581–99.

Filler, Louis. *The Muckrakers*. 1968. Stanford, CA: Stanford University Press, 1976.

Firkins, O. W. "Literature and the Stage: A Question of Tactics." *The Atlantic Monthly* 109 (1912): 477–83.

Fitzgerald, P. A. *The Exhibition Reader*. New York: Sheldon, Blakeman, 1856.

Flory, Claude R. "Notes on the Antecedents of *Anna Christie*." *PMLA* 86.1 (1971): 77–83.

Flower, B. O. "The Theater as a Potential Factor for Higher Civilization, and a Typical Play Illustrating Its Power." *The Arena* 37 (1907): 497–509.

Flynn, Joyce. "A Complex Causality of Neglect." *American Quarterly* 41 (1989): 123–27.

"Melting Plots: Patterns of Racial and Ethnic Amalgamation in American Drama Before Eugene O'Neill." *American Quarterly* 38.3 (1986): 416–38.

Foerster, Norman. "Factors in American Literary History." *The Reinterpretation of American Literature*, ed. Norman Foerster. New York: Harcourt, Brace, 1928. 23–38.

Toward Standards. 1928. New York: Farrar & Rinehart, 1930.

Ford, Paul Leicester. "The Beginnings of American Dramatic Literature." *The New England Magazine* 9 (1894): 673–87.

Forte, Jeanie. "Realism, Narrative, and the Feminist Playwright – A Problem of Reception." *Modern Drama* 32.1 (1989): 115–27.

Freedman, Morris. *American Drama in Social Context*. Carbondale: Southern Illinois University Press, 1971.

Fry, Emma Sheridan. *Educational Dramatics*. 1913. The Educational Players Publications. New York: Lloyd Adams Noble, 1917.

Fuller, Harold de Wolf. "The Realism of the American Stage: The Drama of Exposure and the Reforming Spirit." *The Nation* 102 (1916): 307–10.

Fuller, S. Margaret. "American Literature." *Literature and Art*. Part II. New York: Fowlers & Wells, 1852. 122–59.

Fussell, Edwin. *Frontier: American Literature and the American West*. Princeton: Princeton University Press, 1965.

Gafford, Lucile. "Transcendentalist Attitudes Toward Drama and the Theatre." *New England Quarterly* 13 (1940): 442–66.

Gagey, Edmond M. *Revolution in American Drama*. New York: Columbia University Press, 1947.

Gardner, Rufus Hallette. *The Splintered Stage: The Decline of the American Theatre*. New York: Macmillan, 1965.

Gassner, John. "An Answer to the New Critics." *Theatre Arts* 36 (1952): 59–61.

"An Appraisal of the Contemporary American Stage." *Dramatic Soundings*. New York: Crown, 1968. 346–55.

"A Hundred Years of American Theatre." *Dramatic Soundings*. New York: Crown, 1968. 241–53.

Masters of the Drama. Third edition. New York: Random House, 1954.

"The Meaning and Scope of Playwriting Study." *Educational Theatre Journal* 9 (1957): 167–76.

"Social Realism and Imaginative Theatre." *Dramatic Soundings*. New York: Crown, 1968. 456–71.

Theatre at the Crossroads – Plays and Playwrights of the Mid-Century American Stage. New York: Holt, Rinehart & Winston, 1960.

"'There Is No American Drama' – a Premonition of Discontent." *Theatre Arts* 36 (1952): 24–25, 84–86.

25 Best Plays of the Modern American Theatre, Early Series. New York: Crown, 1949.

Gates, Robert Allan, ed. *18th- and 19th-century American Plays*. New York: Irvington, 1984.

Gayley, Charles Mills. "English at the University of California." *The Dial* 26 (1894): 29–32.

Geddes, Virgil. "The Rebirth of Drama." *The Drama*, March 1931, 7.

Gerstle, Gary. *Working-class Americanism: The Politics of Labor in a Textile City, 1914–1960*. Cambridge: Cambridge University Press, 1989.

Gibbons, Reginald. "Academic Criticism and Contemporary Literature." *Criticism in the University*. Series on Criticism and Culture, ed. Gerald Graff and Reginald Gibbons. Evanston, IL: Northwestern University Press, 1985. 15–34.

Gilbert, Sandra, and Susan Gubar, eds. *The Norton Anthology of Literature by Women*. New York: Norton, 1985.

Gilman, Richard. "The Drama Is Coming Now." *The Modern American Theatre: A Collection of Essays*, ed. Alvin B. Kernan. 1963. Englewood Cliffs, NJ: Prentice Hall, 1967. 155–69.

Gilmore, Michael T. "The Drama." *The Cambridge History of American Literature, I, 1590–1820*, gen. ed. Sacvan Bercovitch. Cambridge: Cambridge University Press, 1994. 573–90.

Glassberg, David. *American Historical Pageantry: The Uses of Tradition in the Early Twentieth Century*. Chapel Hill: University of North Carolina Press, 1990.

Golden, Joseph. *The Death of Tinkerbell: The American Theater in the 20th Century*. Syracuse, NY: Syracuse University Press, 1967.

Golding, Alan C. "A History of American Poetry Anthologies." *Canons*, ed. Robert von Hallberg. Chicago: University of Chicago Press, 1984. 279–307.

Goldman, Arnold, et al., eds. *American Literature in Context*. 4 vols. London: Methuen, 1983.

Goldman, Harry, and Mel Gordon. "Workers' Theatre in America: A Survey 1913–1978." *Journal of American Culture* 1 (1978): 169–81.

Goodman, Edward. "The American Dramatic Problem." *The Forum* 43 (1910): 182–91.

Gostwick, Joseph. *Hand-book of American Literature*. 1856. New York: Kennikat, 1971.

Gottesman, Ronald, et al., eds. *The Norton Anthology of American Literature*. First edition. New York: Norton, 1979.

Gottlieb, Lois C. "The Antibusiness Theme in Late Nineteenth Century American Drama." *The Quarterly Journal of Speech* 64 (1978): 415–26.

Graff, Gerald. *Professing Literature: An Institutional History*. Chicago: University of Chicago Press, 1987.

Graff, Gerald, and Michael Warner, eds. *The Origins of Literary Studies in America: A Documentary Anthology*. New York: Routledge, 1989.

Grant, Robert. "The Conduct of Life." *Scribner's Magazine* 18 (1895): 581–92.

Granville-Barker, Harley. *The Use of the Drama*. Princeton: Princeton University Press, 1945.

Grau, Robert. "The Prosperity of American Playwrights." *Lippincott's Magazine* 89 (1912): 617–19.

Gray, Giles Wilkeson. "Some Teachers and the Transition to Twentieth-Century Speech Education." *History of Speech Education in America*, ed. Karl R. Wallace. New York: Appleton-Century-Crofts, 1954. 422–46.

Green, Paul. "The Dying American Theatre." *The Hawthorne Tree*. Chapel Hill: University of North Carolina Press, 1943.

Grimsted, David. *Melodrama Unveiled: American Theater & Culture, 1800–1850*. University of Chicago Press, 1968. Berkeley: University of California Press, 1987.

Grossberg, Michael. "Institutionalizing Masculinity: The Law as a Masculine Profession." *Meanings for Manhood: Constructions of Masculinity in Victorian America*, ed. Mark C. Carnes and Clyde Griffen. Chicago: University of Chicago Press, 1990. 133–51.

Haber, Samuel. *The Quest for Authority and Honor in the American Professions, 1750–1900*. Chicago: University of Chicago Press, 1991.

Hackett, James. "A University for the Drama." *The Independent* 55.2838 (1903): 973–74.

Halline, Allan G. "American Dramatic Theory Comes of Age." *Bucknell University Studies* 1.2 (1949): 1–11.

Halline, Allan G., ed. *American Plays*. New York: American Book Company, 1935.

Hamar, Clifford Eugene. "College and University Theatre Instruction in the Early Twentieth Century." *History of Speech Education in America*, ed. Karl R. Wallace. New York: Appleton-Century-Crofts, 1954. 572–94.

Hamilton, Clayton Meeker. *Conversations on American Drama*. New York: Macmillan, 1924.

"Drama and the War." *The Bookman* 47 (1918): 289.

"Literature and the Drama." *Problems of the Playwright*. New York: Holt, 1917. 292–99.

"Organizing an Audience." *The Bookman* 34.2 (1911): 161–66.

"Something to Say in the Theatre." *The Bookman* 43 (1916): 166.

"What Is Wrong with the American Drama?" *The Bookman* 39 (1914): 314–19.

"The Younger American Playwrights." *The Bookman* 32 (1910): 249–57.

Hammond, Percy. *But – Is It Art?* New York: Doubleday, Page, 1927.

Hapgood, Norman. "Our Only High Class Theatre." *The Stage in America 1897–1900*. New York: Macmillan, 1901.

Harper, William Rainey. *The Trend in Higher Education*. Chicago: University of Chicago Press, 1905.

Harris, Wendell V. *Interpretive Acts: In Search of Meaning*. Oxford: Clarendon, 1988.

Hart, James D. *The Popular Book: A History of America's Literary Taste*. 1950. Berkeley: University of California Press, 1963.

Hart, John Seely. *A Manual of American Literature: A Text-Book for Schools and Colleges*. Philadelphia: Eldredge & Brother, 1872.

Hennequin, Alfred. "Characteristics of the American Drama." *Arena* 1 (1890): 700–709.

Henry, George H. "Toward a Theatre for Our Time." *Educational Theatre Journal* 10 (1958): 1–10.

Hewitt, Barnard. "The Americanism of the American Theater." *The American Theater Today*, ed. Alan Downer. New York: Basic, 1967. 3–14.

Hill, Howard C. "The Americanization Movement." *The American Journal of Sociology* 24 (1919): 609–42.

Hinckley, Theodore B. "The Drama Progresses." *The Drama* 11 (1921): 139.

Hodge, Francis. "European Influences on American Theatre: 1700–1969." *The American Theatre: A Sum of Its Parts*. New York: Samuel French, 1971. 3–24.

Hodgson, John, and Martin Banham, eds. *Drama in Education 1: The Annual Survey*. London: Pitman Publishing, 1972.

Hoffman, Daniel, ed. *Harvard Guide to Contemporary American Writing*. Cambridge, MA: Harvard University Press, 1979.

Hoffman, Theodore. "American Theatre Is Un-American." *Theatre Arts* 37 (1953): 70–73, 94–96.

Hornblow, Arthur. "A Foreword." *The Theatre* 1 (1901): 1.

The Theatre in America. 2 vols. Philadelphia: J. B. Lippincott, 1919.

Howard, Leon. *Literature and the American Tradition*. Garden City, NY: Doubleday, 1960.

Howells, William Dean. *Criticism and Fiction and Other Essays*, ed. Clara M. and Rudolph Kirk. New York: New York University Press, 1959.

Editor's Study, ed. James W. Simpson. January 1886–March 1892. Troy, NY: Whitson, 1983.

Hristič, Jovan. "The Problem of Realism in Modern Drama." *New Literary History* 8.2 (1977): 311–18.

Hubbard, Louise Shipman. "The Rise of Amateur Drama." *The Drama* 28 (Nov. 1917): 621–29.

Hubbell, Jay Broadus. *Who Are the Major American Writers? A Study of the Changing Literary Canon.* Durham, NC: Duke University Press, 1972.

Hubbell, Jay Broadus, ed. *American Life in Literature.* Abridged edition. New York: Harper & Brothers, 1951.

Hubbell, Jay Broadus, and John O. Beaty. *An Introduction to Drama.* 1927. New York: Macmillan, 1929.

Huber, Bettina J. "Today's Literature Classroom: Findings from the MLA's Survey of Upper-division Courses." *ADE Bulletin* 101 (Spring 1992): 36–60.

"What's Being Read in Survey Courses? Findings from a 1990–91 MLA Survey of English Departments." *ADE Bulletin* 110 (Spring 1995): 40–48.

Hughes, Glenn. *A History of the American Theatre, 1700–1950.* New York: Samuel French, 1951.

Humiston, Beatrice. "The Theatre as Educational Institution." *Quarterly Journal of Speech* 5 (1919): 120–27.

Hunter, Frederick J. "The Technical Criticism of Clayton Hamilton." *Educational Theatre Journal* 7.3 (1955): 285–93.

Hutton, Laurence. *Curiosities of the American Stage.* New York: Harper & Brothers, 1891.

Ingarden, Roman. *The Literary Work of Art: An Investigation on the Borderlines of Ontology, Logic, and the Theory of Literature,* trans. George G. Grabowicz. Evanston, IL: Northwestern University Press, 1973.

Jacobus, Lee A., ed. *The Longman Anthology of American Drama.* New York: Longman, 1982.

James, Henry. "Notes on the Theatres: New York." *The Scenic Art: Notes on Acting & the Drama, 1872–1901.* Henry James. 1875. New Brunswick, NJ: Rutgers University Press, 1948. 22–27.

Johns, Elizabeth. "Scholarship in American Art: Its History and Recent Developments." *American Studies International* 22.2 (1984): 3–40.

Johnson, Claudia. "A New Nation's Drama." *Columbia Literary History of the United States,* gen. ed. Emory Elliott. New York: Columbia University Press, 1988. 324–41.

"That Guilty Third Tier: Prostitution in Nineteenth-Century American Theaters." *American Quarterly* 27.5 (1975): 575–84.

Johnson, Gertrude. "Dramatic Production and the Educational Curriculum." *Quarterly Journal of Speech* 5 (1919): 158–70.

Jones, Henry Arthur. *The Foundations of a National Drama.* New York: George H. Doran, 1913.

Jones, Howard Mumford. "Arms of the Anglo-Saxons." *The Theory of American Literature.* Ithaca, NY: Cornell University Press, 1965. 98–117.

"The Orphan Child of the Curriculum." *The English Journal* 25.5 (1936): 376–88.

Jones, Howard Mumford, and Ernest Leisy, eds. *Major American Writers.* New York: Harcourt, Brace, 1935.

Kaplan, E. Ann. "The Realist Debate in the Feminist Film: A Historical Overview of Theories and Strategies in Realism and the Avant-garde Theory of Film (1971–81)." *Women & Film: Both Sides of the Camera*. E. Ann Kaplan. New York: Methuen, 1983. 125–41.

Kazin, Alfred. *An American Procession*. New York: Knopf, 1984.

Kenyon, Elmer. "The Aim of the Drama League." *Drama League Review* 1 (Season 1923–24, 1924): 1.

"Drama in Education." *Drama League Review* 17 (Season 1924–25, 1925): 1.

Kernodle, George R. "Theatre Practice and Theatre Theory in the Liberal Arts Curriculum." *Educational Theatre Journal* 1 (1949): 82–85.

Kinne, Wisner Payne. *George Pierce Baker and the American Theatre*. New York: Greenwood, 1968.

Kiper, Florence. "Some American Plays; from the Feminist Viewpoint." *The Forum* 51 (1914): 921–31.

Klein, Charles. "Religion, Philosophy and the Drama." *The Arena* 37 (1907): 492–97.

Knapp, James. *Literary Modernism and the Transformation of Work*. Evanston, IL: Northwestern University Press, 1988.

Knapp, Margaret. "Narrative Strategies in Selected Studies of American Theatre Economics." *The American Stage*, ed. Ron Engle and Tice L. Miller. Cambridge: Cambridge University Press, 1993. 267–77.

Knapp, Samuel L. *Lectures on American Literature: With Remarks on Some Passages of American History*. New York: Elam Bliss, 1829.

Knight, Marietta. *Dramatic Reader for Grammar Grades*. New York: American Book Company, 1910.

Knox, George A., and Herbert M. Stahl. "Dos Passos and 'The Revolting Playwrights.'" *Essays and Studies on American Language and Literature, XV*. Upsala: Lund, 1964.

Kolodny, Annette. "The Integrity of Memory: Creating a New Literary History of the United States." *American Literature* 57 (1985): 291–307.

Kostelanetz, Richard. "The New American Theatre." *The New American Arts*, ed. Richard Kostelanetz. New York: Horizon, 1965. 50–87.

The Theatre of Mixed Means. New York: Dial, 1968.

Kozelka, Paul. "Dramatics in the High Schools, 1900–1925." *History of Speech Education in America*. New York: Appleton, 1954. 595–616.

Kronenberger, Louis. "The Decline of the Theater." *Commentary* 1 (1935): 47–51.

Kruger, Loren. *The National Stage: Theatre and Cultural Legitimation in England, France, and America*. Chicago: University of Chicago Press, 1992.

Krutch, Joseph Wood. "How Modern Is the Modern American Drama?" *"Modernism" in Modern American Drama*. Ithaca, NY: Cornell University Press, 1953.

Kuhn, Thomas S. *The Structure of Scientific Revolutions*. 1962. Chicago: University of Chicago Press, 1970.

Lauter, Paul. *Canons and Contexts*. Oxford: Oxford University Press, 1991.

"Melville Climbs the Canon." *American Literature* 66.1 (1994): 1–22.

Lauter, Paul, ed. *Reconstructing American Literature: Courses, Syllabi, Issues.* Old West-
bury, NY: Feminist Press, 1983.

Lauter, Paul, gen. ed. *The Heath Anthology of American Literature.* Lexington, MA:
D. C. Heath, 1990.

Lawrenson, Helen. "The Decline of the American Drama Critics." *Esquire* 53 (March
1960): 94–97.

Lawson, John Howard. *The International.* New York: Macauley, 1927.
Theory and Technique of Playwriting and Screenwriting. New York: Putnam, 1949.

Lepenies, Wolf. *Between Literature and Science: The Rise of Sociology,* trans. R. J. Holling-
dale. Cambridge: Cambridge University Press, 1985.

Levine, Lawrence W. *Highbrow/Lowbrow: The Emergence of Cultural Hierarchy in
America.* Cambridge, MA: Harvard University Press, 1988.

Lewis, Theophilus. "Theatre: Ideas in Drama." *America* 9.1 (1954): 629, 631.

Lewisohn, Ludwig. *The Story of American Literature.* New York: Harper & Brothers, 1932.

Lippman, Monroe. "The American Playwright Looks at Business." *Educational Theatre
Journal* 12 (1960): 98–106.

Londré, Felicia Hardison. *The History of World Theater from the English Restoration to
the Present.* New York: Continuum, 1991.

Lowenthal, David. "The American Scene." *Geographical Review* 58 (1968): 61–88.

McCandless, Stanley. "A Map of These United States Showing the Influence of the
Work of George Pierce Baker (1890–1924)." *Theatre Arts Monthly* 9 (1925): 106–8.

McCarthy, Mary. "The American Realist Playwrights." *Theatre Chronicles 1937–1962.*
New York: Farrar, 1963. 209–29.
"Americans, Realists, Playwrights." *Encounter* 17.1 (1961): 24–31.

McConachie, Bruce A. "New Historicism and American Theater History : Toward an
Interdisciplinary Paradigm for Scholarship." *The Performance of Power: Theatrical
Discourse and Politics,* ed. Sue-Ellen Case and Janelle Reinelt. Iowa City: Univer-
sity of Iowa Press, 1991. 265–71.

McCormick, John. *The Middle Distance: A Comparative History of American Imaginative
Literature, 1919–1932.* New York: Free Press, 1971.

McDermott, Douglas. "The Theatre That Nobody Knows: Workers' Theatre in America, 1926–1942." *Theatre Journal* 6 (1965): 65–82.

McGarth, John. "Behind the Clichés of Contemporary Theatre." *Literature in the
Modern World,* ed. Dennis Walder. Oxford: Oxford University Press, 1990.
257–63.

Macgowan, Kenneth. "The Educational Theatre for Tomorrow." *Educational Theatre
Journal* 9 (1957): 85–95.
Footlights Across America. New York: Harcourt, Brace, 1929.
The Theatre of Tomorrow. New York: Liveright, 1921.

Macgowan, Kenneth, and Robert Edmond Jones. *Continental Stagecraft.* New York:
Harcourt, 1922.

Macgowan, Kenneth, and Herman Rosse. *Masks and Demons.* New York: Harcourt,
Brace, 1923.

McGranahan, Donald V., and Ivor Wayne. "German and American Traits Reflected in Popular Drama." *Human Relations* 1 (1948): 429–55.

McGuffey, William Holmes. *New High School Reader.* New York: Wilson, Hinkle, 1857.

MacIver, R. M. *Society: A Textbook of Sociology.* New York: Farrar, Rhinehart, 1937.

Mackay, Constance D'Arcy. *The Little Theatre in the United States.* New York: Holt, 1917.

MacKaye, Percy. "The Drama of Democracy." *The Playhouse and the Play.* 1908. New York: Greenwood, 1968. 100–117.

"George Pierce Baker." *The American Magazine* 73 (1911): 180–82.

McLaws, Lafayette. "A Master of Playwrights." *The North American Review* 200 (1914): 459–67.

McMichael, George, ed. *Anthology of American Literature. Realism to the Present.* New York: Macmillan, 1974.

Anthology of American Literature. 2 vols. New York: Macmillan, 1989.

McQuade, Donald, et al., eds. *The Harper American Literature.* New York: Harper & Row, 1987.

Mandeville, H. *A Course of Reading for Common Schools.* New York: Appleton, 1846.

March, F. A. "English at Lafayette College." *The Dial* 26 (1894): 294–96.

Marranca, Bonnie. *Theatrewriting.* New York: Performing Arts Journal Publications, 1984.

Matlaw, Myron, ed. *Nineteenth-century American Plays.* New York: Applause Theatre Book Publishers, 1967.

Matthews, Brander. "The American on the Stage." *Scribner's Monthly* 18.3 (1879): 321–33.

A Book About the Theatre. New York: Scribner, 1916.

The Development of the Drama. 1903. New York: Scribner, 1914.

"Forty Years of the Drama – A Retrospect." *Journal of the National Institute of Social Sciences* 12 (1927): 13–19.

An Introduction to the Study of American Literature. New York: American Book Company, 1896.

"The Relation of Drama to Literature." *The Historical Novel and Other Essays.* New York: Scribner, 1914. 217–38.

A Study of the Drama. Boston: Houghton Mifflin, 1910.

Studies of the Stage. New York: Harper & Brothers, 1894.

Matthiessen, F. O. *American Renaissance.* 1941. Oxford: Oxford University Press, 1968.

Mayorga, Margaret G. *A Short History of the American Drama: Commentaries on Plays Prior to 1920.* New York: Dodd, Mead, 1932.

Mayorga, Margaret G., ed. *Representative One-Act Plays by American Authors.* Boston: Little, Brown, 1919.

Mazzocco, Robert. "Sam Shepard's Big Roundup." *The New York Review of Books* 32.6 (1985): 21–27.

Meinig, D. W. "Symbolic Landscapes: Some Idealizations of American Communities." *The Interpretation of Ordinary Landscapes*, ed. D. W. Meinig. New York: Oxford University Press, 1979. 164–92.

Melnitz, William W. "Theatre Arts as an Academic Discipline: Recent Theatrical Literature in German." *Educational Theatre Journal* 3 (1951): 135–41.

Mercier, Vivian. "Who Killed the Drama?" *Commonweal* 47 (1948): 374–75.

Mersand, Joseph. "When Ladies Write Plays." *The American Drama 1930–1940.* Joseph Mersand. New York: Modern Chapbooks, 1941. 145–61.

Meserve, Walter J. *An Emerging Entertainment: The Drama of the American People to 1828.* Bloomington: Indiana University Press, 1977.

Meserve, Walter J., ed. *The Complete Plays of William Dean Howells.* New York: New York University Press, 1960.

Metcalfe, James S. "Dramatic Criticism in the American Press." *The Atlantic Monthly,* April 1918, 495–99.

"The Theatrical Season in New York." *The Cosmopolitan* 18 (1895): 279–85.

Miller, Arthur. "The American Theater." *Holiday* 17 (1955): 90–104.

Miller, Jordan Y., ed. *American Dramatic Literature.* New York: McGraw-Hill, 1961.

Miller, Jordan Y., and Winifred L. Frazer. *American Drama Between the Wars: A Critical History.* Boston: G. K. Hall, 1991.

Moffatt, James. *Teaching the Universe of Discourse.* New York: Houghton Mifflin, 1968.

Mogen, David. "Frontier Myth and American Gothic." *Genre* 14 (1981): 329–46.

Moody, Richard, ed. *Dramas from the American Theatre 1762–1909.* New York: World, 1966.

Moore, Charles Leonard. "The Interregnum in American Literature." *The Dial* 48.573 (1910): 307–9.

Morison, Samuel Eliot. *Three Centuries of Harvard 1636–1936.* Cambridge, MA: Harvard University Press, 1936.

Morton, Dixon M. "The Theatre Goes to Yale." *Theatre Arts Monthly* 10 (1926): 254–60.

Moses, Montrose J. *The American Dramatist.* Boston: Little, Brown, 1911.

"American Plays of Our Forefathers." *The North American Review* 215 (1922): 790–804.

"American Professors of Dramatic Literature." *Independent* 71 (1911): 813–16.

"Cobwebs of Antiquity: A Plea for Folk Basis in American Drama." *The North American Review* 231 (1931): 81–88.

"The Disintegration of the Theatre." *Forum* 45 (1911): 465–71.

"The Drama, 1860–1918." *Cambridge History of American Literature,* ed. Trent et al. Vol 3. New York: Putnam, 1921. 266–98. 4 vols.

"A Hopeful Note on the Theatre." *The North American Review* 234 (1932): 528–35.

"Is There an American Drama?" *Drama League Monthly* 2.5 (1917): 505–9.

"The Regeneration of the Theatre." *Forum* 45 (1911): 584–88.

"A Study Course on the American Drama." *Drama League Monthly* 1.1 (1916): 24–38.

"The Theatre in America." *The North American Review* 219 (1924): 82–91.

Moses, Montrose J., ed. *Representative American Dramas.* Boston: Little, Brown, 1929.

Representative Plays by American Dramatists. New York: Benjamin Blom, 1918.

Moses, Montrose J., and John Mason Brown, eds. *The American Theatre as Seen by Its Critics, 1752–1934.* New York: Norton, 1934.

Mott, Frank Luther. *A History of American Magazines, 1741–1905.* Cambridge, MA: Harvard University Press, 1957.

Mueller, John H. "The Folkway of Art: An Analysis of the Social Theories of Art." *The American Journal of Sociology* 44.2 (1938): 222–38.

"Is Art the Product of Its Age?" *Social Forces* 13.3 (1935): 367–75.

Mulford, Carla. "Re-presenting Early American Drama and Theatre." *Resources for American Literary Study* 17 (1990): 1–24.

Murphy, Brenda. *American Realism and American Drama, 1880–1940.* Cambridge: Cambridge University Press, 1987.

"Breaking the Constraints of History: Recent Scholarly Treatment of Nineteenth-century American Drama." *Resources for American Literary Study* 17 (1990): 25–34.

A Realist in the American Theatre. Athens: Ohio University Press, 1992.

Murray, Lindley. *Introduction to the English Reader.* Philadelphia: Uriah Hunt & Son, 1845.

Nathan, George Jean. "Dramatic Criticism in America." *The Critic and the Drama.* London: John Lane: The Bodley Head, 1924. 133–52.

The Theatre, the Drama, the Girls. New York: Knopf, 1921.

National Council of Teachers of English. "Preparation of High-school Teachers of English." *The English Journal* 4 (1915): 323–32.

Nelson, Richard, ed. *Strictly Dishonorable and Other Lost American Plays.* New York: Theatre Communications Group, 1986.

Nichols, Harold J. "The Prejudice Against Native American Drama from 1778 to 1830." *Quarterly Journal of Speech* 60 (1974): 279–88.

Nietz, John. *The Evolution of American Secondary School Textbooks.* Rutland, VT: Charles E. Tuttle, 1966.

Old Textbooks. Pittsburgh: University of Pittsburgh Press, 1961.

Nightingale, Benedict. *Fifth Row Center. A Critic's Year On and Off Broadway.* New York: Times Books, 1986.

Norton, Elliot. "Puffers, Pundits, and Other Play Reviewers: A Short History of American Dramatic Criticism." *The American Theatre: A Sum of Its Parts.* New York: Samuel French, 1971. 317–37.

Nuhn, Ferner. "Teaching American Literature in American Colleges." *American Mercury* 13.49 (1928): 328–31.

Nye, Russel B., ed. *New Directions in Popular Culture.* Bowling Green, OH: Bowling Green University Press, 1972.

Odenwald-Ungar, Mrs. J. "The Fine Arts as a Dynamic Factor in Society." *The American Journal of Sociology* 12 (1907): 656–74.

Ohmann, Richard. "The Shaping of a Canon: U.S. Fiction, 1960–1975." *Critical Inquiry* 10.1 (1983): 199–223.

Oliver, William. "Theatre Aesthetics in Crisis." *Educational Theatre Journal* 21 (1969): 20.

Owens, Rochelle, ed. *Spontaneous Combustion: Eight New Plays.* New York: Winter House, 1972.

Page, Eugene R. "Rediscovering American Drama." *The American Scholar* 8 (1939): 250–52.

Parrington, Vernon Lewis. *The Beginnings of Critical Realism in America, 1860–1920.* New York: Harcourt, Brace, 1930.

Pattee, Fred Lewis. "Anthologies of American Literature Before 1861." *Colophon* 4.16 (1934): n. p.

　Century Readings for a Course in American Literature. New York: Century Co., 1924.

　The New American Literature, 1890–1930. New York: Century Co., 1930.

　"The Old Professor of English: An Autopsy." *Tradition and Jazz.* New York: Century Co., 1925. 175–255.

Patterson, Charlotte A., comp. *Plays in Periodicals: An Index to English Language Scripts in Twentieth Century Journals.* Boston: G. K. Hall, 1970.

Paulding, James Kirk. "American Drama." *American Quarterly Review* 1.2 (1827): 331–57.

Peck, Mary Grey. "The Educational Movement for the New American Drama." *The English Journal* 1 (1912): 129–37.

Perkins, George, and Barbara Perkins, eds. *The American Tradition in Literature.* Eighth edition. New York: McGraw-Hill, 1994.

Pettet, Edwin Burr. "Thespis Mis-cast in Liberal Arts." *Educational Theatre Journal* 1 (1949): 109–14.

Phelps, William Lyon. *Twentieth Century Theatre: Observations on the Contemporary English and American Stage.* New York: Macmillan, 1918.

Philbrick, Norman. "A Plan for a Graduate Program in Drama." *Educational Theatre Journal* 5 (1953): 97–105.

Philbrick, Norman, ed. *Trumpets Sounding: Propaganda Plays of the American Revolution.* New York: Benjamin Blom, 1972.

Poe, Edgar Allan. "The American Drama." *The Works of Edgar Allan Poe,* ed. E. C. Stedman and G. E. Woodberry. New York: Scribner, 1895. Volume 6 of *Literary Criticism.* 1845.

Popkin, Henry. "American Theater in Transition." *College English* 23 (1962): 567–70.

Porter, Carolyn. "What We Know That We Don't Know: Remapping American Literary Studies." *American Literary History* 6.3 (1994): 467–526.

Postlewait, Thomas. "The Criteria for Periodization in Theatre History." *Theatre Journal* 40.3 (1988): 299–318.

　"From Melodrama to Modern Drama: A Problem in Understanding the History of American Drama." Paper Presented at American Studies Convention. Toronto, Canada, 1989.

Postlewait, Thomas, and Bruce A. McConachie, eds. *Interpreting the Theatrical Past: Essays in the Historiography of Performance.* Iowa City: University of Iowa Press, 1989.

Price, Guernsey. "American Undergraduate Dramatics." *The Bookman* 18.4 (1903): 373–88.

Quinn, Arthur Hobson. "American Literature as a Subject for Graduate Study." *Educational Review* 64 (1922): 7–15.

"The Early Drama, 1756–1860." *Cambridge History of American Literature*, ed. Trent et al. Vol. 1. New York: Putnam, 1917. 215–32.

A History of the American Drama from the Beginning to the Civil War. 1923. New York: Irvington, 1979.

A History of the American Drama from the Civil War to the Present Day. 1936. New York: Irvington, 1980.

"Modern American Drama." *The English Journal* 12 (1923): 653–62.

"Modern American Drama." *The English Journal* 13 (1924): 1–10.

Quinn, Arthur Hobson, ed. *Contemporary American Plays.* New York: Scribner, 1923.

Representative American Plays. New York: Century Co., 1917. Reprinted 1953.

Rabe, Margaret. "The Princess's Choice." *Quarterly Journal of Speech* 5 (1919): 277–86.

Rahv, Philip. "The Cult of Experience in American Writing," ed. Philip Rahv. *Literature in America.* 1940. New York: Meridian, 1957. 358–72.

Reardon, William R. "The American Drama and Theatre in the Nineteenth Century: A Retreat from Meaning." *ESQ: A Journal of the American Renaissance* 20.3 (1974): 170–86.

Reising, Russell. *The Unusable Past: Theory and the Study of American Literature.* New York: Methuen, 1986.

Renker, Elizabeth. "Resistance and Change: The Rise of American Literature Studies." *American Literature* 64.2 (1992): 347–65.

Reston, James, Jr. "Coming to Terms." *American Theatre* 2.2 (1985): 16–18.

Rich, Frank. "Play: *Angels Fall*, Lanford Wilson's Apocalypse." *New York Times*, October 18, 1982, C15.

Richards, Stanley, ed. *America on Stage.* New York: Doubleday, 1976.

Richardson, Charles. *American Literature, 1607–1885.* New York: Putnam, 1889.

Richardson, Gary A. *American Drama from the Colonial Period Through World War I: A Critical History.* New York: Twayne, 1993.

Richardson, Lyon N. *A History of Early American Magazines, 1741–1748.* New York: Octagon Books, 1966.

Roach, Joseph. "Mardi Gras Indians and Others: Genealogies of American Performance." *Theatre Journal* 44.4 (1992): 461–83.

Robbins, Bruce. *Secular Vocations: Intellectuals, Professionalism, Culture.* London: Verso, 1993.

Robinson, Marc. *The Other American Drama.* Cambridge: Cambridge University Press, 1994.

Roe, Clifford G. *The Great War on White Slavery or Fighting for the Protection of Our Girls.* 1911, n. p.

Rosen, Robert C. *John Dos Passos: Politics and the Writer.* Lincoln: University of Nebraska Press, 1981.

Rosenblatt, Louise. *The Reader, the Text, the Poem: The Transactional Theory of the Literary Work.* Carbondale: Southern Illinois University Press, 1978.

Ross, Dorothy. *The Origins of American Social Science.* New York: Cambridge University Press, 1991.

Roudané, Matthew. "Mamet's Mimetics." *David Mamet: A Casebook*, ed. Leslie Kane. New York: Garland, 1992. 3–32.

Ruland, Richard. *The Rediscovery of American Literature: Premises of Critical Taste, 1900–1940.* Cambridge, MA: Harvard University Press, 1967.

Salem, James M. "American Drama Between the Wars: The Effects of Sociology." *Ball State University Forum* 10 (1969): 47–54.

Sargent, Epes. *The Intermediate Standard Reader.* Philadelphia: Charles Desilver, 1859.

Schechner, Richard. *Performance Theory.* New York: Routledge, 1988.

Sedgwick, William Ellery. "The Materials for an American Literature: A Critical Problem of the Early Nineteenth Century." *Harvard Studies and Notes in Philosophy and Literature* 17 (1935): 141–62.

Selden, Samuel. "Academic Shadows on the American Theatre." *Educational Theatre Journal* 6 (1954): 97–105.

Seller, Maxine Schwartz, ed. *Ethnic Theatre in the United States.* Westport, CT: Greenwood, 1983.

Shank, Thomas J. "Provincialism in College and University Play Selection, a Five Year Study." *Educational Theatre Journal* 13 (1961): 112–17.

Shaw, T. B., and Truman J. Backus. *Shaw's New History of English Literature.* New York: Sheldon & Company, 1884.

Shaw's New History of English Literature. New York: Sheldon & Company, 1897.

Shumway, David R. *Creating American Civilization: A Genealogy of American Literature as an Academic Discipline.* Minneapolis: University of Minnesota Press, 1994.

Sifton, Paul. *The Belt.* New York: Macauley, 1927.

Simon, John. "Can Drama Be Saved?" *Singularities.* New York: Random House, 1974. 55–57.

Small, Albion. "The Era of Sociology." *The American Journal of Sociology* 1 (1895): 1–15.

General Sociology. Chicago: University of Chicago Press, 1905.

Small, Albion, and George Vincent. *An Introduction to the Study of Society.* New York: American Book Company, 1894.

Smith, Barbara Herrnstein. "Contingencies of Value." *Canons*, ed. Robert von Hallberg. Chicago: University of Chicago Press, 1983. 5–39.

Smith, Henry Nash. *Virgin Land: The American West as Symbol and Myth.* New York: Vintage/Random House, 1950.

Smith, Susan Harris. "Generic Hegemony: American Drama and the Canon." *American Quarterly* 41 (1989): 112–22, 138–40.

Smith, Sydney. "Review of *Statistical Annals of the United States of America 1818.*" *The Edinburgh Review* 33.65 (1820): 69–80.

Smyth, Albert Henry. *American Literature.* Philadelphia: Eldredge & Brother, 1889.

Sontag, Susan. *Against Interpretation.* New York: Octagon Books, 1966.

Spencer, Benjamin T. *The Quest for Nationality.* Syracuse, NY: Syracuse University Press, 1957.

Spengemann, William. "American Things/Literary Things: The Problem of American Literary History." *American Literature* 57 (1985): 456–81.

Spiller, Robert E. "The Cycle and the Roots: National Identity in American Literature." *Toward a New American Literary History*, ed. Louis J. Budd, Edwin H. Cady, and Carl L. Anderson. Durham, NC: Duke University Press, 1980. 3–18.

The Cycle of American Literature. New York: New American Library, 1955.

The Oblique Light. New York: Macmillan, 1968.

Spiller, Robert E., et al., eds. *Literary History of the United States*. Fourth edition, revised. 1948. New York: Macmillan, 1978.

Spingarn, Joel Elias. "Dramatic Criticism and the Theatre." *Creative Criticism and Other Essays*. New York: Harcourt, Brace, 1931. 52–93.

Stafford, John. *The Literary Criticism of "Young America": A Study in the Relationship of Politics and Literature, 1837–1850*. Berkeley: University of California Press, 1952.

Stall, Sylvanus, D.D. *What a Young Husband Ought to Know*. Philadelphia: Vir, 1897.

Stambusky, Alan A. "The 'America First' Attitude in U.S. College and University Play Selection: A Five-year Report." *Educational Theatre Journal* 18 (1966): 136–39.

"American College and University Play Production: 1963–1964." *Educational Theatre Journal* 17 (1965): 122–27.

Stephenson, Nellie A. "Required American Literature." *English Journal* 1 (1915): 566–70.

Stern, Milton, and Seymour Gross, eds. *American Literature Survey*. 4 vols. New York: Viking, 1975.

Straumann, Heinrich. *American Literature in the Twentieth Century*. 1951. New York: Harper & Row, 1968.

Styan, John. *Drama, Stage and Audience*. Cambridge: Cambridge University Press, 1975.

Sullivan, T. R. "A Standard Theatre." *Atlantic Monthly* 75 (1895): 686–89.

Szondi, Peter. *On Textual Understanding and Other Essays*, trans. Harvey Mendelsohn. Minneapolis: University of Minnesota Press, 1986.

Taubman, Howard. *The Making of American Theatre*. New York: Coward-McCann, 1965.

Taylor, Frederick Winslow. *Scientific Management*. New York: Harper & Brothers, 1947.

Taylor, Walter Fuller. *The Story of American Letters*. Chicago: Henry Regnery, 1956.

"Theater Issue." *Kenyon Review* 15.2 (1993).

Thorp, Willard. *American Writing in the Twentieth Century*. Cambridge, MA: Harvard University Press, 1960.

Tichi, Cecilia. *Shifting Gears: Technology, Literature, Culture in Modernist America*. Chapel Hill: University of North Carolina Press, 1987.

Trilling, Lionel. *The Liberal Imagination: Essays of Literature and Society*. Garden City, NY: Doubleday, 1953.

Tukesbury, Beatrice L. "Emma Sheridan Fry and Educational Dramatics." *Educational Theatre Journal* 16 (1964): 341–48.

Tupper, James W. "Guide to the Contemporary Drama." *The Dial* 56 (1914): 56–57.

Turner, Frederick Jackson. "The Significance of the Frontier in American History." *Annual Report of the American Historical Association for the Year 1893*. Washington, DC: GPO, 1894.

Turner, Ronnie E., and Charles Edgley. "Death as Theatre: A Dramaturgical Analysis of the American Funeral." *Sociology and Social Research* 53 (1968): 377–92.

Tyler, Moses Coit. *A History of American Literature During the Colonial Time, 1607–1765*. 1878. Ithaca, NY: Cornell University Press, 1949.

The Literary History of the American Revolution, 1763–1783. 2 vols. 1897. New York: Frederick Ungar, 1957.

Uricchio, William, and Roberta Pearson. *Reframing Culture: The Case of Vitagraph Quality Films*. Princeton: Princeton University Press, 1993.

Vanden Heuvel, Michael. *Performing Drama/Dramatizing Performance*. Ann Arbor: University of Michigan Press, 1991.

"Textual Harassment: Teaching Drama to Interrogate Reading." *Theatre Topics* 3.2 (1993): 159–66.

Vanderbilt, Kermit. *American Literature and the Academy: The Roots, Growth, and the Maturity of a Profession*. Philadelphia: University of Pennsylvania Press, 1986.

Vaughn, Jack A. *Early American Dramatists from the Beginnings to 1900*. New York: Frederick Ungar, 1981.

Veltrusky, Jiri. "Drama as Literature and Performance." *Das Drama und Seine Inszenierung*. Fischer-Lichte. Tübingen: Max Niemeyer Verlag, 1985. 12–21.

Vince, Ron. "Theatre History as an Academic Discipline." *Interpreting the Theatrical Past: Essays in the Historiography of Performance*, ed. Thomas Postlewait and Bruce A. McConachie. Iowa City: University of Iowa Press, 1989. 1–18.

Vincent, Melvin J. "Fiction, Drama, and Sociology." *The Journal of Applied Sociology* 9 (1924): 124–28.

"The Influence of Drama upon Human Attitudes." *Sociology and Social Research* 7 (1932): 142–52.

"Social Drama Notes." *The Journal of Applied Sociology* 10 (January/February 1926): 294.

"Social Drama Notes." *The Journal of Applied Sociology* 10 (May/June 1926): 396–97.

"Social Drama Notes." *Sociology and Social Research* 14 (1930): 595.

"Social Drama." *Sociology and Social Research* 22 (1938): 497–98.

"Social Drama." *Sociology and Social Research* 25 (1940): 98.

"Social Drama." *Sociology and Social Research* 32 (1948): 906.

"Social Poetry Notes." *The Journal of Applied Sociology* 10 (1925): 94.

Wager, Willis. *American Literature: A World View*. New York: New York University Press, 1968.

Wagner, Linda W. *Dos Passos: Artist as American*. Austin: University of Texas Press, 1979.

Wallis, Wilson D. "Environmentalism." *International Encyclopedia of the Social Sciences*, ed. Edwin R. Seligman. Vol. 5. New York: Macmillan, 1931. 561–66.

Ward, Lester F. "The Place of Sociology Among the Sciences." *The American Journal of Sociology* 1 (1895): 16–27.

Warner, Charles Dudley. "Literature and the Stage." *The Critic* 15 (1889): 285–86.

Weales, Gerald. "Theatre Without Walls." *A Time of Harvest*, ed. Robert E. Spiller. New York: Hill & Wang, 1962. 130–43.

Webb, Winifred. "The Spirit of American Literature." *Arena* 36 (1906): 121–25.

Weimann, Robert. *Structure and Society in Literary History: Studies in the History and*

Theory of Historical Criticism. Expanded edition. Baltimore: Johns Hopkins University Press, 1984.

Wellek, René, and Austin Warren. *Theory of Literature.* New York: Harcourt, Brace & World, 1957.

Wendell, Barrett. *A Literary History of America.* New York: Scribner, 1901.

Wernaer, Robert M. "The Drama League of Boston." *The Nation* 99 (1914): 310–11.

Wetzsteon, Ross. "The Most Populist Playwright." *New York,* November 8, 1982, 40–41, 44–45.

"What We Stand For." Editorial. *Theatre Arts Magazine* 1 (1917): 149.

Whitman, Walt. "Democratic Vistas." *"Leaves of Grass" and Selected Prose.* 1871. New York: Random House, 1981.

"Miserable State of the Stage – Why Can't We Have Something Worth the Name of American Drama?" *The American Theatre as Seen by Its Critics, 1752–1934,* ed. Montrose J. Moses and John Mason Brown. 1847. New York: Cooper Square, 1969. 70–72.

"Why Do Theatres Languish? And How Shall the American Stage Be Resuscitated?" *The Gathering of Forces,* ed. Cleveland Rodgers and John Black. 1847. Vol. 2. New York: Putnam, 1920. 314–18.

Williams, Raymond. *Writing in Society.* Thetford, Norfolk: Thetford Press, n.d.

Williams, Stanley. *American Literature.* The Folcroft, 1933.

Wilson, Edmund. "The All-star Literary Vaudeville." *The New Republic* 43 (1926): 158–63.

Wilstach, Paul. "The American Library and the Drama." *The Bookman* 8.2 (1898): 134–38.

Winter, William. "A Critic's Review of the Subject." *Harper's Weekly* 33 (1889): 101.

Winters, Yvor. *The Function of Criticism.* Denver: Alan Swallow, 1957.

Wolter, Jürgen C. *The Dawning of American Drama: American Dramatic Criticism, 1746–1915.* Westport, CT: Greenwood, 1993.

Woodbridge, Homer E. "Eugene O'Neill." *O'Neill and His Plays: Four Decades of Criticism,* ed. O. Cargill, N. Bryllion Fagin, and W. J. Fisher. New York: New York University Press, 1961. 307–8.

Woodbury, George E. *America in Literature.* New York: Harper & Brothers, 1903.

Wrenn, John H. *John Dos Passos.* New York: Twayne, 1961.

Wyatt, David. "Shepard's Split." *The South Atlantic Quarterly* 91.2 (1992): 333–60.

Zachos, J. C. *The New American Speaker.* New York: A. S. Barnes, 1857.

Index

Abbey Theatre, 142
Abe Lincoln in Illinois (Sherwood), 71
Abraham Lincoln (Drinkwater), 145
Abraham's Bosom (Green), 107
Abstract Expressionism, 111
academics/academe, 4, 29, 42, 49, 81, 112, 114, 115; bias against drama, 12–29; and New Criticism, 46; study of American drama, 57; and theatre, 120, 140
Achilles Had a Heel (Flavin), 203
adaptations, 69
Addison, Joseph, 134
Adler, Mortimer J., 138
Adler, Thomas P., 4, 205
aesthetic/aesthetics, 72, 150, 169, 170; drama, 97; movements, 103; of New Playwrights' Theatre, 193
African Americans, 7, 12, 70
Aiken, Conrad, 28
Aiken, G. L., 64
Airways, Inc. (Dos Passos), 189
Akins, Zoe, 203
Albee, Edward, 44, 49, 90, 106, 155, 179
Aldrich, Thomas Bailey, 175
Alexander, Doris, 30–1
Alfred, William, 29
All My Sons (Miller), 178, 181
All Over (Albee), 179
Allen, Ralph G., 81–2
Allen, Woody, 29
alternative drama, 74
Alvarez, Ruth, 100
amateur theatres/theatricals, 80, 85, 88; Howells's contribution to, 175
amateurism, 147, 148
American Buffalo (Mamet), 55

American drama: Baker on, 141; beginning of, 66–7, 68, 96, 98–9, 176, 200; beyond hegemony and canonicity, 197–207; bias against, 2, 10–11, 12–29, 36, 53; characteristics of, 206; charges against, 42–5; cultural location of, 7, 75–83; current status of, 48–53; in curriculum, 1, 114–58, 199; descriptive and journalistic, 102; development of, 68; Drama League and, 88, 89; geographical determination, 108–13; goals of, 76; and higher education, 126–34; Howells on, 174–5; literary and aesthetic qualities of, 2–3; as masculine science, 103–8; modern, 50; neglect of, 6, 9, 10, 11–12, 30, 34–42; and realism, 179–83; reputation of, 23–4; roots of, 13; separation from Europe, 96–103; and social education, 134–8; as subject of scholarly work, 3; trope of organic evolution, 89–96; *see also* exclusion of drama
American Drama (journal), 3–4
American Drama Society, 83
American Dramatists Club, 91
American Dream (O'Neil), 37, 178
American Educational Theatre Association, 153
"American" experience, 60, 62, 64, 71
American Journal of Sociology, The, 53, 73–4, 162, 163, 164, 167
American Library Association, 147
American literature, 2, 7, 48, 55, 158, 200; as academic discipline, 116–17; American drama and, 205, 206; American studies and, 117, 150, 195; courses in, 49, 122, 130; in curriculum, 10, 134–5, 137, 149–50; drama in/and, 52, 53; isolation of Ameri-

232

can dramatic literature from, 29–34; the
     land in, 110; in secondary schools, 125–6;
     theoretical approaches to, 51
American Quarterly, 2, 30, 117
American School of Playwriting, 103
American Society of Dramatic Art, 168
Americanism/Americanness, 7, 82, 95, 96, 101;
     in American drama, 1, 57–113; in antholo-
     gies, 65–9, 70–2; in curriculum, 144; the
     land in, 109–10, 111, 112–13; in literature, 4,
     77–8, 80; measurement of, 113; standard
     for, 67–8
Anderson, Carl L., 51
Anderson, John, 180
Anderson, Mary, 51, 140
Anderson, Maxwell, 40, 74, 153, 168
Anderson, Sherwood, 154
Androborus (Hunter), 67
Angels in America (Kushner), 55
Anglo-American drama, 93
Anglophilia, 3, 12, 34, 36, 117, 156, 207
Angoff, Charles, 35
Anna Christie (O'Neill), 99
Anouilh, Jean, 155
Anspacher, Louis, 85, 88
anthologies, 29, 50–1, 88, 96; American
     drama, 65–75, 123; bias against American
     drama in, 2; compilers of, 59; criteria for
     inclusion in, 72–3, 74–5; dominant para-
     digm in, 62; exclusion of drama from, 32,
     33–4, 116; women playwrights ignored in,
     106
Applebee, Arthur N., 4, 18, 89, 120–1, 157
Arabesque, 204
Archer, William, 16–17, 90, 93, 142; and real-
     ism, 178–9
Ardrey, Robert, 29
Arent, Arthur, 37
Aristotle, 196
Arnold, Matthew, 11
Arnold, Sarah Lewis, 124
Arnoldian model, 37
arts (the), 170; drama in, 138; expansion of, 84;
     sociology and, 165, 167–8
Asahina, Robert, 62
Atkinson, Brooks, 89, 95
audiences, 43, 54, 76, 93, 114, 142, 203; decadence
     of, 84; effect of drama on, 167; feminized,
     104; training through education and art, 85
Auerbach, Doris, 62
autochthonic paradigm, 111, 112–13

Babbitt, Irving, 41, 121–2, 129
Backus, Truman J., 126
Baker, Harry T., 121
Baker, George Pierce, 14, 129, 138–44, 139*f*,
     153, 155; and drama in higher education,
     133–4; 47 Workshop, 133, 134; at Harvard,

81, 87, 131, 132, 141; legacies of, 144–9; map
     of influence of, 146–7*f*; at Radcliffe, 133,
     141; students of, 148–9
Bakhtin, M. M., 199
Baldwin, James, 41
Ballard, John Frederick, 148
Balzac, Honoré, 179
Bank, Rosemarie K., 188
Banker's Daughter, The (Howard), 177
Baraka, Imamu Amiri, 28, 49
Barish, Jonas, 20–3
Barker, James Nelson, 36, 59, 171
Barnes, Clive, 44, 74
Barnes, Djuna, 28
Barnes, Douglas, 157
Barnett, James, 170
Barnum, Phineas T., 35
Baron Rudolph (Howard), 177
Barron, Samuel, 90, 94
Basic Training of Pavlo Hummel, The (Rabe), 49
Basshe, Em Jo, 188–9, 192
Battle of Bunker's-Hill, The (Brackenridge), 67,
     123, 172
Baym, Nina, 39
Beach, Lewis, 164
Beard, Charles, 105, 110
Beard, Mary, 105, 110
Beatty, Richmond Croom, 33
Beaty, John, 99
Becker, William, 47
Beckerman, Bernard, 14, 127
Beckett, Samuel, 31, 179
Beers, Henry, 126, 175
Beggar on Horseback (Kaufman and Connelly),
     177
Behn, Aphra, 96
Behrman, S. N., 154
Beiswanger, George, 10
Belasco, David, 24, 136, 180
Bel Geddes, Norman, 151
Believe Me, Xantippe! (Ballard), 148
Bell, Michael Davitt, 206
Bellamy Societies, 83
belles lettres, 122, 150
Bellow, Saul, 28, 42–3
Belt, The (Sifton), 189, 192–3, 194
Ben Hur, 79, 97
Benavente y Martínez, Jacinto, 189
Benedict, John, 33
Bennett, Arnold, 148
Bennett, Benjamin, 198
Benrimo, J. H., 88
Bentley, Eric, 10, 29, 30, 32, 46, 47, 54, 90, 183;
     and death of drama, 94
Bercovitch, Sacvan, 2, 41, 48, 51, 117
Berkowitz, Gerald, 183
Berlin, James, 130
Berthoff, Warner, 39, 172

Best, Mrs. A. Starr, 84, 85, 86, 88
Betti, Ugo, 28
Bewley, Marius, 110
Beyond the Horizon (O'Neill), 27, 50, 98, 99
Big Bonanza, The (Daly), 177
Bigsby, C. W. E., 2, 3, 42, 55, 58, 106, 177, 198;
    on New Playwrights' Theatre, 188, 191
Bird, Robert Montgomery, 73, 126
Black, Alexander, 24
Black Pit (Maltz), 100
Black Revolutionary Theatre, 186
Blackmur, R. P., 46
blacks, 64; works by, 49; *see also* African
    Americans
Blair, Hugh, 125
Blair, Karen, 84, 85
Blair, Walter, 32, 33
Blake, Ben, 195
Blake, Warren Barton, 58–9
Blankenship, Russell, 35–6, 40
Blau, Herbert, 44
Bledstein, Burton J., 129
Blitzstein, Marc, 37
Bloom, Harold, 55, 106
Bloomfield, Maxwell, 176
Blues for Mister Charlie (Baldwin), 41
Boal, Augusto, 196
Bogard, Travis, 3, 54, 98, 102, 111, 134, 171–2
Bogardus, Emory S., 167, 170
Boker, George Henry, 29, 34, 67, 161
Bolton, Gavin, 156
Bonnet, Henri, 20
Bordman, Gerald, 36
Born Yesterday (Kanin), 178
Boss, The (Sheldon), 178
*Boston Prize Poems and Other Specimens of
    Dramatic Poetry*, 123
Boucicault, Dion, 9, 17, 19, 53, 67, 68, 69, 79,
    160, 177
Bourdieu, Pierre, 114, 115
Bowles, Jane, 28
Boyd, James Robert, 125–6
Boynton, Percy, 35, 36, 40
Brackenridge, Hugh Henry, 67, 123, 172
Bradbury, Ray, 28
Bradley, Sculley, 33
Brecht, Bertolt, 28, 46
Brief Candle (Powel), 203
Brieux, Eugène, 92
British model of instruction, 18
Broadhurst, George, 92
Broadway, 19, 20, 24, 26, 27, 28, 41, 94, 120,
    138, 189; power of, 26
Bronson, Howard, 29
Brooklyn Polytechnic, 132
Brooks, Cleanth, 46
Brooks, Van Wyck, 39
Brotherhood (Wells), 168

Brougham, John, 64, 67, 82, 160
Broun, Heywood, 148
Brown, Alice, 88
Brown, Herbert, 104
Brown, John Mason, 38, 148, 195
Browne, Maurice, 72, 98
Browning Clubs, 83
Bruntière, Ferdinand, 142
Brustein, Robert, 26–7, 43, 44, 45, 55, 90, 103
Brutus (Payne), 67
Bryer, Jackson R., 3, 100
Budd, Louis J., 51
Burd, Henry, 134–5
Buried Child (Shepard), 111
Burke, Kenneth, 171, 199–200
burlesque, 13, 62, 78, 82, 186, 193, 195, 206;
    "new," 79
Bury the Dead (Shaw), 69
Butler, James H., 14, 140
Butsch, Richard, 75, 104

Cadden, Michael, 2
Cady, Edwin H., 51
Cain, William, 108
Cairns, William, 68
Calder, Chester, 42, 108
Call Me Ishmael, 112
Calverton, V. F., 35, 99–100, 169
Cambridge History of American Literature, 15,
    34, 41, 48, 73, 127, 149, 205–6; established
    legitimacy of American literature as aca-
    demic subject, 117; sexism of, 103
"Cambridge thesis," 119
Campbell, Bartley, 97
Camus, Albert, 28
canon (American drama), 36, 57–9, 69, 83,
    203; Drama League and course of, 86;
    female playwrights in, 74; the feminine
    and, 106; masculinity in, 112; opening, 82;
    O'Neill in, 32; virility of, 107
canon (American literature), 7, 9, 11, 46,
    108–9, 201, 204; challenges to, 39, 51; crit-
    ics and, 116; drama in, 41, 48, 175; exclusion
    of drama from, 3, 55, 202; masculine es-
    sence of, 112; Matthiessen and, 117; open-
    ing of, 48–9; revision of, 6, 11–12, 205
canon: creation, 158; English literary, 117; for-
    mation, 4, 6–7, 31, 109; development as
    seen through anthologies, 65–6
canonicity, 197–207
Capitol, The (Thomas), 177
Capote, Truman, 28
Capus, Alfred, 92
Carafiol, Peter, 4–5, 206
Carlson, Marvin, 18, 51, 133
Carnegie Institute of Technology, 138
Carolina Playmakers (University of North
    Carolina), 107

Carpenter, Charles A., 31–2
Carpenter, George, 121
Carter, Everett, 39
Carter, Jean, 85, 107
Cartmell, Van H., 69, 71
Case, Sue-Ellen, 56, 185
Cassady, Edward, 177
Cathcart, George, 126
Cather, Willa, 150
Cato (Addison), 134
Centuries, The (Basshe), 189
Cerf, Bennett, 69, 71
Chadwick, F. E., 149
Chandler, F. W., 132
Chaney, Stewart, 148
Chapman, George, 96
character: essence of drama, 174; realism of,
    101; types, 116
Chase, Mary, 72
Chaudhuri, Una, 119
Chautauqua Literary and Scientific Cir-
    cle/Chautauquas, 83, 85
Chekhov, Anton, 181
Cheney, Sheldon, 24–6, 38, 97–8
Children of the Earth (Brown), 88
Children's Educational Theatre, 136
Chorus Lady, The (vaudeville sketch), 97
Christakes, George, 163
Chubb, Percival, 85, 88–9, 121
City, The (Fitch), 73, 88, 177
Civil War, 19, 64, 68
Claire, or the Maid of Milan (Payne), 69
Clark, Barrett H., 15, 35, 71, 72–3, 74, 203–4;
    and Drama League, 87; on evolution of
    American drama, 100, 101
Clark, Eleanor, 47
Clark, Harry Hayden, 39
Clemens, Samuel, 136
Clurman, Harold, 54, 94
Cody, William, 109
Coghill, Nevill, 155
Cohan, George M., 178
Cohn, Ruby, 3, 9, 44–5
Colacurcio, Michael, 5
Colum, Padraic, 30
Columbia Literary History of the United States,
    9, 48, 115–16, 172; Howells in, 173
Columbus el Filibusters (Brougham), 82
comedy, 82, 175; comic types, 71
Command Decision (Haines), 71
commercial theatre, 30, 82, 83, 142, 191; man-
    ager-dominated, 120
commercialism, 19, 26, 41, 83, 84, 94
community theatres, 148
Comte, Auguste, 163, 167
conflict model of drama, 61, 80, 142, 170
Connelly, Marc, 73, 107, 168, 177
Conquest of Canaan (Dwight), 34

Conrad, R. T., 67
Contrast, The (Tyler), 50, 51, 63–4, 72, 73, 74,
    75, 76, 79, 82; in curriculum, 144; first suc-
    cessful American play, 96
Cook, Albert S., 130
Cooke, Alistair, 148
Cooper, James Fenimore, 77, 110
Copperhead, The (Thomas), 88
copyright, 13, 16, 17, 18, 75–6
Copyright Law of 1856, 17; revision of, 91
Corbin, John, 83, 90, 91–2
Cordell, Richard, 16, 72, 98
Corson, Hiram, 121, 153
Coward, Noel, 103
Cowards (Lovett), 136
Cradle Will Rock, The (Blitzstein), 37
Craig, Gordon, 97
Craig's Wife (Kelly), 169
Crane, R. S., 179
Crane, Stephen, 28
Crane, William, 122, 150
Cravens, Hamilton, 162
creative dramatics, 18
critical theory, 202–5; new, 204–5
criticism, 29, 75–6, 169; Archer's effect on, 179;
    dominant paradigm in, 62–3; Film Stud-
    ies, 19; formalist, aesthetic focus of, 48;
    Gilman on, 13–14; in magazines and jour-
    nals, 75; prestige of, 115–16
critics, 2, 7, 34–5, 37–8, 41–2, 44–5, 59, 93, 96,
    198; biases of, 23, 24; change in view of
    drama, 51; disdain for American drama, 12,
    38, 45–8; and dominant paradigm, 64; and
    gendering of drama, 106, 108; and literary
    status of American drama, 54–5, 57; medi-
    ocrity of, 95; and nationalism, 61–2; on
    O'Neill, 99; as playwrights, 28–9; and
    playwrights' political involvement, 178–9;
    and realism, 185; and separation of Ameri-
    can drama from European models, 101, 102
Croce, Benedetto, 153
Crosby, Thomas, 147
Crothers, Rachel, 73, 169
Crouse, Russel, 69
Crucible, The (Miller), 49, 69
cultural artifact, drama as, 12, 56
cultural bias against drama, 12–29
cultural capital, 116–17, 156, 157–8, 197
cultural conservatism, 37
cultural diversity (American), 53–4, 71, 74, 201;
    see also multiculturalism
cultural form, and social process, 202
cultural hegemony, Anglo-American, 65
cultural history, 5, 6, 204
cultural issues, in canon of American drama,
    19–20, 58
cultural location of American drama, 1–2, 75–83
cultural mission of American drama, 61–2, 73–4

cultural value of American drama, 114, 115–16
culture, 63; American drama in, 1, 3, 7, 55–6;
    effect of technology on, 187–8; patriarchal,
    11; and sociology, 162; studies, 6, 19; and
    theatre-performance dyad, 118–19; women
    and, 84–5
cummings, e. e., 28, 30, 33
Cunliffe, Marcus, 39, 40
Cure for the Spleen, A (Sewall), 172
curriculum, 7, 201; American drama in, 1, 2, 145,
    147, 149–57, 199; drama in, 37, 134–5, 138; revi-
    sionist approaches to, 137; theatre in, 137

Daly, Augustin, 79–80, 177
Dartmouth College, 137, 157
Dasgupta, Gautam, 49
Daughters of Men, The (Klein), 92, 168
Davenport, William H., 71, 74
Davies, Henry, 24
Davis, Owen, 88
Davis, Vincent, 124
Death of a Salesman (Miller), 49, 50, 55, 111, 199
Decision of the Court (Matthews), 127
decline of American drama, 23, 89, 94–5, 104
delegitimation crisis, 7
Demastes, William, 183–4
democracy, 42, 64; and art, 53
Denby, David, 180
Dessoir, Max, 15
determinism, 99, 184; geographic, 109–10
De Voto, Bernard, 39
De Walden, T. B., 175
Dial, The (journal), 16, 30, 68, 97, 130, 131, 185
Diamond, Elin, 185
Dibble, Vernon, 163
Dickinson, Thomas H., 53, 61, 69, 72, 88, 90,
    134, 145; on Americanness, 109; on evolu-
    tion of drama, 93
disciplinary fields/disciplines, 1, 2, 3, 115, 201,
    207; boundaries, 201–2; creation and
    justification of, 4, 6–7, 115, 116, 118–19; pro-
    fessional journals, 137–8; status of drama
    as, 32
Disraeli (Parker), 86
Distant Drums (Totheroh), 203
District Attorney, The (Klein), 92
Dolan, Jill, 19
Donleavy, J. P., 28
Donnay, Maurice, 92
Donoghue, Denis, 29, 60
Dorey, J. Milnor, 135
Dos Passos, John, 28, 39–40; and New Play-
    wrights' Theatre, 188–9, 190, 191, 194–5, 196
Douglas, Wallace, 126–7
Downer, Alan S., 38, 99, 153
drama, 2, 197–8; as academic discipline, 135;
    conflict with theatre, 118–19, 120; in cur-
    riculum, 134–5, 138, 145; different from lit-

erature, 141; in early American textbooks,
    122–6; generic distinctions within, 203–4;
    lowly status of, 23; moral and didactic pur-
    pose of, 65, 76, 137, 168, 169; origins of,
    119; in/and sociology, 164–9, 170–1; split
    with theatre, 3, 143, 152; study of, 143; *see
    also* American drama
Drama, The (magazine), 42, 135–6, 145, 147, 148
drama departments, 140, 154, 155; first, 138;
    Yale, 142
Drama League, 16, 18, 83–9, 93, 103, 140, 147;
    publications of, 85, 86, 87; and cultural val-
    ues, 85
"Drama of Democracy," 38
drama of ideas, 92
drama/theatre binarism, 199–200
"dramas of attack," 177
dramatic discourse versus modern manage-
    ment, 187–96
dramatic literature, 5, 96, 147–8, 199–200; cul-
    tural reception and position of, 1; literary
    status of, 2–3; multiple positions of, 157–8;
    reevaluation of, 203, 207; study of, 115; and
    theatrical practice, 201–7
dramatic theory, 55, 94, 133
dramatics, 137–8
Dramatists Guild, 17, 91
dramaturgical literacy, 13
dramaturgy, 168; experimental, 183, 187; New
    Playwrights' Theatre, 192–3, 194
Dreiser, Theodore, 74, 93
Drinkwater, John, 145
Drummond, Alexander, 205
Dryden, John, 126, 175
Duberman, Martin, 29
Dunlap, William, 34, 52, 59, 69, 75, 76–7, 96
Dunlap Society, 17
Dutchman (Baraka), 33, 49
Dwight, Timothy, 34, 128
Dynamo (O'Neill), 188

Eagleton, Terry, 52
Early, Michael, 49
Earth (Basshe), 189, 192
Easiest Way, The (play), 18
East Lynne (play), 47
Eaton, Walter Prichard, 35, 43, 90, 92, 104,
    144–5, 153, 159 61, 196
Eberhart, Richard, 28
Edgar, Neal, 75
Edgley, Charles, 171
education, 136–7, 156, 161; by Drama League,
    86–7
Educational Alliance, 136
Educational Dramatic League, 136
Educational Dramatics, 136–7, 156
educational institutions: drama in, 143–4;
    theatre as, 136–7

educational movement(s), 83, 85
Educational Theatre Journal, 42, 138, 150, 153, 155
Edwards, Thomas, 86
Efficiency Movement, 188
Ehrenpreis, Irvin, 129
Elevator (Howells), 126
Elfinbein, Josef Aaron, 104
Eliot, Charles W., 136
Eliot, T. S., 28, 29, 33, 55, 133
Elliott, Emory, 2, 48, 107
elocution, 123, 137, 140
Emerson, Ralph Waldo, 47, 100, 117, 150
Emery, Gilbert, 73
emotion in/and drama, 103, 108, 121, 142,
    152–3, 161
emotionalism, 42–3, 122, 156–8, 161
Emperor Jones, The (O'Neill), 32, 99, 100, 170
Engle, Ron, 56
English: as discipline, 127; relationship with
    drama, 140; as subject in high school, 120;
    teaching of, 130, 131
English departments, 14, 116, 118, 129, 130, 149,
    151, 158; study of drama in, 15, 132, 134, 152
English drama, 103; study of, 140, 143, 151
"English 47" (course, Harvard), 14, 133
English literature, study of, 117, 126
English taste, 36
entertainment, 20, 43, 94; American drama as,
    27–8, 161; popular, 79, 81, 82, 97; ritual
    and, 119; theatre of, 141
Entrikin, Knowles, 203
epic theatre, 179
essentialism, 57, 65, 102, 103; Green spokes-
    man for, 107; nationalist, 62
Esslin, Martin, 119, 157, 205
Estrin, Mark W., 205
ethnic drama/theatre, 54, 73–4
Europe, study of drama in, 15, 16
European drama, 10, 46; American drama in-
    ferior to, 58–9
European models, 3, 12, 13, 38, 45, 46, 61, 200;
    competition with, 42; separation from,
    96–103
European plays, 62, 91, 92, 205
European playwrights, 26, 27
exceptionalism (American), 101, 161
exclusion of drama, 1, 3, 9–56; from college an-
    thologies, 32; dominant paradigm and,
    64–5; in study of American literature, 130;
    from textbooks, 122–4, 125–6; from univer-
    sity curriculum, 116, 119
experimental theatre, 120, 142, 147, 184, 193
expressionism, 94–5, 99, 100, 191, 192
extracurricular activity, theatre as, 115, 127, 129,
    134

Falk, Robert, 177
Falk, Sawyer, 154–5

Fall of British Tyranny, The (Leacock), 172
Faragoh, Francis, 188–9, 193
Farrell, James, 30
Fashion (Mowatt), 88, 92
Father, The: or, American Shandyism (Dunlap),
    75, 96
Father of an Only Child, The (Dunlap), 59, 96
Fatted Calf (Kinne), 203
Federal Theatre, 54
Feiffer, Jules, 29
feminine (the): drama and, 103, 104, 105; and
    dramatic canon, 106
feminism/feminists, 11, 12, 19, 92, 108, 135; re-
    sistance to realism, 185–7
Fences (Wilson), 50, 55
Ferber, Edna, 28, 74
Fergusson, Francis, 53–4, 119, 181–2
Ferlinghetti, Lawrence, 28
fiction, 23, 112; in canon, 11, 31; dramatization
    of, 142; narrative essence of, 141; in sociol-
    ogy, 165
Fiddler on the Roof, 74
"field-coverage model," 52
Field God, The (Green), 72, 107
Figaro! (periodical), 78
Filler, Louis, 177
film, 141, 180
Film Studies, 19
Firkins, O. W., 20
Fisher, Philip, 206
Fitch, Clyde, 35, 73, 88, 99, 177
Fitzgerald, P. A., 123
Flavin, Martin, 203
Flory, Claude R., 30
Flower, B. O., 81, 168
Flynn, Joyce, 2, 204
Foerster, Norman, 72, 95
folk drama, 81, 107–8; movement, 69
"folk" playwriting movement, 106–8
for colored girls . . . (Shange), 49, 183
Ford, Paul Leicester, 96–7, 128
Foreman, Richard, 63
formalist problem, 59, 72
Fornes, Maria Irene, 63, 183
Forte, Jeanie, 186
Fortune Theatre, 132
47 Workshop, 133–4, 141, 147–8, 153
Foucault, Michel, 1
Fourth Estate, The (Patterson), 178
Francesca da Rimini (Boker), 34, 67, 83, 161
Frazer, Winifred L., 188
Frederic, Harold, 28
Freedman, Morris, 27–8
Freud, Sigmund, 47, 94
Friedman, Bruce Jay, 28
Friel, Brian, 31
frontier (the), 60, 72, 109
Frost, Robert, 28, 30

Fry, Emma Sheridan, 136, 156
Fuller, Harold de Wolf, 176
Fuller, Margaret, 77–8
Fussell, Edwin, 109

Gafford, Lucile, 78
Gagey, Edmond, 180
Galley Slave, The (Campbell), 97
Galsworthy, John, 97
Garbage Man, The (Dos Passos), 192
Gardner, Rufus Hallette, 47
Garland, Hamlin, 28, 171, 175
Gassner, John, 10, 43–4, 45, 46, 93, 153–4, 181;
    anthology, 106; defense of American
    drama, 47; and New Critics, 108; on
    O'Neill, 99–100; on realism, 184
Gates, Robert Allan, 70
Gayley, Charles Mills, 130–1, 132
Geddes, Virgil, 90, 93–4
Gelber, Jack, 28
gender, 6, 106, 122, 161–2
generic hegemony, 1, 7, 9–56, 157, 207; causes
    of, 26–7; explanation for, 12–13
genre(s): academic hegemony of, 11; in Ameri-
    can culture, 63–4; critics and, 116; drama
    as, 156, 199–200, 202, 203–4; hierarchy
    and, 12, 169, 197; and national culture,
    53–6; studies, 49, 129; theory, 205
geographical determination, 108–13
Gerstle, Gary, 65
Get-Rich-Quick Wallingford (Cohan), 178
Ghost Sonata (Strindberg), 80
Gibbons, Reginald, 45
Gilbert, Charles B., 124
Gilbert, Sandra, 48
Gilded Age, 40
Gillette, William, 79
Gilman, Richard, 10, 13–14
Gilmore, Michael, 48, 206
Giraudoux, Jean, 155
Girl of the Golden West, The (play), 18
Girl with the Green Eyes, The (Fitch), 88
Gladiator, The (Bird), 73, 83, 126
Glaspell, Susan, 48, 49, 74
Glass, Montague, 178
Glass Menagerie, The (Williams), 33, 51, 55, 74
Glassberg, David, 141
Gnesin, Maurice, 148
Godfrey, Thomas, 34, 67, 82–3, 106, 144
Gods of the Lightning (Anderson and Hicker-
    man), 168
Goffman, Erving, 171
Gold, Michael, 74, 188–9, 191, 192
Golden, Joseph, 54
Golden Age, 89, 95, 96
Golden Boy (Odets), 181
Golding, Alan C., 66
Goldman, Arnold, 40

Goldman, Harry, 62, 187
Goldsmith, Oliver, 35, 63
Goodman, Edward, 90, 92
Goose Hangs High, The (Beach), 164, 165
Gordon, Mel, 62, 187
Gostwick, Joseph, 34
Gottesman, Ronald, 33, 50
Gottlieb, Lois, 177
Graceful Generation, A (Entrikin), 203
Graff, Gerald, 4, 52–3, 122, 130
Grant, Robert, 84
Granville-Barker, Harley, 154
Grau, Robert, 97
Gray, Giles, 133
Great Divide, The (Moody), 27, 88, 92, 99
Green, Paul, 28, 53, 69, 72, 74, 90, 94, 203;
    spokesman for American essentialism, 107
Green Bay Tree, The (Shairp), 168
Green Grow the Lilacs (Riggs), 74
Green Pastures, The (Connelly), 107, 168
Gregory, Montgomery, 168
Grimsted, David, 4, 56
Gross, Seymour, 33
Grossberg, Michael, 104
Group, The (Warren), 55, 67, 172
Group Theatre, 54, 184; "close embrace" pro-
    ject, 181
Guare, John, 183
Gubar, Susan, 48

Haber, Samuel, 115
Hackett, James, 135
Haines, William Wister, 71
Hairy Ape, The (O'Neill), 33, 51, 71, 99
Hale, Edward Everett, 35
Hall, Stanley G., 121
Halline, Allan Gates, 72, 90, 94
Hamar, Clifford, 134
Hamilton, Clayton, 16, 24, 27, 43, 84–5, 86, 93,
    99, 110
Hammond, Percy, 81
Hapgood (Stoppard), 103
Hapgood, Norman, 73
Harkness, Edward, 143
Harper, William Rainey, 127
Harrigan, Edward, 79, 174
Harris, Mark, 28
Harris, Wendell V., 198
Hart, James D., 39
Hart, John Seely, 122, 126
Hart, Moss, 74
Harte, Bret, 28, 29, 110, 173, 175
Harvard, 35, 129, 145, 148; Baker at, 131, 132,
    133–4, 138, 140, 141, 142, 150; Dramatic
    Club, 134; elective system, 126–7; Wendell
    Collection of American Plays, 149
Harvey (Chase), 72
Hauptmann, Gerhart, 92

Hawkes, John, 28
Hawthorne, Nathaniel, 47, 110, 116, 117
Hayes, Alfred, 28
Hazel Kirke (MacKaye), 68
Hazelton, George, 88
Hearst, Phoebe, 131
Heath, D. C., 140
hegemony, 63, 80, 187; American West in
    tradition of, 109; Anglo-American cul-
    tural, 65; cultural, 73, 81, 82; moving
    beyond, 197–207; *see also* generic
    hegemony
Heillman, Robert, 46
Hell-Bent Fer Heaven (Hughes), 164, 165
Heller, Joseph, 28
Hellman, Lillian, 28, 49, 57, 74, 90, 106
Hemingway, Ernest, 28, 39
Henley, Beth, 183
Hennequin, Alfred, 24, 142, 172
Henrietta, The (Howard), 177
Henry, George H., 138
Hergesheimer, Joseph, 108
Herne, James A., 35, 68, 79, 171
Hero, The (Emery), 73
Herrmann, Max, 15, 151
Herts, Alice Minnie, 136
Hewitt, Barnard, 98, 205
Hickerman, Harold, 168
hierarchy(ies), 5; canonical, 10; eliminating,
    193; genre, 197; legitimation of, 158; rejec-
    tion of, 202
high art, drama as, 83, 135–6
high culture, 11, 14, 41, 54, 84, 112, 117
High Tor (Anderson), 74
higher education: American drama in, 126–34;
    American literature in, 10; bias against
    drama in, 12–29
Hillebrand, H. M., 152
Hinckley, Theodore B., 147
Hippolytus (Howe), 73
historians, 1, 7; and gendering of drama, 106;
    see also literary historians
historical issues in American drama, 9
Historical Pageant of Illinois, An, 109
historical plays, 67, 69
histories of American literary and theatrical
    practice, 4; *see also* literary histories
Hoboken Blues (Gold), 189, 191
Hodge, Francis, 101
Hoffman, Theodore, 47
Hornblow, Arthur, 59, 135, 195
House of Blue Leaves, The (Guare), 183
House of Games (Mamet), 50
Howard, Bronson, 17, 79–80, 91, 127, 174,
    177
Howard, Leon, 40
Howard, Sidney, 35, 69, 98
Howe, Irving, 45–6

Howe, Julia Ward, 19, 29, 68, 73
Howells, William Dean, 28, 29, 72, 73, 81, 126,
    136; and death of drama, 90; "fidelity"
    principle, 94; and realism, 173–5
Hristič, Jovan, 179
Hubbell, Jay Broadus, 32, 41, 99
Hubbard, Louise Shipman, 148, 164
Huber, Bettina J., 116
Hughes, Glenn, 37–8
Hughes, Hatcher, 164
Hughie (O'Neill), 51
humanist-reformist social science, 162–3, 164
Humiston, Beatrice, 137
Hunecker, James Gibbons, 35, 37–8
Hunter, Governor, 67
Hurston, Zora Neal, 28
Hutchins, Robert, 138
Hutton, Laurence, 79

Ibsen, Henrik, 27, 46, 92, 99, 179, 181
Icebound (Davis), 88
Iceman Cometh, The (O'Neill), 55
Ide, Leonard, 203
ideology(ies), 37, 40, 48, 71, 158; dominant,
    186; drama and, 61–2, 195–6
immigrants/immigration, 64, 93, 112, 200; and
    theatre, 71, 73–4
Indians (Kopit), 50
Ingarden, Roman, 198–9
Inge, William, 40, 57, 153
interdisciplinary theory, 6, 204
International, The (Lawson), 178, 189, 192, 193,
    195
intertextuality, 160, 205
Irving, Washington, 28, 29
isolation of American drama, 26, 29; *see also*
    exclusion of drama; patterned isolation

Jack Cade (Conrad), 67
Jackson, President, 177
Jacobus, Lee A., 74–5, 106
James, Henry, 28, 29, 42, 43, 109, 110, 175
James, William, 162
Jarrell, Randall, 28
Jay, Gregory S., 206
Jeffers, Robinson, 28, 33
Jefferson, Joseph, 160
Jefferson, Thomas, 81
Joe Turner's Come and Gone (Wilson), 55
Johns, Elizabeth, 111
Johnson, Claudia, 23, 115–16
Johnson, Gertrude, 137
Jones, Henry Arthur, 105, 128, 172
Jones, Henry Dixon, 140
Jones, Howard Mumford, 10, 32, 36, 117,
    180
Jones, Robert Edmond, 38, 80, 151
Jonson, Ben, 96

journalism: drama's ties with, 178, 179; dra-
    matic realism and, 182; theatre and, 26; *see
    also* muckraking journalism
journals, 42, 46, 103, 120; and cultural position-
    ing of American drama, 75–6; drama in,
    78–9; education of people through, 78; pro-
    fessional, 117, 137–8, 145; *see also* scholarly
    journals
Joyce, James, 181

Kahn, Otto, 188
Kanin, Garson, 178
Kaplan, Ann, 186
Kaufman, George S., 73, 74, 177–8
Kauffmann, Stanley, 29, 54
Kazan, Elia, 148
Kazin, Alfred, 39–40, 46
Keene, Laura, 19, 68
Kelly, George, 169, 180
Kennedy, Adrienne, 31, 50, 63, 183
Kenyon, Charles, 27, 85–6, 88, 98
Kenyon Review, The, 10, 30, 90, 94
Kernodle, George R., 150–1
Kerr, Walter, 95
Kettell, Samuel, 52, 66
Kindling (Kenyon), 18, 27, 85–6, 88
Kingsley, Sidney, 57, 178
Kinne, Burdette, 203
Kinne, Wisner Payne, 140, 141, 148
Kiper, Florence, 92–3
Kirkland, Joseph, 175
Klein, Charles, 81, 92, 168, 176, 177
Knapp, James, 187–8, 190, 191
Knapp, Margaret, 95–6
Knapp, Samuel L., 34
Knight, Marietta, 124
Knoblock, Edward, 148
Knox, George, 195
Knudsun, Hans, 151
Koch, Frederick, 107
Koch, Kenneth, 28, 45
Kolodny, Annette, 7, 202–3
Kopit, Arthur, 50
Kostelanetz, Richard, 26, 45
Kotzebue, August von, 69
Kraus, Herman, 93
Kronenberger, Louis, 90, 94
Kruger, Loren, 4
Krutch, Joseph Wood, 27, 28, 195
Kuhn, Thomas, 200–1
Kushner, Tony, 55, 103
Kutscher, Artur, 151

Lafayette College, 130
land (the): Americanness in, 109–10, 111,
    112–13; as theme, 109
Lauter, Paul, 5, 49, 51, 108–9, 112
Lavedan, Henri, 92

Lawrence, D. H., 112
Lawrenson, Helen, 90, 95
Lawson, John Howard, 28, 40, 72, 88, 178,
    188–9, 191, 192, 193
Lazarus Laughed (O'Neill), 55, 143, 203
Leacock, John, 172
Left (the), 7, 36–7, 100, 195
legitimation, 7, 132; American drama, 72, 108,
    158; American literature, 117; discourse of,
    6, 119–20; Drama League and, 83–9; of lit-
    erature as subject, 121–2; scholarly, 136, 137;
    of sociology, 162; of theatre, 135
Leisy, Ernest, 32, 36, 180
Leonora or The World's Own (Howe), 19, 68
Lepenies, Wolf, 162
Letter of Introduction, A (Howells), 73
Levine, Lawrence W., 4, 56
Lewis, R. W. B., 46
Lewis, Theophilus, 180
Lewisohn, Ludwig, 71–2, 98
library(ies), drama collections of, 141, 149
Life with Father (Lindsay and Crouse), 69, 169
Lindsay, Howard, 69
Linn, John Blair, 34
Lion and the Mouse, The (Klein), 18, 97, 168,
    176, 177
Lippman, Monroe, 177, 178
literary criticism/critics, 1, 4, 118, 161; as play-
    wrights, 28; *see also* critics
literary drama, 93, 97
literary historians, 2, 7, 59, 96; on muckraking
    drama, 177
literary histories, 5, 12, 17, 26, 29, 34–42, 51–2,
    75, 101; exclusion of American drama, 2,
    64–5; Howells in, 173
literary status of American drama, 2–3, 13–16,
    18, 23, 31, 32–3, 46, 54–5, 57, 58, 65, 72, 73,
    79, 91, 93, 95, 107–8, 172, 175, 179, 198, 206;
    dramatics and, 138; Eaton on, 159–61; play-
    wrights and, 26–9; universities and, 143
Literary Work of Art, The (Ingarden), 198–9
literature, 3, 20; as academic subject, 121–2;
    Americanness in, 80; drama as, 11, 12, 91,
    97, 107–8, 155, 165 (*see also* literary status of
    drama); drama different from, 37, 40–1,
    141; narrowing of definition of, 37; as prod-
    uct of sociology, 169; science and, 161–2;
    separate from performance/stage, 15, 23–4,
    204; *see also* literature studies
literature courses, plays in, 14–15; *see also* cur-
    riculum
literature studies, 201, 202–3; drama in, 127–8;
    drama separated from, 128; multicultural-
    ism and, 206–7; rhetoric in, 122; in secon-
    dary schools, 125–6; *see also* literature
Little Foxes, The (Hellman), 49
Little Theatre (Chicago), 72, 98
Little Theatre movement, 85, 93

"little theatre" practitioners, 83
Little Theatres, 120, 147, 176
"Living Newspapers," 37, 178
local theatres, 80–1
Locke, Alain, 168
Londré, Felicia, 138
Lonesome Road (Green), 69, 109
Lonesome West (Riggs), 203
Long, E. Hudson, 33
Long Day's Journey into Night (O'Neill), 50, 55, 164–5
Longfellow, Henry Wadsworth, 29, 37
Loud Speaker (Lawson), 189, 193, 194
Lovett, Robert, 136
low culture, 41–2, 78
Lowell, Robert, 28, 33, 45
Lowenthal, David, 112

Macbeth, 46–7
McCandless, Stanley, 145
McCarthy, Mary, 30, 44, 182
McClure, Michael, 28
McConachie, Bruce, 56, 173, 204
McCormick, John, 39
McCullers, Carson, 28, 49, 182
McDermott, Douglas, 187
MacDowell Club, 83, 148
McGarth, John, 199
Macgowan, Kenneth, 38, 80–1, 99, 133, 134, 138–40, 153
McGranahan, Donald V., 102
McGuffey, William Holmes, 123–4
MacIver, R. M., 170
Mackay, Constance D'Arcy, 84
MacKaye, Percy, 27, 38, 85, 88, 92, 97, 141
MacKaye, Steele, 38, 67, 68, 79, 136
McLaws, Lafayette, 142
MacLeish, Archibald, 28, 33
McMichael, George, 33, 51
McQuade, Donald, 50
magazines, 80, 135–6; and cultural positioning of American drama, 75–6; plays published in, 18, 30
Maggie Pepper (play), 18
Mailer, Norman, 28
Malamud, Bernard, 45
Malevinsky, M. L., 103
Malquerida, La (The Passion Flower) (Bena-vente y Martínez), 189
Maltz, Albert, 100
Mamet, David, 28, 50, 55, 106, 111
Man (Schlick), 203
Man of La Mancha (Wasserman), 89–90
Man of the Hour, The (Broadhurst), 92
management, modern, and dramatic discourse versus, 187–96
Mandeville, H., 123
Mann, Emily, 186

March, F. A., 130
Marco Millions (O'Neill), 178
Margaret Fleming (Herne), 68
Margery's Lovers (Matthews), 127
"marginal" generic forms, 51
marginal works, 12; canon opened to, 39, 48
marginalization of American drama, 1, 4, 5–6, 11
Marmion; or, The Battle of Flodden Field (Barker), 36, 59
Marranca, Bonnie, 44, 49
Marston, John, 96
Marx, Karl, 47, 94
Marx, Leo, 46
masculine paradigm, 59, 61, 112
masculine science, 122; American drama as, 103–8
masculinity, 77, 84, 103, 104, 112, 133; of American drama, 158; of American social science, 162; of playwriting, 148–9; study of theatre and, 150
Masks and Demons (Macgowan and Rosse), 80
Masque of Alfred, The, 68
Masque of American Drama (Trombly), 82–3
Matlaw, Myron, 70
Matthews, Brander, 56, 71, 132, 133, 155; on beginning of drama, 99; chair of dramatic literature, 131; and decline of drama, 90–1; and drama as masculine science, 103, 104, 105–6; on place of drama in literature, 127–8
Matthiessen, F. O., 39, 41, 112, 117
Mayorga, Margaret G., 36, 145–7
Mazzocco, Robert, 30
Mead (playwright), 177
Meinig, D. W., 111
Melnitz, William W., 151–2
melodrama, 26, 34, 59, 62, 63, 68, 75, 91, 119, 176, 195; as form in its own right, 203; move from, to realism, 62, 100, 172–3; realism antidote to, 95; sensation, 104
Melville, Herman, 32, 47, 109, 112, 117
Member of the Wedding (McCullers), 49
Mercier, Vivian, 44, 90, 94–5
Merrill, James, 28
Mersand, Joseph, 185
Meserve, Walter J., 3, 19–20, 175
Metamora (Stone), 73, 126, 160
Metcalfe, James, 24, 98–9
Michael Bonham, or the Fall of Bexar (Simms), 64
Midnight, 203–4
Mighty Dollar, The (Woolf), 73
Millay, Edna St. Vincent, 28
Miller, Arthur, 26, 27, 28, 31, 40, 44, 49, 50, 55, 57, 69, 90, 106, 107, 153, 154, 178; in curriculum, 116, 138; the land in works of, 111; and realism, 182; social drama, 181; stage

Miller, Arthur *(cont.)*
    directions, 199; status of, 183; tragedy of
    the common man, 94
Miller, Joaquin, 175
Miller, Jordan Y., 72, 188
Miller, Perry, 107
Miller, Sigmund, 178
Miller, Tice L., 56
mimetic and idealistic art (theory), 76
Minimum Basic Agreement of 1926, 17
minstrel show, 13, 56, 62, 64, 81, 82, 95, 160,
    161, 174, 206
mirror of life, drama as, 70–1, 81, 84, 170–1
Mitchell, Langdon, 27, 88
Modern Drama (journal), 4, 32, 42
Modern Language Association, 2, 116, 153
modernism/modernity, 103, 187–8, 189; art,
    190–1; European, 101
Moffatt, James, 156
Mogen, David, 110
Money Makers, The (Klein), 18, 177
Moody, Richard, 73, 205
Moody, William Vaughn, 27, 88, 92, 99
Moore, Charles, 185
moral opposition to theatre, 75, 79
moral purpose of drama, 57, 65, 76, 137, 168, 169
Morison, Samuel Eliot, 134
Morning Glory (Akins), 203
Morrison, Toni, 28
Mortimer, Lillian, 72–3
Morton, Dixon, 145
Mose the Fireman, 161
Moses, Montrose J., 15, 18, 34, 38, 55, 73, 100,
    117, 127–8, 145; anthologies, 66–7, 88, 106;
    and drama in curriculum, 131–2; and folk
    movement, 107; and realism, 172, 176–7, 180
Mott, Frank, 75, 76, 78
Mourning Becomes Electra (O'Neill), 179, 199
Movie Star Has to Star in Black and White, A
    (Kennedy), 50
Mowatt, Cora (Mrs. Mowatt), 88, 92
Mrs. Tony Trentor (Ide), 203
muckraking: dramas, 92; journalism, 26, 175–9
Mueller, John, 169–70
Mukarovsky, Jan, 15
Mulford, Carla, 3, 204–5
multiculturalism, 6, 200, 205, 206–7
Mumford, Lewis, 29
Murphy, Brenda, 3, 173–4, 184, 205
Murray, Lindley, 123
"Myth-symbol Critics," 46

Nathan, George Jean, 24, 90, 93
national character, 60, 63, 70, 71, 102
National Council of Teachers of English, 122,
    137
national culture, 12; genre and, 53–6
national drama, 59

national identity, 63, 64
National Police Gazette, 78
national theatre, 81, 144–5, 191
nationalism, 6, 36, 102, 108, 195; critics and,
    62; idealized, 200; literary, 66; new, 100
Native American Indians, 50, 70, 160; works
    by, 12, 49
native character, 174–5
native drama, 59, 61, 81, 82, 88, 96, 101; differ-
    ence between cultural imports and, 73;
    folk movement and, 107; national drama
    distinct from, 59; and theatre, 191; virility
    in, 106–7
native themes, 68, 69, 71, 113
naturalism, 68, 70, 183–4
Neighborhood Players, 98
Nelson, Richard, 70
New Blood (Thomas), 177
New Criticism, 37, 46, 98, 116, 197; effect of, 46–7
New Critics, 3, 10, 11, 12, 46, 108
*New-England Magazine of Knowledge and
    Pleasure, The*, 75
New Historicism, 12, 19, 204
New Literary History (journal), 31
New Playwrights' Theatre, 186, 187, 188–9,
    190, 191, 192–6
New York Clipper (magazine), 78
New York Drama Critics Circle, 181
New York Drama League, 89
New York Idea, The (Mitchell), 27, 88
New York Illustrated Times, 78
"New York Intellectuals," 45–6
New-York Magazine, 75
New York Mirror, 78–9
New York Times, 31
Nice People (Crothers), 73
Nichols, Harold J., 36
Nicholson, Kenyon, 74
Niebuhr, Reinhold, 60
Niessen, Carl, 151
Nietz, John, 124–5, 126
Nightingale, Benedict, 157
No Mother to Guide Her (Mortimer), 73
Norman, Marsha, 183
Norris, Frank, 93, 177
Norton, Elliot, 38
Not I (Beckett), 179
Novak, Barbara, 111
novel (the), 44, 58, 91, 174; Americanness in,
    110; divorce between drama and, 110–11,
    142; drama compared to, 182, 206; dramati-
    zation of, 24; and realism, 179; study of, 150
novelists, 28
Nuhn, Ferner, 149
Nye, Russel, 41

Oates, Joyce Carol, 28
Obey, André, 181

Octoroon, The (Boucicault), 160
Odell, George C. D., 152
Odenwald-Ungar, Mrs. J., 168
Odets, Clifford, 40, 46, 49, 50, 57, 90, 94; realism in, 181
Ogden, Jess, 85, 107
Ohmann, Richard, 31
Oklahoma!, 94
Old Homestead, The (Thompson), 174
Old Times (Pinter), 179
Oliver, William, 186
Olson, Charles, 28, 112
One Bright Day (Miller), 178
O'Neil, George, 37, 178
O'Neill, Eugene, 27, 31, 32, 33, 38, 39, 41, 44, 46, 47, 50, 51, 55, 71, 80, 90, 94, 98, 103, 106, 107, 143, 170, 172, 178, 203; in American canon, 32; in Baker's course, 133–4; in curriculum, 116, 138, 149; effect of status of, on contemporaries, 205; first serious American playwright, 14, 35, 57; impact on American theatre, 98–9; opposition to technology, 188; place in American drama, 74; psychological drama yoked to classical tragedy in, 179; as realist playwright, 182, 184; reviews of works of, 164–5; as savior of American drama, 40; stage directions, 199; as transitional playwright, 99–100
Oppenheim, James, 30
oral reading, 121, 124
oral tradition, 13
oratory, 122, 123, 125, 127, 130, 156
organic evolution (trope), 89–96, 183
Orphan, The (Addison), 134
Owens, Rochelle, 28, 106
Oxford Drama Commission, 154

Page, Eugene, 17–18
pageant drama, 37
Paid in Full (play), 18
"pamphlet plays," 178
Parker, Dorothy, 29
Parker, Louis, 86
Parrington, Vernon Lewis, 171
Party, The (Powell), 203
Patriarch, The (Smith), 143
Pattee, Fred Lewis, 39, 123, 143, 144
patterned isolation of drama, 12, 29–34
Patterson, Joseph Medill, 98, 178
Paul Kauver (MacKaye), 67
Paulding, James Kirk, 36, 59, 109, 171
Payne, John Howard, 34, 65, 67, 69
Peale, Norman Vincent, 39
Pearson, Roberta, 56
Pease, Donald, 31
Peck, Mary Grey, 87
Pere Indian, Le (Villaneuve), 96

Perelman, S. J., 29
performance, 15, 51, 55, 154, 155, 197–8, 199; articles on, 31; Baker's focus on, 141–2; emphasis on, 14, 51, 131, 132–3; extracurricular status of, 156; pedagogical interest in, 18–19; reevaluation of practices, 203; separated from literature, 15, 23–4, 204; studies, 6, 115, 198–9, 205; tension between text and, 118–19; theory, 52, 205; values, 44–5
periodicals, 75–6; drama in, 78–9; *see also* journals; magazines
Persecution and Assassination of Marat/Sade (Weiss), 89–90
Peter Stuyvesant (Matthews and Howard), 127
Peters, Paul, 100
Pettet, Edwin Burr, 151
Phelps, William Lyon, 128–9, 132, 135
Philbrick, Norman, 151, 152, 178
"Photography in Fiction: 'Miss Jerry,' the First Picture Play" (Black), 24
Pilgrim Spirit, The (Baker), 141
Pinter, Harold, 31, 179
Pinwheel (Faragoh), 193
Pirandello, Luigi, 151
Pit, The (Norris), 93, 177
Plath, Sylvia, 28
plays: demand for, 85; first American, 82–3; foreign, 69; markets for, 86; novelizing of, 18; published, 13, 17–18, 87, 88; published in magazines, 18, 30; publishers of, 83, 85; readership for, 145–7; as score to be performed/as literary text, 15
Plays in Periodicals, 30
Plays of the 47 Workshop, 141–2
Playshop (Chicago), 142
playwrights, 28–9, 49, 81, 94, 118, 120, 148; blamed for low status of drama, 24–6; and copyright, 17; criticism of, 43, 44; culturally elite core of, 54; failure of, 23; female, in American canon, 74; feminist, 186–7; first career, 91; and future American drama, 79–80; and generic hegemony, 26–9; opposition to scientific management, 191–2, 195; realist, 178, 182; and study of American literature, 116; universities' responsibility for, 153–4; white male, 41, 50, 51; women, 74, 105–6, 183
playwriting, American, 149; beginning of, 67; in curriculum, 131, 132, 133, 143, 153–4; as masculine and academic enterprise, 77, 148–9
Plumes (Stallings), 164
PMLA, 30–1
Pocahontas, or The Gentle Savage, (Brougham), 64, 160
Poe, Edgar Allan, 28, 29, 37, 124
poetic drama/dramatists, 46, 52, 120, 128, 147–8

poetry, 23, 51, 52, 58, 112; in American litera-
    ture, 117; in canon, 11; dominance of, 1, 3,
    12; drama as, 15; lack of, in American
    drama, 98; and literary drama, 97
poetry anthologies, 66
poets as playwrights, 28, 50
political agenda(s), 96, 116; in higher educa-
    tion, 127
political issues in drama, 9, 48, 100, 104–5, 156,
    178, 195–6; New Playwrights' Theatre, 192
Pollock, Channing, 177
Ponteach (Rogers), 67, 68, 122
Poor of New York, The (Boucicault), 177
Popkin, Henry, 90, 95
popularity of plays, 72–3; *see also* entertain-
    ment, popular
Porter, Carolyn, 206
Portrait of a Madonna (play), 51
Postlewait, Thomas, 56, 96, 99, 203
Potash and Perlmutter (Glass), 178
Potter's Field (Green), 203
Powel, J. H., 203
Powell, Dawn, 203
pragmatism, 99, 171–3
Price, William Thompson, 142
Prince Hagen (Sinclair), 177
Prince of Parthia, The (Godfrey), 34, 67, 68,
    82–3; in curriculum, 144
Princess's Choice, The (play), 137
problem of American drama, 1–8, 119–20,
    197–8; in curriculum, 116–17
"problem" play(s), 36, 180
Processional (Lawson), 88
Producing Centre Report, 86
production, 13, 16, 20, 153; Baker's focus on,
    141; Drama League, 86, 87; emphasis on,
    137, 155; equivalent to text, 31; and inclu-
    sion in anthologies, 67, 68; primacy of, 133;
    profitability of, 97; simultaneous, 144–5;
    text and, 13, 14, 15; in universities, 155–6
professional journals, 117, 137–8, 145
professionalism/professionalization, 2, 4, 58,
    82, 84, 104, 140, 147, 200; of academics, 84,
    109; of actors, 135; drama in curriculum
    and, 129–30
professionals (American literary), 103–4
progressive movement/progressivism, 18, 65,
    138
prose, 51, 52; in American literature, 117; domi-
    nance of, 1, 3, 12; nonfictional, in canon, 11
Provincetown Players, 98
Przkwzi, Leon, 93
psychologic drama, 97, 179
psychological realism, 176, 179, 184
psychology, 138, 171
publishers' catalogues, 30, 83
publishing industry, 29–30, 145–6
Pudd'nhead Wilson (play), 24

Purdy, James, 28
Puritan distaste for theatre and drama, 3, 12,
    13, 23, 34–6, 72, 204–5

Quarterly Journal of Speech, 137
Quinn, Arthur Hobson, 17, 19, 52, 59, 64, 107,
    117, 159, 160; and American literature in
    curriculum, 149; anthologies, 65–6, 67–9,
    73, 88, 106; course in American drama,
    136; criteria for American drama, 61; dis-
    tinction between American and European
    drama, 101; on folk drama, 107–8; history
    of American drama, 26; on Howells, 173,
    174; and isolation of American dramatic
    literature, 29; and muckraking drama, 177;
    on O'Neill, 99; and organic growth of
    drama, 89; values espoused by, 168

Rabe, David, 49, 55, 186
Racine, Jean Baptiste, 151
Rahv, Philip, 43
Raisin in the Sun, A (play), 51
Rand, Ayn, 28
Random House, 18
Ratzenhofer, Gustav, 163
reading: drama in teaching of, 123; modes of, 198
reading plays, 13, 16–17; readership for, 145–7;
    and "reading versions," 18
realism, 1, 26, 38, 44, 46, 57, 63, 68, 69, 70, 72,
    79, 94, 95, 116, 119, 179–83, 197; antidote to
    melodrama, 95; avoiding, 92; Eaton on,
    159–60; expanded understanding of, 183–5;
    Howells and, 173–5; move from melo-
    drama to, 62, 100, 203; "new," 184–5;
    propagandistic, 184; resistance to, 185–7; as
    salvation of drama, 171–3; schools of, 184;
    and social science, 162; sociology and,
    159–96
realistic drama, American school of, 176
Reardon, William, 19
Recruiting Officer, The (Addison), 134
Reed, P. I., 172
regional drama, 20, 54, 74
regional theatre movement/theatres, 80–1, 106
Reinelt, Janelle, 56
Reinhardt, Max, 97
Reising, Russell, 48, 51
Removal of the Deposits, The (Mead), 177
Removing the Deposits (Mead), 177
Renker, Elizabeth, 103–4
Reston, James, 186–7
"revolting playwrights," the, 188, 189
Rexroth, Kenneth, 28
rhetoric, 36, 121, 122, 125, 130; decentering of,
    130; devaluation of, 156
Rice, Elmer, 40, 72, 74, 98, 100, 154, 172, 188
Rich, Frank, 62
Richards, Stanley, 69

Richardson, Charles F., 34, 117
Richardson, Gary, 4
Richardson, Lyon, 75
Richman, Arthur, 72
Riggs, Lynn, 74, 203
Rinehart, Mary Roberts, 28
Rip Van Winkle (Boucicault), 24, 83, 160
Roach, Joseph, 205
Robbins, Bruce, 4
Robinson, Marc, 57–8, 62–3
Robinson, R. R., 124
Rockefeller, John D., 176
Roe, Clifford G., 20
Roger Bloomer (Lawson), 88, 191
Rogers, Robert, 67, 68
Roman Father, The (Addison), 134
romance, 29, 68, 69, 100, 174–5
Romance (Sheldon), 27
romantic period, 48, 69
romanticism, 72, 98, 171
Rosen, Robert C., 195
Rosenblatt, Louise, 198
Ross, Dorothy, 161–2
Rosse, Herman, 80
Roth, Philip, 45
Roudané, Matthew, 111
Ruland, Richard, 42

Saldívar, José David, 206
Salem, James, 44
Sanford, Charles, 46
Sargent, Epes, 124
Saroyan, William, 28, 40, 57, 182
Scarecrow, The (MacKaye), 27, 83, 88
Schechner, Richard, 118–19
Schenkar, Joan, 183
Scheville, James, 29
Schlick, Frederick, 203
scholarly journals, 2, 30–1, 32, 120, 137–8; and
    legitimation of drama, 135
"school of sincerity," 97, 98
"schools" of American criticism, 45–6
Schwartz, Delmore, 28
science, 115, 121, 122; drama and/as, 150–1;
    dramatics as, 138; equated with objectivity,
    103–4; and literature, 161–2
scientific management movement, 187–96
Scott, Fred Newton, 121
Scott, Sir Walter, 91, 124
Scribner's Magazine, 24, 73; "Art of Living"
    series, 84
Second Story Man, The (Sinclair), 177
secondary schools: teaching of literature in,
    125–6
Sedgwick, W. E., 64–5
"Segregated Drama," 38
Selden, Samuel, 151, 152–3
Seldes, Gilbert, 30

"Self and Sex" series, 20
Seller, Maxine Schwartz, 73–4
Seven Arts, The (magazine), 30
Seven Plays (Shepard), 55
Sewall, Jonathan, 172
Sexton, Anne, 28
Shairp, Mordaunt, 168
Shakespeare, William, 14, 28, 36, 76, 117, 118,
    129, 141, 176, 197; in curriculum, 123–4, 128,
    130, 132, 143, 151; student productions of, 155
Shakespeare studies, 19, 158
Shange, Ntozake, 49, 50, 183
Shank, Thomas, 155
Shaw, George Bernard, 27, 97, 165, 199
Shaw, Irwin, 28, 69, 154, 155
Shaw, T. B., 126
Sheldon, Edward, 27, 98, 148, 176, 178
Shenandoah (Howard), 174
Shepard, Sam, 28, 50, 55, 63, 106, 107, 111;
    Americanness of, 62; in curriculum, 116;
    mythologizing impulse in, 112
Sheridan, Richard Brinsley, 35, 63
Sherwood, Robert, 57, 71, 98, 138
Shirer, William, 29
Shumway, David, 5, 52, 103, 117, 150
Sifton, Paul, 189, 192–3
Simms, William Gilman, 64
Simon, John, 43
Simonson, Lee, 148, 151
Sinclair, Upton, 28, 177, 189, 193
Singing Jailbirds (Sinclair), 189, 193
Sklar, George, 100
Slade, Peter, 156
Slavs! (Kushner), 103
Sleeping-Car (Howells), 126
Small, Albion, 120–1, 162–4, 167
Smith, Barbara Herrnstein, 202
Smith, Boyd, 143
Smith, Elihu Hubbard, 66
Smith, Henry Nash, 109
Smith, Penn, 69
Smith, Sydney, 9
Smyth, Albert, 126
Social Darwinism, 120
social drama, 69, 181
social education, American drama and,
    134–8
social issues/problems in drama, 9, 37, 99,
    100, 104–5
social process, cultural form and, 202
sociocultural approach, 160, 161
sociological approach to drama, 70, 164–70,
    171, 180, 181, 196
sociology, 1, 7, 138, 167; and drama, 170–1;
    emergent, 161–4; and realism, 159–96
Sociology and Social Research (journal), 165, 170–1
Solid Gold Cadillac, The (Teichmann and
    Kaufman), 178

Sontag, Susan, 182
Spanish Student, The (Longfellow), 37
Speed-the-Plow (Mamet), 55
Spencer, Benjamin, 171
Spengemann, William, 5
Spiller, Robert E., 39, 40–1, 63–4, 107, 133, 173; on O'Neill, 100
Spingarn, Joel Elias, 129, 132–3
Spirit of the Times (magazine), 78, 89
Sporting and Theatrical Journal, 78
Spread Eagle (Brooks and Lister), 178
Spumenti, Giacomo, 93
Stafford, John, 23
stage: American drama linked to, 118, 128; directions, 198–9; premodern conventions, 70; set(s), 112; stage-as-mirror-of-life, 170–1; types, 70–2, 174
stagecraft, 101, 180
Stahl, Herbert, 195
Stall, Sylvanus, 20
Stallings, Laurence, 164
Stambusky, Alan A., 155–6
star system, 23, 26, 110
Stedman, Edmund Clarence, 91
Stein, Gertrude, 28, 31, 32, 39, 63, 112, 181, 183
Stephenson, Nellie A., 134
Stern, Milton, 33
Stevedore (Sklar and Peters), 100, 184
Stevens, Wallace, 28
Still Life (Mann), 186
Stone, John Augustus, 73, 126, 160
Stoppard, Tom, 103
Strange Interlude (O'Neill), 184
Straumann, Heinrich, 99
Streamers (Rabe), 55, 186
Street Scene (Rice), 74
Streetcar Named Desire, A (Williams), 49, 50, 55, 169
Strindberg, August, 46, 80
Stuart, Gilbert, 76
Studies in American Drama, 1945–Present (journal), 4
Styan, John, 199
subliterary quality of American drama, 42, 43–4
Sudermann, Hermann, 92
Sullivan, T. R., 23
Sully, Thomas, 76
Sunshine Boys, The (play), 75
Sun-Up (Vollmer), 69, 107–8
Superstition (Barker), 59
Susan and God (Crothers), 169
Symposium on the Responsibility of the Universities to the Theatre, 154–5
Szondi, Peter, 15

Tarbell, Ida, 92, 176
Tarkington, Booth, 28

Taubman, Howard, 19
Taylor, Charles, 34
Taylor, Frederick Winslow, 189–90, 191, 193
Taylor, Walter Fuller, 100
Taylorism, 186, 187, 191–2, 193, 194–5
Teichmann, Howard, 178
Ten Million Ghosts (Kingsley), 178
Ten Nights in a Bar Room (play), 47
Terry, Megan, 49, 183
text(s), 13, 18, 46, 51, 198–9; drama as, 118–19, 145–6; and performance, 118; printed, 6; privileged, 203; and production, 14, 15; reading, 16; in sociology, 169; taught, studied, valued, 116
textbook anthologies/textbooks, 50–1, 107, 122–6; genre studies, 129
textual analysis, performance emphasized over, 132–3
theatre, 76, 115, 197–8; academic attitude toward, 145; as academic discipline, 135; bias against, 3, 11; cultural and social antipathy toward, 20–3; in curriculum, 131–2; distribution and reification of dramatized images of America by, 70; and drama, 8, 16, 114, 118–19, 120; extracurricular location of, in academe, 134; history of, 95; and journalism, 26; and literature, 15; as "male club," 75; manager-dominated, 36, 44, 68, 120; moral bias against, 35; in sociology, 164; split with drama, 152
Theatre, The (magazine), 135
Theatre Arts Magazine, 38, 132, 135, 140, 144, 147
Theatre departments, 14, 15, 52, 118, 131, 134, 140, 143, 150, 156, 158
Theatre Journal, 4, 32, 205
theatre managers: "anti-syndicate" of, 91–2; financial success of, 97
theatre of the absurd, 179
Theatre Union, 184
theatre-within-the-theatre, 179
Theatre Workshop of New York, 142
theatres: clerical ban on, 78; college and university, 138–40, 143; commercial, manager-dominated, 36; rowdy behavior in, 75, 78; subsidized, 93
theatrical practice, dramatic literature and, 201–7
theatrical study versus literary, 133
theatricality, 42, 44–5, 94
themes (American drama), 49–50, 59, 72, 87, 102, 104–5; the land, 109; native, 68, 69, 71, 113
They Knew What They Wanted (Howard), 69
They Shall Not Die (Wexley), 37, 168, 180
Third Little Show, 203
Thomas, Augustus, 24, 27, 88, 97, 99, 177
Thompson, Denman, 174
Thoreau, Henry David, 109, 117
Thorp, Willard, 40

Tichi, Cecilia, 187, 188, 191
To the Ladies! (Kaufman and Connelly), 73
Tocqueville, Alexis de, 42
topical drama, 54, 180
Tortesa, the Usurer (Willis), 37, 67
Totheroh, Dan, 203
Toynbee, Arnold, 39
Toy-Shop, The (play), 75
tragedy, 44, 68, 87, 196
Transcendentalists, 78
Trifles (Glaspell), 48, 51
Trilling, Lionel, 46, 110
Triple-A Plowed Under (Arent), 37
Triumph of Plattsburg, The (Smith), 69
Trojan Women, The (Euripides), 98
Trollope, Frances, 64, 76
Trombly, Albert, 83
True West (Shepard), 50
Truth, The (Fitch), 88
Tucker, Samuel Marion, 132
Tukesbury, Beatrice L., 136
Tupper, James, 97
Turner, Frederick Jackson, 60
Turner, Ronnie E., 171
Twain, Mark, 28, 29, 109, 110, 173, 175
Tyler, Moses Coit, 65, 117, 122–3
Tyler, Royall, 50, 63–4, 72, 73, 76, 82, 106, 107, 126; in curriculum, 144; first successful American play was by, 96
Tyndall, John, 106

un-Americanness of American drama, 58–9
Unchastened Woman, The (Anspacher), 88
Uncle Remus, 107
Uncle Tom's Cabin; or, Life Among the Lowly (Aiken), 47, 64, 79, 160, 180
Under the Gaslight (play), 47
universities: drama in curriculum, 114–58; exclusion of American dramatic literature, 1; play production in, 155–6; responsibility of, 153–5
University of California, 130–1, 132
University of Chicago, 120, 129, 149, 162
University of Pennsylvania, 83, 136, 149
Uricchio, William, 56

Van Doren, Mark, 28
Vanden Heuvel, Michael, 184–5, 204
Vanderbilt, Kermit, 52
Vassar Workshop, 142
vaudeville, 13, 38, 62, 186, 193, 195, 206; circuits, 79
Vaughn, Jack, 95, 182–3
Veltrusky, Jiri, 15
verse drama, 29, 69
Vidal, Gore, 28
Vietnam War, 186
Villaneuve, Le Blanc de, 96

Villard, Léonie, 180
Vince, Ron, 118
Vincent, George E., 163–4
Vincent, Melvin J., 161, 164–9, 170
virile drama/virility, 77, 106–7, 122
vitality, 95; masculine, 108–9; rhetoric of, 103
vocational theatre practice programs, 120
Volkenburg, Ellen Van, 98
Vollmer, Lula, 69, 107–8
Vonnegut, Kurt, 28

Wager, Willis, 40
Wagner, Linda W., 192
Waiting for Lefty (Odets), 49, 50, 51
Walker, Alice, 116
Wall Street, or Ten Minutes Before Three (Mead), 177
Wall Street as It Is Now (Mead), 177
Wallack, "the elder," 19, 68
Wallis, Wilson D., 109
Walter, Eugene, 97, 176
Ward, Lester F., 163, 167–8
Warner, Charles, 24, 79
Warner, Michael, 4
Warren, Austin, 46
Warren, Mercy Otis (Mrs. Warren), 34, 49, 55, 67, 172
Warren, Robert Penn, 28
Washington Square Players, 98
Wasserman, Dale, 89–90
Wasserstein, Wendy, 183
Way, Brian, 156
Way Out, A (Frost), 30
Wayne, Ivor, 102
We the People (Rice), 100
Weales, Gerald, 183
Webb, Winifred, 80
Weimann, Robert, 51
Weiss, Peter, 89–90
Wellek, René, 46
Wells, William H., 168
Wendell, Barrett, 34, 43, 65, 117, 129, 140
Wetzsteon, Ross, 62
Wexley, John, 37, 168
Whitman, Walt, 29, 37, 47, 54, 71, 90, 117
Why Marry? (Williams), 27, 73
Widow Ranter, The: or, Bacon in Virginia (Behn), 96
Wilde, Oscar, 36
Wilder, Thornton, 26–7, 28, 40, 46, 54, 138, 181
Williams, Jesse Lynch, 27, 73
Williams, Raymond, 201
Williams, Stanley, 39
Williams, Tennessee, 27, 28, 33, 40, 44, 49, 50, 55, 63, 74, 90, 106, 107, 153, 154, 182; in curriculum, 116; as realist playwright, 182; status of, 183

Williams, William Carlos, 28
Willis, Nathaniel, 67
Willis, N. P., 29, 37
Wilson, August, 50, 55, 58, 107
Wilson, Edmund, 28, 30, 32
Wilson, John Grosvenor, 79
Wilson, Lanford, 62
Wilstach, Paul, 24
Winter, William, 175
Winters, Yvor, 23, 46–7
Wisconsin Dramatic Society, 134
Witching Hour, The (Thomas), 27, 88
Wolf, The (play), 18
Wolfe, Thomas, 28, 148
Wolter, Jürgen, 172
women, 7, 84, 112; in anthologies, 50, 51;
    Baker's exclusion of, 148–9; and culture,
    84–5; playwrights, 74, 105–6, 183; and real-
    ism, 185; in teaching profession, 149; works
    by, 12, 49
Woodbridge, Homer E., 32–3, 159, 160
Woodbury, George, 17

Woolf, Benjamin, 73
Workers' Theatre movement, 60, 62, 194
World War I, 101
Wrenn, John H., 189
Wunderlich, Hermann, 15
Wyatt, David, 112

Yale, 35, 130, 132, 148, 150; Baker at, 131, 140,
    142–4; Department of Drama, 14, 138, 145;
    Institute, 49
Yankee Hill, 161
Yellow Jacket, The (Hazelton and Benrimo), 88
Yiddish Theatre, 64
You Can't Take It with You (Hart and Kauf-
    man), 74
Young, Karl, 150
Young Mrs. Winthrop (Howard), 177

Zachos, J. C., 124
Ziegfeld Follies, 28
Zoo Story (Albee), 33, 49, 51